鳥　山　明

At the end of October, I became the father of a second child. This time it was a baby girl. The mother and my daughter are both doing fine so I am very happy. When my son was first born, I vowed to be a strict father, but I turned out to be very doting. Losing faith in myself, I vowed that with the next one I'll be strict! But I don't see how I can be strict with a baby girl. Recently, I'm thinking better of myself because I've been thinking that there's nothing wrong with spoiling your kids!

–Akira Toriyama, 1991

Artist/writer Akira Toriyama burst onto the manga scene in 1980 with the wildly popular **Dr. Slump**, a science fiction comedy about the adventures of a mad scientist and his android "daughter." In 1984 he created his hit series **Dragon Ball**, which ran until 1995 in Shueisha's bestselling magazine **Weekly Shonen Jump**, and was translated into foreign languages around the world. Since **Dragon Ball**, he has worked on a variety of short series, including **Cowa!**, **Kajika**, **Sand Land**, and **Neko Majin**, as well as a children's book, **Toccio the Angel**. He is also known for his design work on video games, particularly the **Dragon Warrior** RPG series. He lives with his family in Japan.

DRAGON BALL Z VOL. 8
The SHONEN JUMP Graphic Novel Edition

This graphic novel is number 24 in a series of 42.

STORY AND ART BY
AKIRA TORIYAMA

ENGLISH ADAPTATION BY
GERARD JONES

Translation/Lillian Olsen
Touch-Up Art & Lettering/Wayne Truman
Cover Design/Sean Lee & Dan Ziegler
Graphics & Design/Sean Lee
Senior Editor/Jason Thompson

Managing Editor/Annette Roman
Editor in Chief/Hyoe Narita
Director, Licensing and Acquisitions/Rike Inouye
V.P. of Sales and Marketing/Liza Coppola
V.P. of Strategic Development/Yumi Hoashi
Publisher/Seiji Horibuchi

In the original Japanese edition, DRAGON BALL and DRAGON BALL Z
are known collectively as the 42-volume series DRAGON BALL. The
English DRAGON BALL Z was originally volumes 17-42 of the Japanese
DRAGON BALL.

Published by VIZ, LLC
P.O. Box 77010 • San Francisco, CA 94107

The SHONEN JUMP Graphic Novel Edition
10 9 8 7 6 5 4 3 2 1
First printing, May 2003

THE WORLD'S
MOST POPULAR MANGA

www.viz.com

GRAPHIC NOVEL
www.shonenjump.com

SHONEN JUMP GRAPHIC NOVEL

DRAGON BALL Z

Vol. 8

DB: 24 of 42

STORY AND ART BY
AKIRA TORIYAMA

THE MAIN CHARACTERS

Bulma

Goku's oldest friend, Bulma is a scientific genius. She met Goku while on a quest for the seven magical Dragon Balls which, when gathered together, can grant any wish.

Son Goku

The greatest martial artist on Earth, he owes his strength to the training of Kame-Sen'nin and Kaiô-sama, and the fact that he's an alien Saiyan. To get even stronger, he has trained under 100 times Earth's gravity.

The Great Elder

The oldest living Namekian, all the current Namekians (except Piccolo) are its children. It created Namek's Dragon Balls.

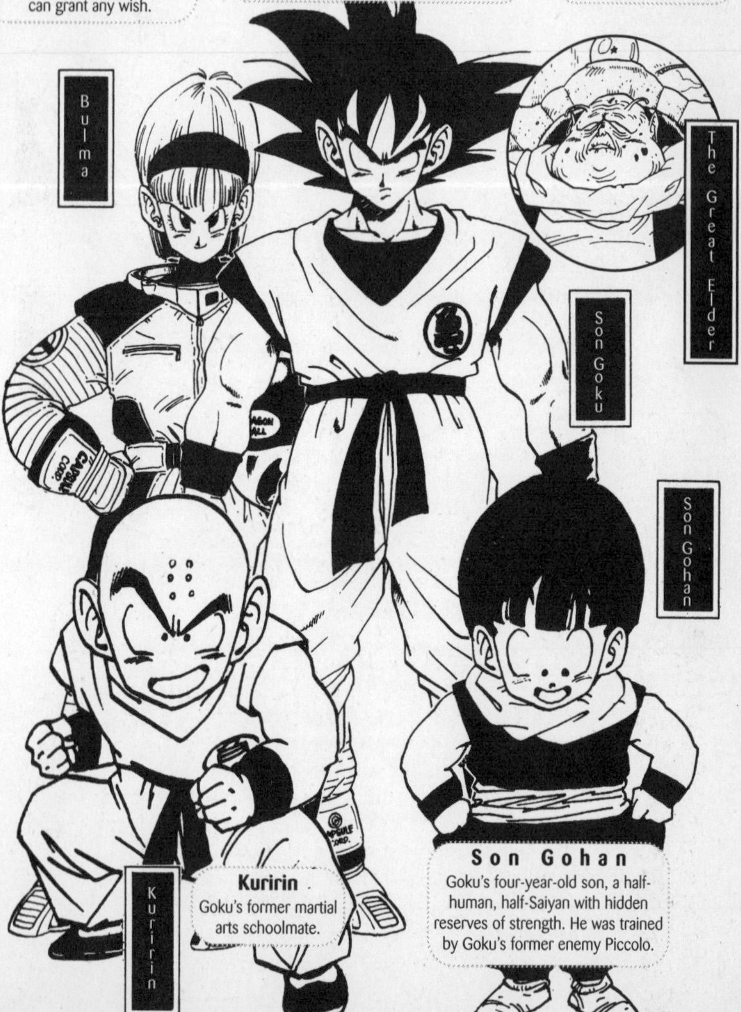
Bulma
The Great Elder
Son Goku
Son Gohan
Kuririn
CAPSULE CORP.
DRAGON BALL

Kuririn

Goku's former martial arts schoolmate.

Son Gohan

Goku's four-year-old son, a half-human, half-Saiyan with hidden reserves of strength. He was trained by Goku's former enemy Piccolo.

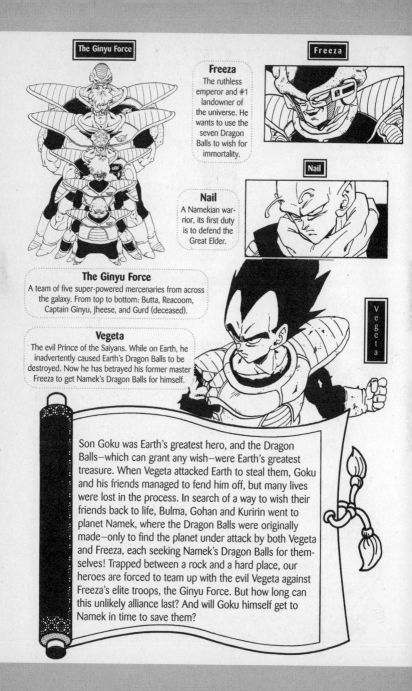

The Ginyu Force

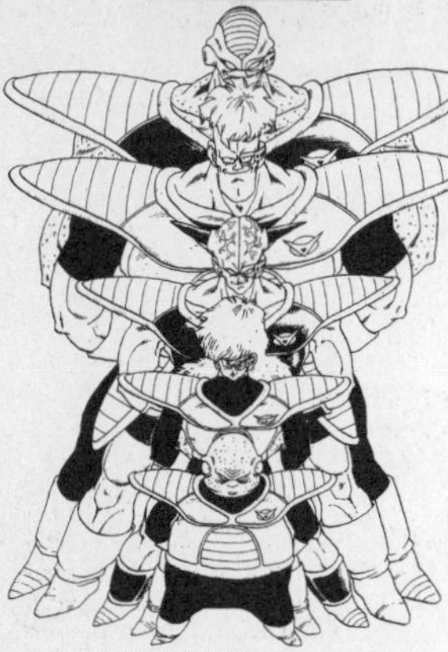

Freeza

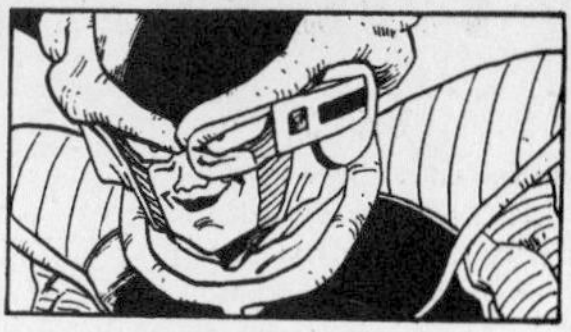

Freeza

The ruthless emperor and #1 landowner of the universe. He wants to use the seven Dragon Balls to wish for immortality.

Nail

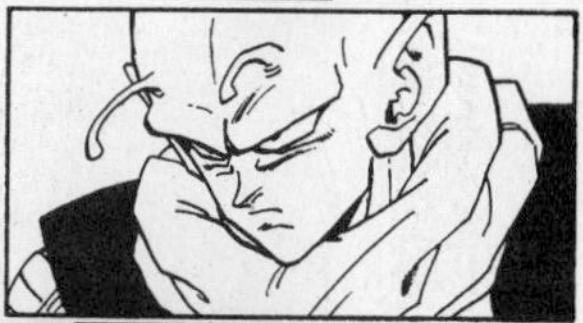

Nail

A Namekian warrior, its first duty is to defend the Great Elder.

The Ginyu Force

A team of five super-powered mercenaries from across the galaxy. From top to bottom: Butta, Reacoom, Captain Ginyu, Jheese, and Gurd (deceased).

Vegeta

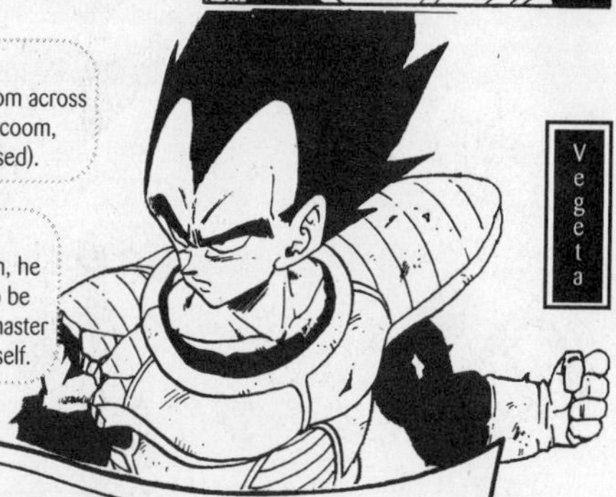

Vegeta

The evil Prince of the Saiyans. While on Earth, he inadvertently caused Earth's Dragon Balls to be destroyed. Now he has betrayed his former master Freeza to get Namek's Dragon Balls for himself.

Son Goku was Earth's greatest hero, and the Dragon Balls—which can grant any wish—were Earth's greatest treasure. When Vegeta attacked Earth to steal them, Goku and his friends managed to fend him off, but many lives were lost in the process. In search of a way to wish their friends back to life, Bulma, Gohan and Kuririn went to planet Namek, where the Dragon Balls were originally made—only to find the planet under attack by both Vegeta and Freeza, each seeking Namek's Dragon Balls for themselves! Trapped between a rock and a hard place, our heroes are forced to team up with the evil Vegeta against Freeza's elite troops, the Ginyu Force. But how long can this unlikely alliance last? And will Goku himself get to Namek in time to save them?

DRAGON BALL Z 8

THE CONTENTS, IF YOU PLEASE... OHO HO HO...

DRAGON BALL

DBZ:83 • Freeza Victorious?!!

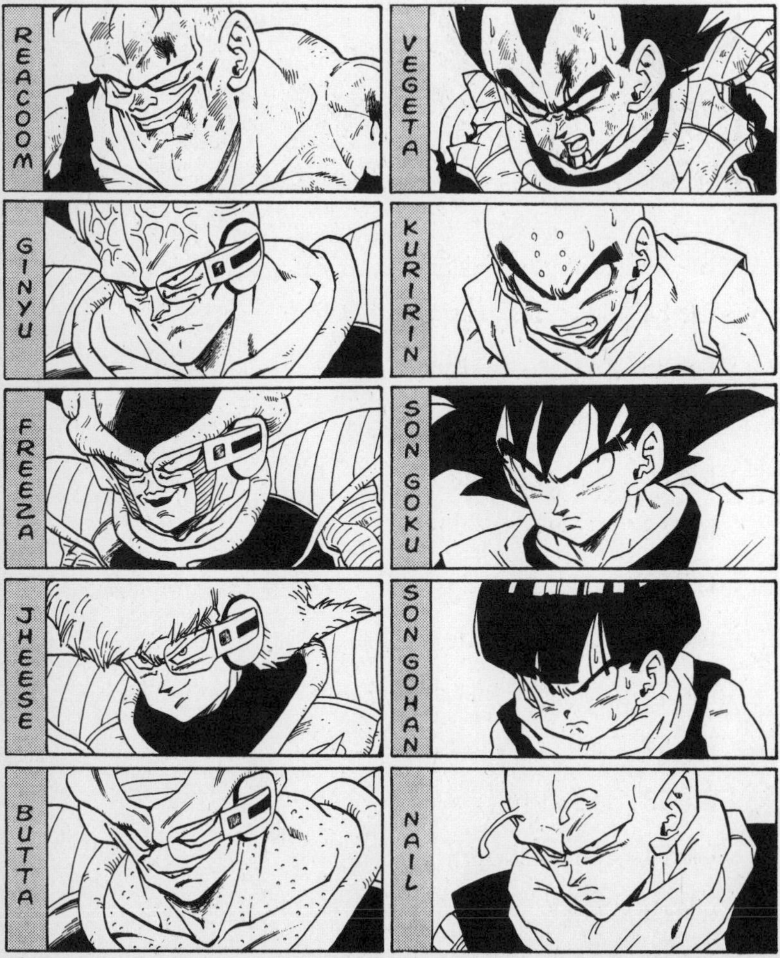
VEGETA
REACOOM
KURIRIN
GINYU
SON GOKU
FREEZA
SON GOHAN
JHEESE
NAIL
BUTTA

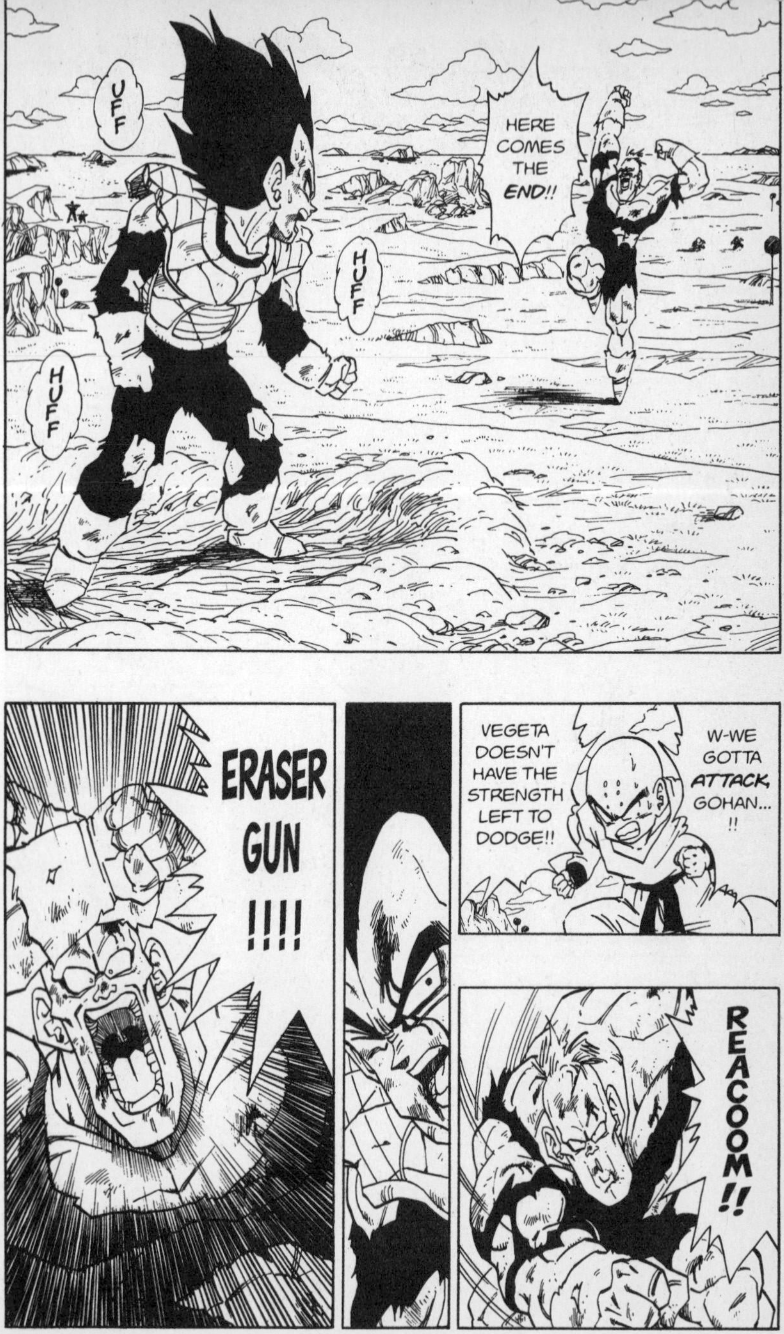
HERE COMES THE END!!
UFF
HUFF
HUFF
W-WE GOTTA ATTACK, GOHAN...!!
VEGETA DOESN'T HAVE THE STRENGTH LEFT TO DODGE!!
REACOOM!!
ERASER GUN!!!!

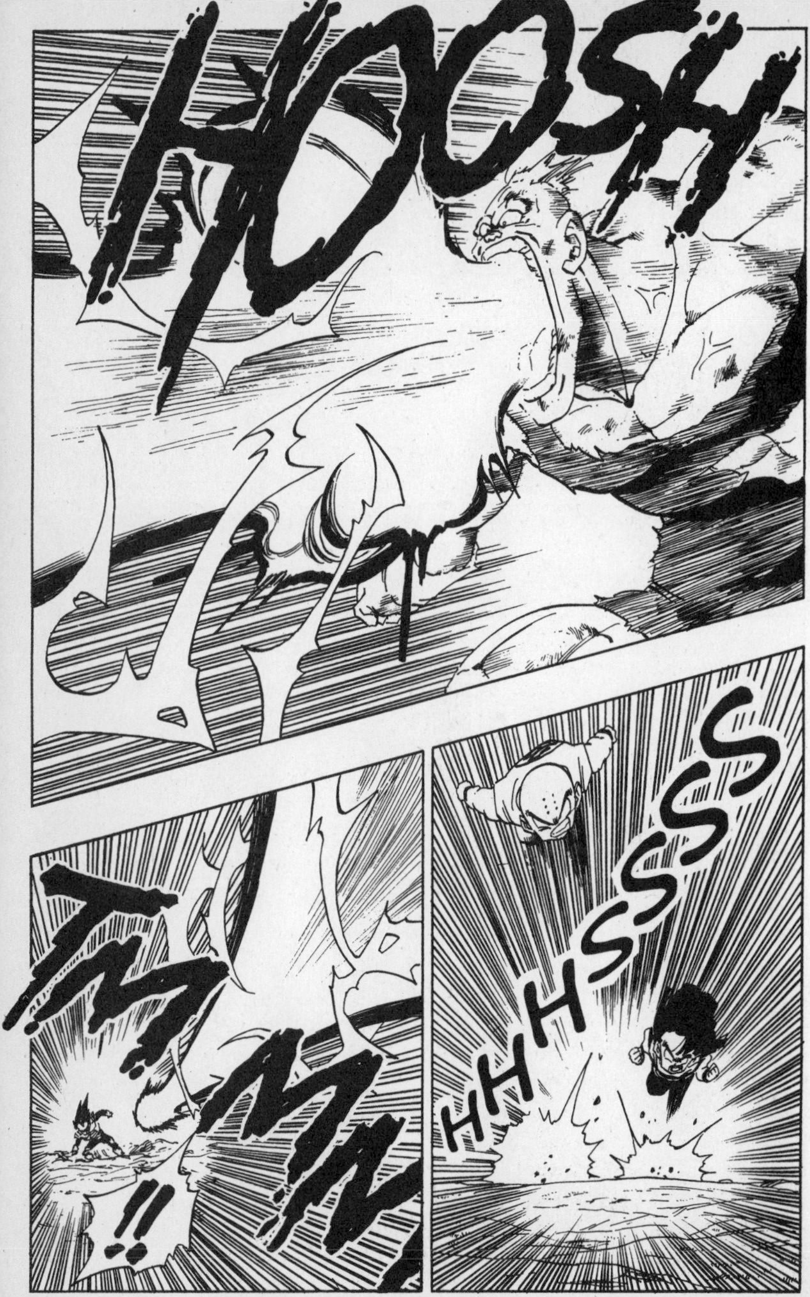
WHOOSH!!
HHHSSSSS

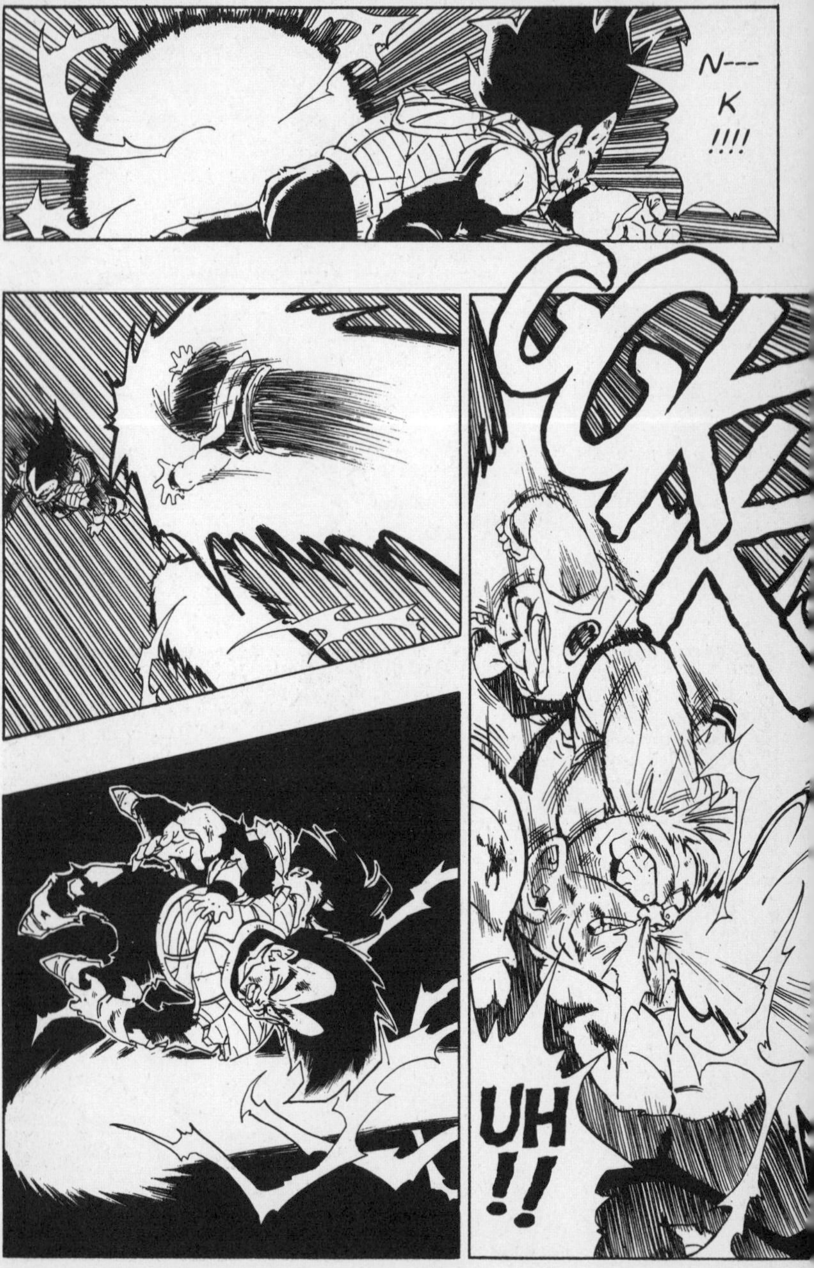
N---
K
!!!!
GGK
UH
!!

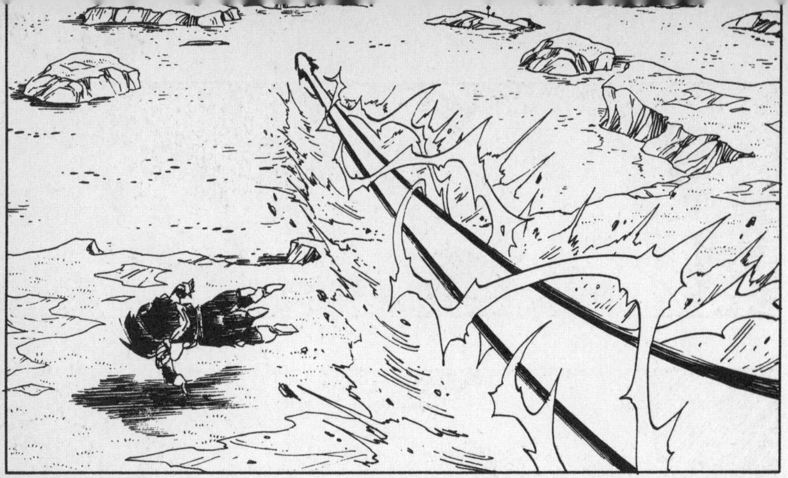

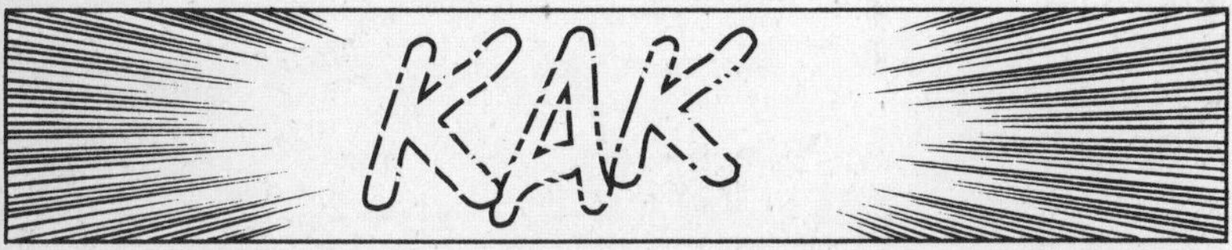
KAK

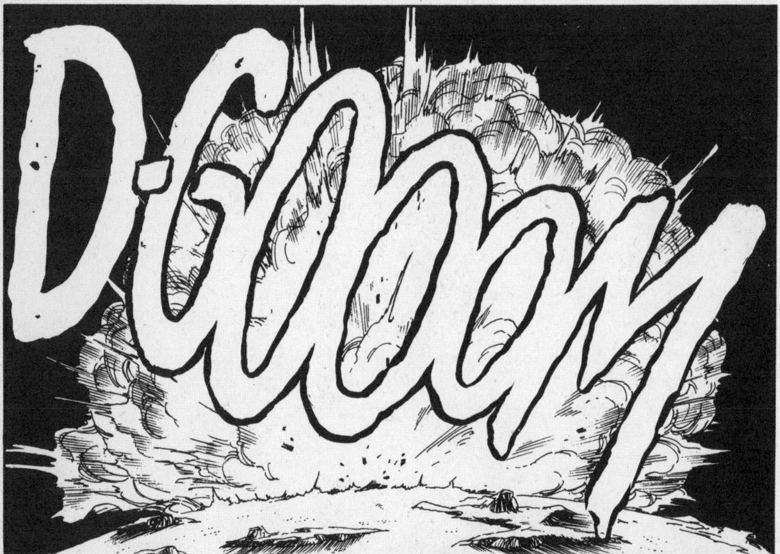
DOOOM

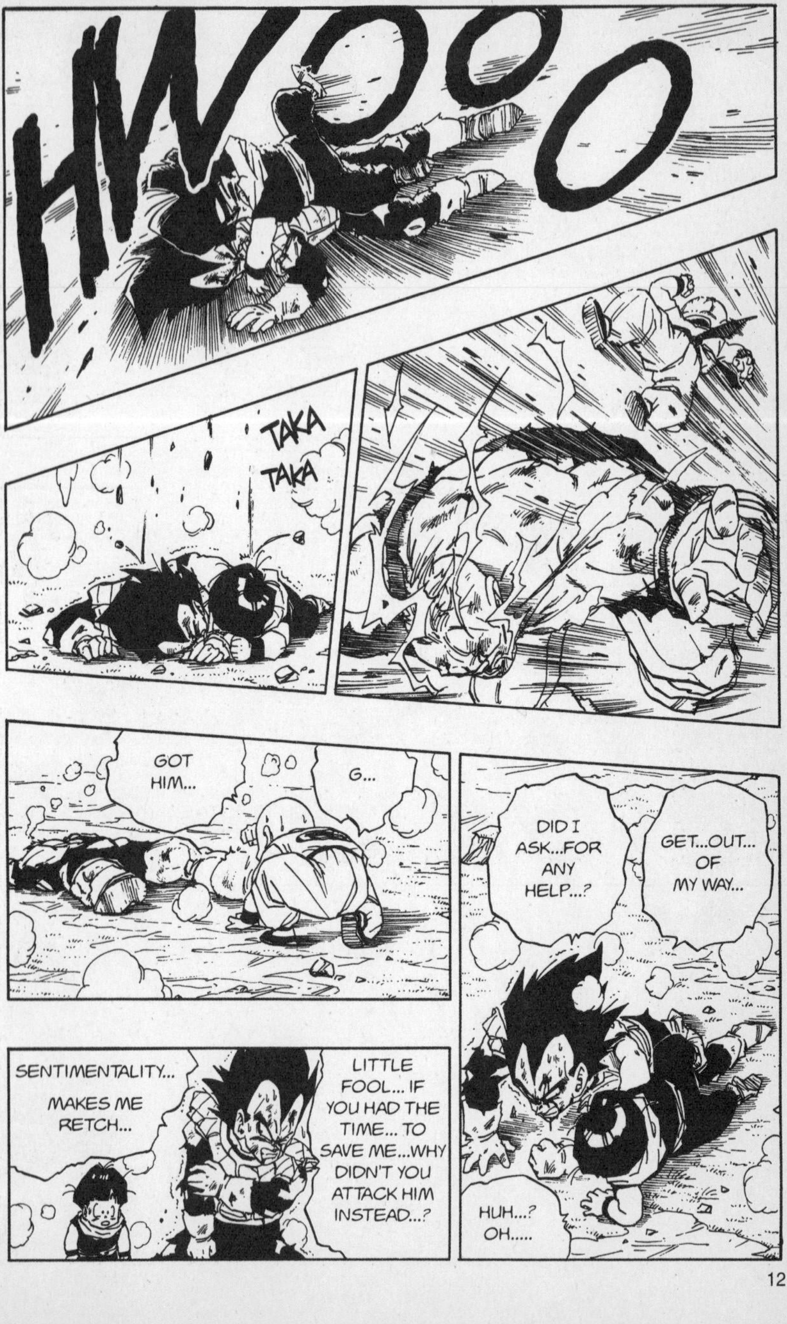
HWOOO
TAKA
TAKA
GET...OUT... OF MY WAY...
DID I ASK...FOR ANY HELP...?
HUH...? OH.....
G...
GOT HIM...
LITTLE FOOL... IF YOU HAD THE TIME... TO SAVE ME...WHY DIDN'T YOU ATTACK HIM INSTEAD...?
SENTIMENTALITY...
MAKES ME RETCH...

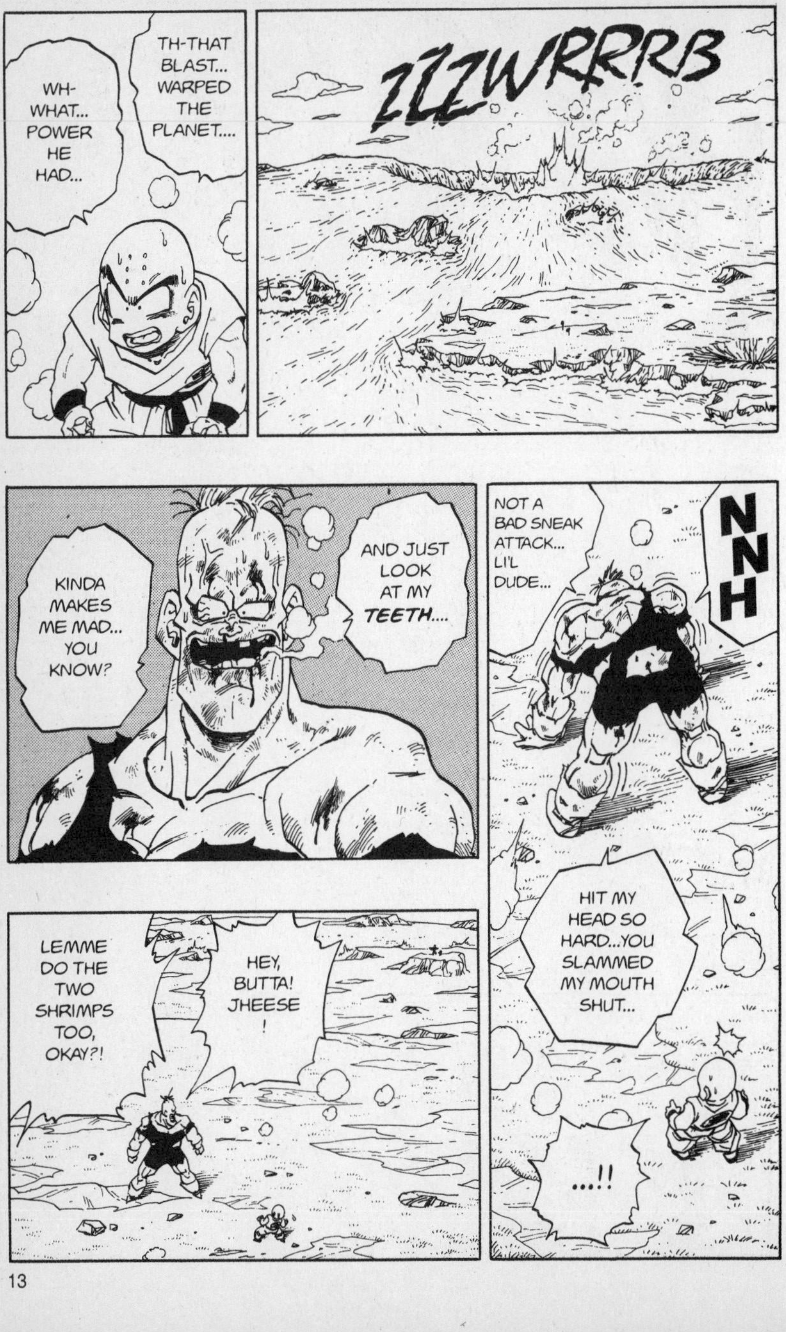
ZZZWRRRB
TH-THAT BLAST... WARPED THE PLANET....
WH-WHAT... POWER HE HAD...
NNH
NOT A BAD SNEAK ATTACK... LI'L DUDE...
HIT MY HEAD SO HARD...YOU SLAMMED MY MOUTH SHUT...
...!!
AND JUST LOOK AT MY *TEETH*....
KINDA MAKES ME MAD... YOU KNOW?
HEY, BUTTA! JHEESE!
LEMME DO THE TWO SHRIMPS TOO, OKAY?!

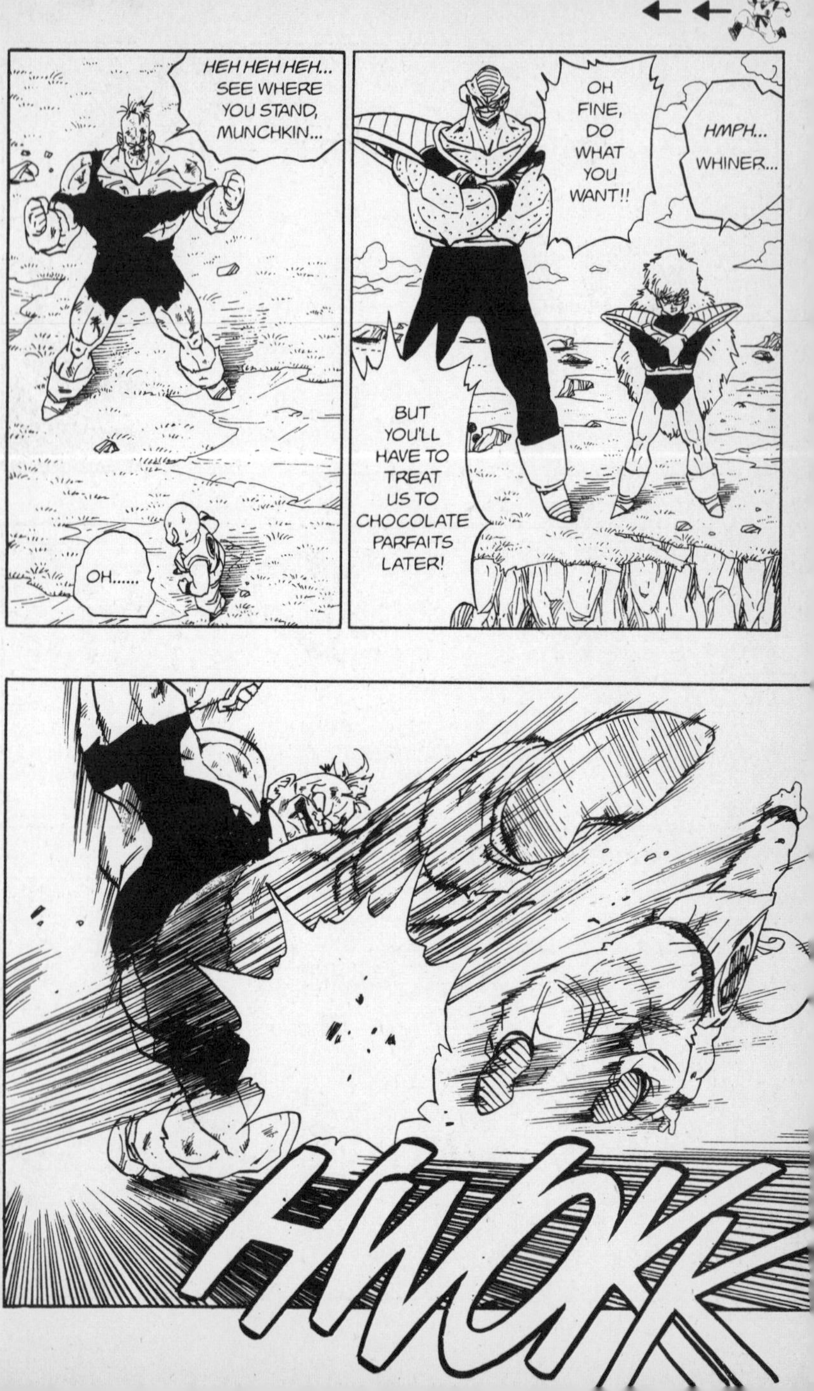
HMPH...
WHINER...
OH FINE, DO WHAT YOU WANT!!
BUT YOU'LL HAVE TO TREAT US TO CHOCOLATE PARFAITS LATER!
HEH HEH HEH... SEE WHERE YOU STAND, MUNCHKIN...
OH......
HWOK

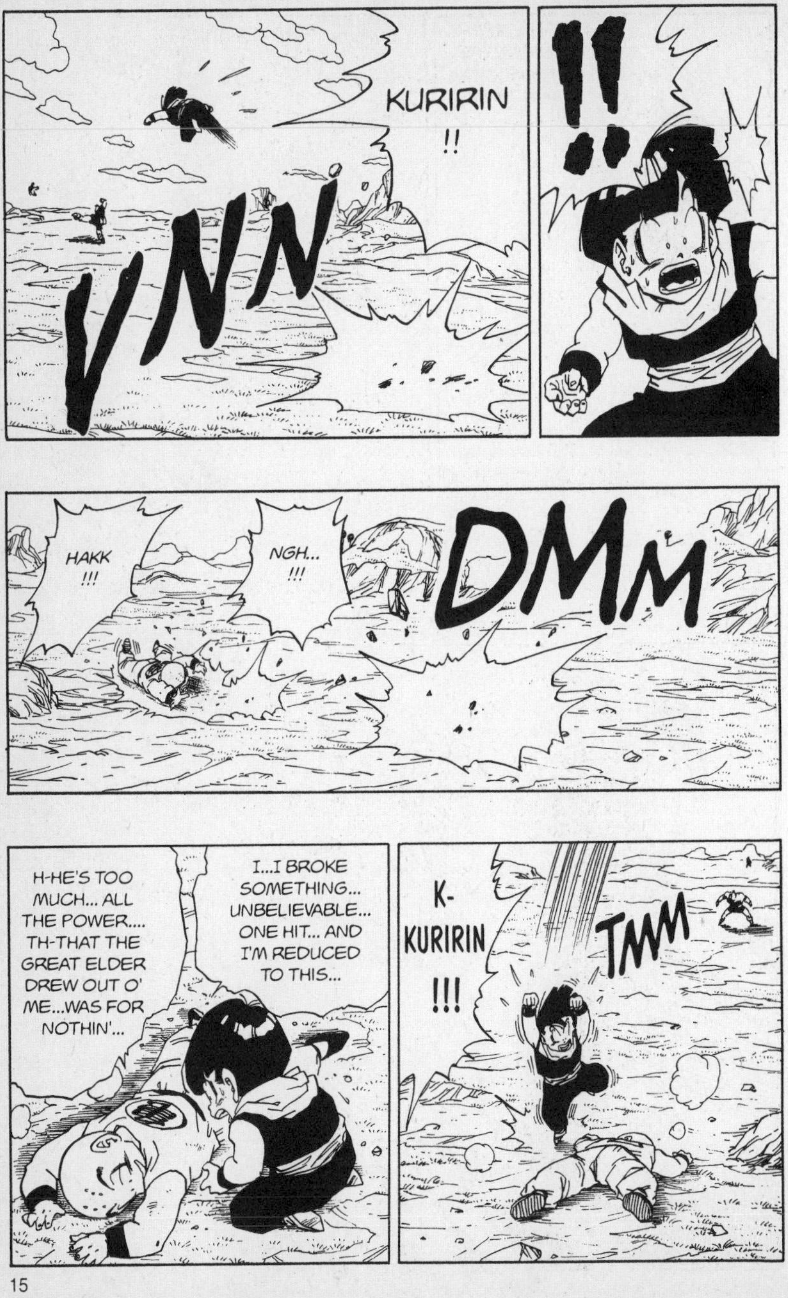
!!
KURIRIN !!
VNN
DMM
NGH... !!!
HAKK !!!
K-KURIRIN !!!
TMM
I...I BROKE SOMETHING... UNBELIEVABLE... ONE HIT... AND I'M REDUCED TO THIS...
H-HE'S TOO MUCH... ALL THE POWER.... TH-THAT THE GREAT ELDER DREW OUT O' ME...WAS FOR NOTHIN'...

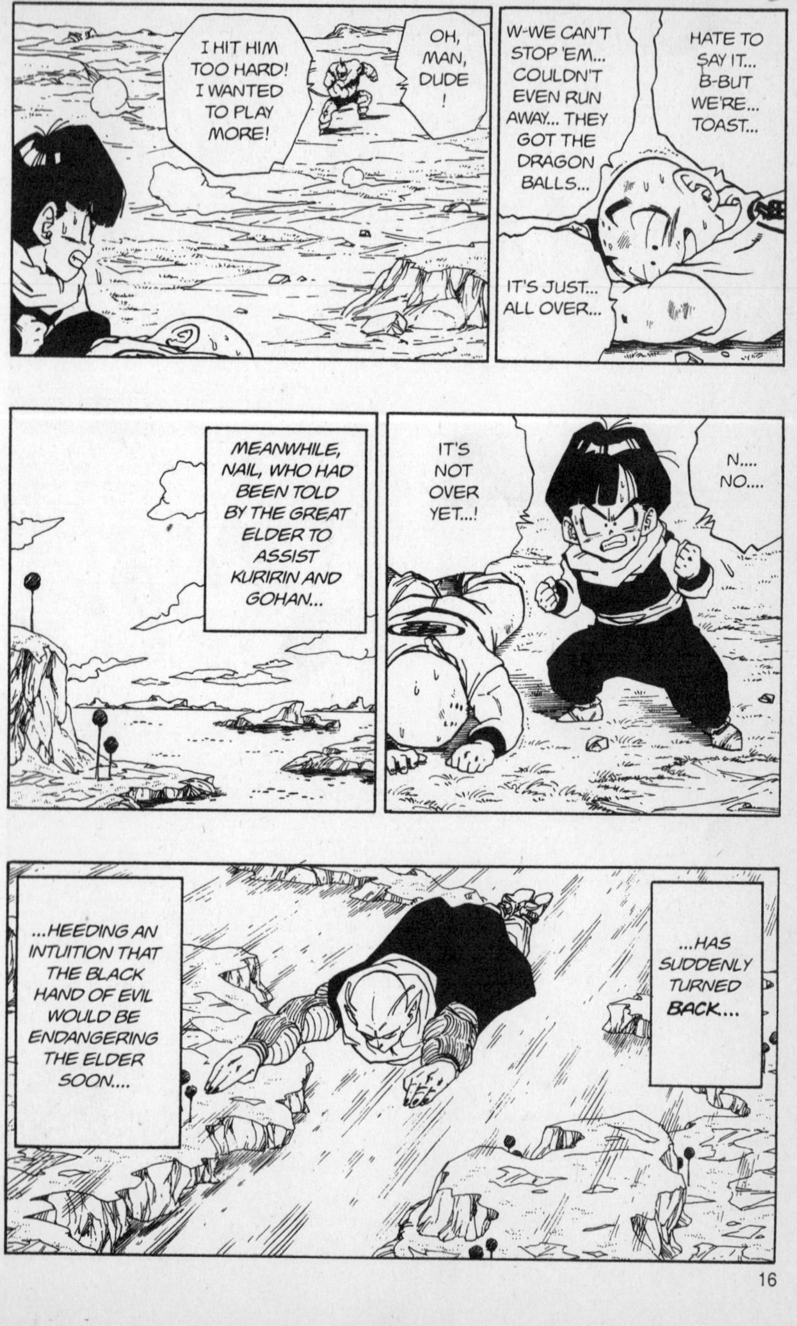
HATE TO SAY IT... B-BUT WE'RE... TOAST...
W-WE CAN'T STOP 'EM... COULDN'T EVEN RUN AWAY... THEY GOT THE DRAGON BALLS...
IT'S JUST... ALL OVER...
OH, MAN, DUDE!
I HIT HIM TOO HARD! I WANTED TO PLAY MORE!
N.... NO....
IT'S NOT OVER YET...!
MEANWHILE, NAIL, WHO HAD BEEN TOLD BY THE GREAT ELDER TO ASSIST KURIRIN AND GOHAN...
...HEEDING AN INTUITION THAT THE BLACK HAND OF EVIL WOULD BE ENDANGERING THE ELDER SOON....
...HAS SUDDENLY TURNED BACK...

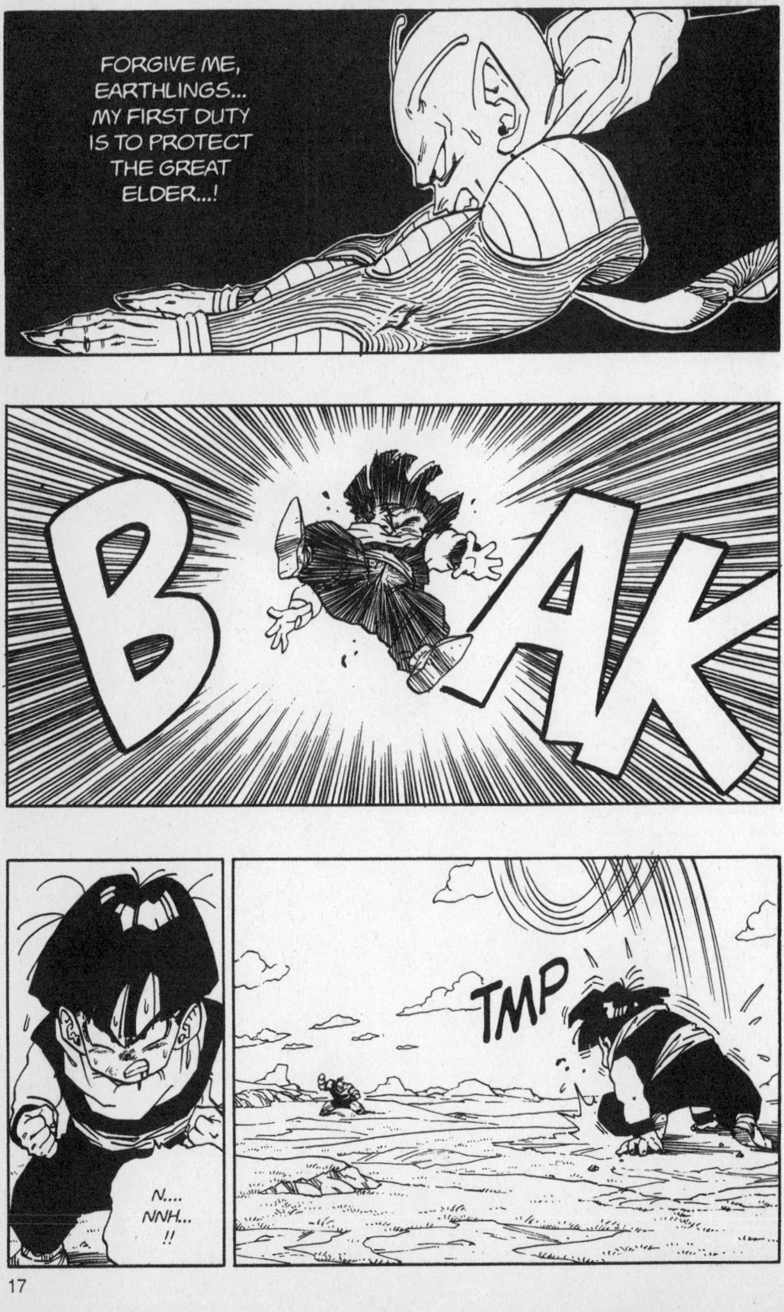
FORGIVE ME, EARTHLINGS... MY FIRST DUTY IS TO PROTECT THE GREAT ELDER...!
BAK
TMP
N.... NNH... !!

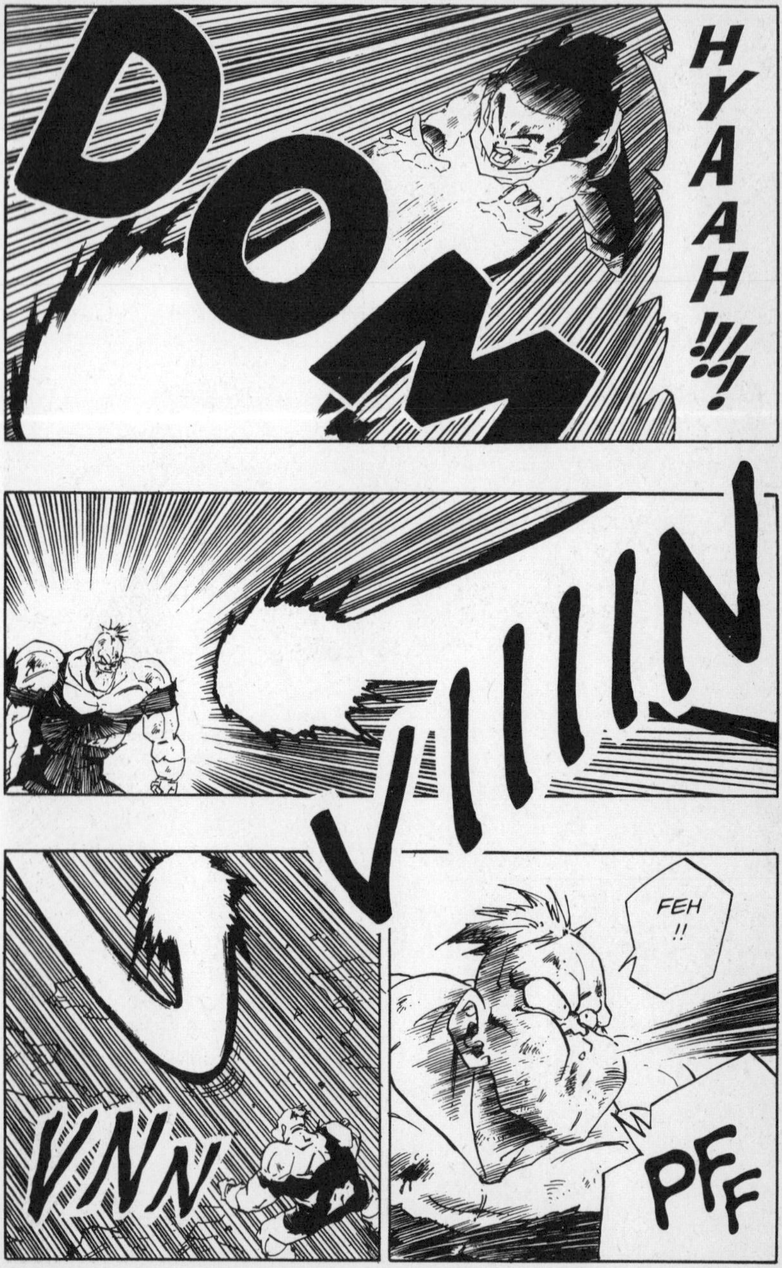
HYAAH!!!!
DOM
VIIIIN
FEH !!
PFF
VNN

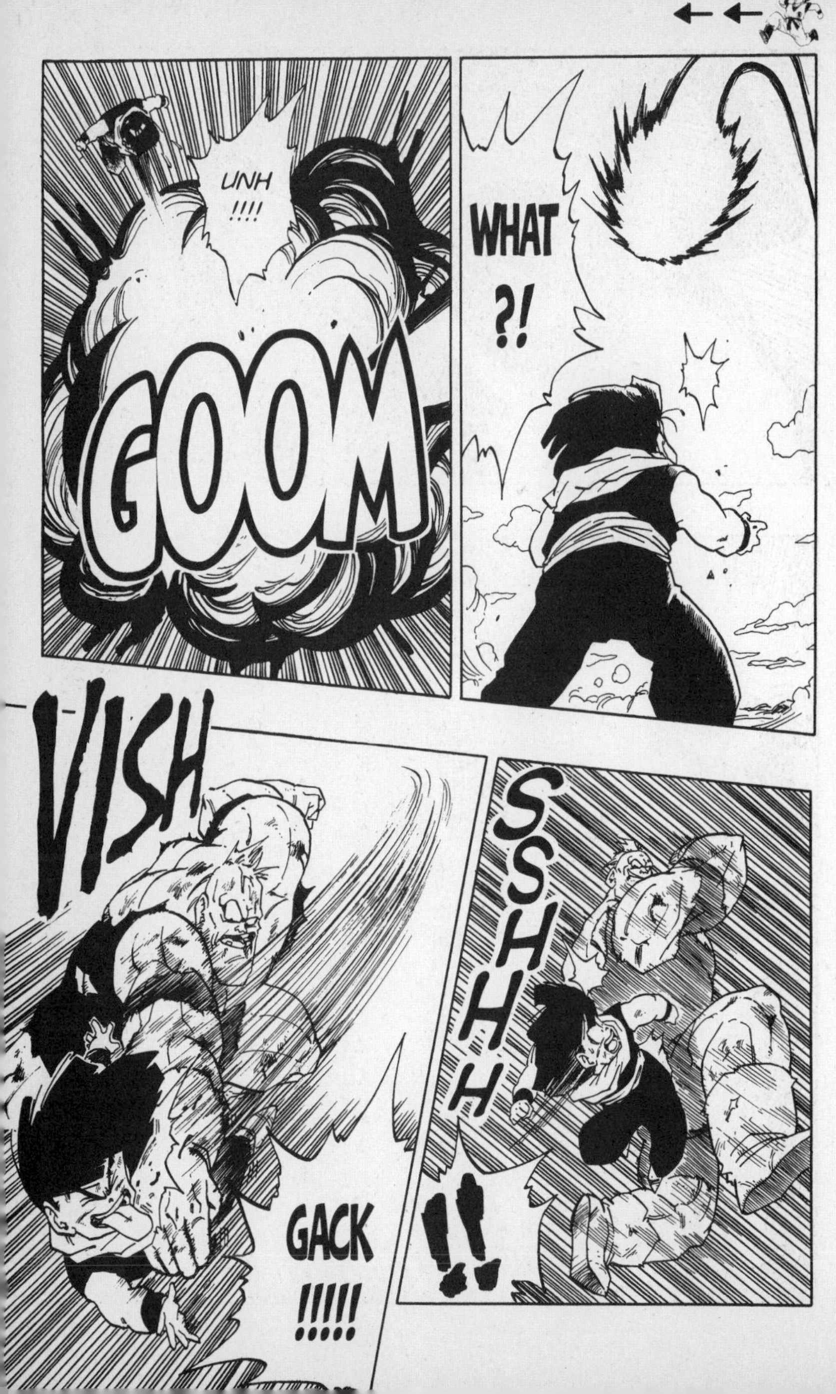
WHAT ?!
UNH !!!!
GOOM
SSHHHH
!!
VISH
GACK !!!!!

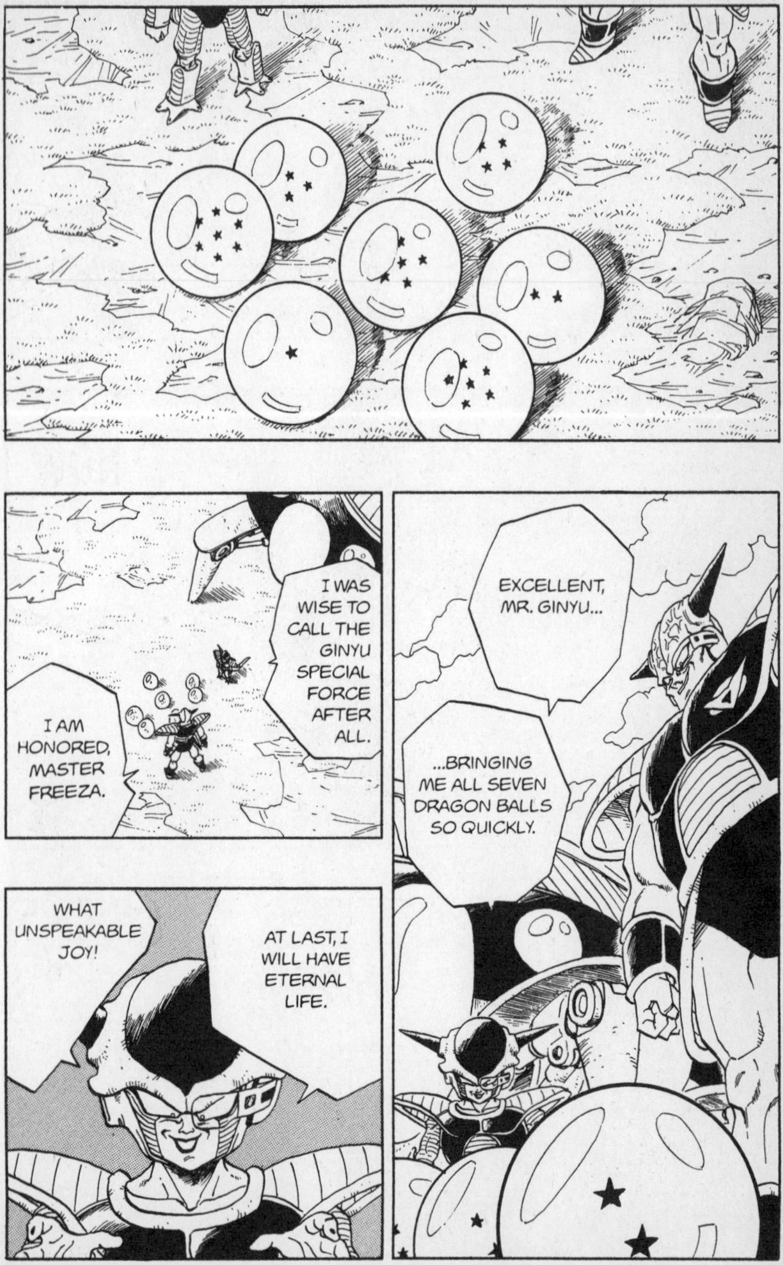
EXCELLENT, MR. GINYU...
...BRINGING ME ALL SEVEN DRAGON BALLS SO QUICKLY.
I WAS WISE TO CALL THE GINYU SPECIAL FORCE AFTER ALL.
I AM HONORED, MASTER FREEZA.
WHAT UNSPEAKABLE JOY!
AT LAST, I WILL HAVE ETERNAL LIFE.

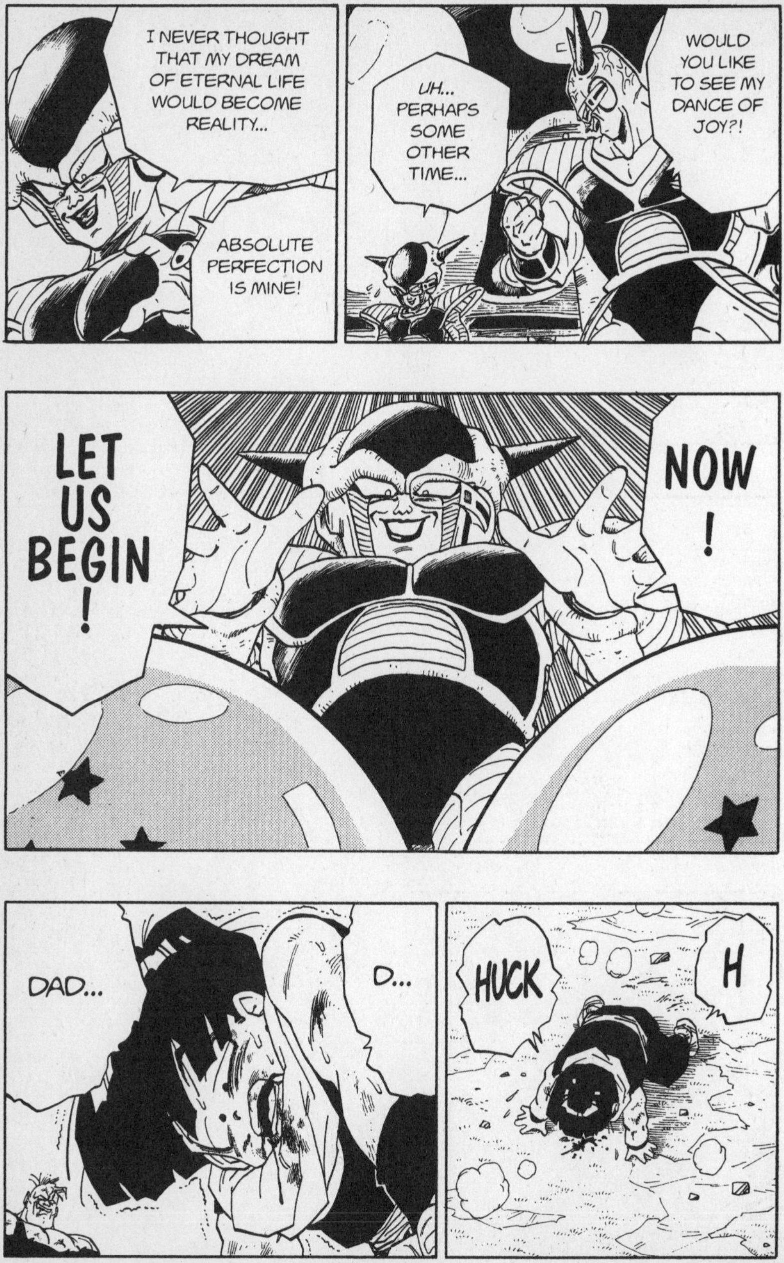
WOULD YOU LIKE TO SEE MY DANCE OF JOY?!
UH... PERHAPS SOME OTHER TIME...
I NEVER THOUGHT THAT MY DREAM OF ETERNAL LIFE WOULD BECOME REALITY...
ABSOLUTE PERFECTION IS MINE!
NOW!
LET US BEGIN!
H
HUCK
D...
DAD...

NEXT: *Freeza's Wish!*

DBZ:84 • Son Gohan's Last Stand

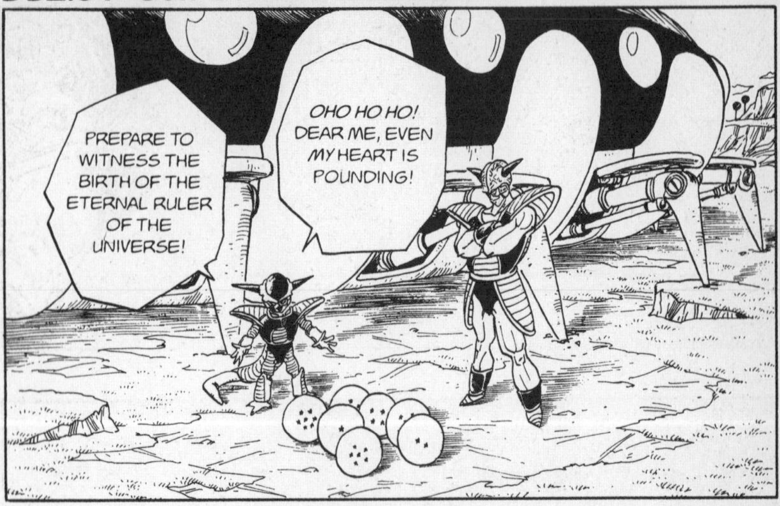
OHO HO HO! DEAR ME, EVEN MY HEART IS POUNDING!
PREPARE TO WITNESS THE BIRTH OF THE ETERNAL RULER OF THE UNIVERSE!

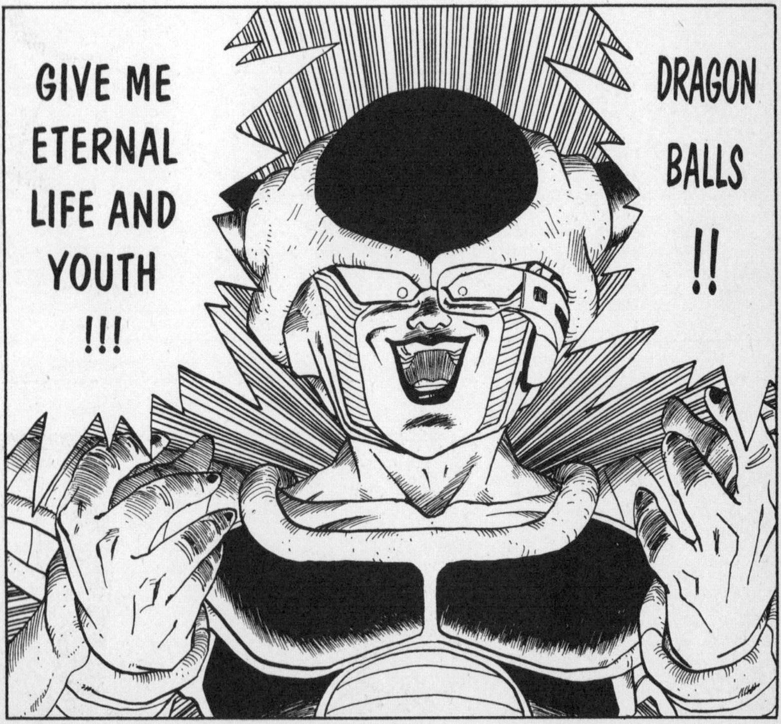
DRAGON BALLS!!
GIVE ME ETERNAL LIFE AND YOUTH!!!

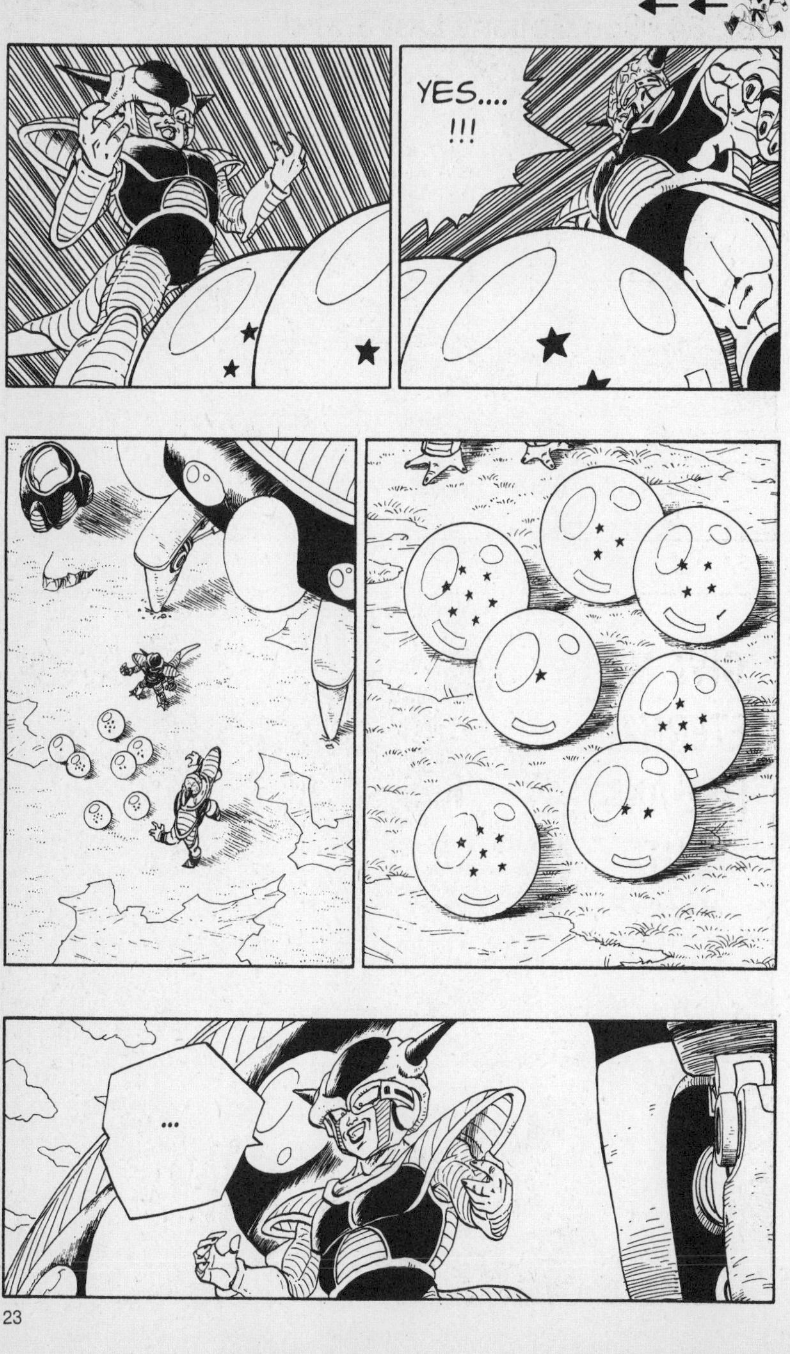
YES....
!!!
...

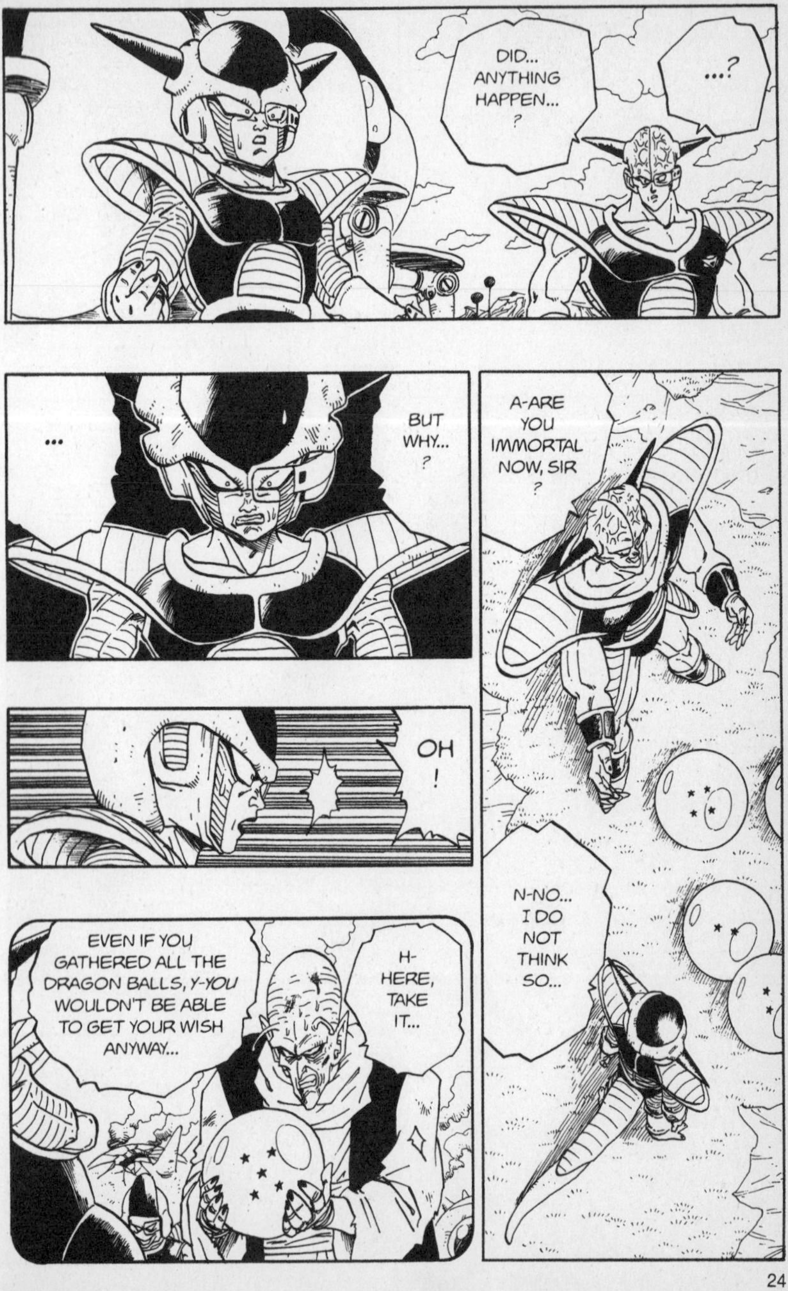
...?
DID... ANYTHING HAPPEN... ?
A-ARE YOU IMMORTAL NOW, SIR ?
N-NO... I DO NOT THINK SO...
BUT WHY... ?
...
OH !
H- HERE, TAKE IT...
EVEN IF YOU GATHERED ALL THE DRAGON BALLS, *Y-YOU* WOULDN'T BE ABLE TO GET YOUR WISH ANYWAY...

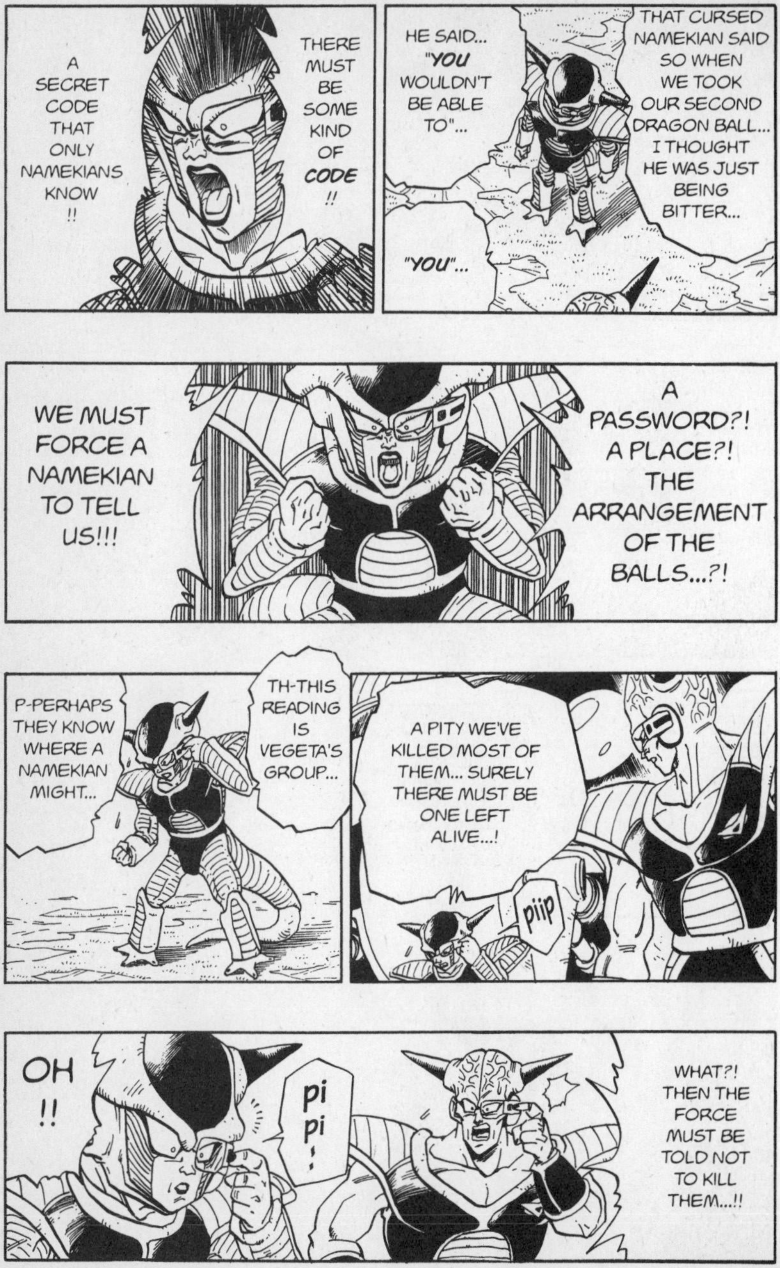
THAT CURSED NAMEKIAN SAID SO WHEN WE TOOK OUR SECOND DRAGON BALL... I THOUGHT HE WAS JUST BEING BITTER...
HE SAID... "***YOU*** WOULDN'T BE ABLE TO"...
"***YOU***"...
THERE MUST BE SOME KIND OF ***CODE*** !!
A SECRET CODE THAT ONLY NAMEKIANS KNOW !!
A PASSWORD?! A PLACE?! THE ARRANGEMENT OF THE BALLS...?!
WE MUST FORCE A NAMEKIAN TO TELL US!!!
A PITY WE'VE KILLED MOST OF THEM... SURELY THERE MUST BE ONE LEFT ALIVE...!
piip
TH-THIS READING IS VEGETA'S GROUP...
P-PERHAPS THEY KNOW WHERE A NAMEKIAN MIGHT...
WHAT?! THEN THE FORCE MUST BE TOLD NOT TO KILL THEM...!!
pi pi!
OH !!

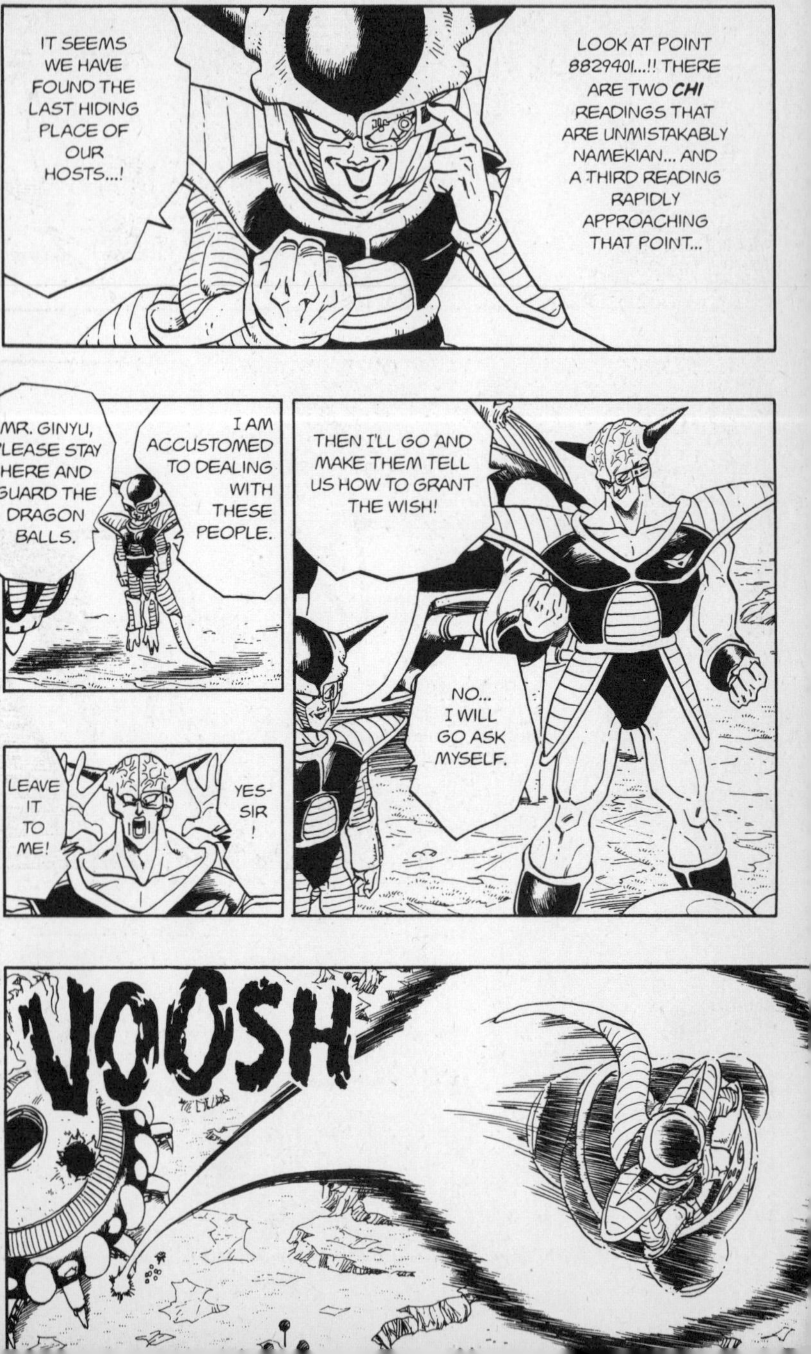
LOOK AT POINT 8829401...!! THERE ARE TWO CHI READINGS THAT ARE UNMISTAKABLY NAMEKIAN... AND A THIRD READING RAPIDLY APPROACHING THAT POINT...
IT SEEMS WE HAVE FOUND THE LAST HIDING PLACE OF OUR HOSTS...!
THEN I'LL GO AND MAKE THEM TELL US HOW TO GRANT THE WISH!
NO... I WILL GO ASK MYSELF.
I AM ACCUSTOMED TO DEALING WITH THESE PEOPLE.
MR. GINYU, PLEASE STAY HERE AND GUARD THE DRAGON BALLS.
YES-SIR!
LEAVE IT TO ME!
VOOSH

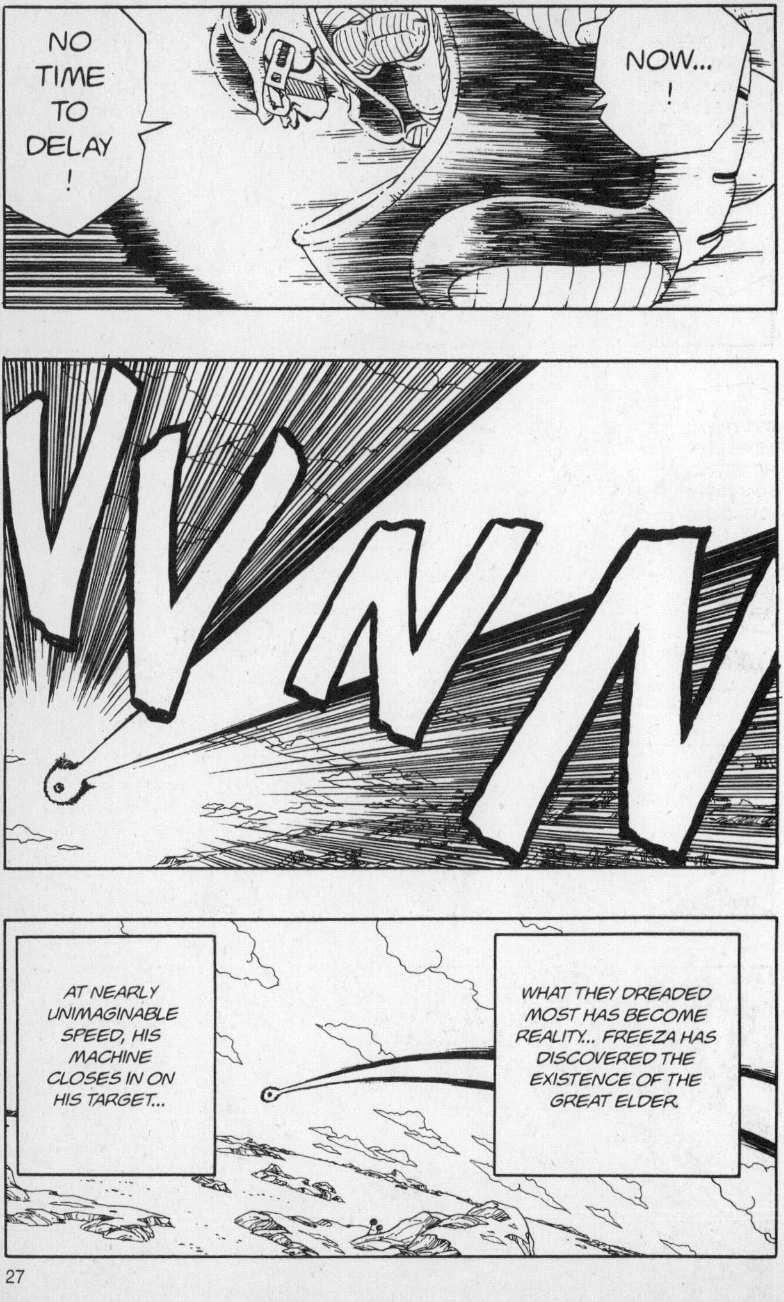
NOW... !
NO TIME TO DELAY !
VVNN
WHAT THEY DREADED MOST HAS BECOME REALITY... FREEZA HAS DISCOVERED THE EXISTENCE OF THE GREAT ELDER.
AT NEARLY UNIMAGINABLE SPEED, HIS MACHINE CLOSES IN ON HIS TARGET...

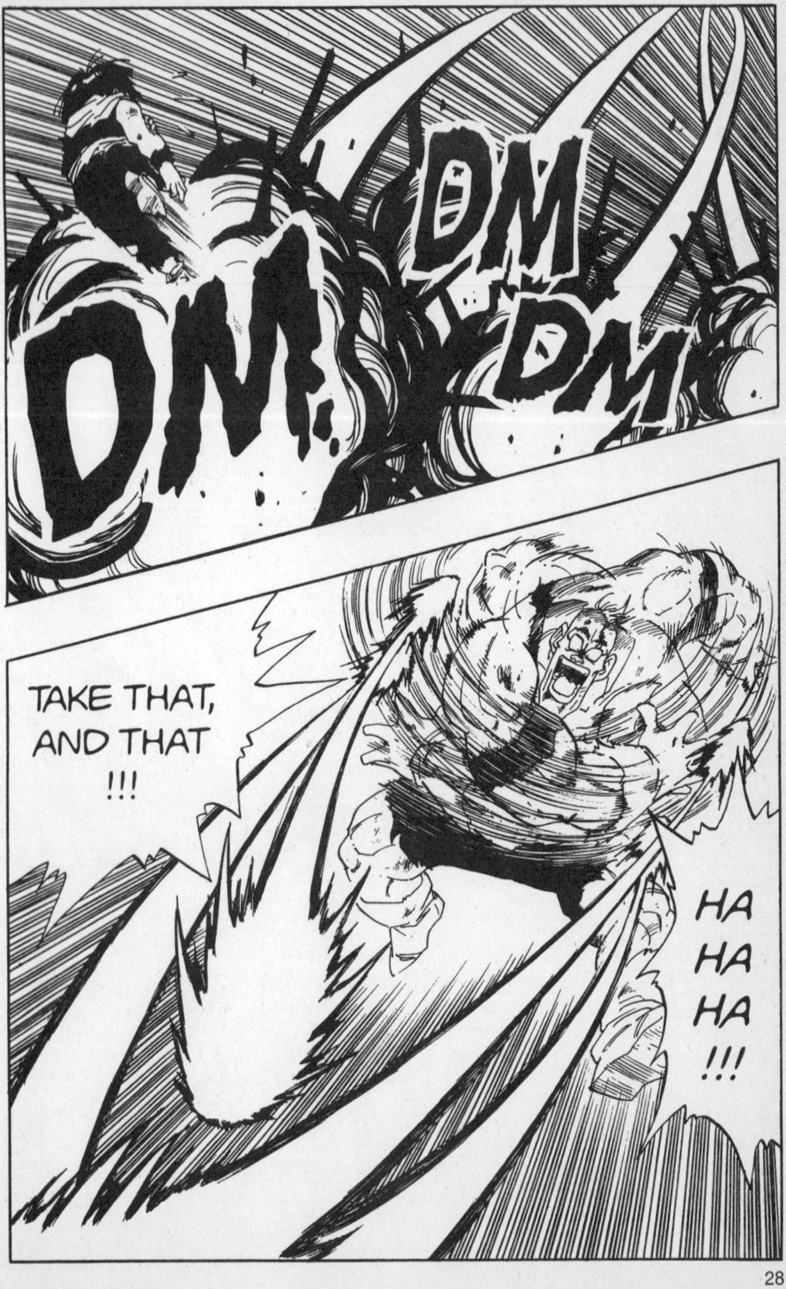
DM
DM
DM
DM
HA
HA
HA
!!!
TAKE THAT,
AND THAT
!!!

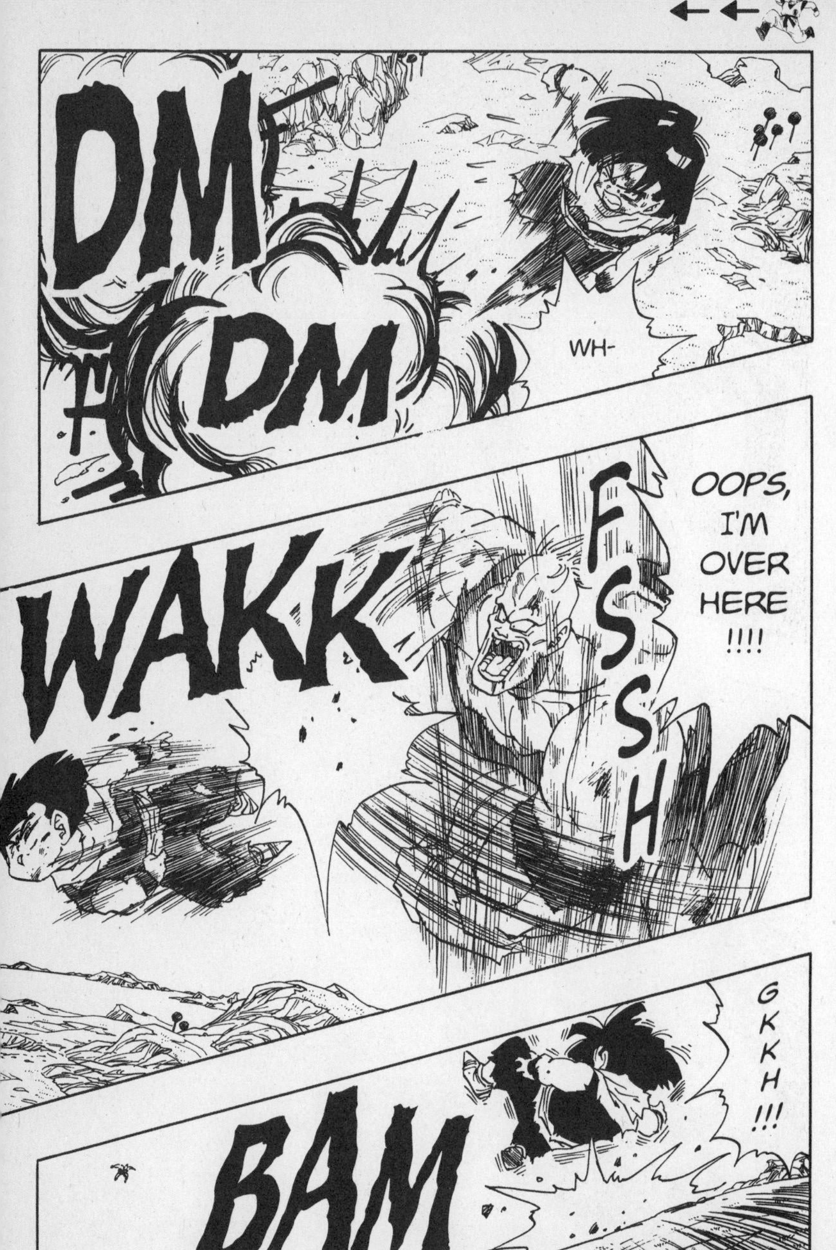
WH-
DM
DM
OOPS, I'M OVER HERE !!!!
FSSH
WAKK
GKKH!!!
BAM

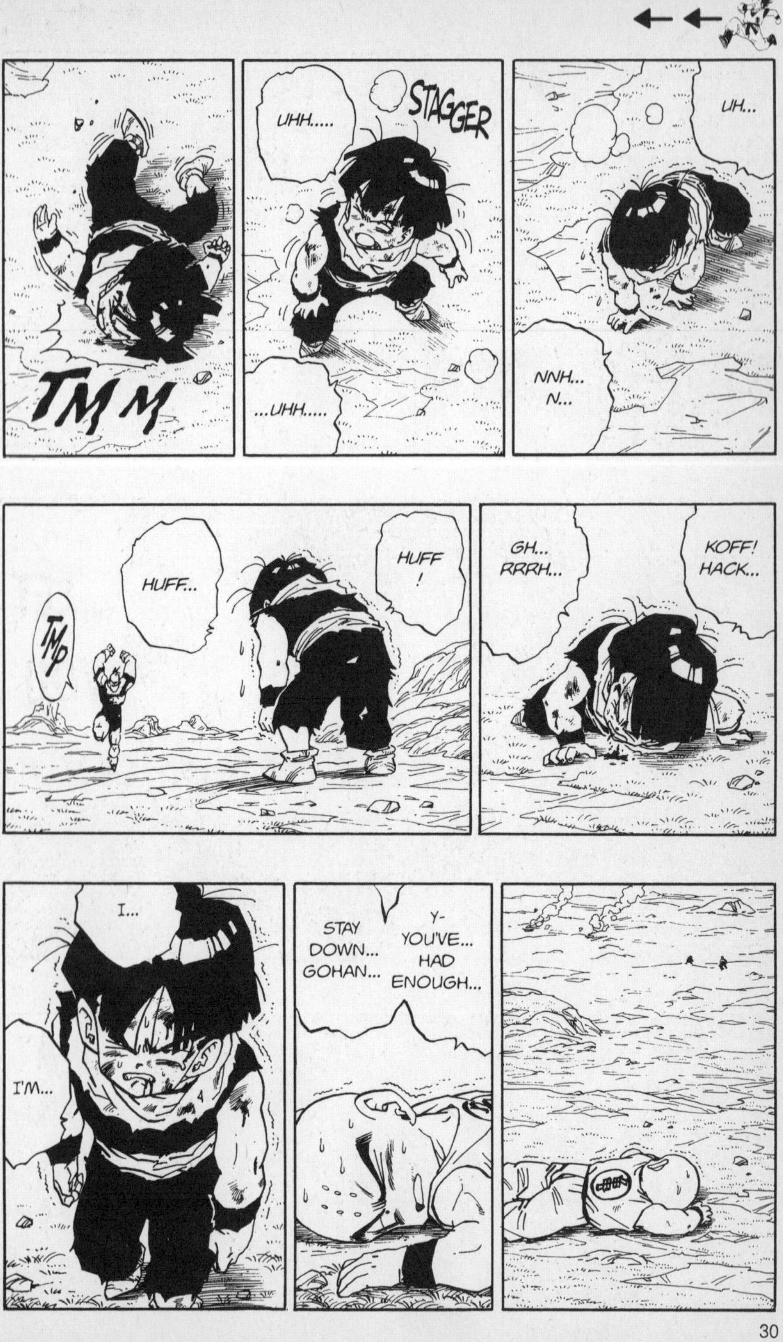
UH...
NNH...
N...
UHH.....
STAGGER
...UHH.....
TMM
KOFF!
HACK...
GH...
RRRH...
HUFF
!
HUFF...
TMP
Y-
YOU'VE...
HAD
ENOUGH...
STAY
DOWN...
GOHAN...
I...
I'M...

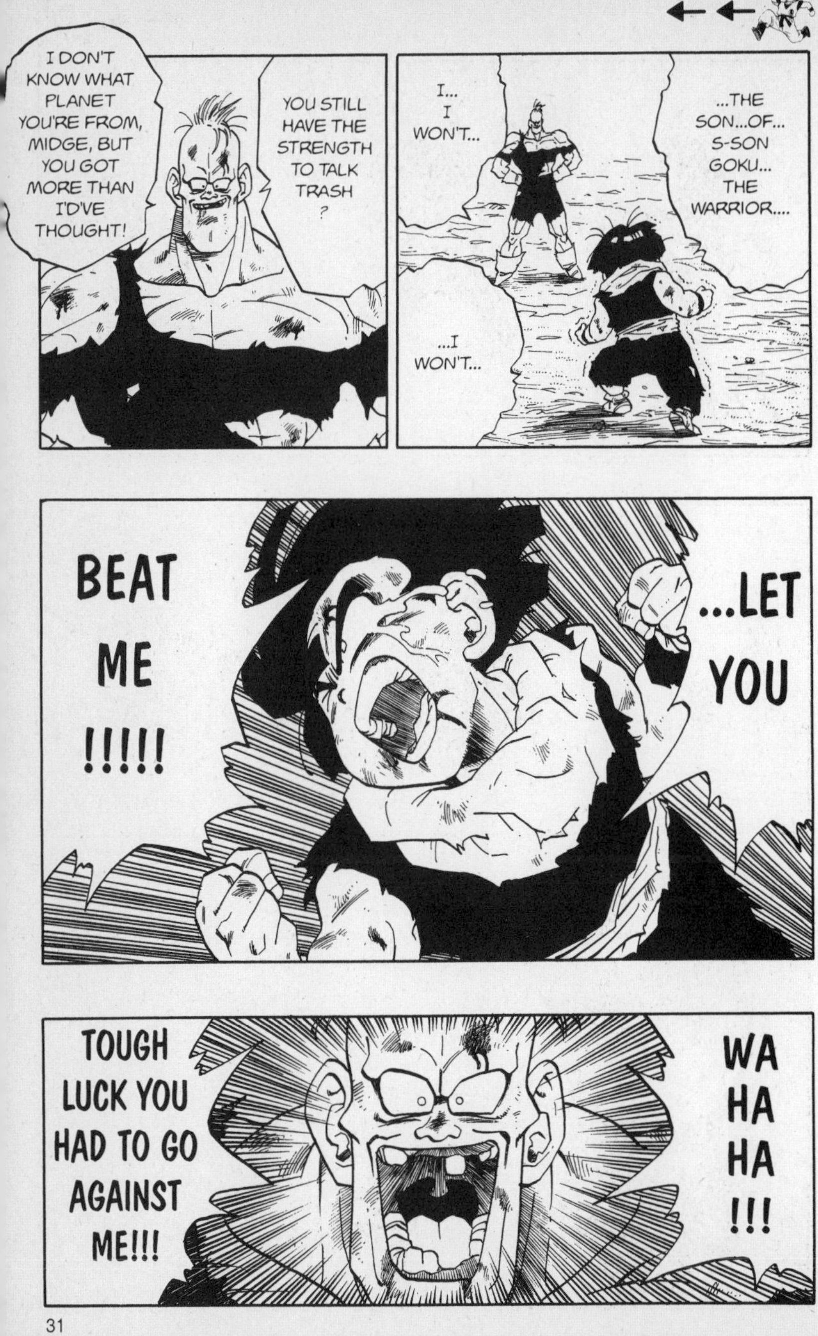
...THE SON...OF... S-SON GOKU... THE WARRIOR....
I... I WON'T...
...I WON'T...
YOU STILL HAVE THE STRENGTH TO TALK TRASH ?
I DON'T KNOW WHAT PLANET YOU'RE FROM, MIDGE, BUT YOU GOT MORE THAN I'D'VE THOUGHT!
...LET YOU
BEAT ME !!!!!
WA HA HA !!!
TOUGH LUCK YOU HAD TO GO AGAINST ME!!!

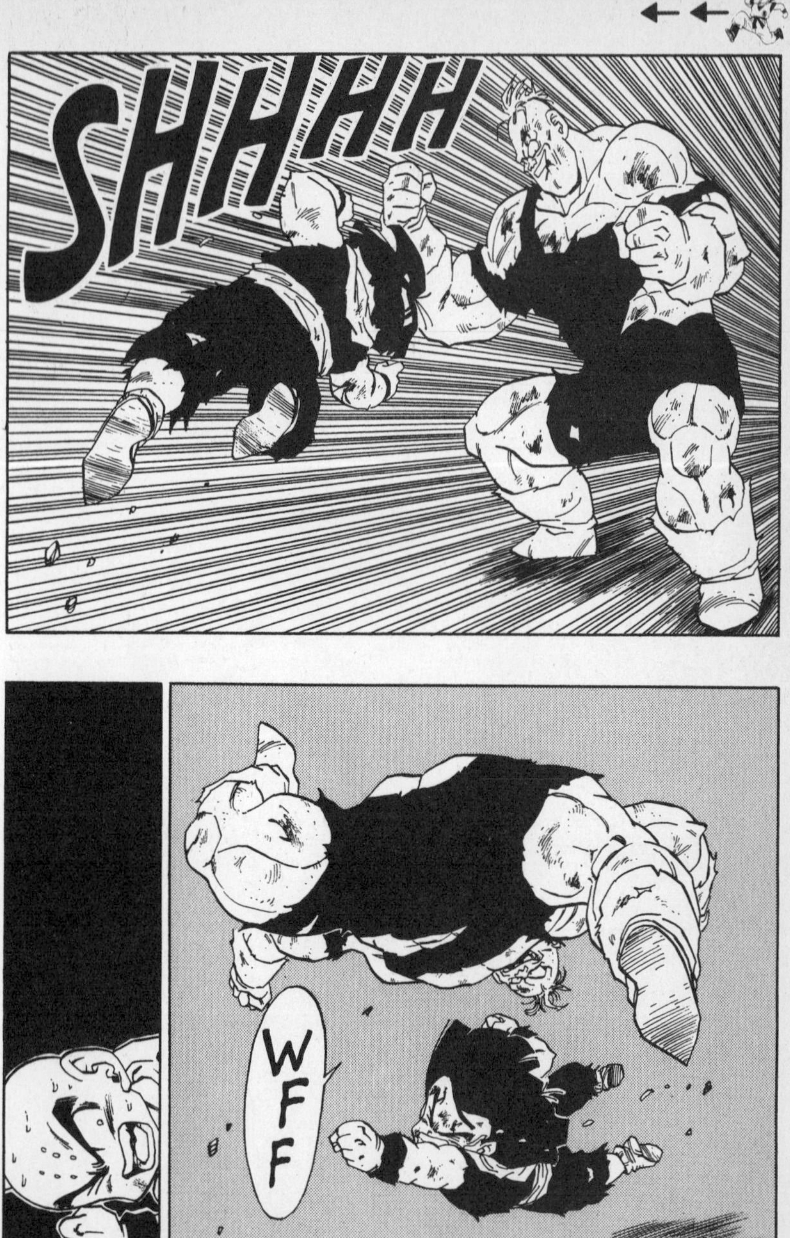
SHHHH
WFF

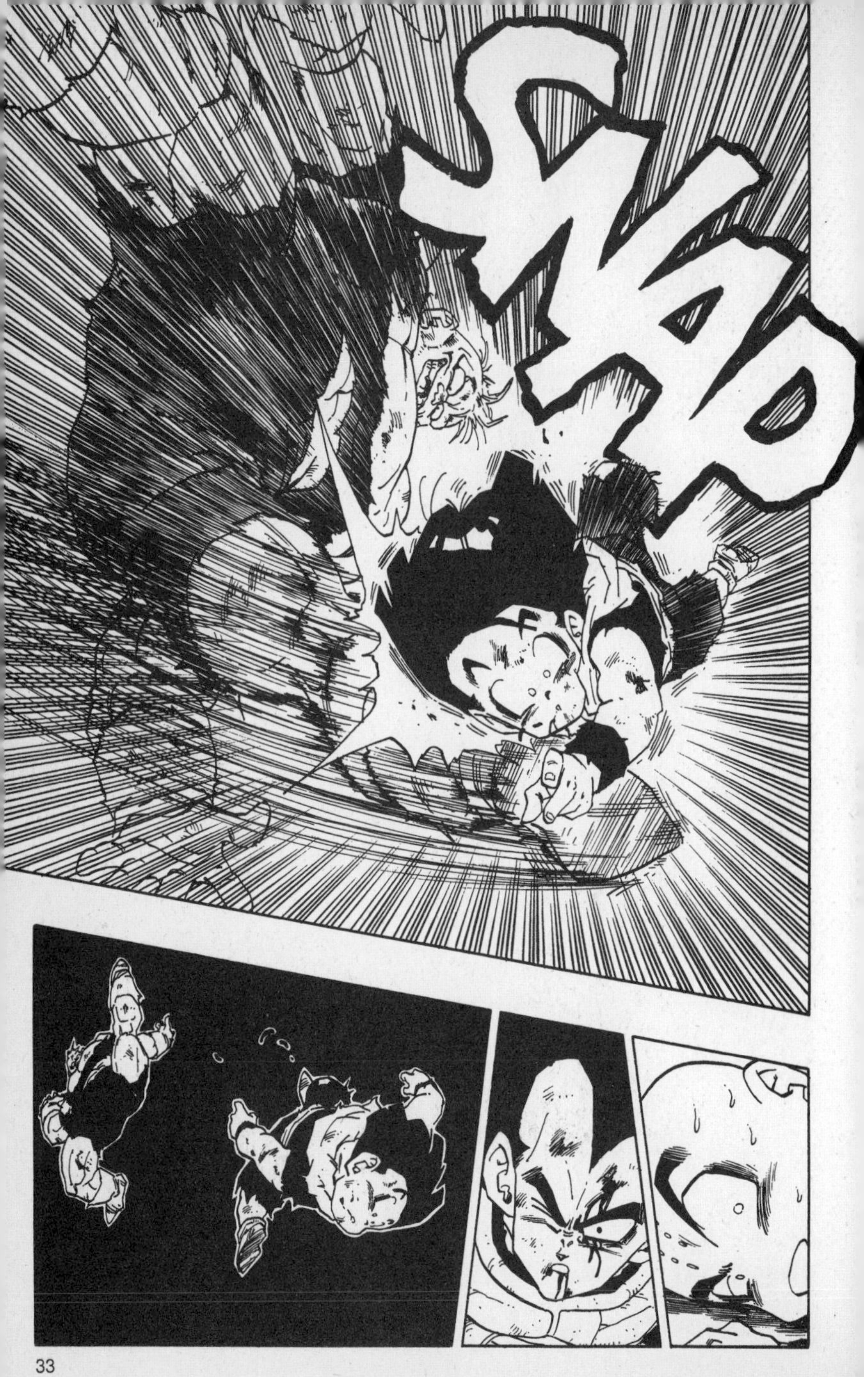
SNAP

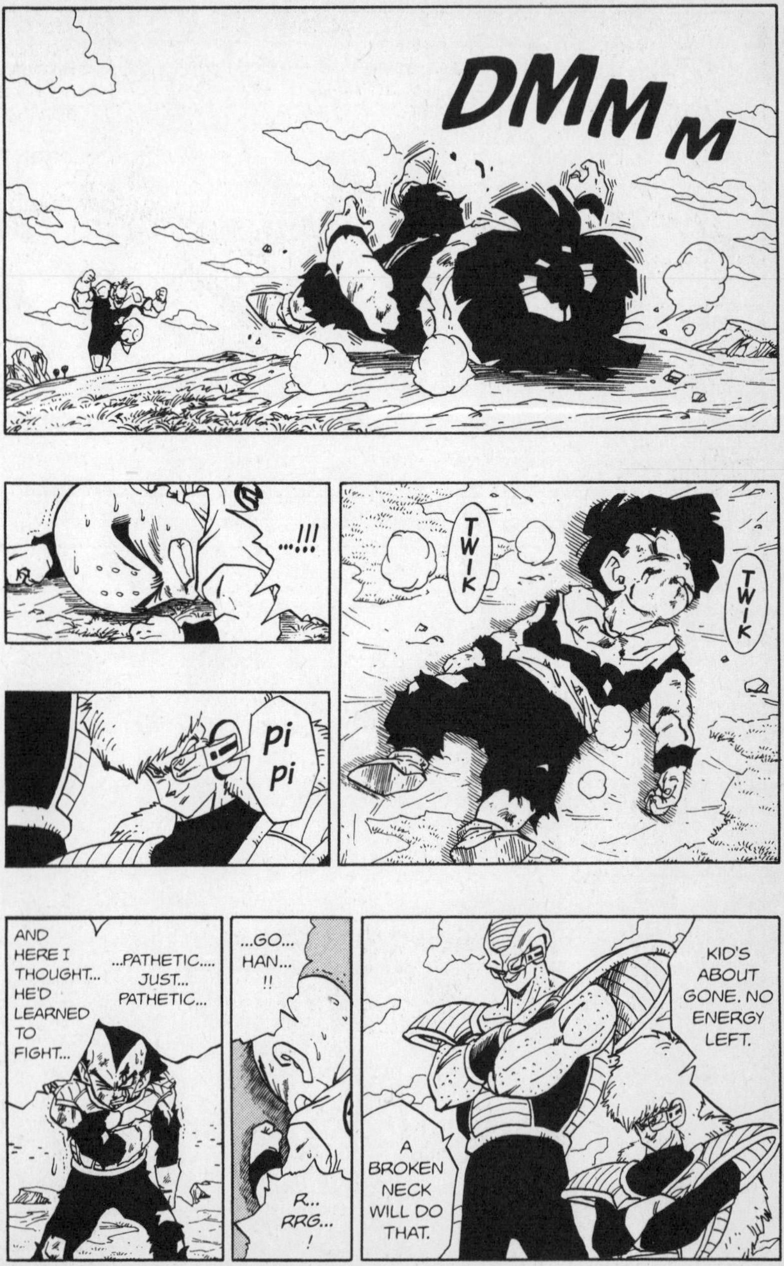
DMMM M
TWIK
TWIK
...!!!
pi pi
KID'S ABOUT GONE. NO ENERGY LEFT.
A BROKEN NECK WILL DO THAT.
...GO... HAN... !!
R... RRG... !
AND HERE I THOUGHT... HE'D LEARNED TO FIGHT...
...PATHETIC.... JUST... PATHETIC...

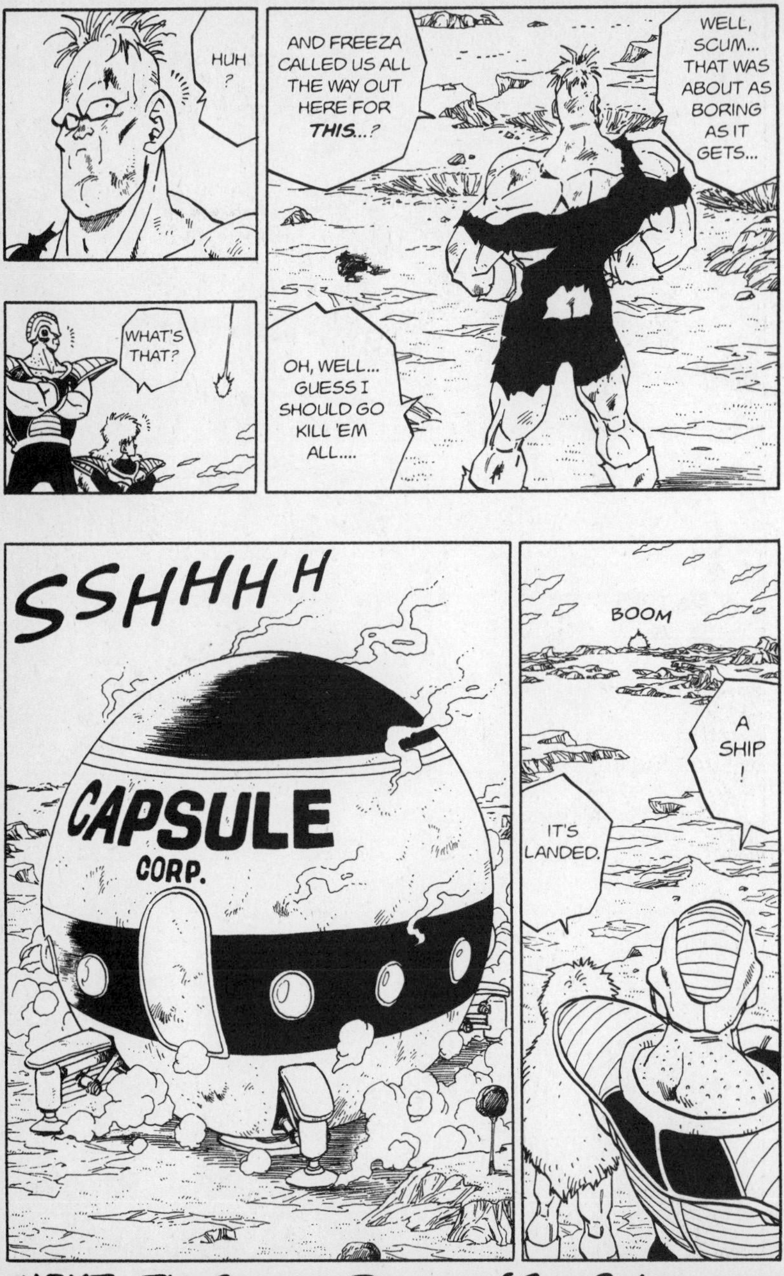
WELL, SCUM... THAT WAS ABOUT AS BORING AS IT GETS...
AND FREEZA CALLED US ALL THE WAY OUT HERE FOR *THIS*...?
OH, WELL... GUESS I SHOULD GO KILL 'EM ALL....
HUH ?
WHAT'S THAT?
BOOM
A SHIP !
IT'S LANDED.
SSHHHH
CAPSULE CORP.

NEXT: *The Strange Powers of Son Goku*

DBZ:85 • Son Goku Has Landed!

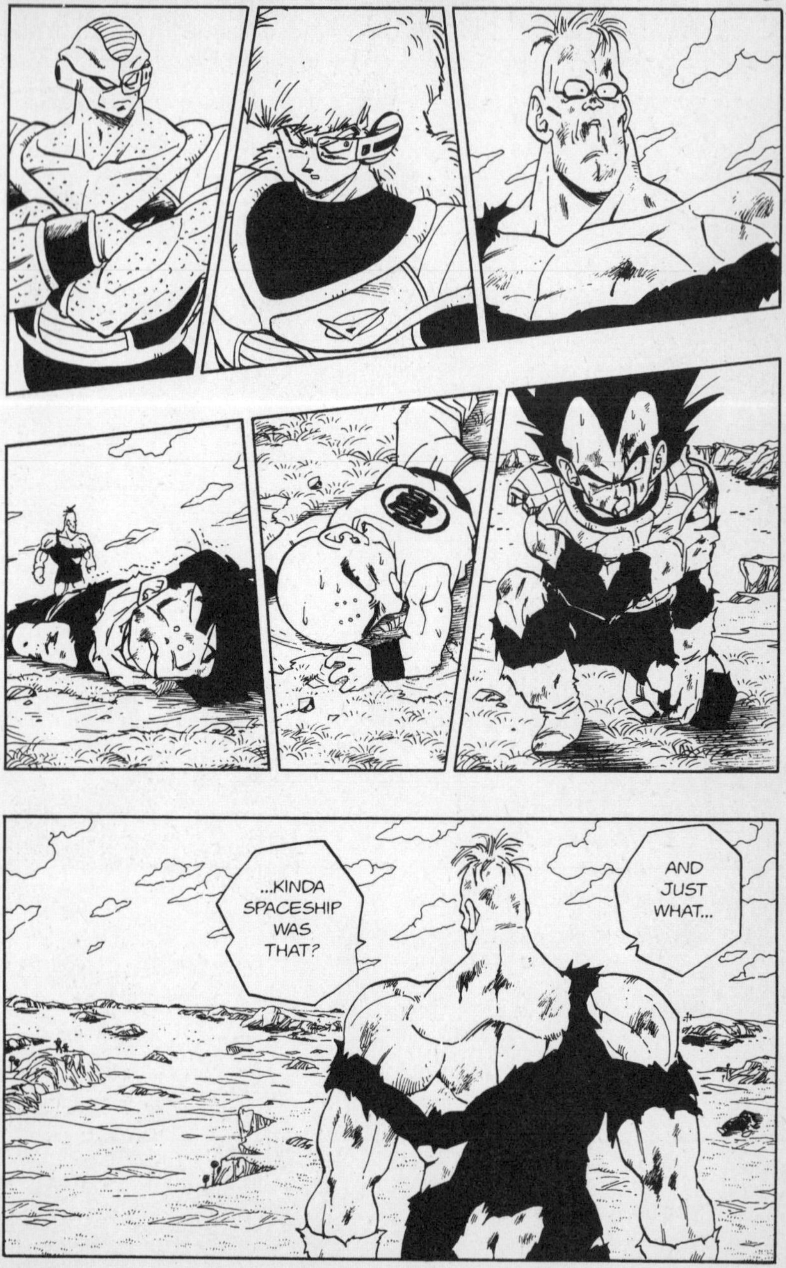
AND JUST WHAT...
...KINDA SPACESHIP WAS THAT?

HAS FINALLY COME...!!!

G-GOKU...

IT'S GOKU...

IT'S...

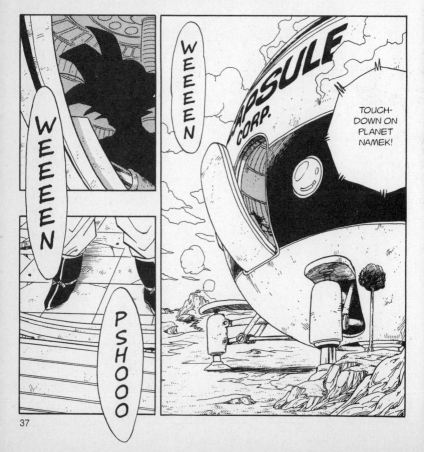

WEEEN

WEEEN

TOUCH-DOWN ON PLANET NAMEK!

P SHOOO

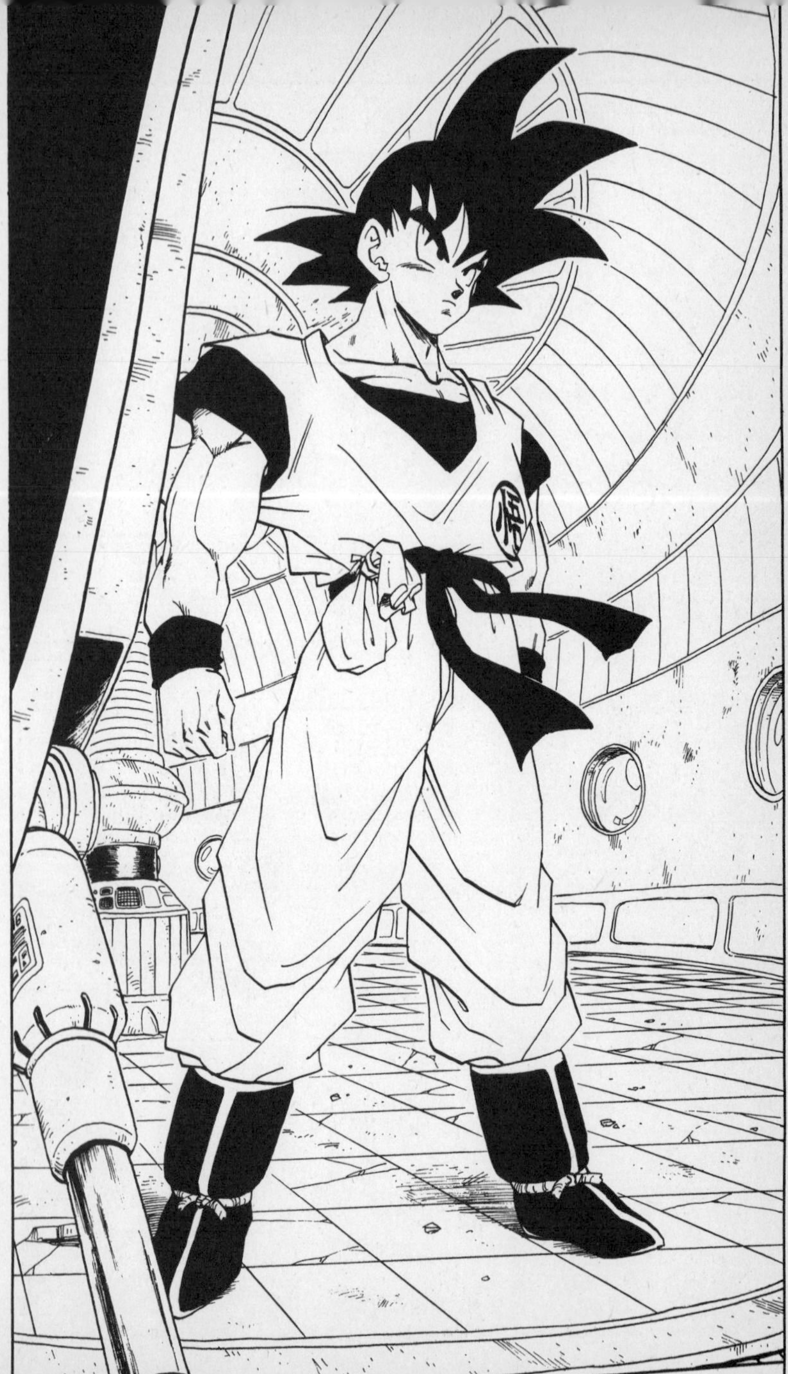

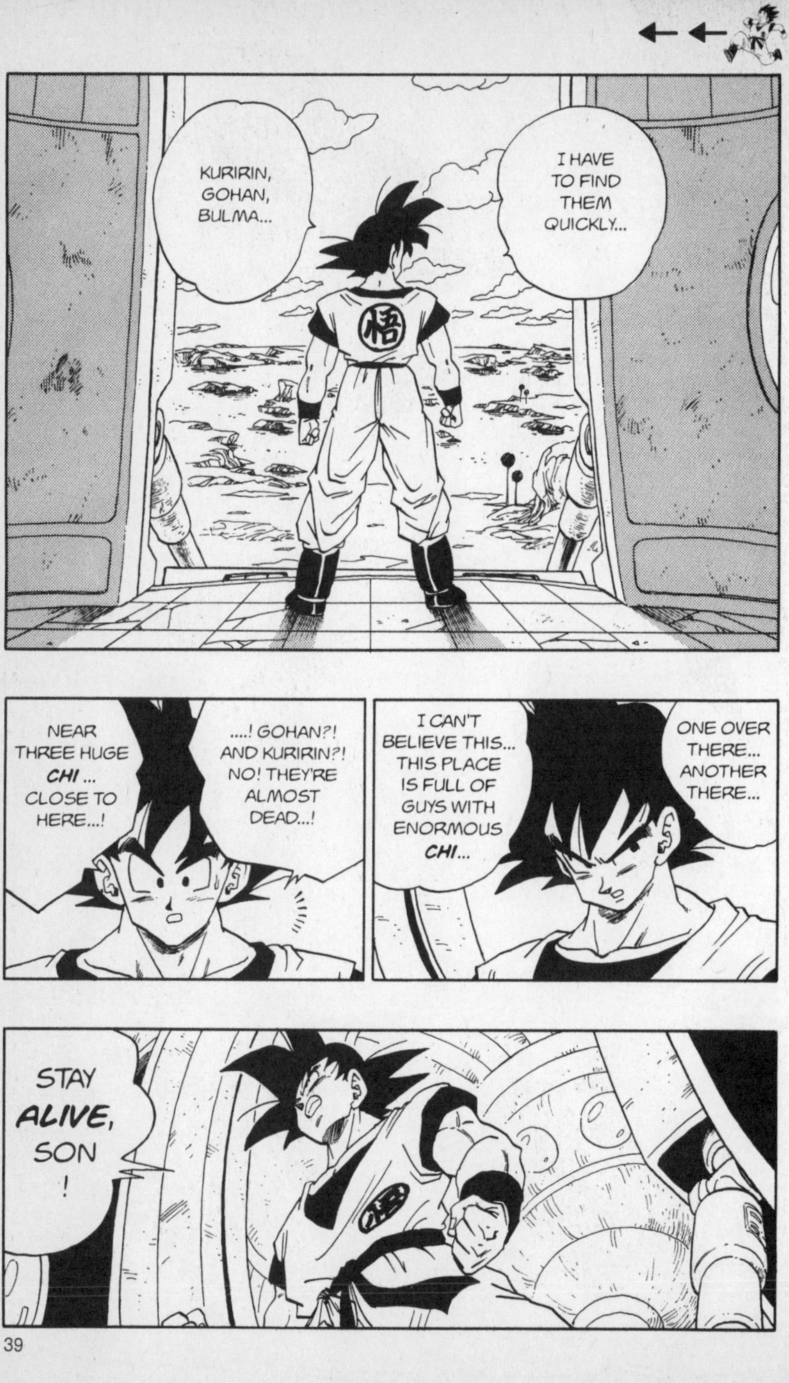

I HAVE TO FIND THEM QUICKLY...
KURIRIN, GOHAN, BULMA...
ONE OVER THERE... ANOTHER THERE...
I CAN'T BELIEVE THIS... THIS PLACE IS FULL OF GUYS WITH ENORMOUS *CHI*...
....! GOHAN?! AND KURIRIN?! NO! THEY'RE ALMOST DEAD...!
NEAR THREE HUGE *CHI* ... CLOSE TO HERE...!
STAY *ALIVE*, SON !

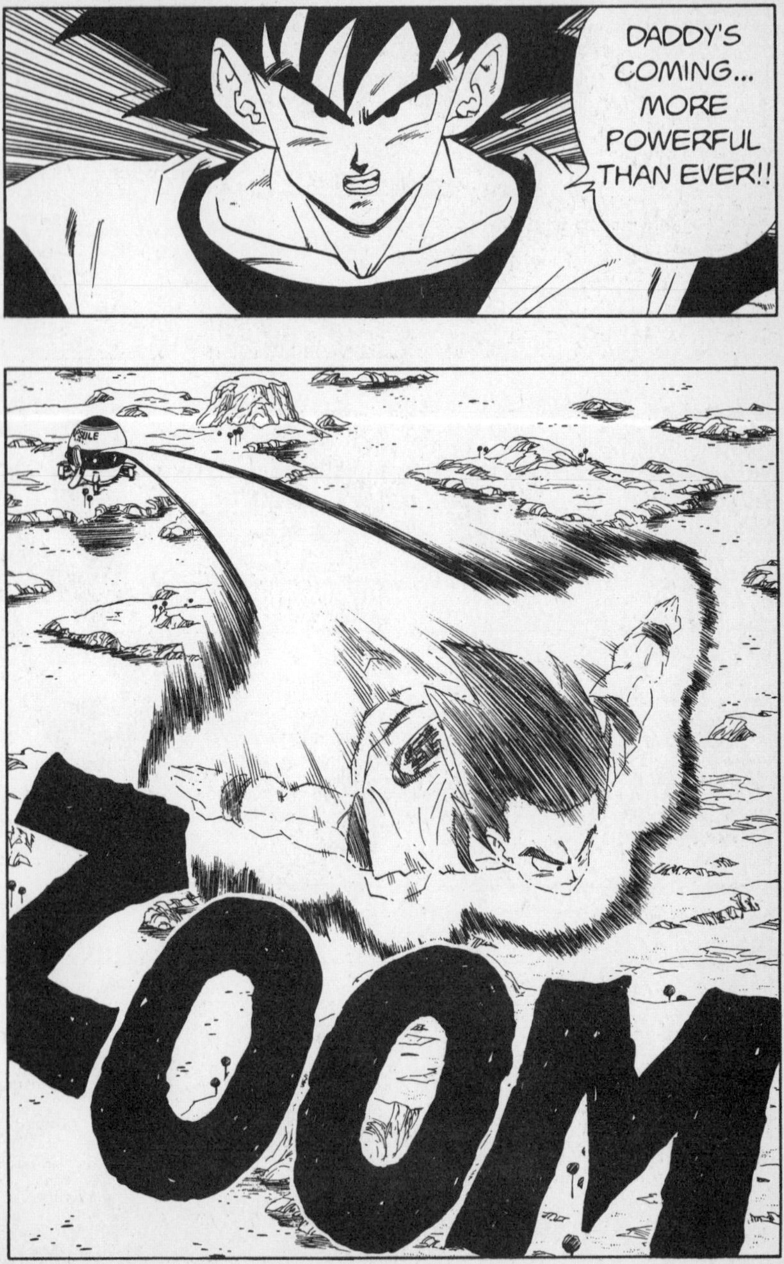
DADDY'S COMING... MORE POWERFUL THAN EVER!!
ZOOM

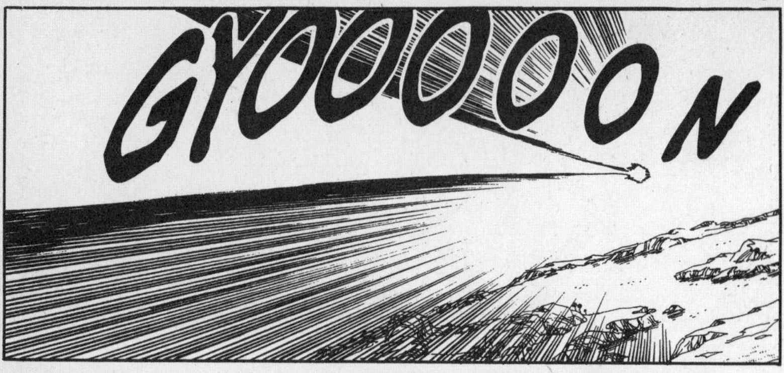
GYOOOOON

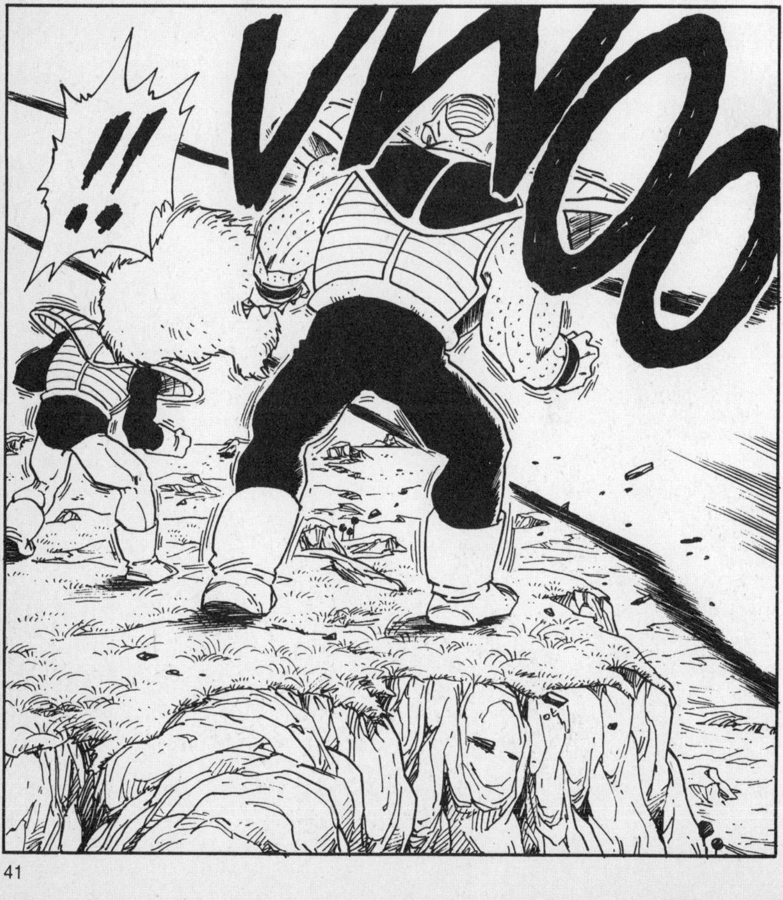
VWOO
!!

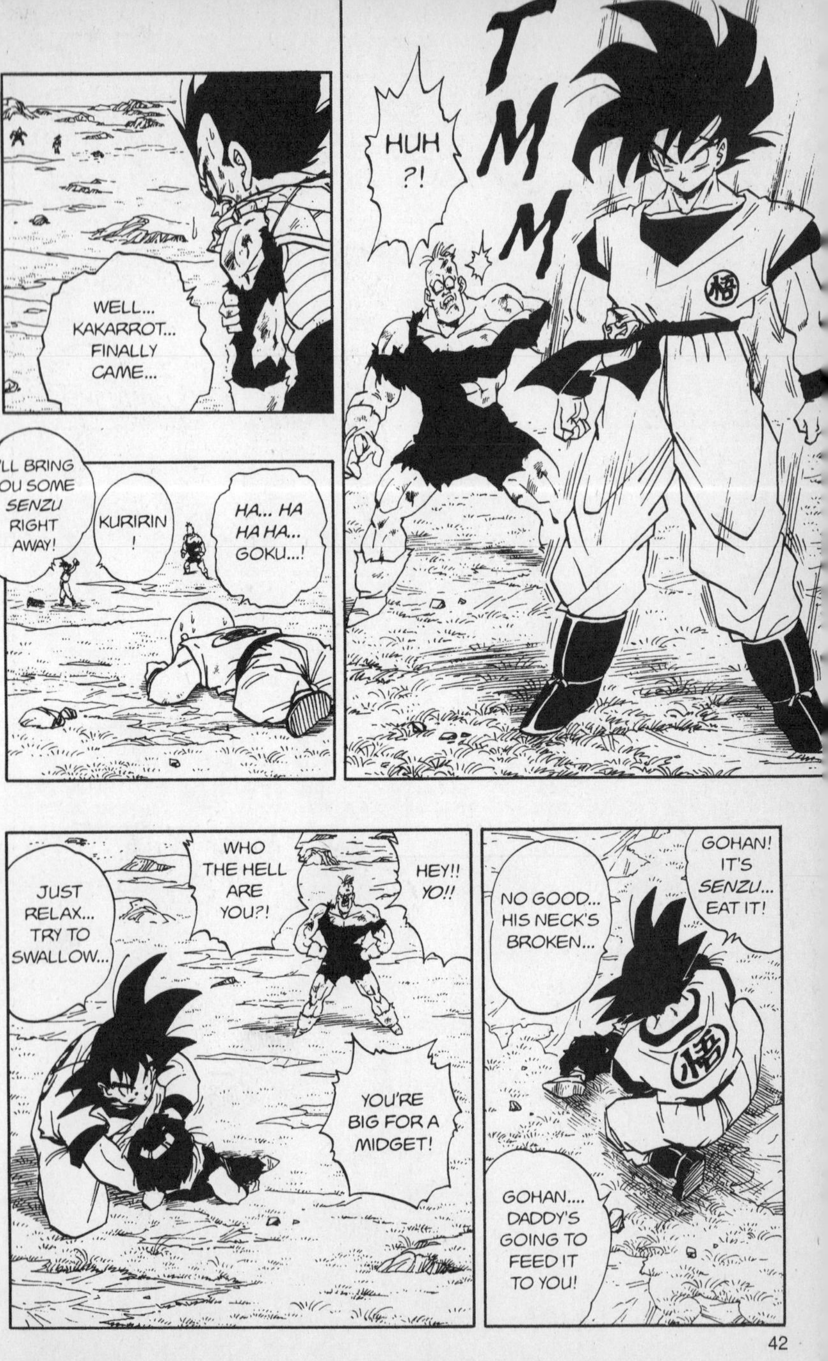
TMM
HUH ?!
WELL... KAKARROT... FINALLY CAME...
HA... HA HA HA... GOKU...!
KURIRIN !
I'LL BRING YOU SOME SENZU RIGHT AWAY!
GOHAN! IT'S SENZU... EAT IT!
NO GOOD... HIS NECK'S BROKEN...
GOHAN.... DADDY'S GOING TO FEED IT TO YOU!
HEY!! YO!!
WHO THE HELL ARE YOU?!
JUST RELAX... TRY TO SWALLOW...
YOU'RE BIG FOR A MIDGET!

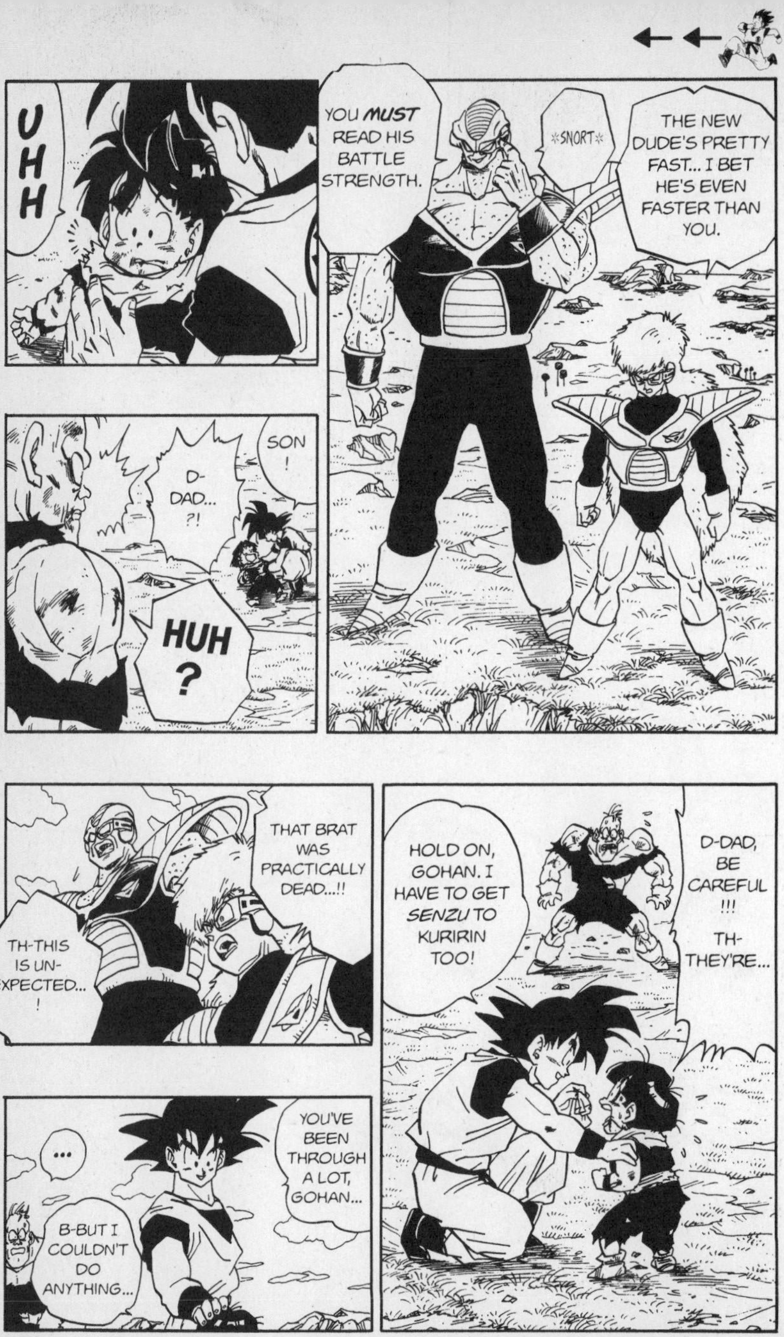
THE NEW DUDE'S PRETTY FAST... I BET HE'S EVEN FASTER THAN YOU.
✲SNORT✲
YOU MUST READ HIS BATTLE STRENGTH.
UHH
SON!
D-DAD...?!
HUH?
D-DAD, BE CAREFUL!!! TH-THEY'RE...
HOLD ON, GOHAN. I HAVE TO GET SENZU TO KURIRIN TOO!
THAT BRAT WAS PRACTICALLY DEAD...!!
TH-THIS IS UN-EXPECTED...!
YOU'VE BEEN THROUGH A LOT, GOHAN...
...
B-BUT I COULDN'T DO ANYTHING...

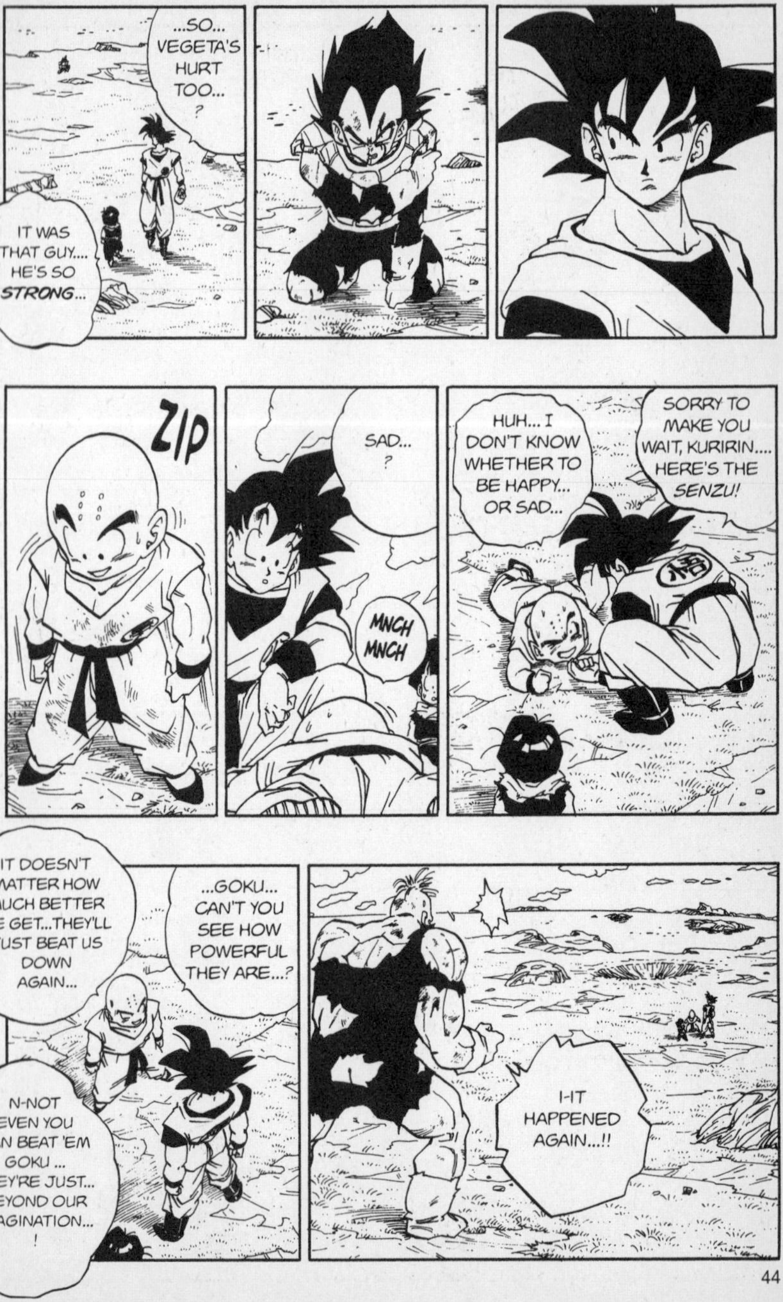
...SO... VEGETA'S HURT TOO...?
IT WAS THAT GUY.... HE'S SO **STRONG**...
SORRY TO MAKE YOU WAIT, KURIRIN.... HERE'S THE SENZU!
HUH... I DON'T KNOW WHETHER TO BE HAPPY... OR SAD...
SAD...?
MNCH MNCH
ZIP
I-IT HAPPENED AGAIN...!!
...GOKU... CAN'T YOU SEE HOW POWERFUL THEY ARE...?
IT DOESN'T MATTER HOW MUCH BETTER WE GET...THEY'LL JUST BEAT US DOWN AGAIN...
N-NOT EVEN YOU CAN BEAT 'EM GOKU ... THEY'RE JUST... BEYOND OUR IMAGINATION...!

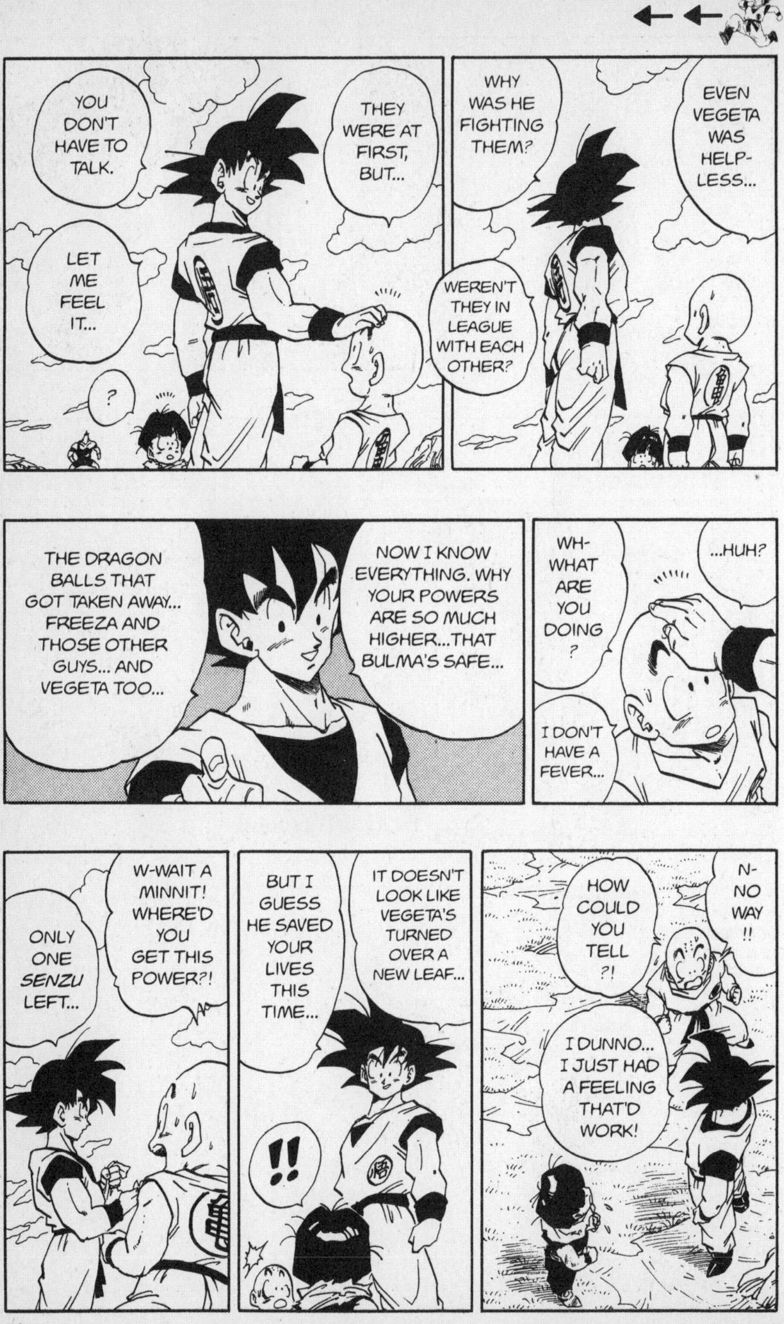
EVEN VEGETA WAS HELPLESS...
WHY WAS HE FIGHTING THEM?
WEREN'T THEY IN LEAGUE WITH EACH OTHER?
THEY WERE AT FIRST, BUT...
YOU DON'T HAVE TO TALK.
LET ME FEEL IT...
?
...HUH?
WH-WHAT ARE YOU DOING?
I DON'T HAVE A FEVER...
NOW I KNOW EVERYTHING. WHY YOUR POWERS ARE SO MUCH HIGHER...THAT BULMA'S SAFE...
THE DRAGON BALLS THAT GOT TAKEN AWAY... FREEZA AND THOSE OTHER GUYS... AND VEGETA TOO...
N-NO WAY!!
HOW COULD YOU TELL?!
I DUNNO... I JUST HAD A FEELING THAT'D WORK!
IT DOESN'T LOOK LIKE VEGETA'S TURNED OVER A NEW LEAF...
BUT I GUESS HE SAVED YOUR LIVES THIS TIME...
!!
W-WAIT A MINNIT! WHERE'D YOU GET THIS POWER?!
ONLY ONE SENZU LEFT...

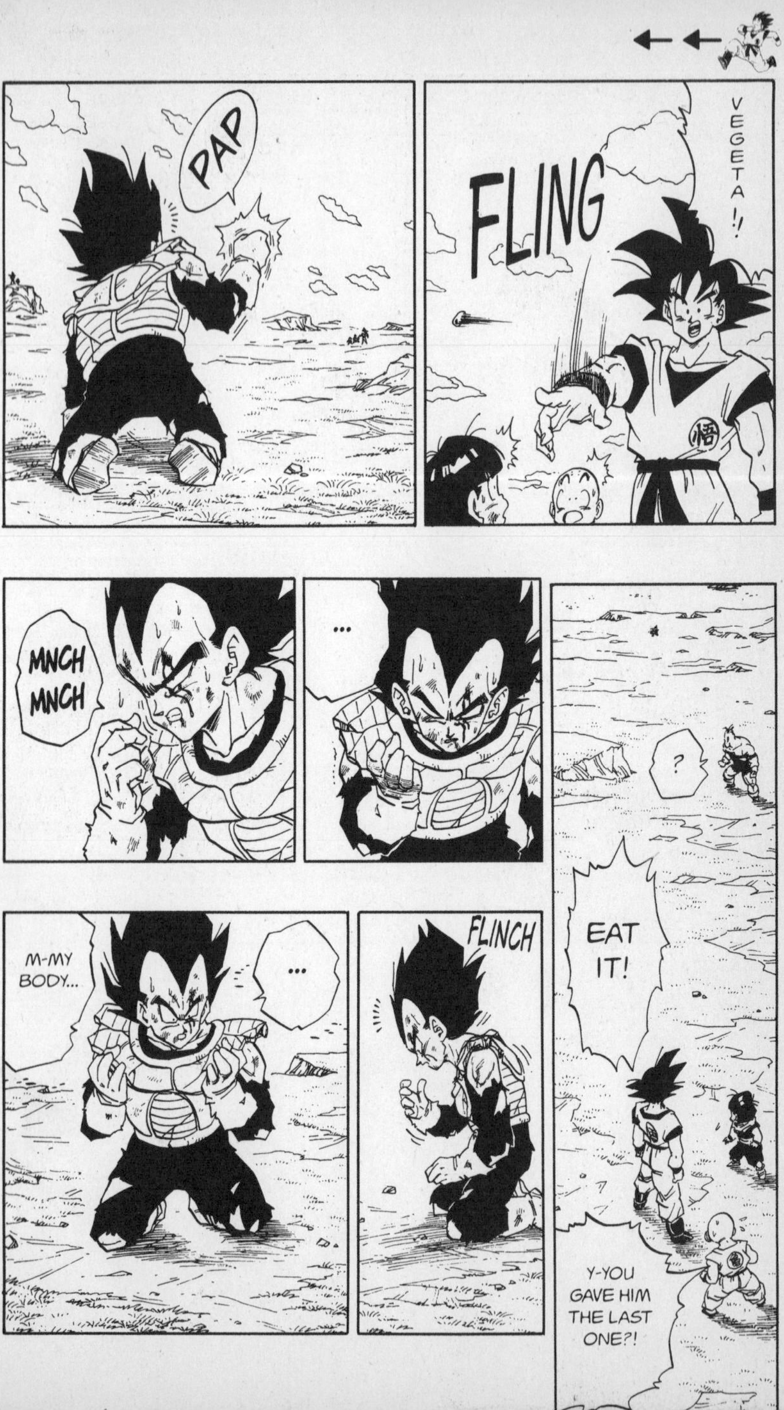
VEGETA!!
FLING
PAP
?
EAT IT!
Y-YOU GAVE HIM THE LAST ONE?!
...
MNCH MNCH
FLINCH
...
M-MY BODY...

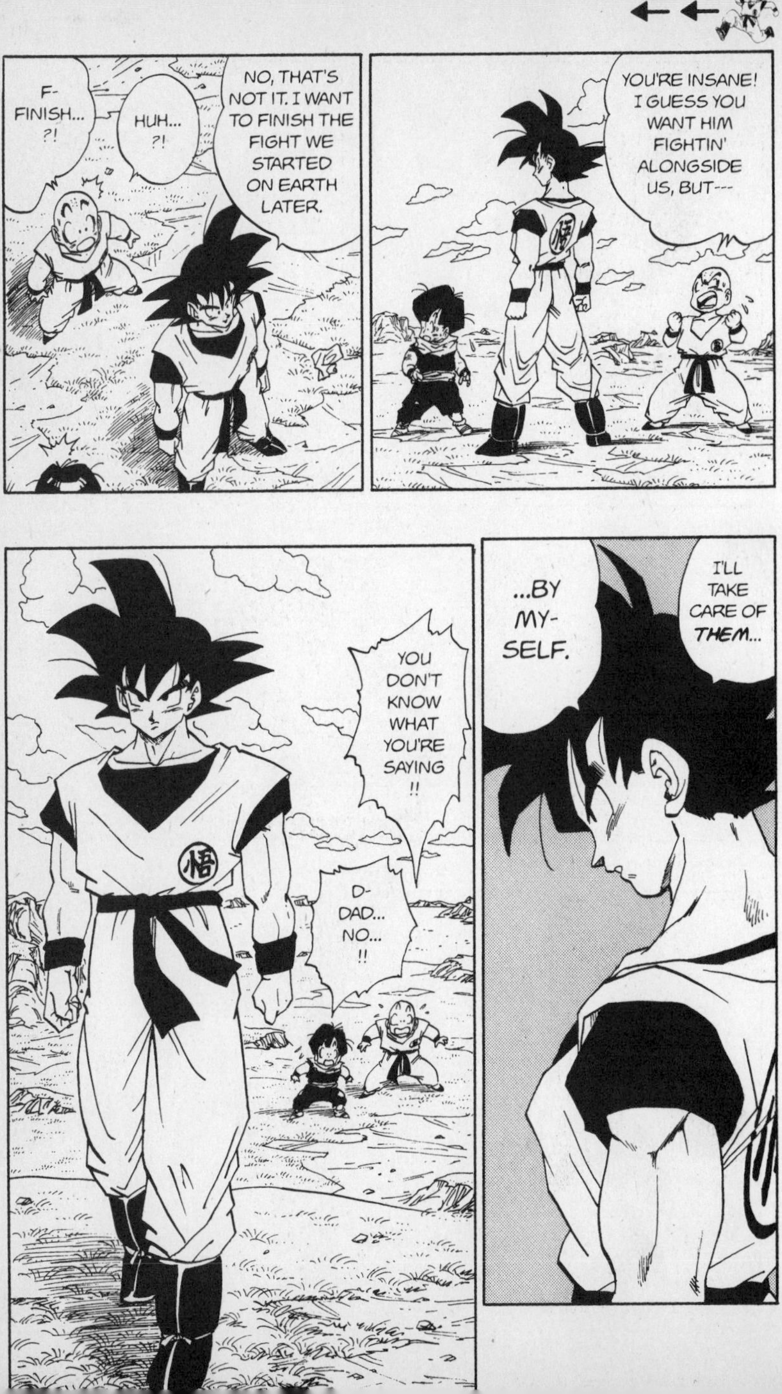
YOU'RE INSANE! I GUESS YOU WANT HIM FIGHTIN' ALONGSIDE US, BUT---
NO, THAT'S NOT IT. I WANT TO FINISH THE FIGHT WE STARTED ON EARTH LATER.
HUH...?!
F-FINISH...?!
I'LL TAKE CARE OF *THEM*...
...BY MY-SELF.
YOU DON'T KNOW WHAT YOU'RE SAYING!!
D-DAD... NO...!!

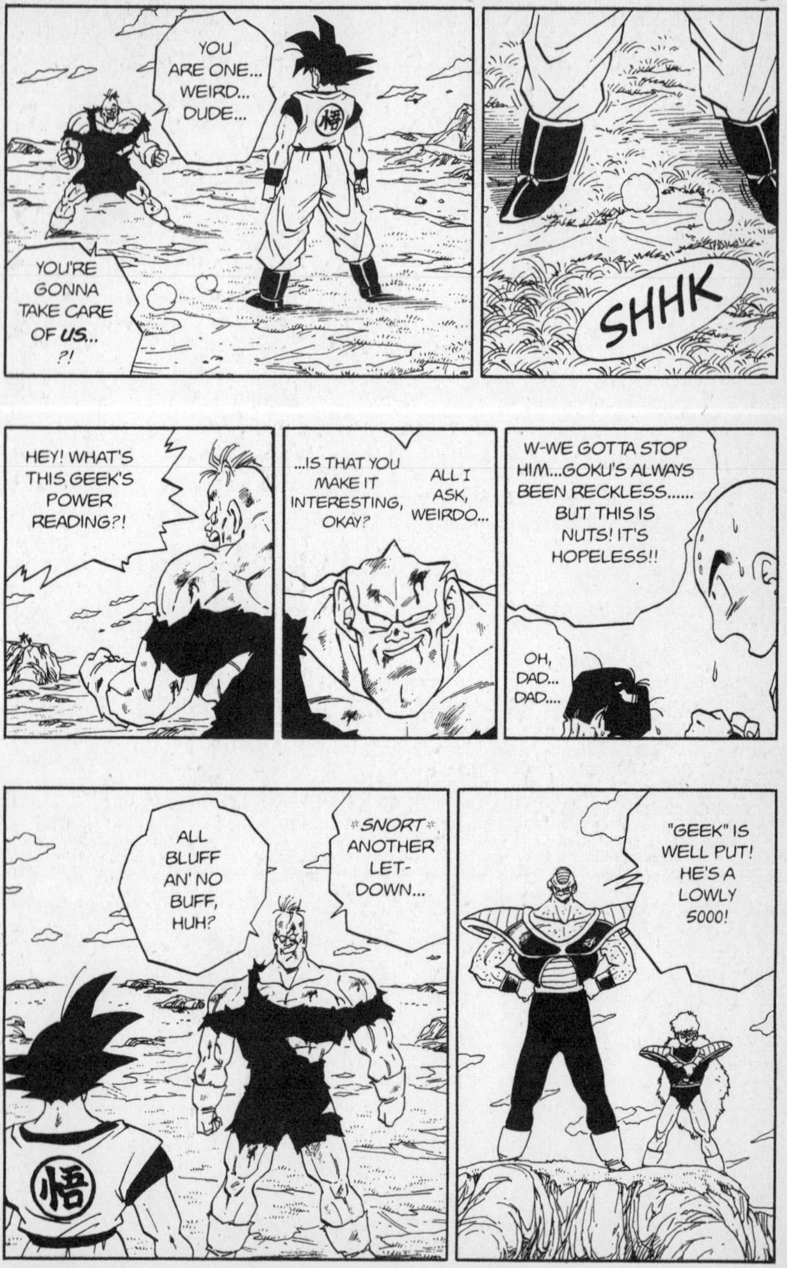
SHHK
YOU ARE ONE... WEIRD... DUDE...
YOU'RE GONNA TAKE CARE OF US...?!
W-WE GOTTA STOP HIM...GOKU'S ALWAYS BEEN RECKLESS...... BUT THIS IS NUTS! IT'S HOPELESS!!
OH, DAD... DAD....
ALL I ASK, WEIRDO...
...IS THAT YOU MAKE IT INTERESTING, OKAY?
HEY! WHAT'S THIS GEEK'S POWER READING?!
"GEEK" IS WELL PUT! HE'S A LOWLY 5000!
SNORT ANOTHER LET-DOWN...
ALL BLUFF AN' NO BUFF, HUH?

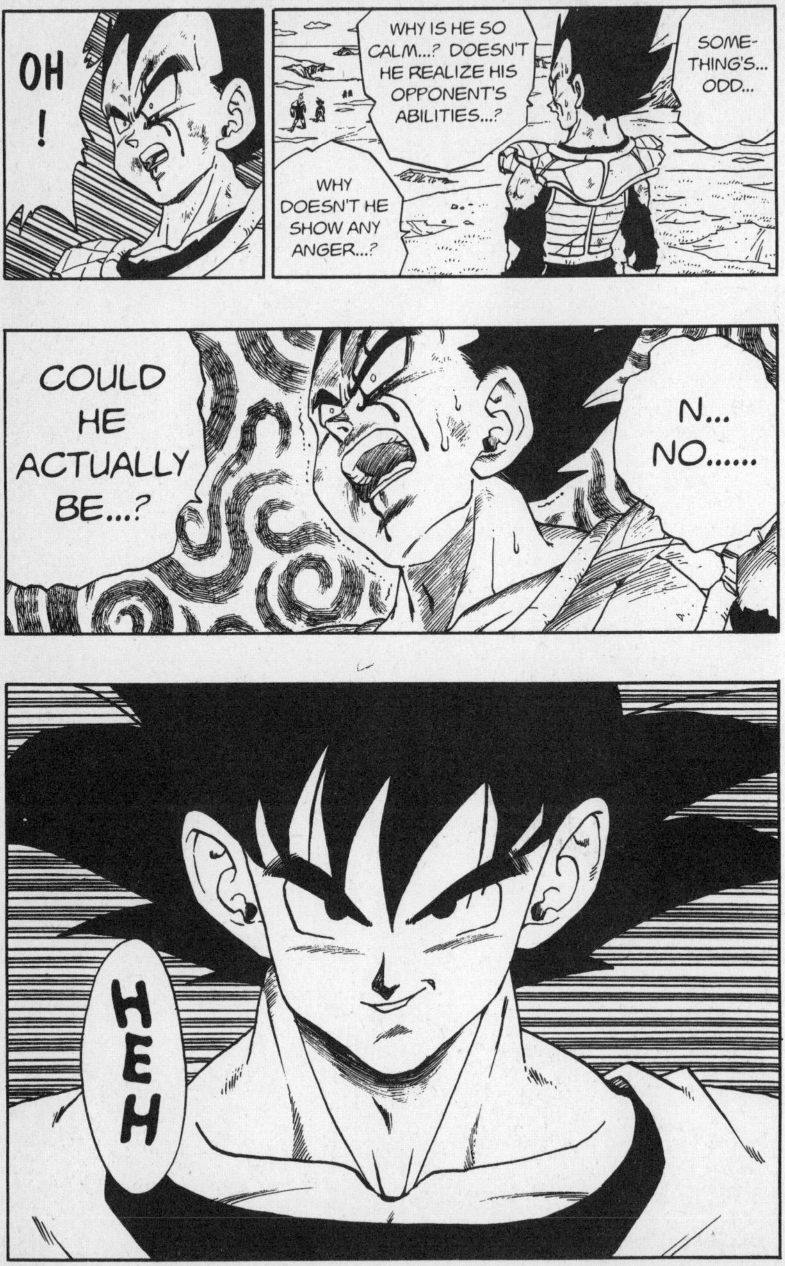
SOME-THING'S... ODD...
WHY IS HE SO CALM...? DOESN'T HE REALIZE HIS OPPONENT'S ABILITIES...?
WHY DOESN'T HE SHOW ANY ANGER...?
OH !
N... NO......
COULD HE ACTUALLY BE...?
HEH

NEXT: A Super Saiyan?!

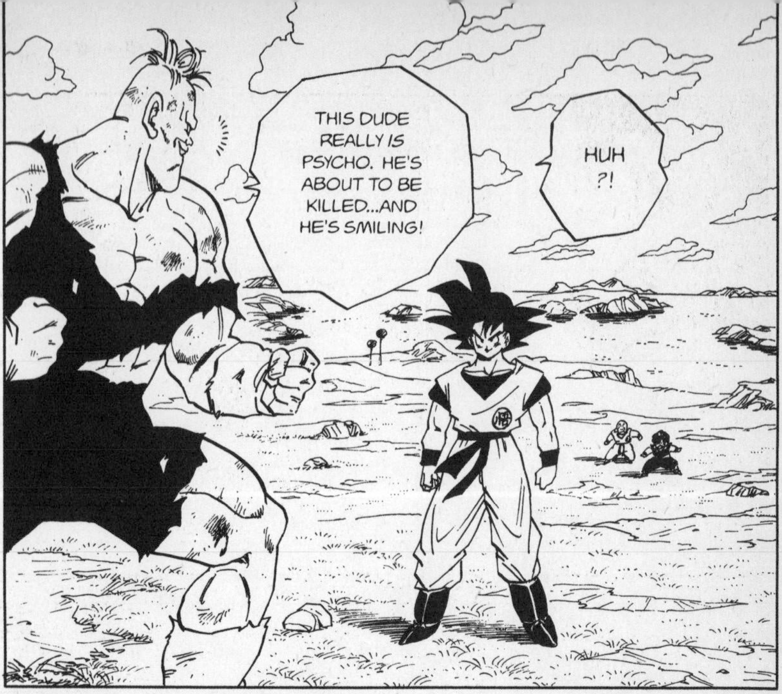
HUH ?!
THIS DUDE REALLY IS PSYCHO. HE'S ABOUT TO BE KILLED...AND HE'S SMILING!

DBZ:86 • Super Saiyan!?

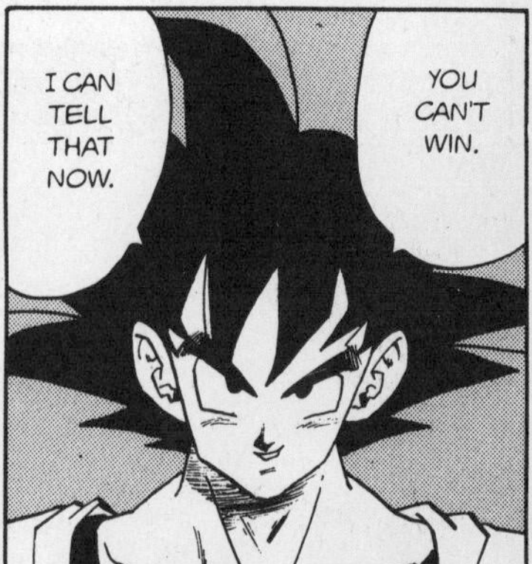
YOU CAN'T WIN.
I CAN TELL THAT NOW.
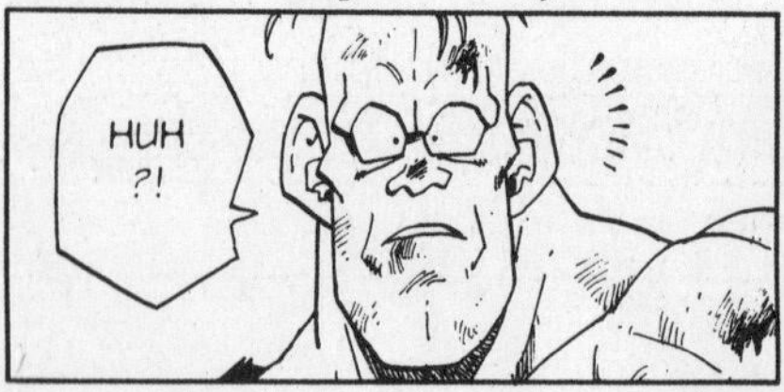
HUH ?!
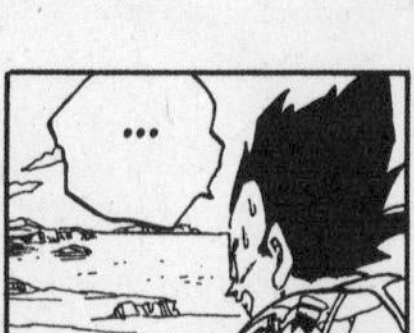
...
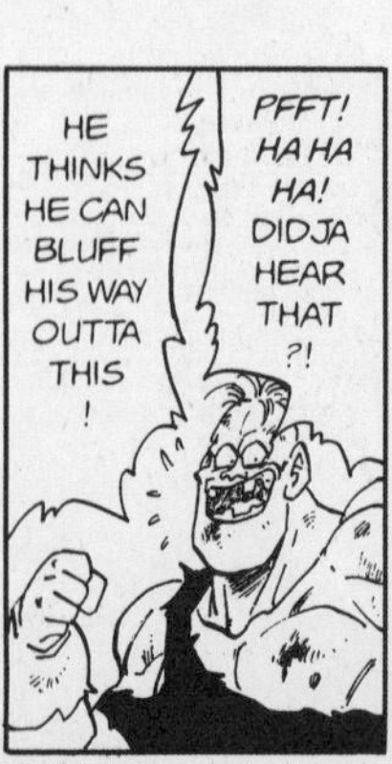
PFFT! HA HA HA! DIDJA HEAR THAT ?!
HE THINKS HE CAN BLUFF HIS WAY OUTTA THIS !

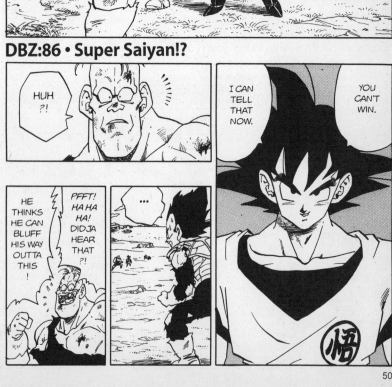

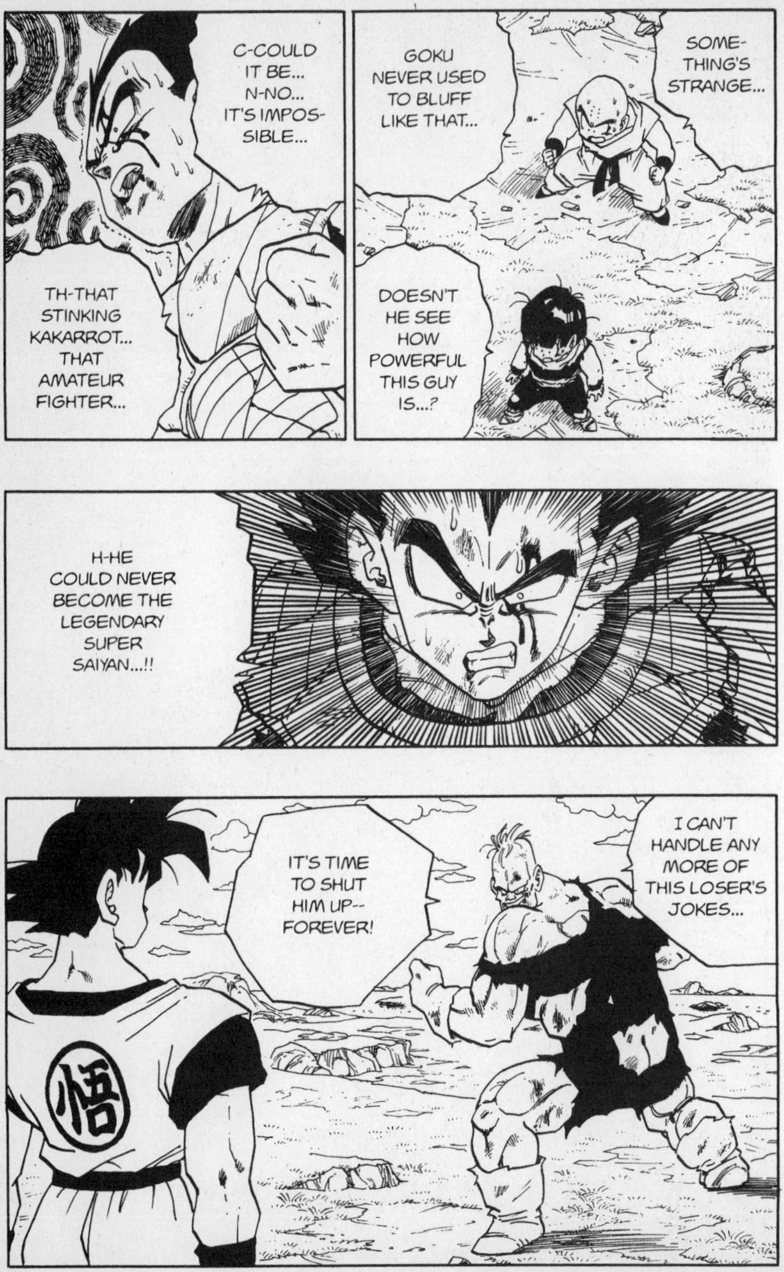
SOME-THING'S STRANGE...
GOKU NEVER USED TO BLUFF LIKE THAT...
DOESN'T HE SEE HOW POWERFUL THIS GUY IS...?
C-COULD IT BE... N-NO... IT'S IMPOSSIBLE...
TH-THAT STINKING KAKARROT... THAT AMATEUR FIGHTER...
H-HE COULD NEVER BECOME THE LEGENDARY SUPER SAIYAN...!!
I CAN'T HANDLE ANY MORE OF THIS LOSER'S JOKES...
IT'S TIME TO SHUT HIM UP--FOREVER!

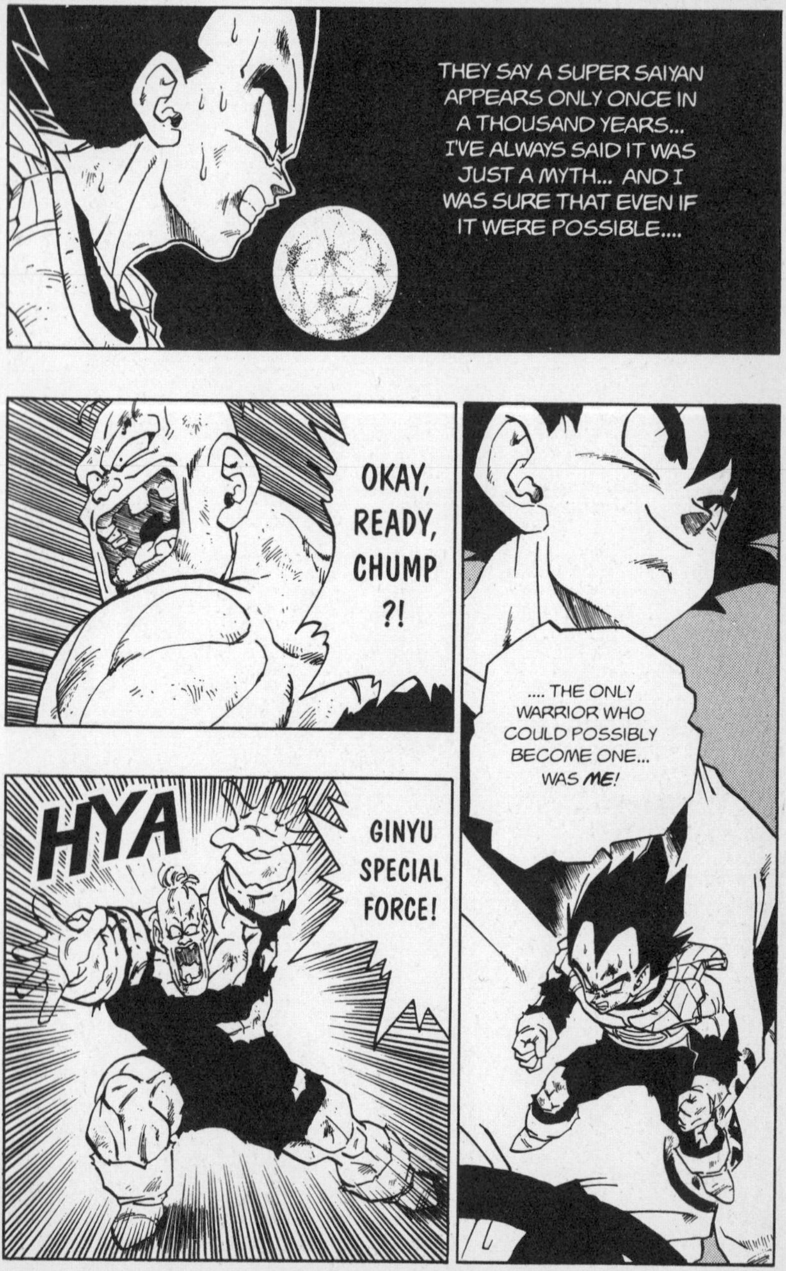
THEY SAY A SUPER SAIYAN APPEARS ONLY ONCE IN A THOUSAND YEARS... I'VE ALWAYS SAID IT WAS JUST A MYTH... AND I WAS SURE THAT EVEN IF IT WERE POSSIBLE....
.... THE ONLY WARRIOR WHO COULD POSSIBLY BECOME ONE... WAS *ME*!
OKAY, READY, CHUMP ?!
GINYU SPECIAL FORCE!
HYA

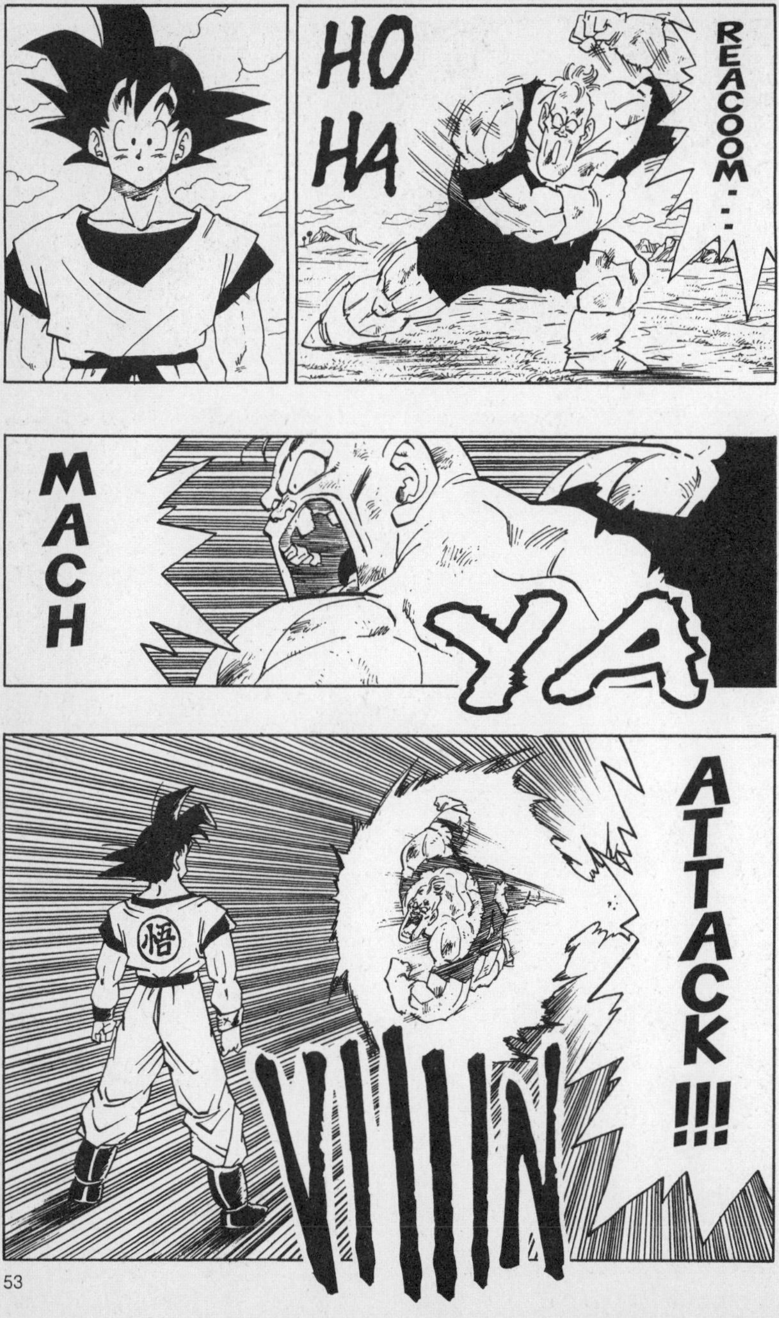
REACOOM...
HO HA
MACH
YA
ATTACK!!!
VIIIN

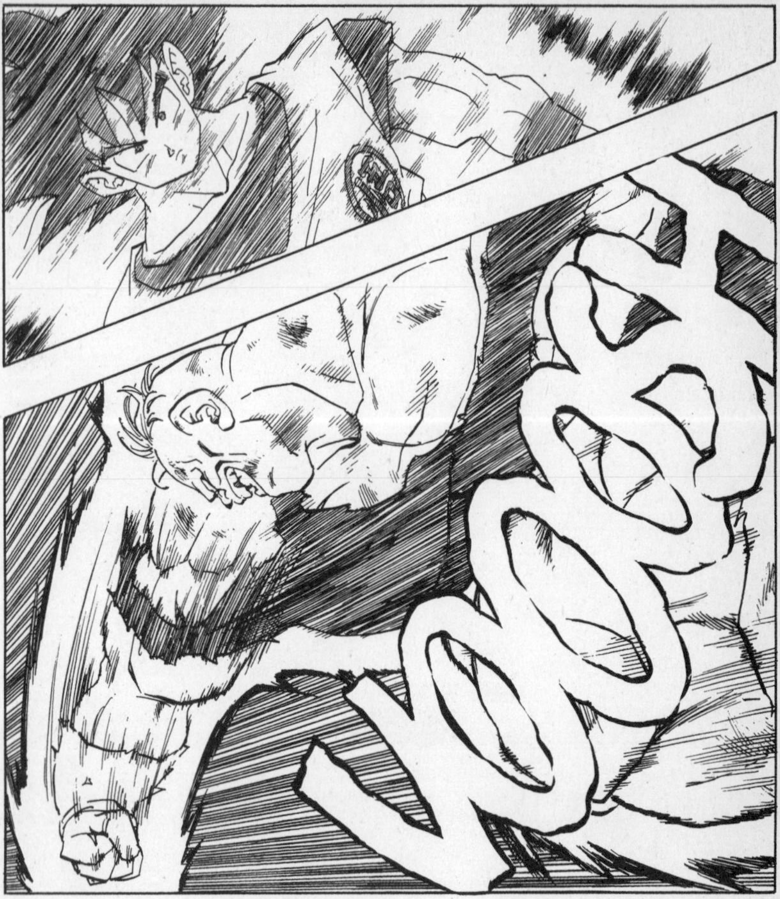

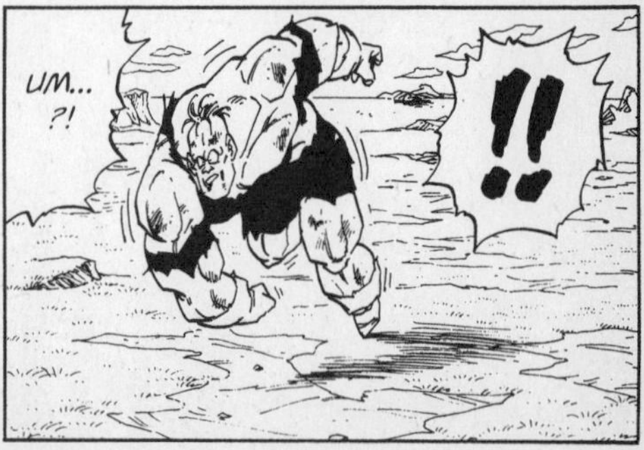
UM...
?!
!!

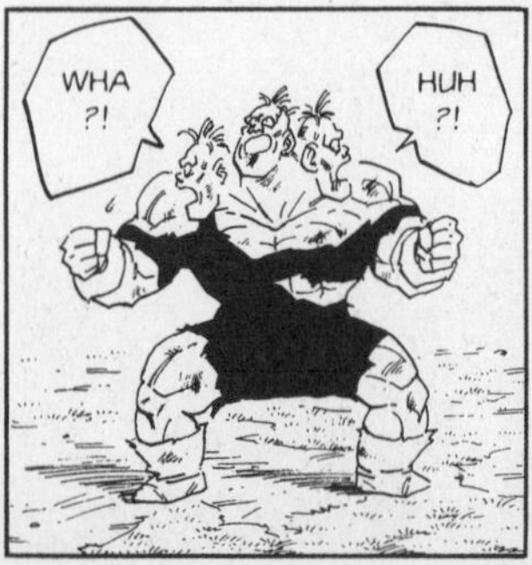
HUH
?!
WHA
?!

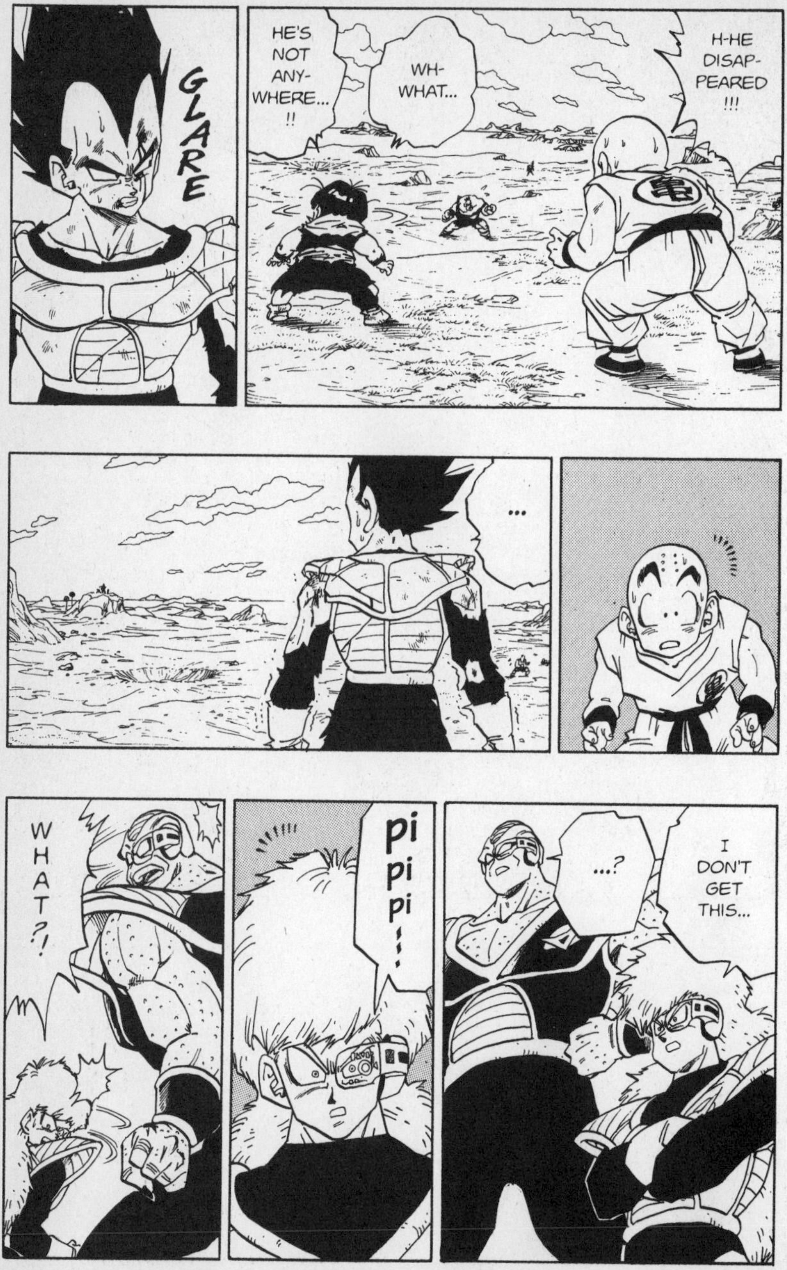
H-HE DISAP-PEARED !!!
WH-WHAT...
HE'S NOT ANY-WHERE... !!
GLARE
...
I DON'T GET THIS...
...?
pi pi pi !!
WHAT?!

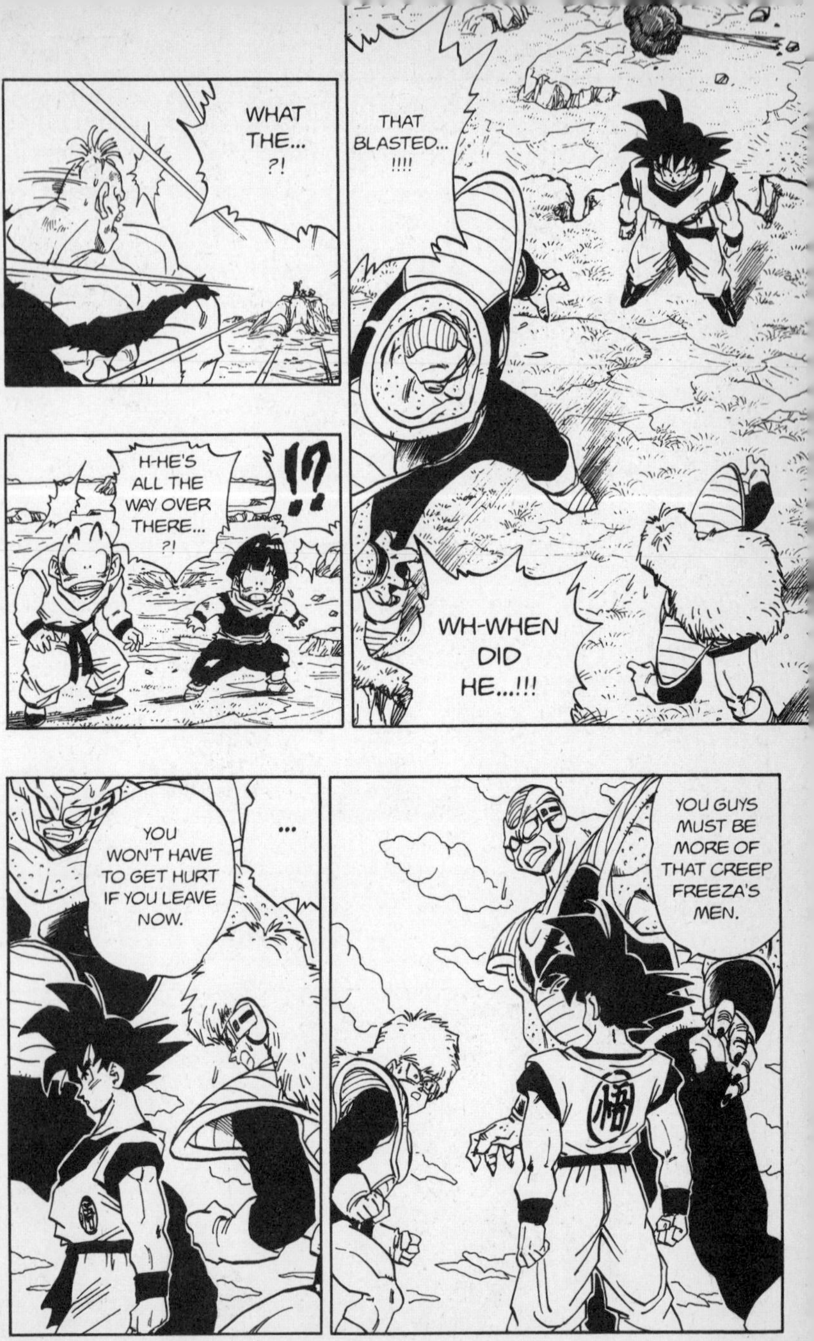
THAT BLASTED... !!!!
WH-WHEN DID HE...!!!
WHAT THE... ?!
H-HE'S ALL THE WAY OVER THERE... ?!
!?
YOU GUYS MUST BE MORE OF THAT CREEP FREEZA'S MEN.
...
YOU WON'T HAVE TO GET HURT IF YOU LEAVE NOW.

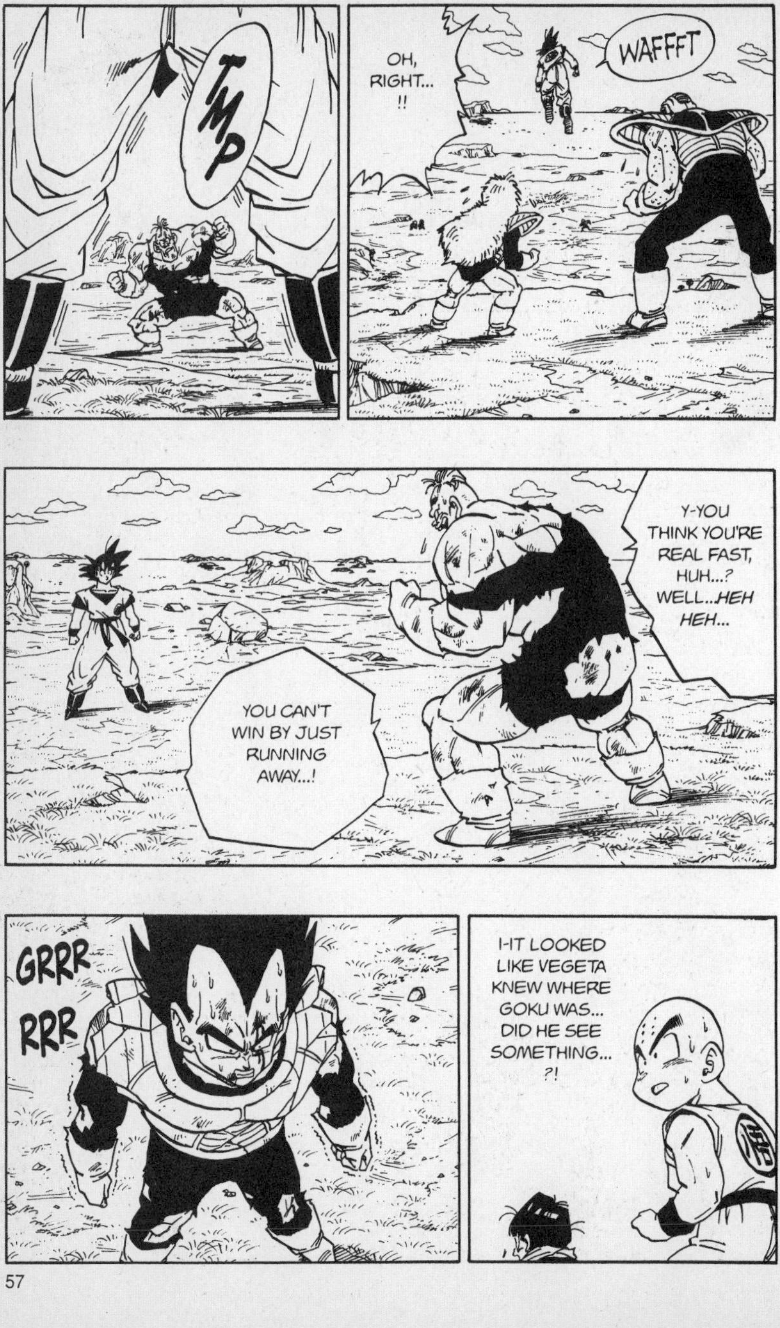
WAFFFT
OH, RIGHT... !!
TMP
Y-YOU THINK YOU'RE REAL FAST, HUH...? WELL...HEH HEH...
YOU CAN'T WIN BY JUST RUNNING AWAY...!
I-IT LOOKED LIKE VEGETA KNEW WHERE GOKU WAS... DID HE SEE SOMETHING... ?!
GRRR RRR

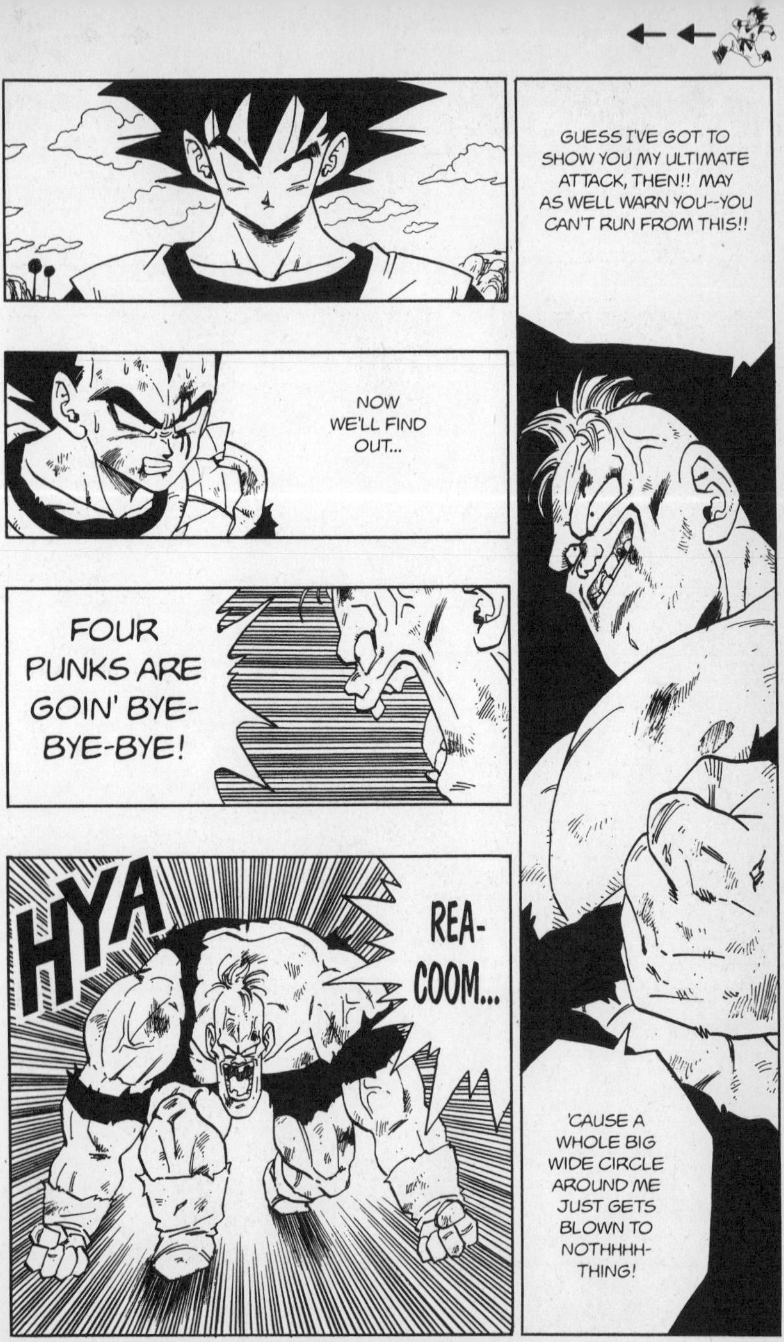
GUESS I'VE GOT TO SHOW YOU MY ULTIMATE ATTACK, THEN!! MAY AS WELL WARN YOU--YOU CAN'T RUN FROM THIS!!
'CAUSE A WHOLE BIG WIDE CIRCLE AROUND ME JUST GETS BLOWN TO NOTHHHH-THING!
NOW WE'LL FIND OUT...
FOUR PUNKS ARE GOIN' BYE-BYE-BYE!
HYA
REA-COOM...

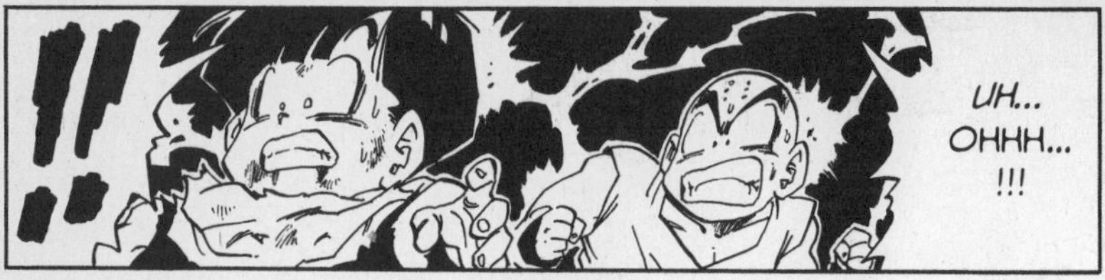
UH...
OHHH...
!!!
!!

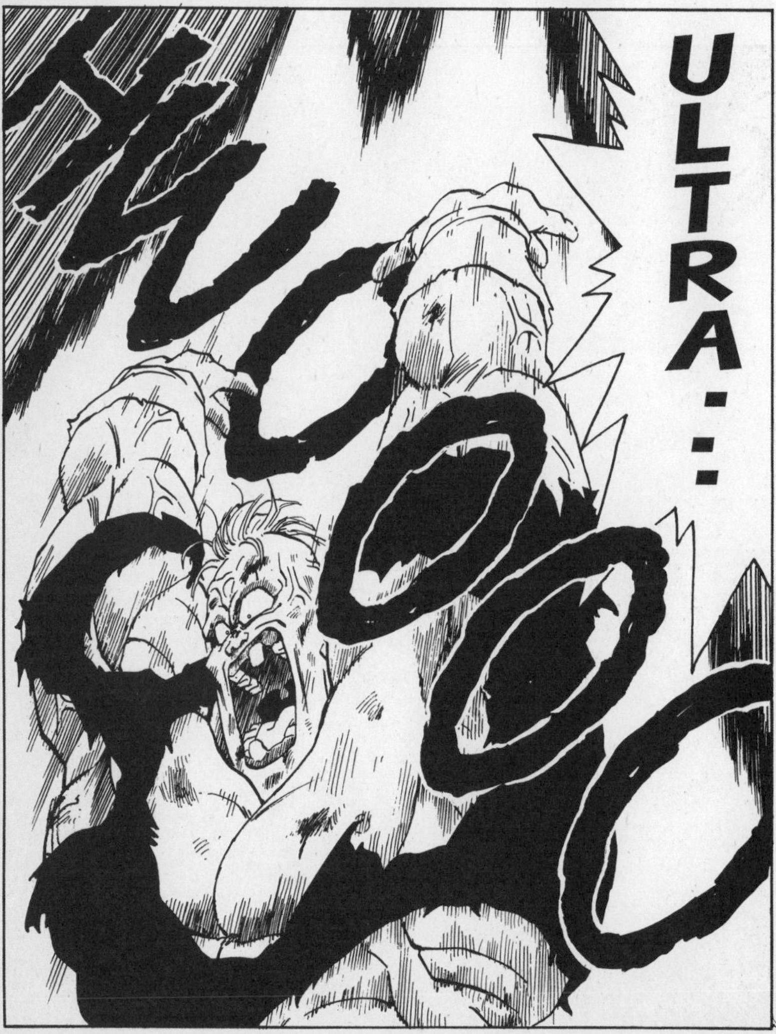
ULTRA...

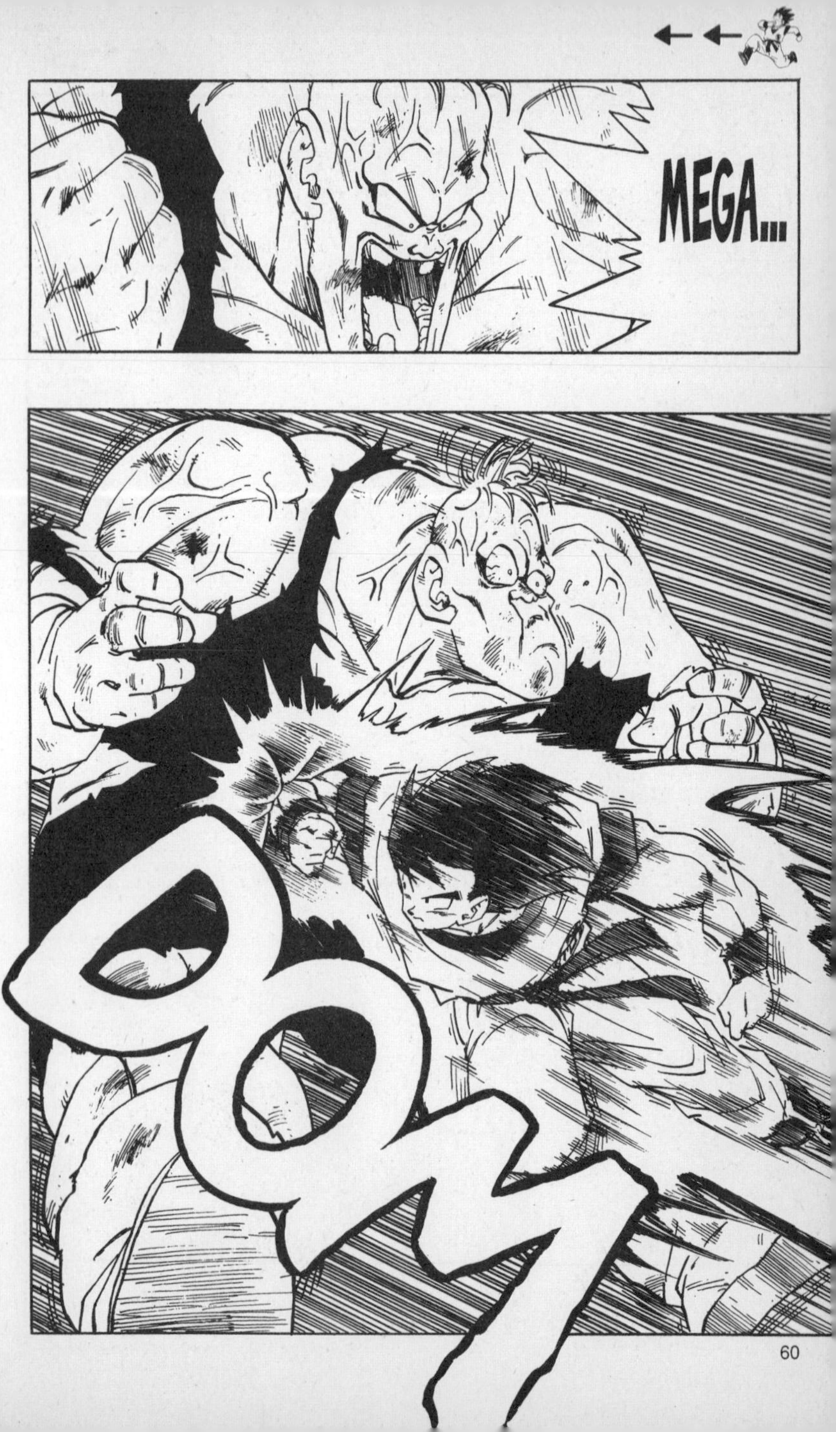
MEGA...

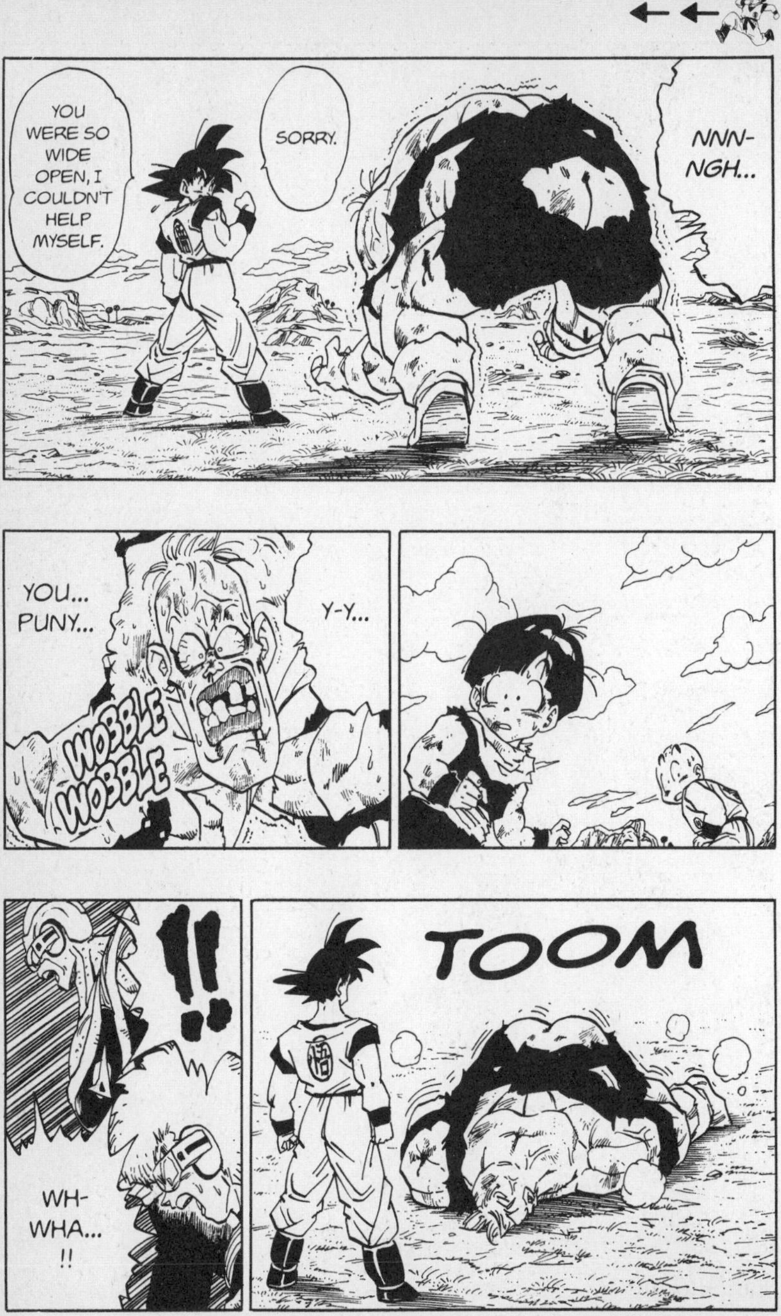
NNN-NGH...
SORRY.
YOU WERE SO WIDE OPEN, I COULDN'T HELP MYSELF.
Y-Y...
YOU... PUNY...
WOBBLE WOBBLE
TOOM
!!
WH-WHA... !!

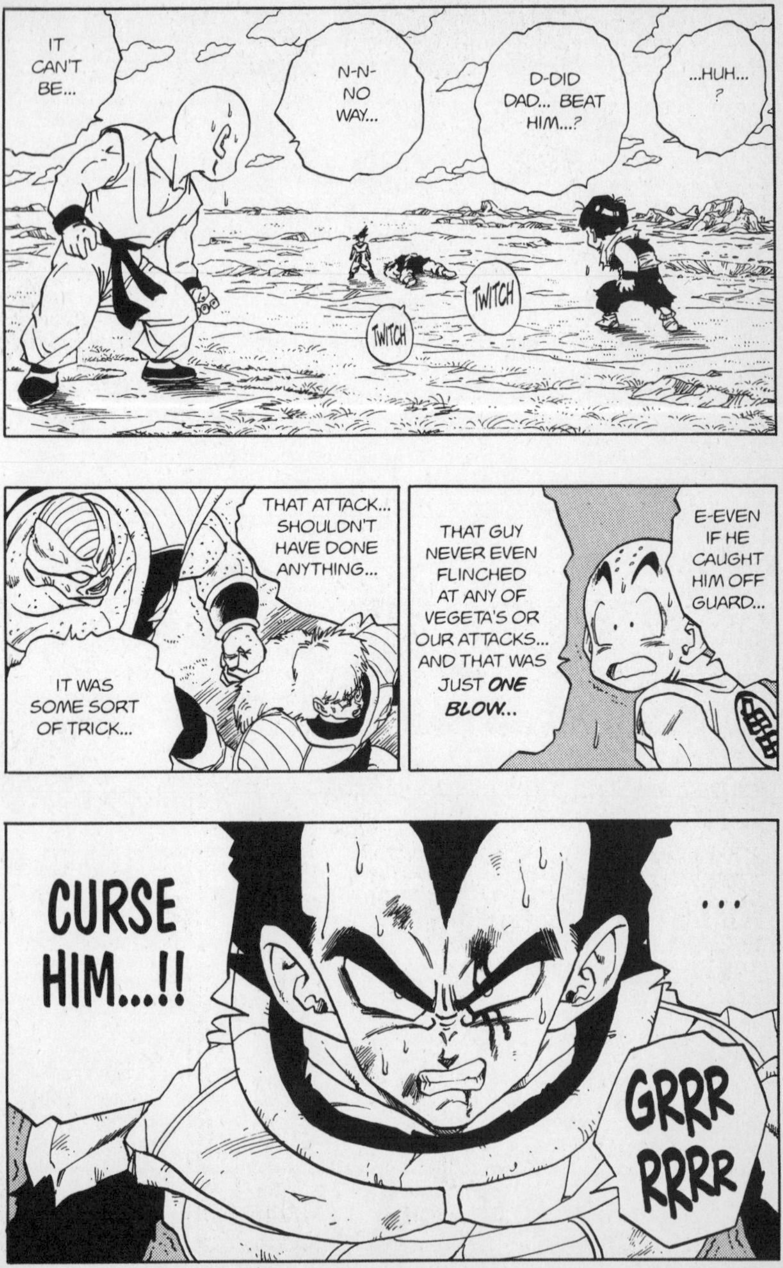

...HUH...?
D-DID DAD... BEAT HIM...?
N-N-NO WAY...
IT CAN'T BE...
TWITCH
TWITCH
E-EVEN IF HE CAUGHT HIM OFF GUARD...
THAT GUY NEVER EVEN FLINCHED AT ANY OF VEGETA'S OR OUR ATTACKS... AND THAT WAS JUST ***ONE BLOW...***
THAT ATTACK... SHOULDN'T HAVE DONE ANYTHING...
IT WAS SOME SORT OF TRICK...
...
GRRR RRRR
CURSE HIM...!!

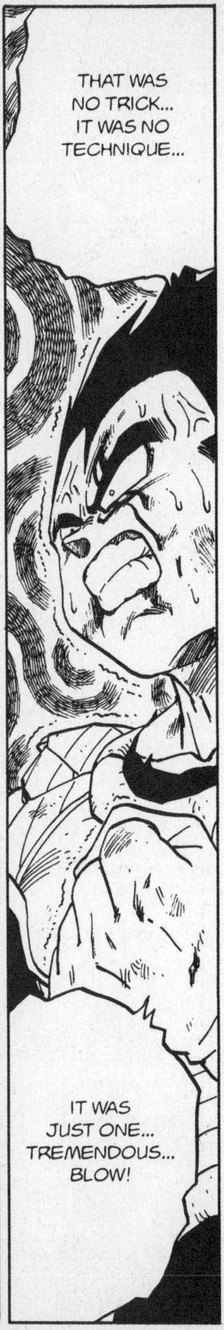
THAT WAS NO TRICK... IT WAS NO TECHNIQUE...
IT WAS JUST ONE... TREMENDOUS... BLOW!

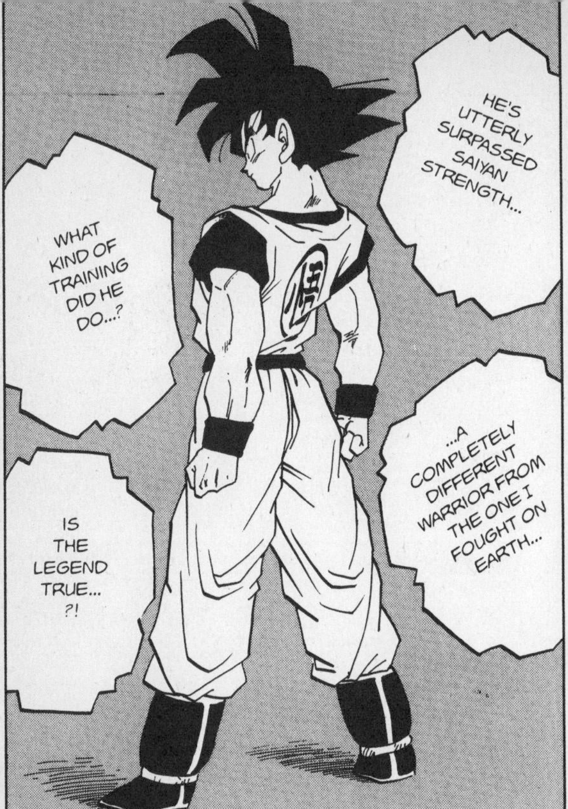
HE'S UTTERLY SURPASSED SAIYAN STRENGTH...
WHAT KIND OF TRAINING DID HE DO...?
...A COMPLETELY DIFFERENT WARRIOR FROM THE ONE I FOUGHT ON EARTH...
IS THE LEGEND TRUE...?!

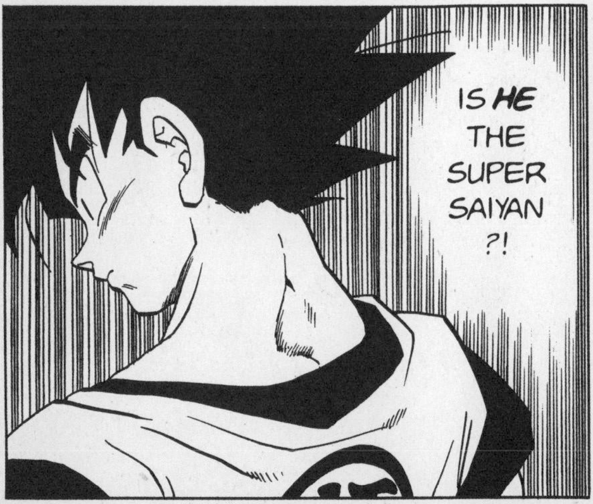
IS *HE* THE SUPER SAIYAN?!

NEXT: *Two Against One!*

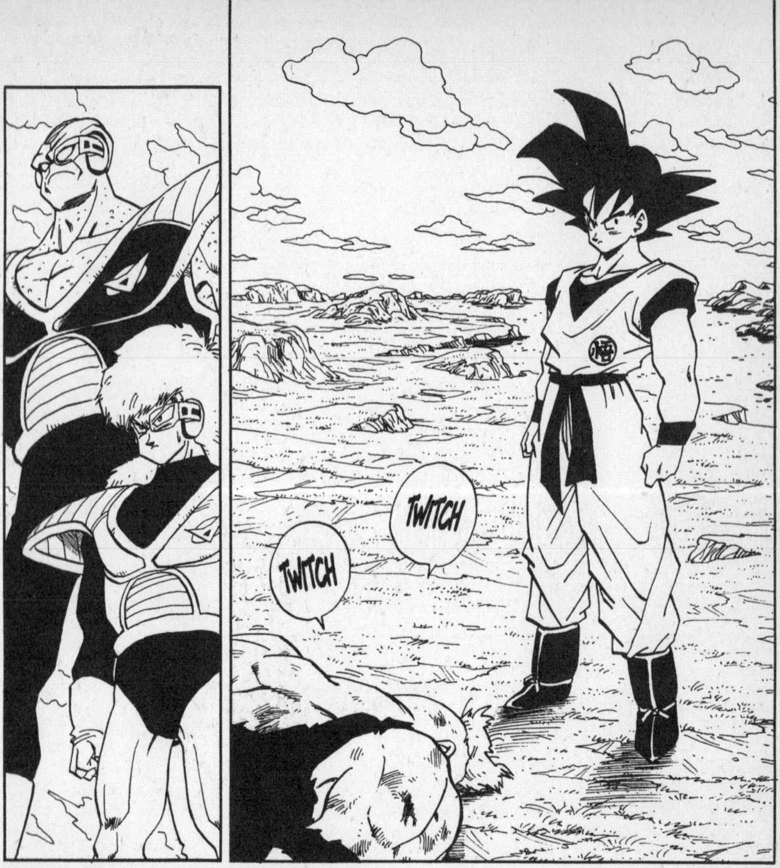
TWITCH
TWITCH

DBZ:87 • Jheese and Butta

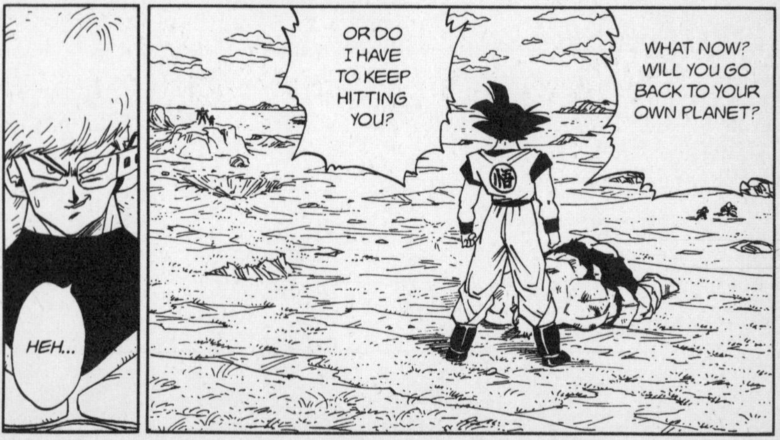
WHAT NOW? WILL YOU GO BACK TO YOUR OWN PLANET?
OR DO I HAVE TO KEEP HITTING YOU?
HEH...

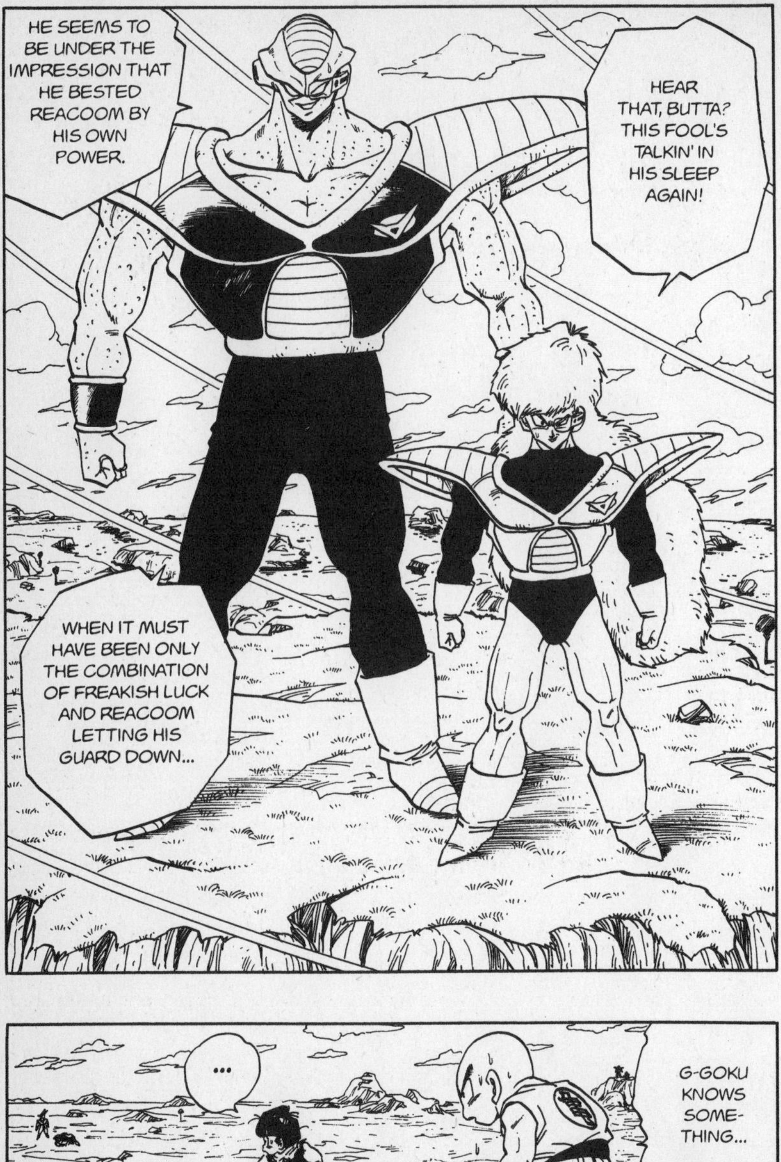
HEAR THAT, BUTTA? THIS FOOL'S TALKIN' IN HIS SLEEP AGAIN!
HE SEEMS TO BE UNDER THE IMPRESSION THAT HE BESTED REACOOM BY HIS OWN POWER.
WHEN IT MUST HAVE BEEN ONLY THE COMBINATION OF FREAKISH LUCK AND REACOOM LETTING HIS GUARD DOWN...
G-GOKU KNOWS SOME-THING...
...

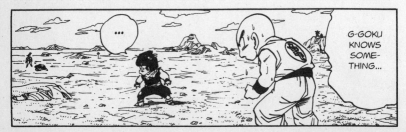

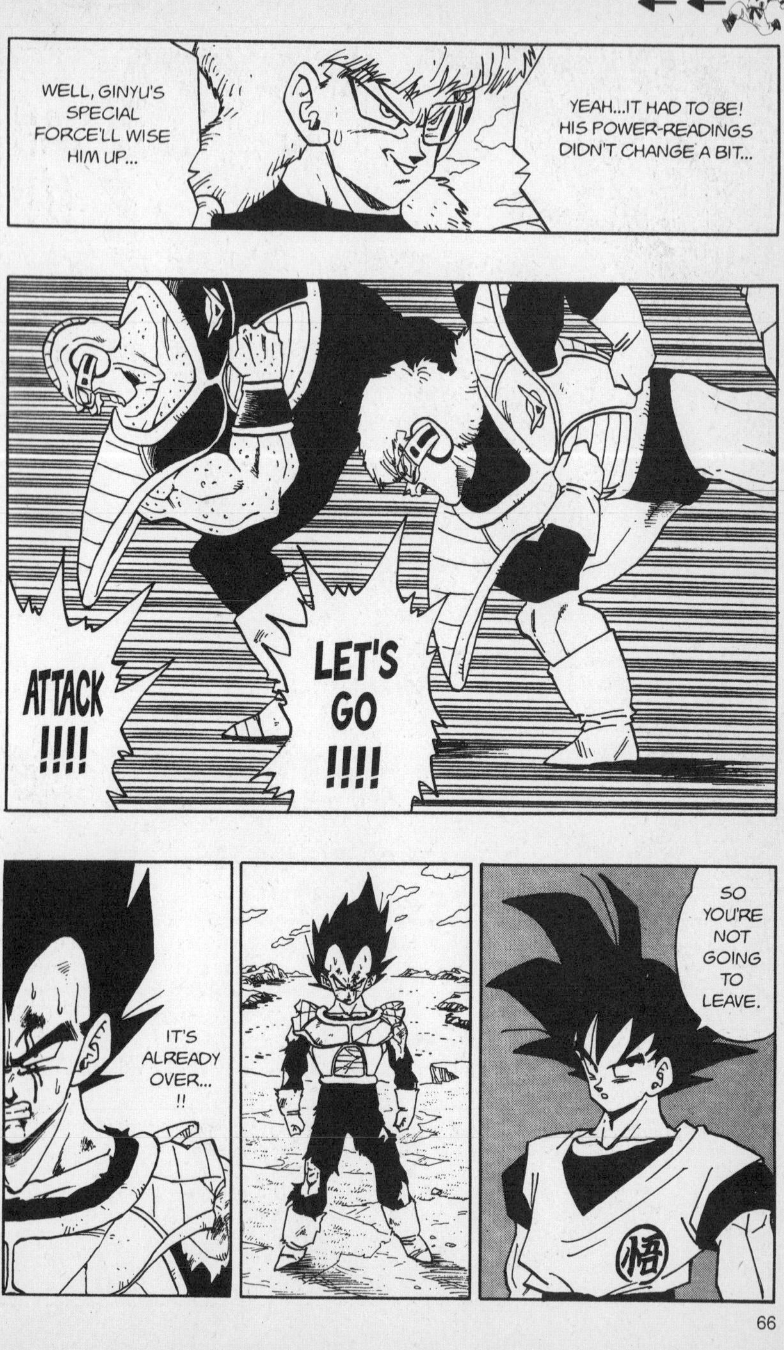
YEAH...IT HAD TO BE! HIS POWER-READINGS DIDN'T CHANGE A BIT...
WELL, GINYU'S SPECIAL FORCE'LL WISE HIM UP...
LET'S GO !!!!
ATTACK !!!!
SO YOU'RE NOT GOING TO LEAVE.
IT'S ALREADY OVER... !!

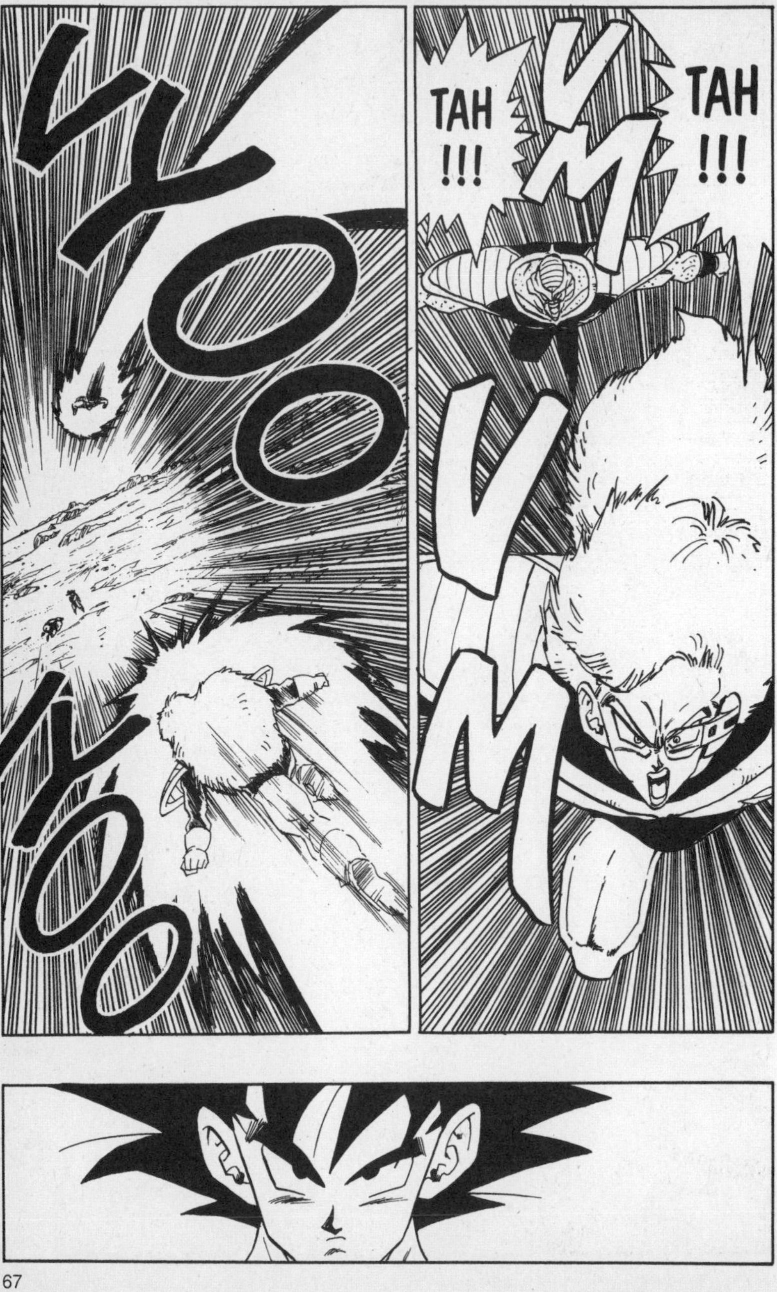
TAH !!!
TAH !!!

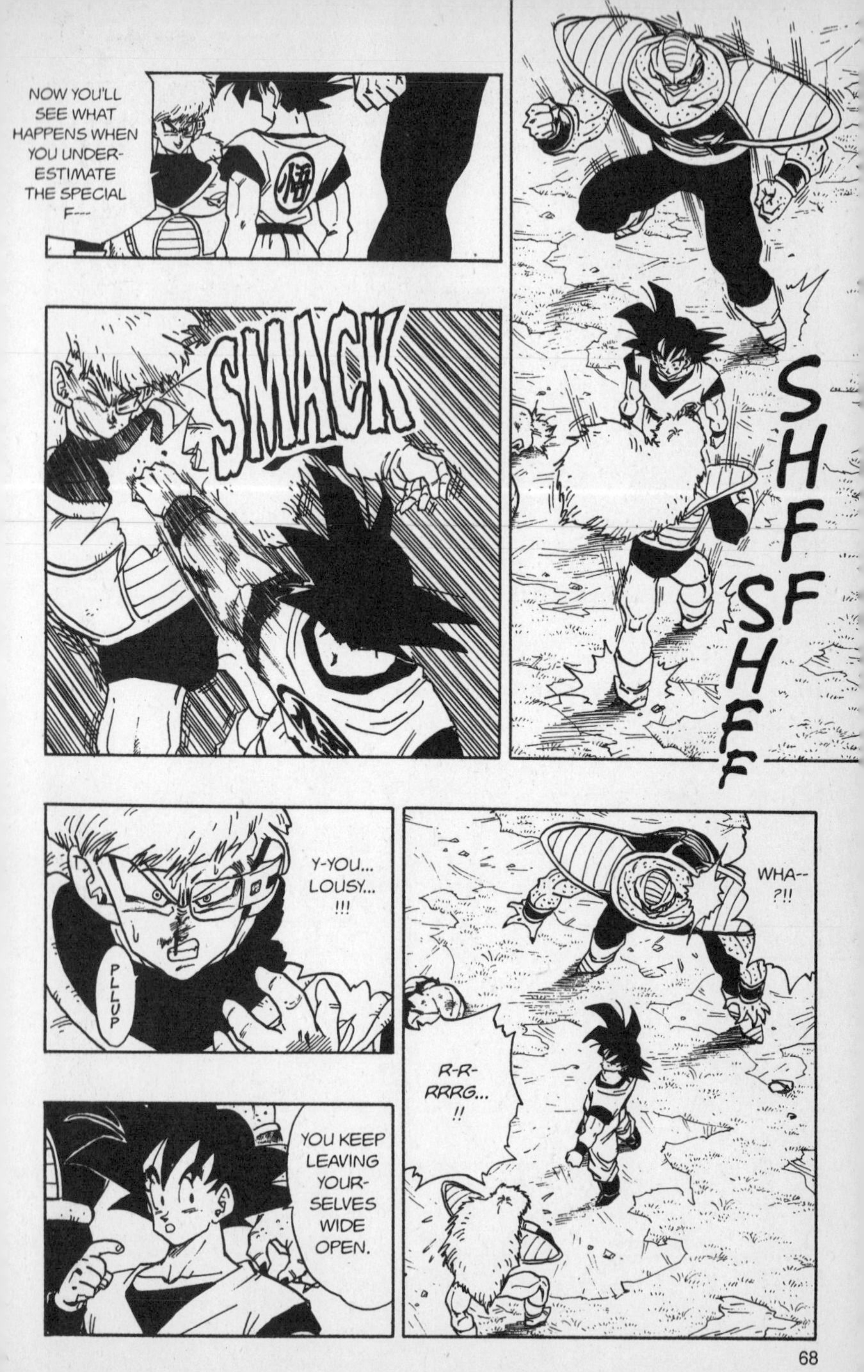

SHFF
SHFF
NOW YOU'LL SEE WHAT HAPPENS WHEN YOU UNDER-ESTIMATE THE SPECIAL F---
SMACK
WHA--?!!
R-R-RRRG...!!
Y-YOU... LOUSY...!!!
PLLUP
YOU KEEP LEAVING YOUR-SELVES WIDE OPEN.

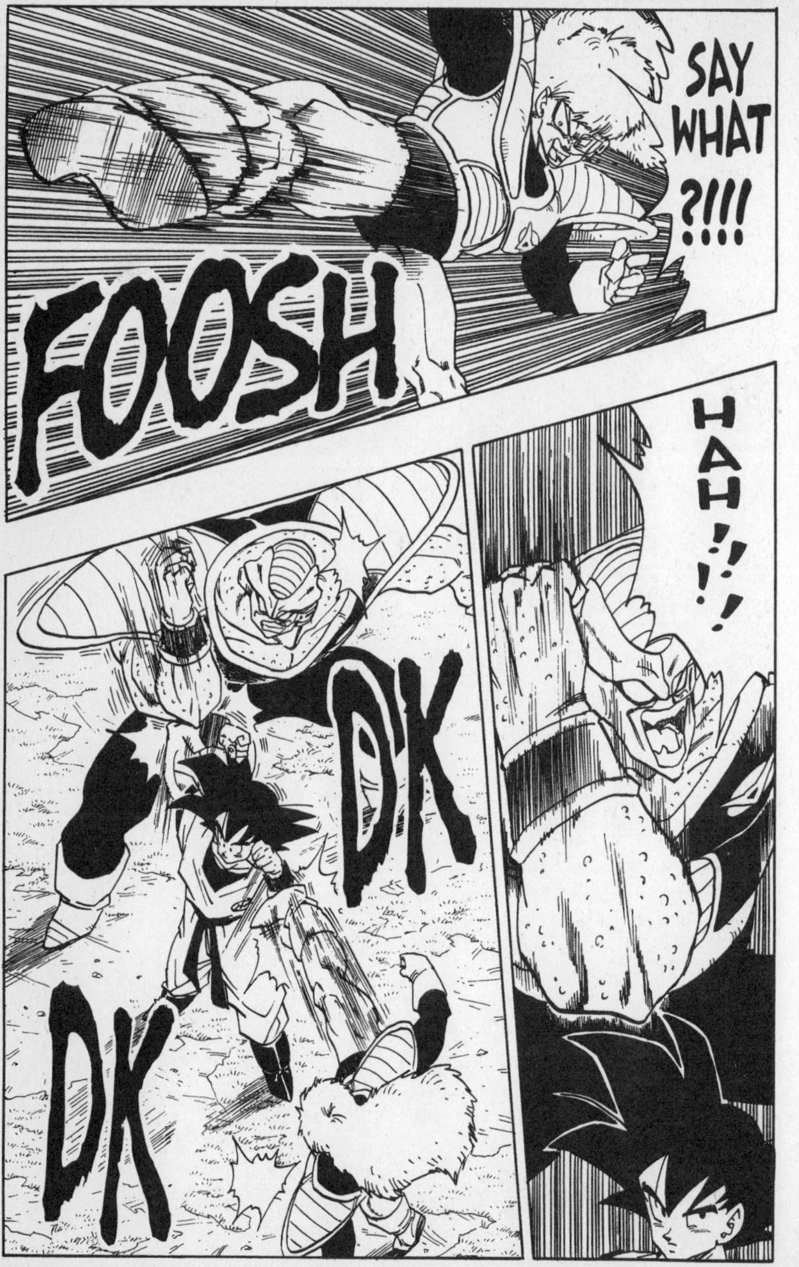
SAY WHAT?!!!
FOOSH
HAH!!!!
DK
DK

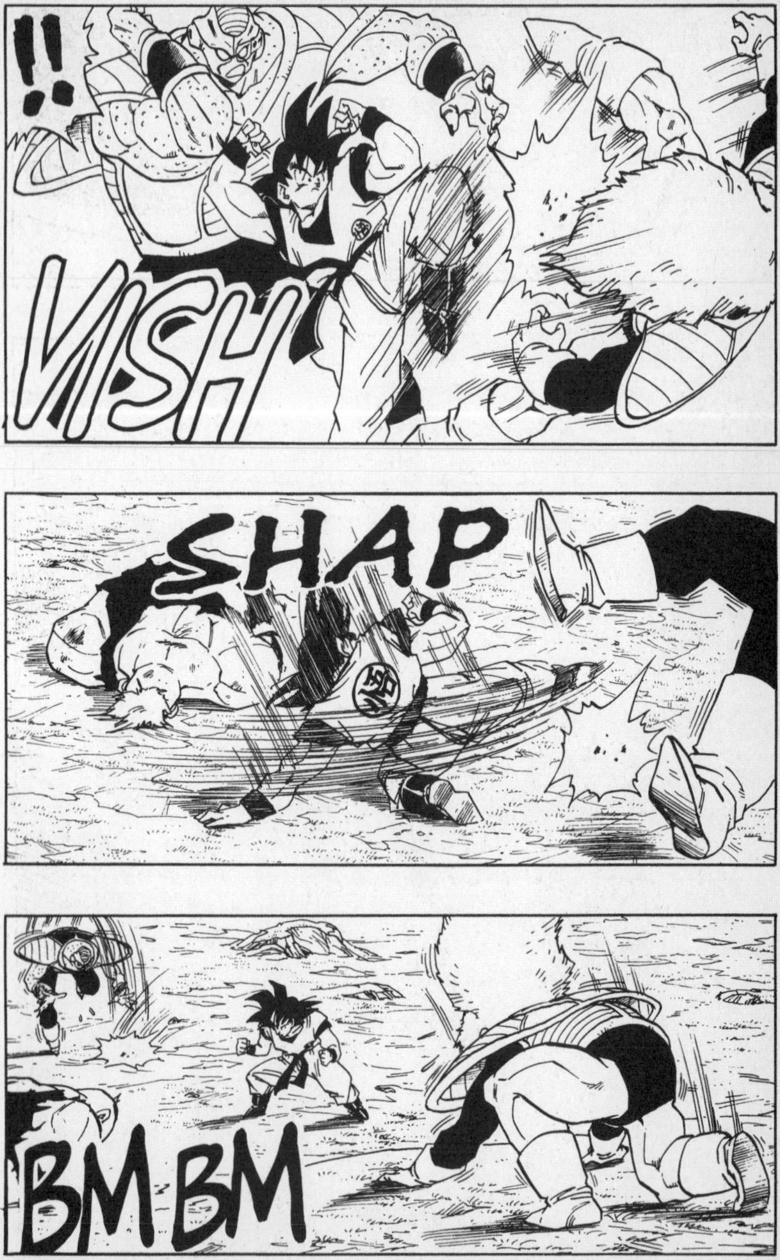
!!
VISH
SHAP
BM BM

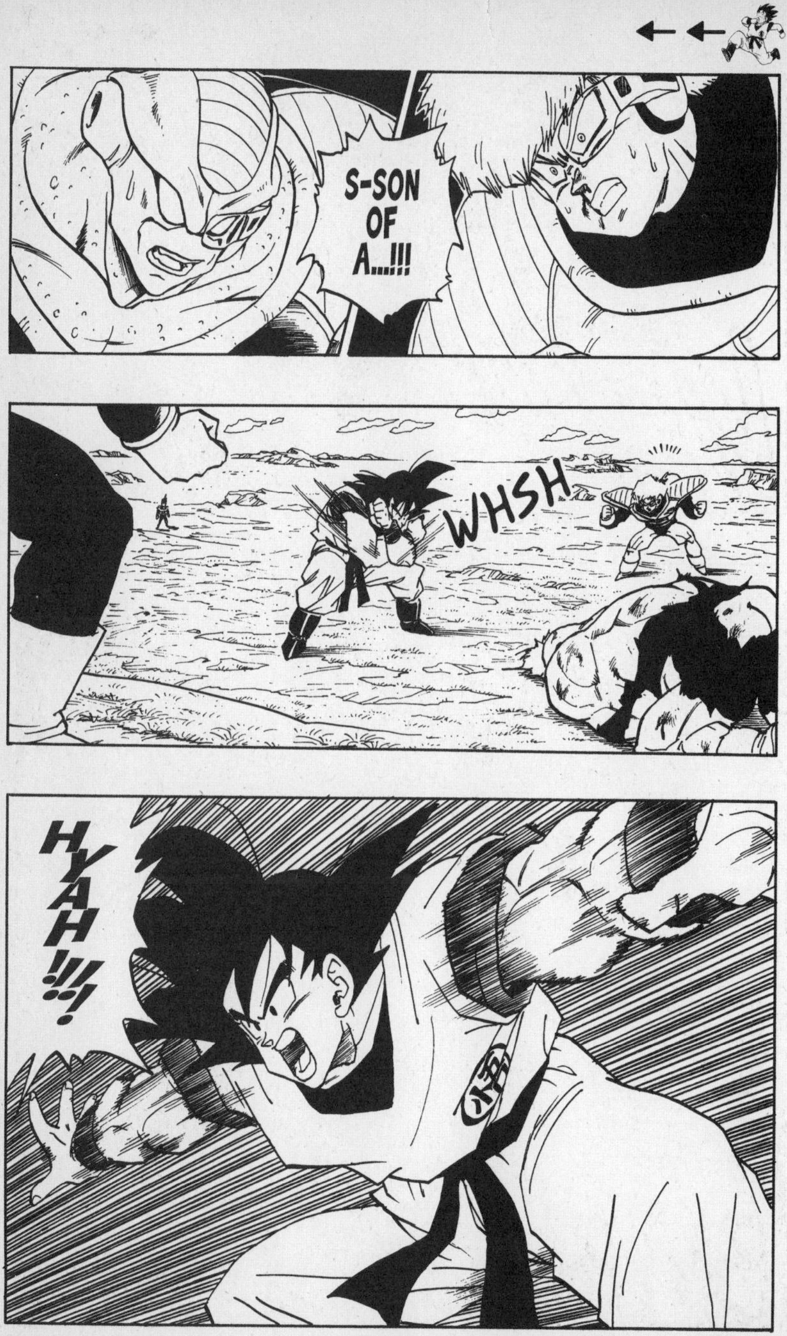
S-SON OF A...!!!
WHSH
HYAH!!!!

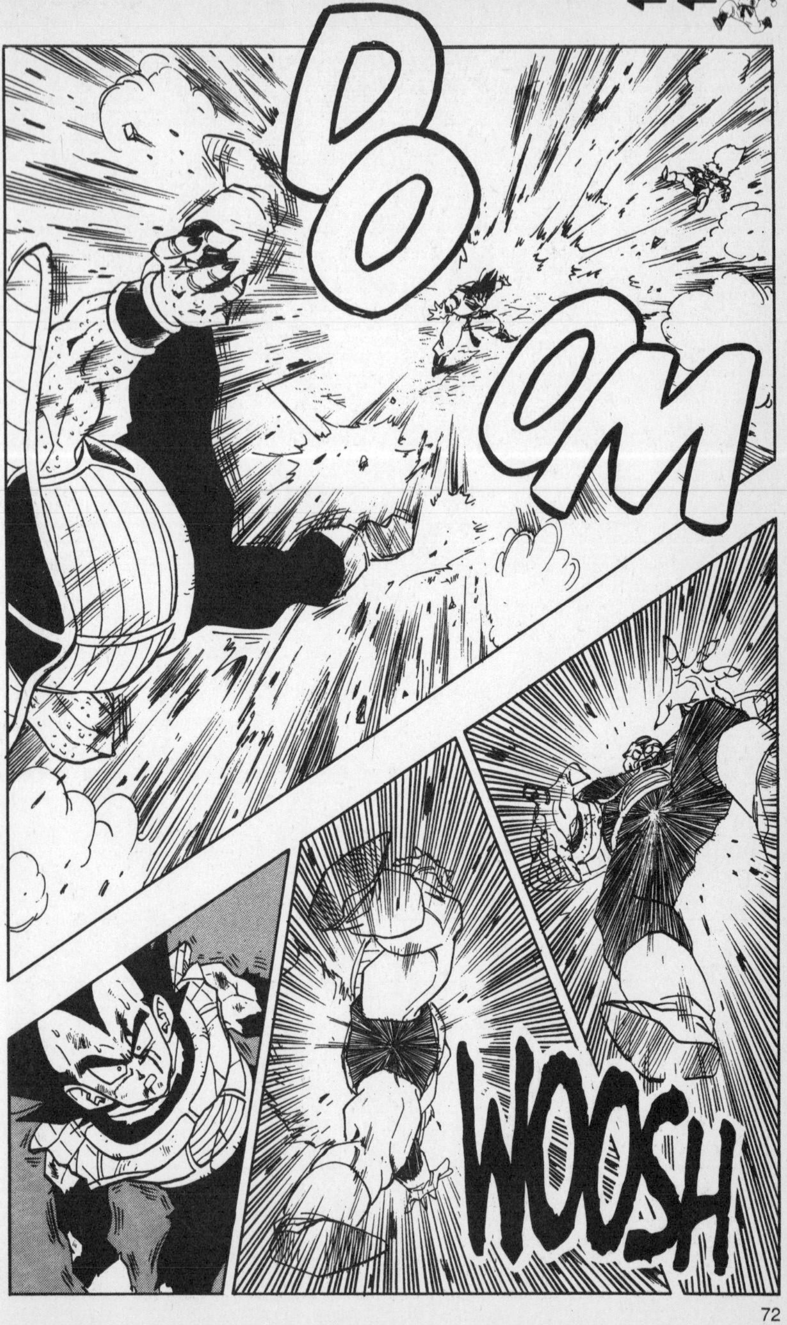
DOOM
WOOSH

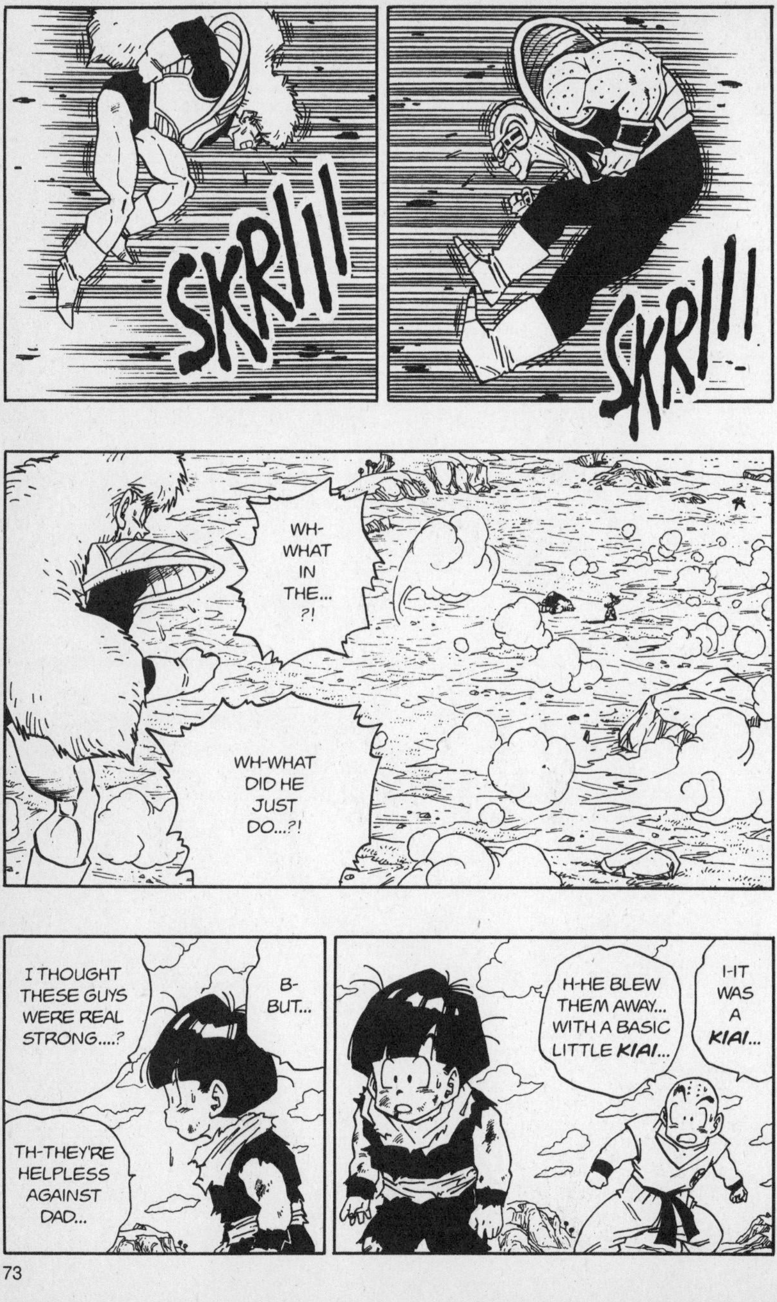
SKRI!!
SKRIII
WH-WHAT IN THE...?!
WH-WHAT DID HE JUST DO...?!
I-IT WAS A *KIAI*...
H-HE BLEW THEM AWAY... WITH A BASIC LITTLE *KIAI*...
B-BUT...
I THOUGHT THESE GUYS WERE REAL STRONG....?
TH-THEY'RE HELPLESS AGAINST DAD...

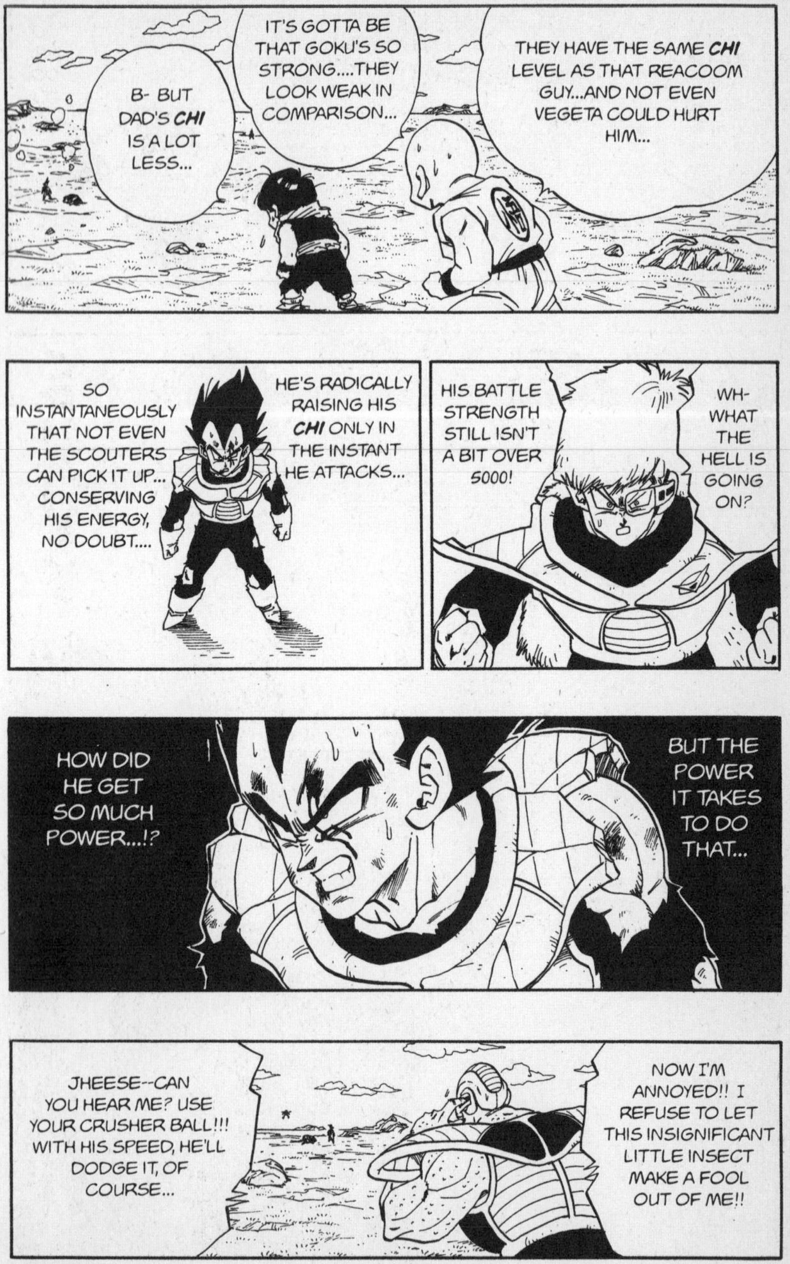
THEY HAVE THE SAME CHI LEVEL AS THAT REACOOM GUY...AND NOT EVEN VEGETA COULD HURT HIM...
IT'S GOTTA BE THAT GOKU'S SO STRONG....THEY LOOK WEAK IN COMPARISON...
B- BUT DAD'S CHI IS A LOT LESS...
WH- WHAT THE HELL IS GOING ON?
HIS BATTLE STRENGTH STILL ISN'T A BIT OVER 5000!
HE'S RADICALLY RAISING HIS CHI ONLY IN THE INSTANT HE ATTACKS...
SO INSTANTANEOUSLY THAT NOT EVEN THE SCOUTERS CAN PICK IT UP... CONSERVING HIS ENERGY, NO DOUBT....
BUT THE POWER IT TAKES TO DO THAT...
HOW DID HE GET SO MUCH POWER...!?
NOW I'M ANNOYED!! I REFUSE TO LET THIS INSIGNIFICANT LITTLE INSECT MAKE A FOOL OUT OF ME!!
JHEESE--CAN YOU HEAR ME? USE YOUR CRUSHER BALL!!! WITH HIS SPEED, HE'LL DODGE IT, OF COURSE...

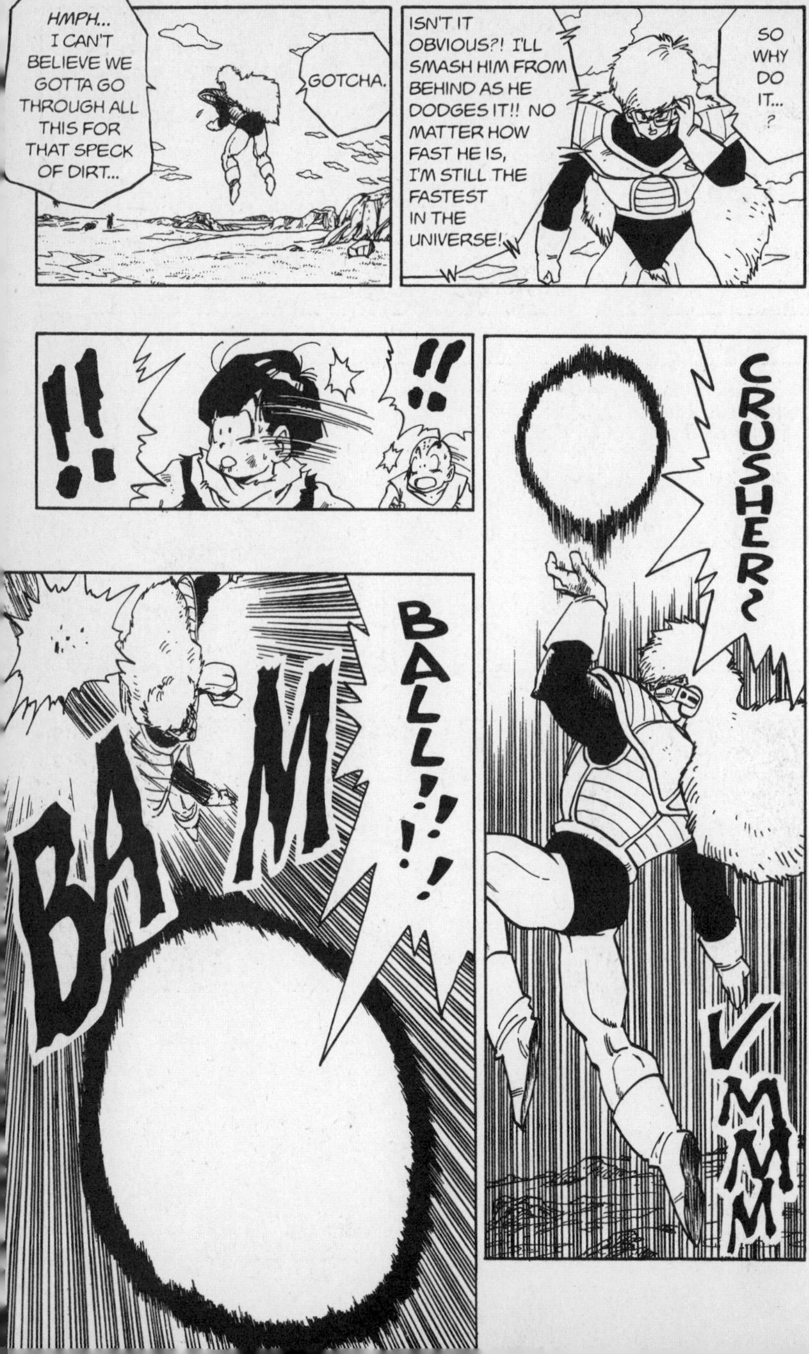
SO WHY DO IT...?
ISN'T IT OBVIOUS?! I'LL SMASH HIM FROM BEHIND AS HE DODGES IT!! NO MATTER HOW FAST HE IS, I'M STILL THE FASTEST IN THE UNIVERSE!
GOTCHA.
HMPH... I CAN'T BELIEVE WE GOTTA GO THROUGH ALL THIS FOR THAT SPECK OF DIRT...
CRUSHER~
VMMMM
!!
!!
BALL!!!!
BAM

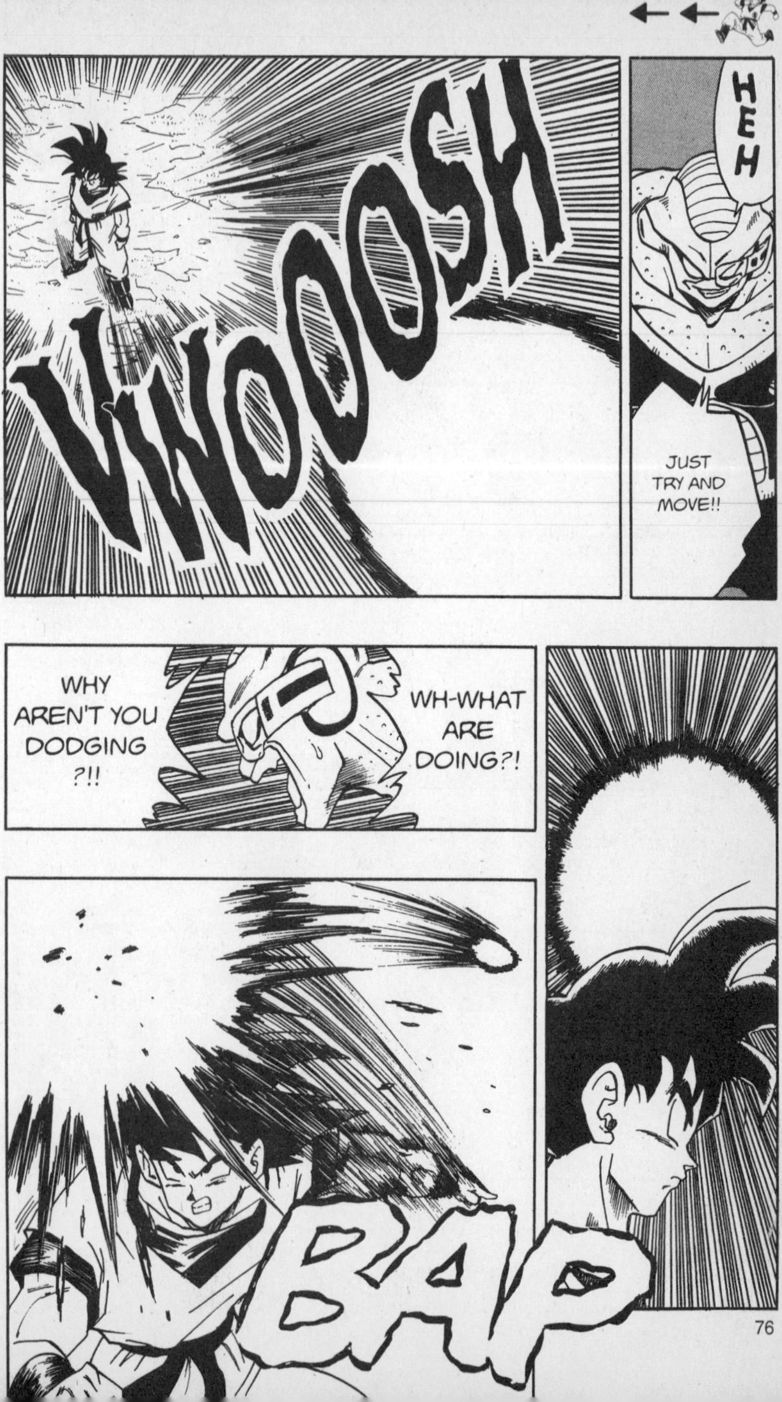
HEH
JUST TRY AND MOVE!!
VWOOOSH
WH-WHAT ARE DOING?!
WHY AREN'T YOU DODGING ?!!
BAP

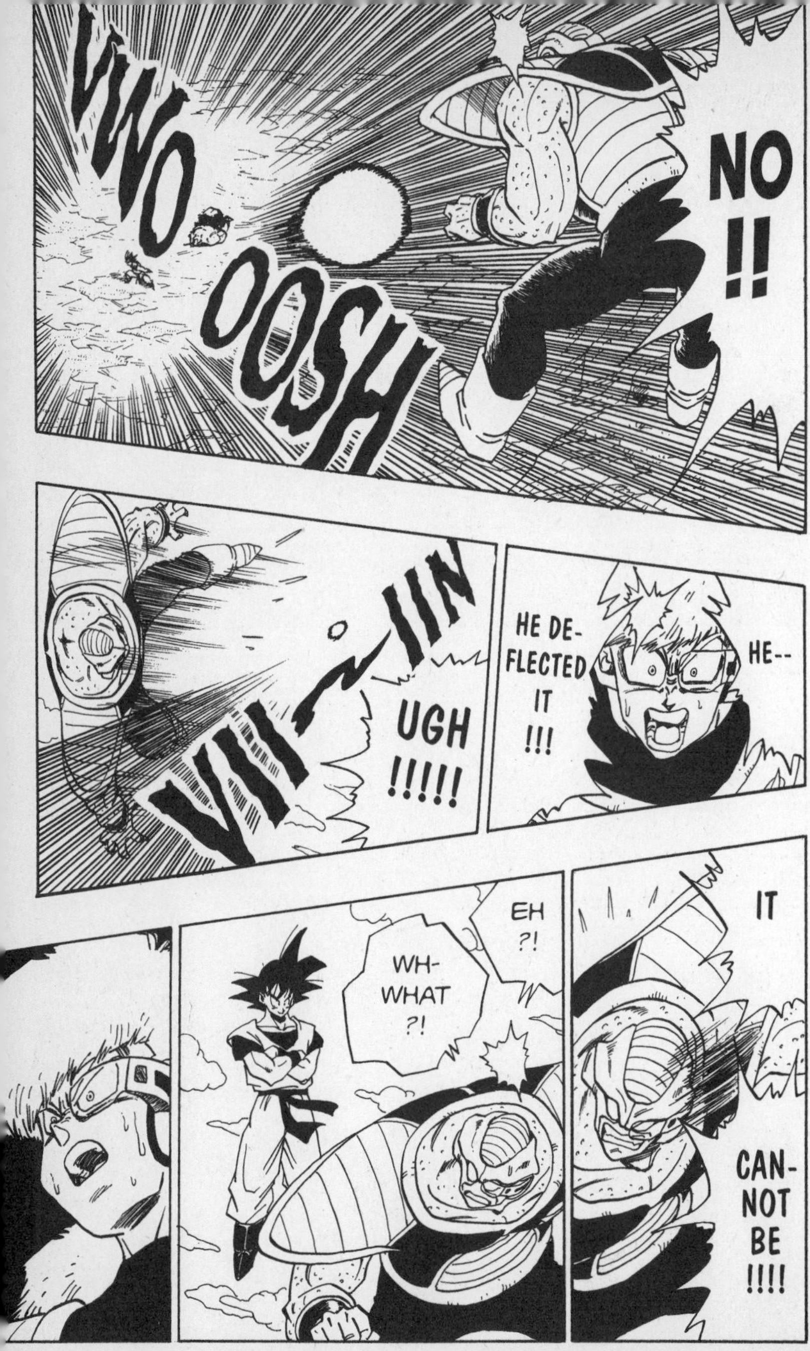
NO!!
VWOOSH
HE--
HE DE-FLECTED IT!!!
VIII~IIN
UGH!!!!!
IT CAN-NOT BE!!!!
EH?!
WH-WHAT?!

DBZ:88 • With Allies Like These...

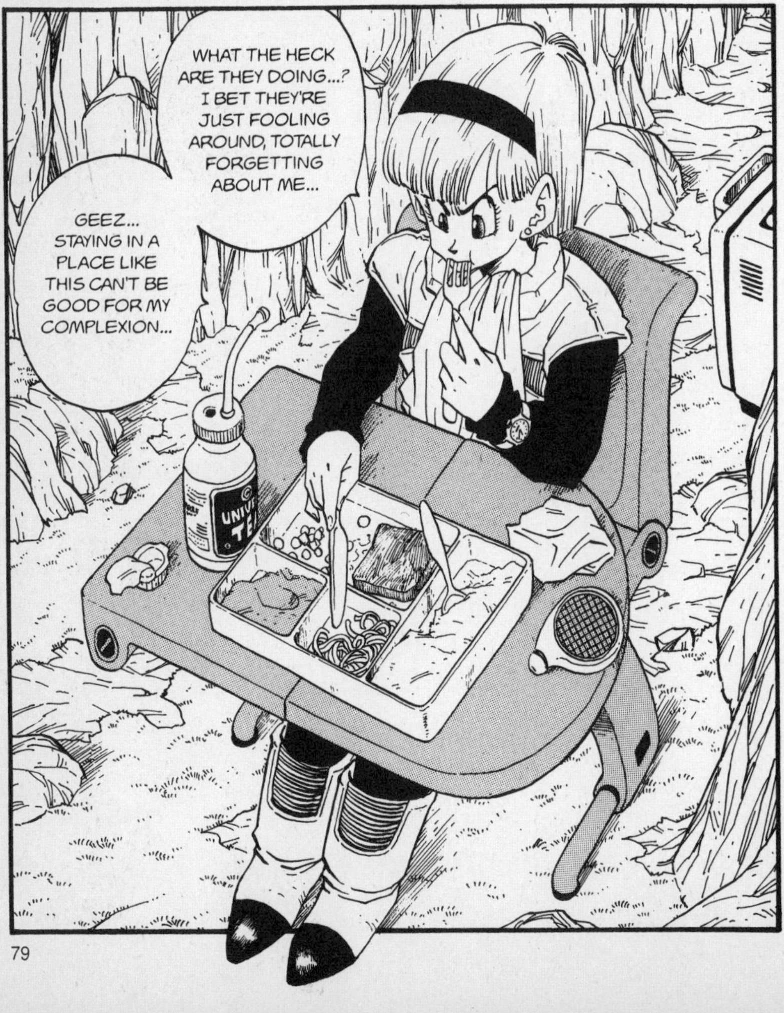
WHAT THE HECK ARE THEY DOING...? I BET THEY'RE JUST FOOLING AROUND, TOTALLY FORGETTING ABOUT ME...
GEEZ... STAYING IN A PLACE LIKE THIS CAN'T BE GOOD FOR MY COMPLEXION...

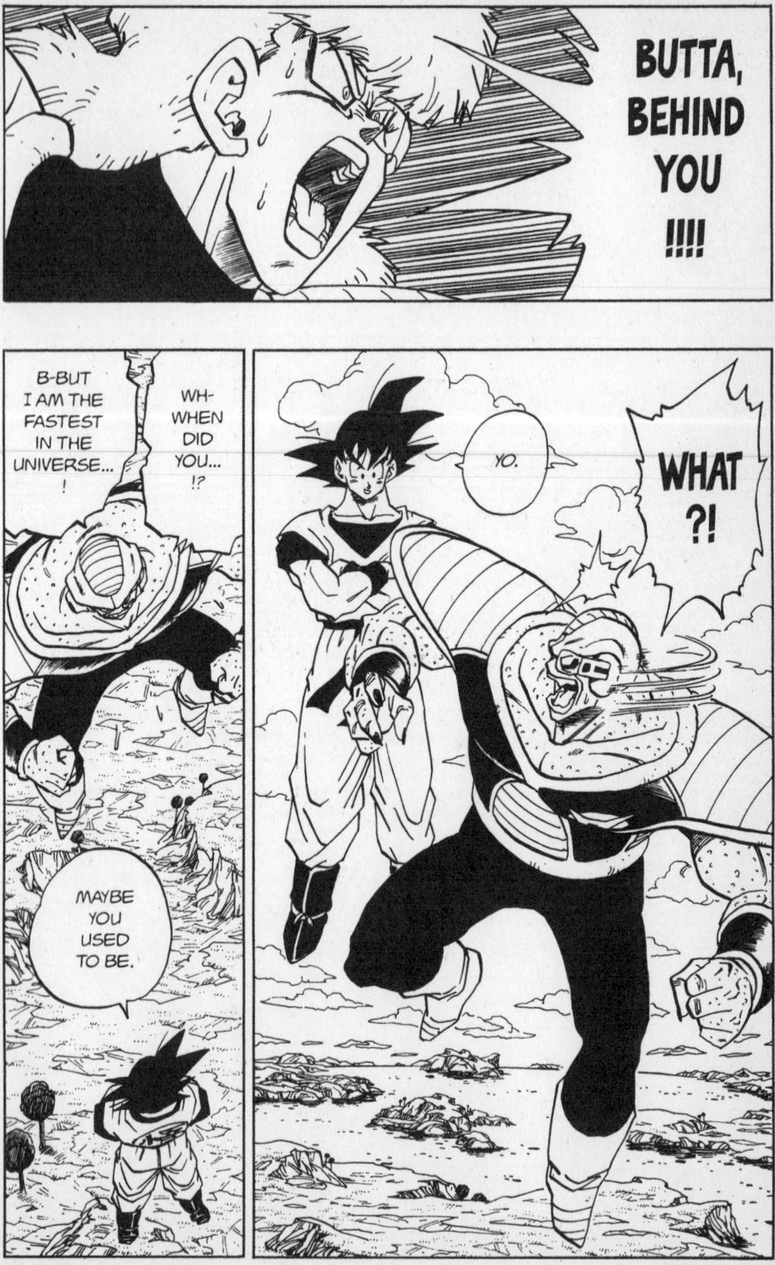
BUTTA, BEHIND YOU !!!!
WHAT ?!
YO.
WH- WHEN DID YOU... !?
B-BUT I AM THE FASTEST IN THE UNIVERSE... !
MAYBE YOU USED TO BE.

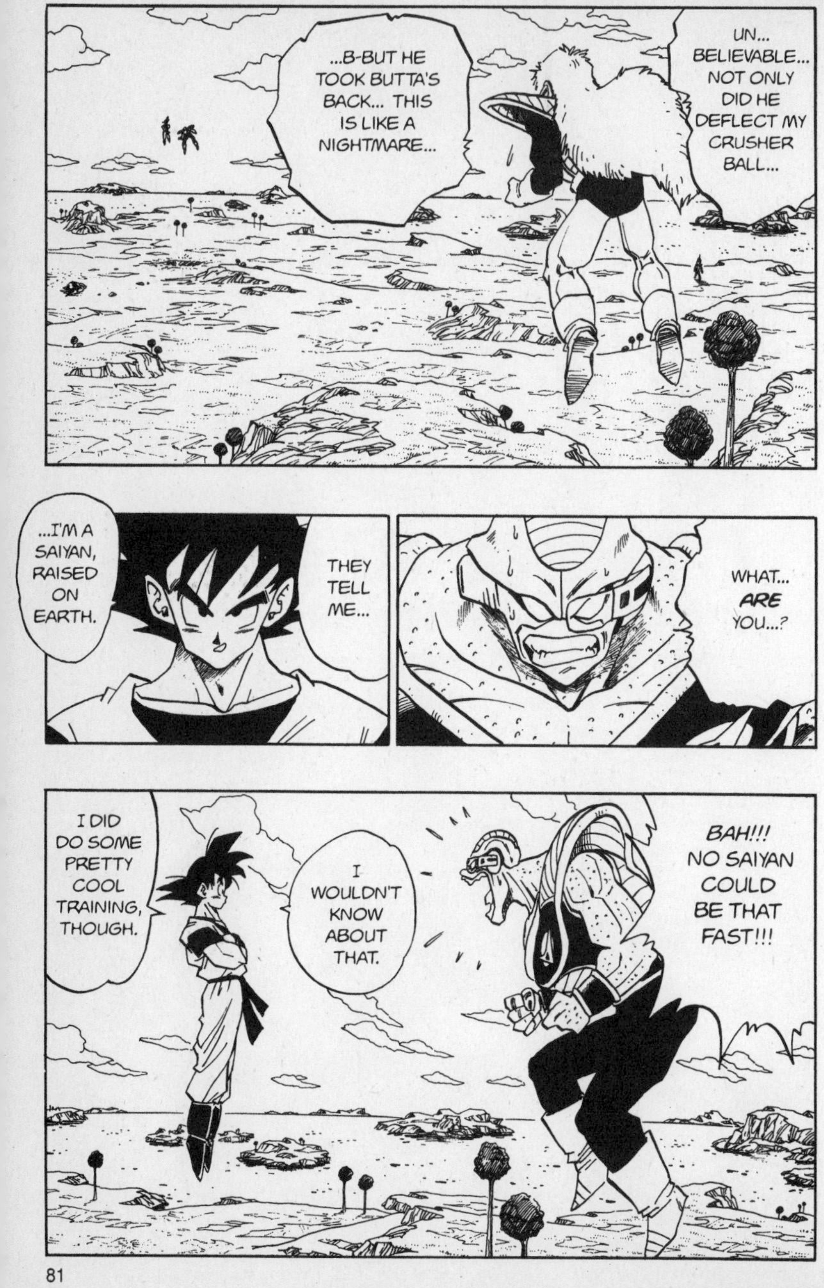
UN... BELIEVABLE... NOT ONLY DID HE DEFLECT MY CRUSHER BALL...
...B-BUT HE TOOK BUTTA'S BACK... THIS IS LIKE A NIGHTMARE...
WHAT... ARE YOU...?
THEY TELL ME...
...I'M A SAIYAN, RAISED ON EARTH.
BAH!!! NO SAIYAN COULD BE THAT FAST!!!
I WOULDN'T KNOW ABOUT THAT.
I DID DO SOME PRETTY COOL TRAINING, THOUGH.

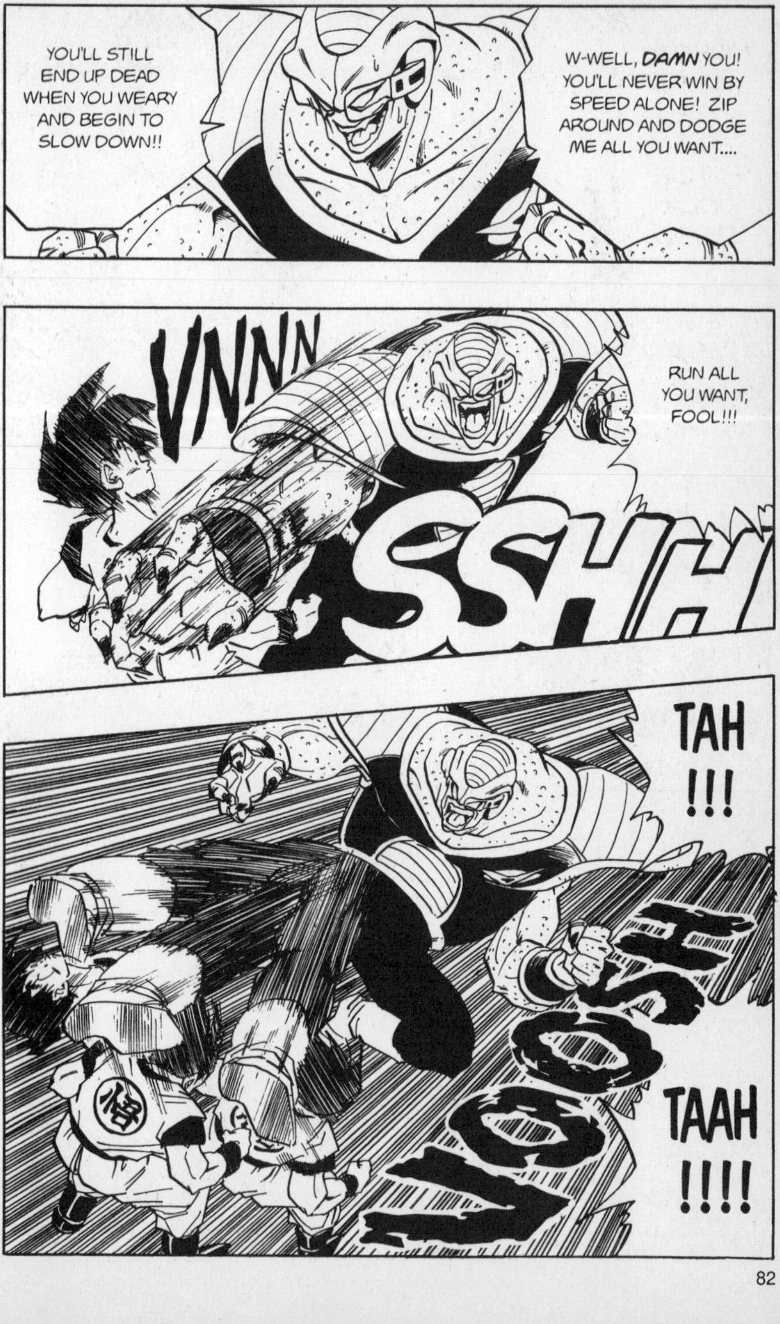
W-WELL, **DAMN** YOU! YOU'LL NEVER WIN BY SPEED ALONE! ZIP AROUND AND DODGE ME ALL YOU WANT....
YOU'LL STILL END UP DEAD WHEN YOU WEARY AND BEGIN TO SLOW DOWN!!
RUN ALL YOU WANT, FOOL!!!
VNNN
SSHH
TAH !!!
VOOSH
TAAH !!!!

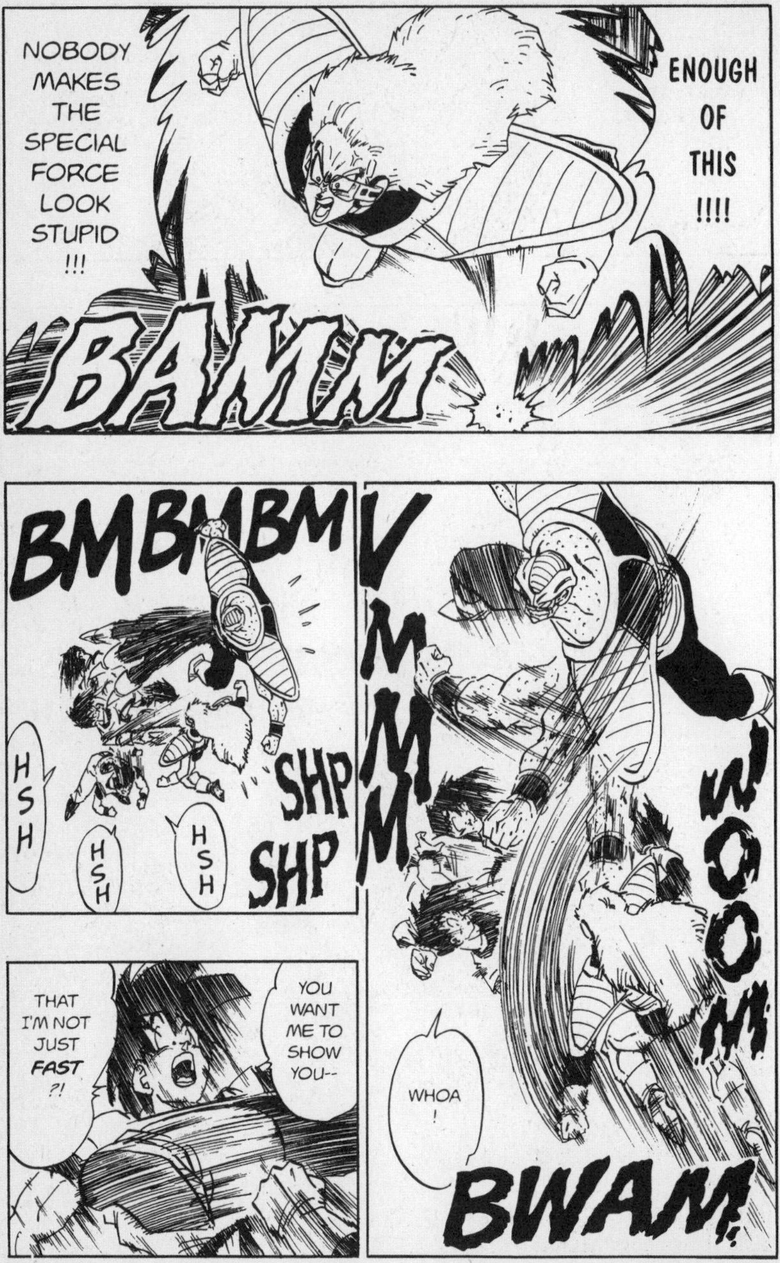
ENOUGH OF THIS!!!!
NOBODY MAKES THE SPECIAL FORCE LOOK STUPID!!!
BAMM
VMMM
WOOM
WHOA!
BWAM
BMBMBM
SHP SHP
HSH
HSH
HSH
YOU WANT ME TO SHOW YOU--
THAT I'M NOT JUST *FAST*?!

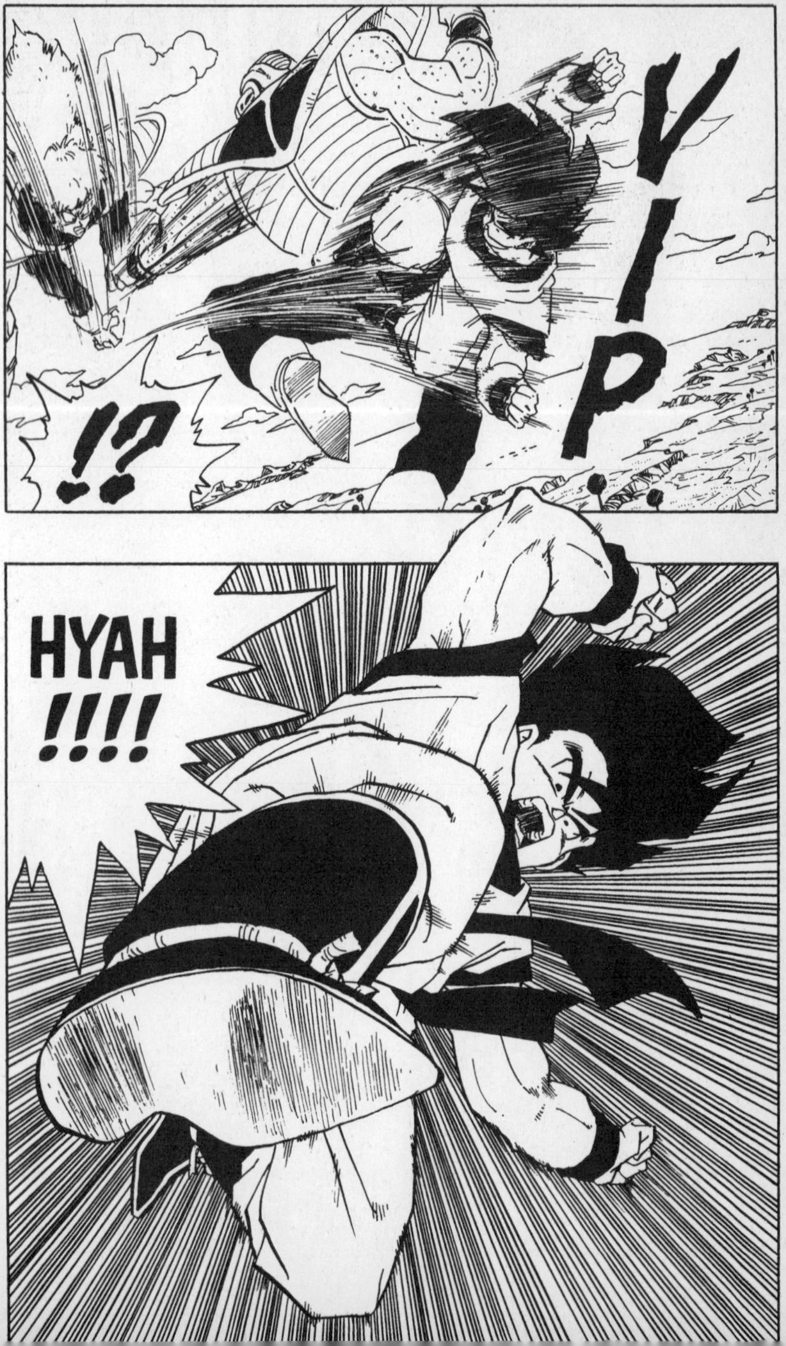
VIP
!?
HYAH!!!!

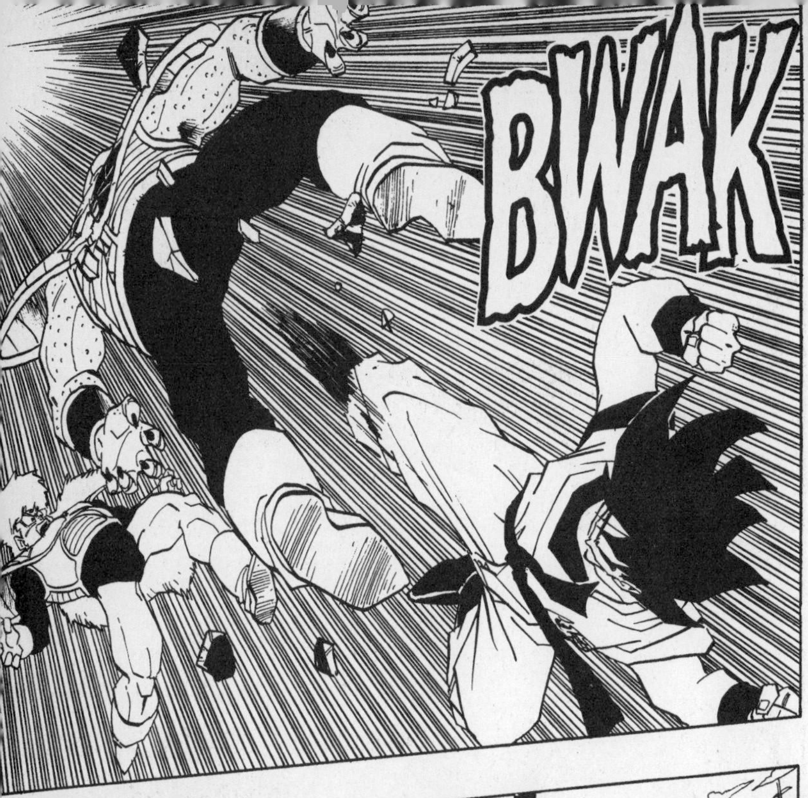
BWAK

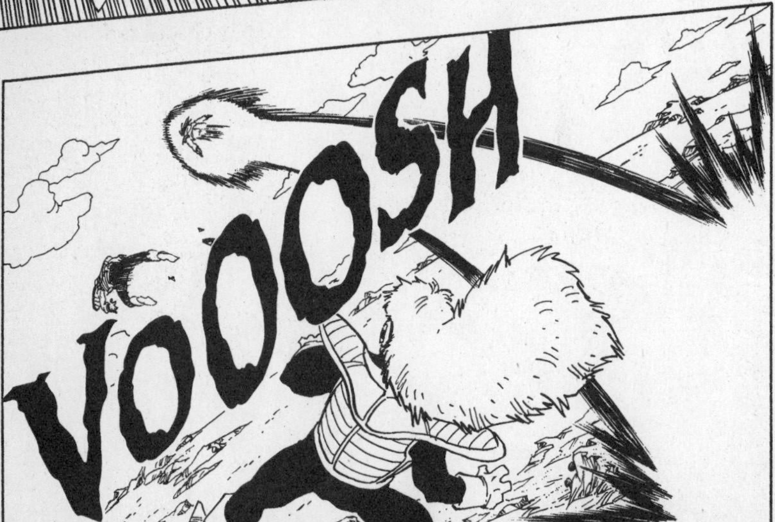
VOOOOSH

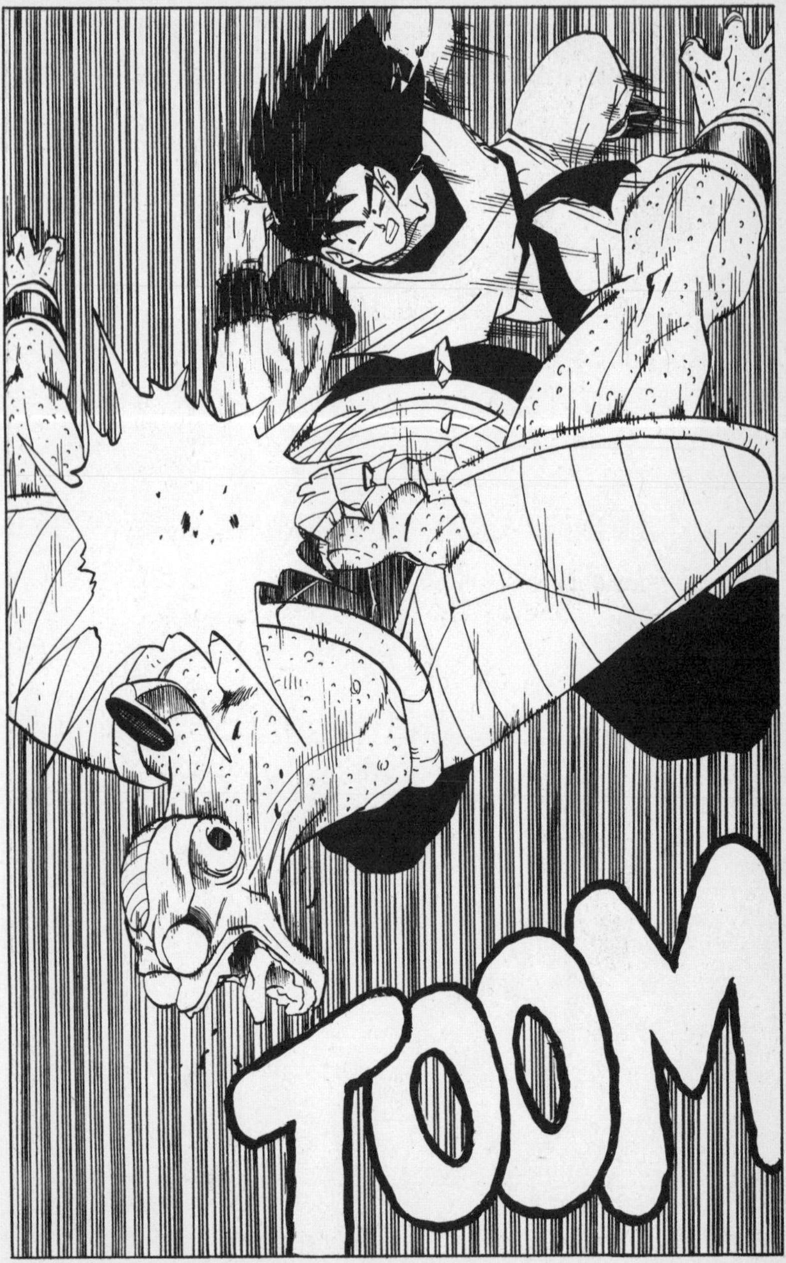
TOOM

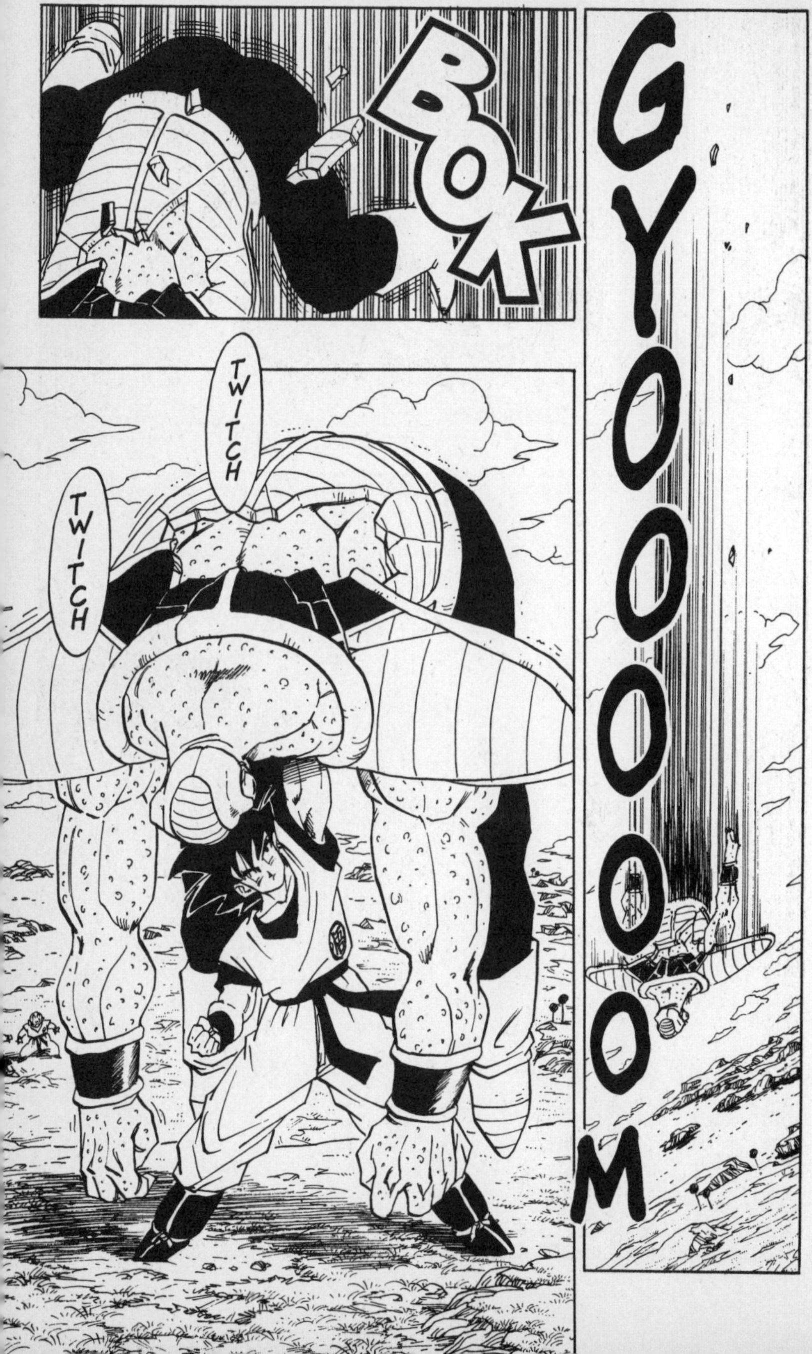
GYOOOOOM
BOK
TWITCH
TWITCH

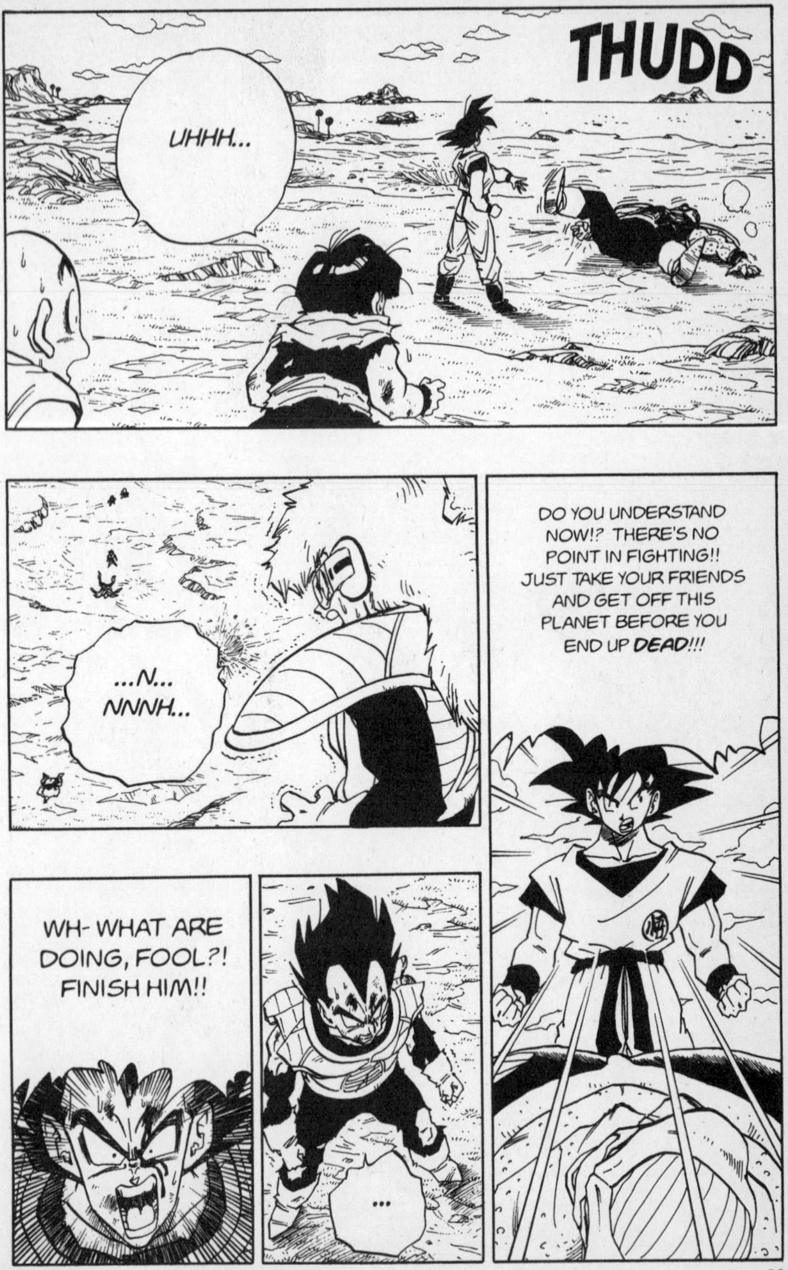
THUDD
UHHH...
DO YOU UNDERSTAND NOW!? THERE'S NO POINT IN FIGHTING!! JUST TAKE YOUR FRIENDS AND GET OFF THIS PLANET BEFORE YOU END UP DEAD!!!
...N... NNNH...
...
WH- WHAT ARE DOING, FOOL?! FINISH HIM!!

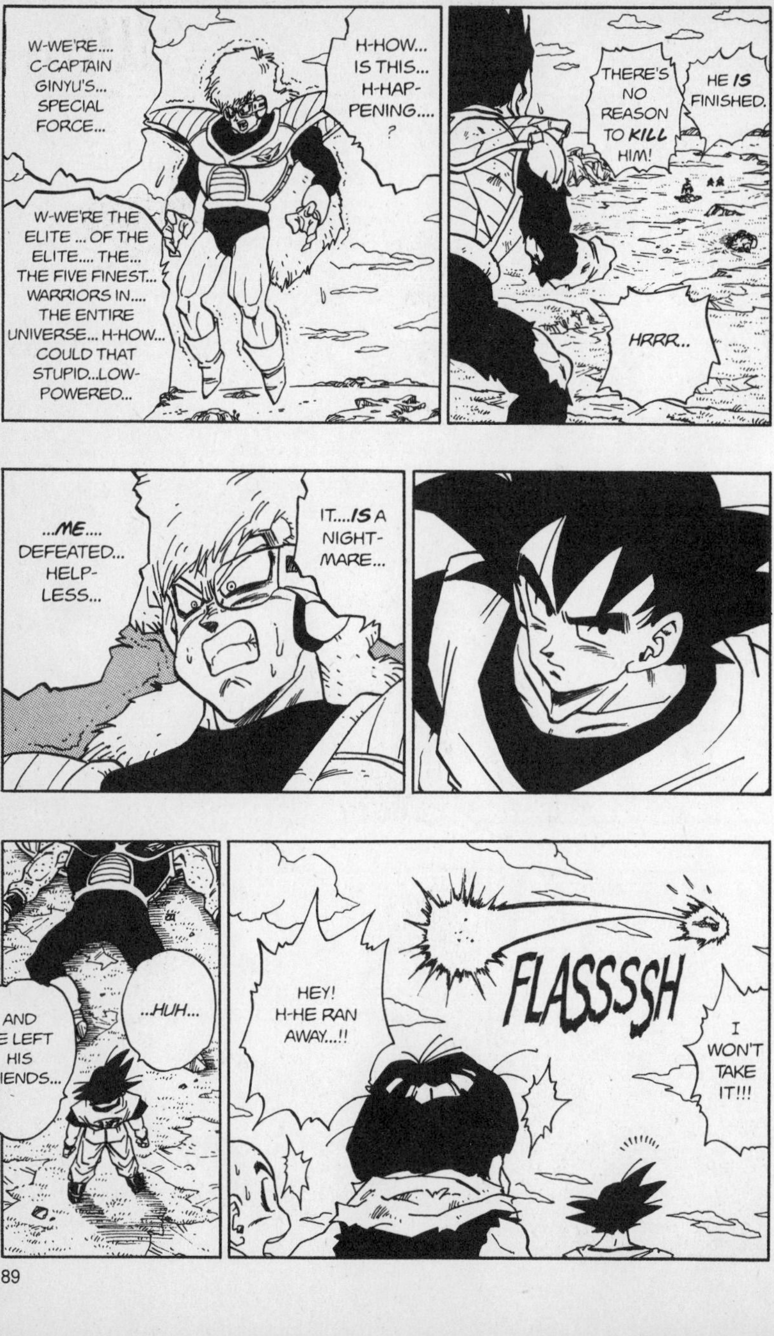
HE IS FINISHED.
THERE'S NO REASON TO KILL HIM!
HRRR...
H-HOW... IS THIS... H-HAPPENING....?
W-WE'RE.... C-CAPTAIN GINYU'S... SPECIAL FORCE...
W-WE'RE THE ELITE ... OF THE ELITE.... THE... THE FIVE FINEST... WARRIORS IN.... THE ENTIRE UNIVERSE... H-HOW... COULD THAT STUPID...LOW-POWERED...
IT....IS A NIGHTMARE...
...ME.... DEFEATED... HELPLESS...
I WON'T TAKE IT!!!
FLASSSSH
HEY! H-HE RAN AWAY...!!
...HUH...
AND HE LEFT HIS FRIENDS...

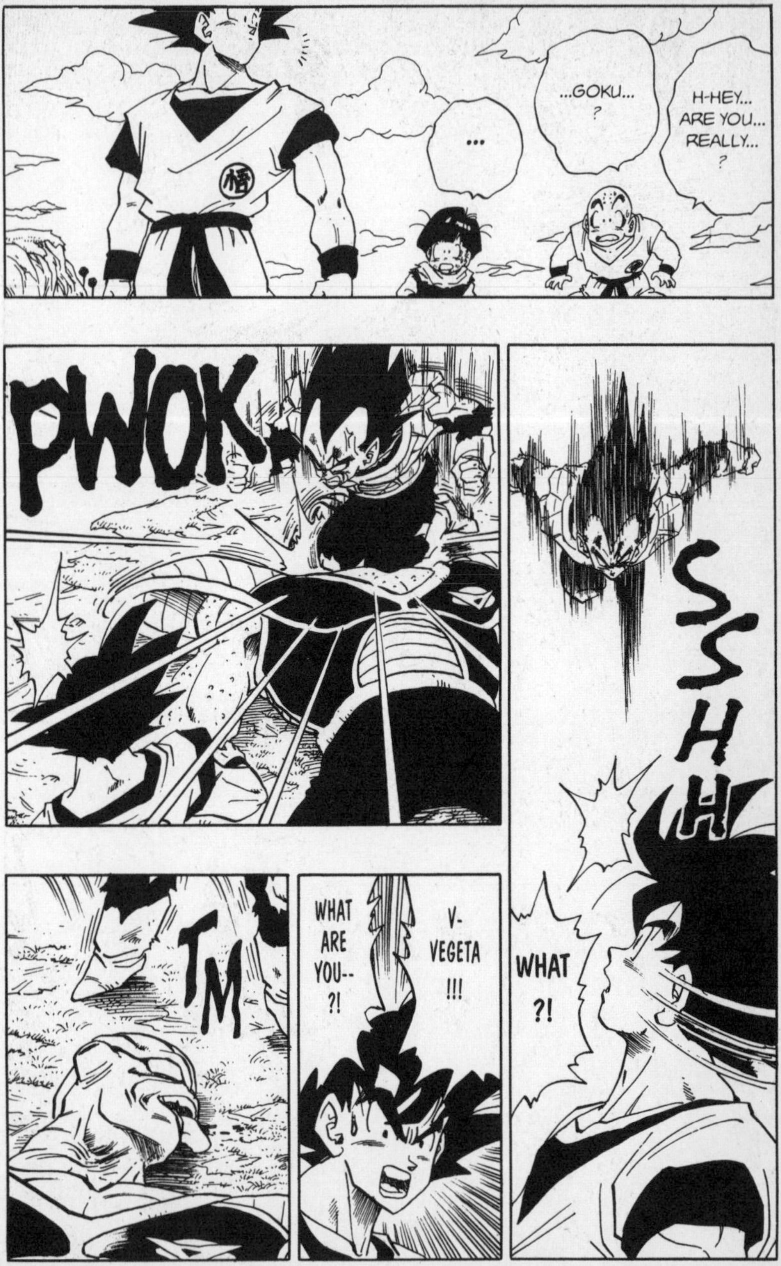
H-HEY... ARE YOU... REALLY...?
...GOKU...?
...
SSHH
WHAT?!
PWOK
V-VEGETA!!!
WHAT ARE YOU--?!
TM

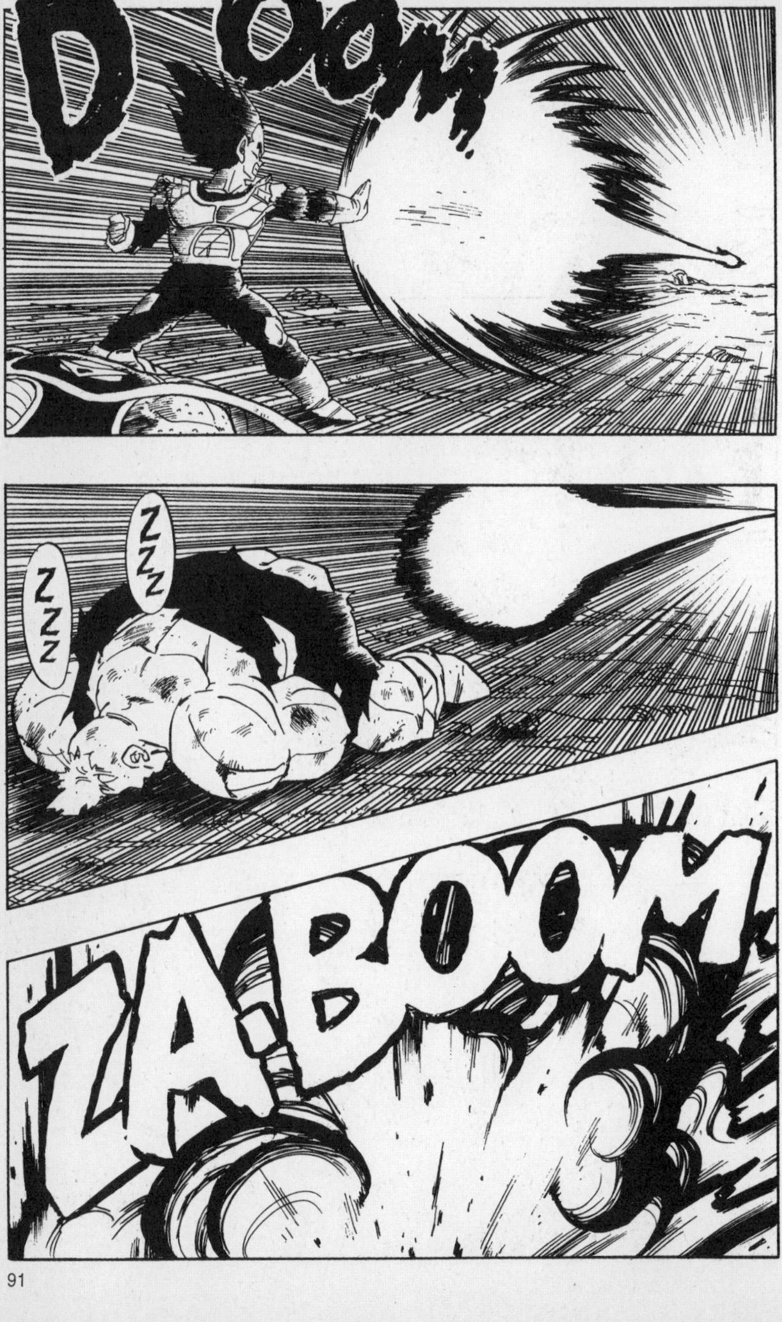
DOOOM
ZZZ
ZZZ
ZABOOM

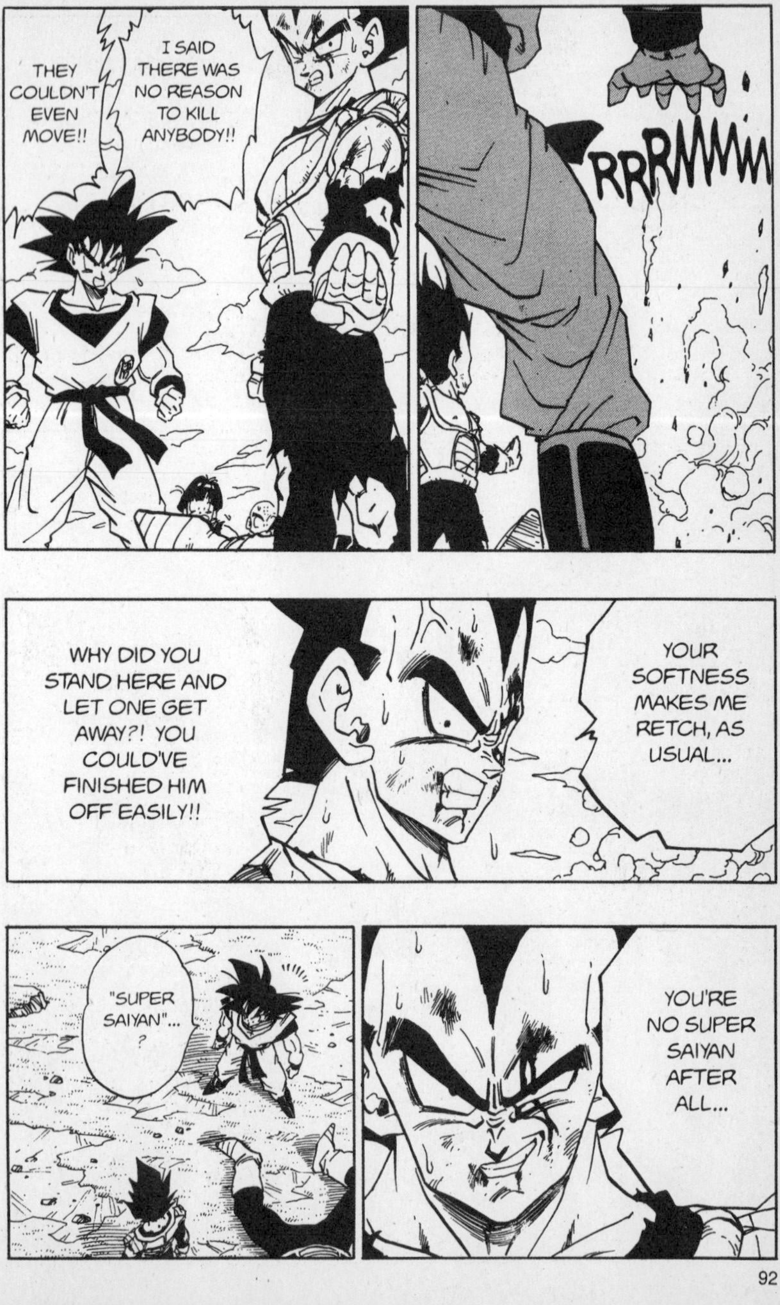
RRRMMMM
I SAID THERE WAS NO REASON TO KILL ANYBODY!!
THEY COULDN'T EVEN MOVE!!
YOUR SOFTNESS MAKES ME RETCH, AS USUAL...
WHY DID YOU STAND HERE AND LET ONE GET AWAY?! YOU COULD'VE FINISHED HIM OFF EASILY!!
YOU'RE NO SUPER SAIYAN AFTER ALL...
"SUPER SAIYAN"... ?

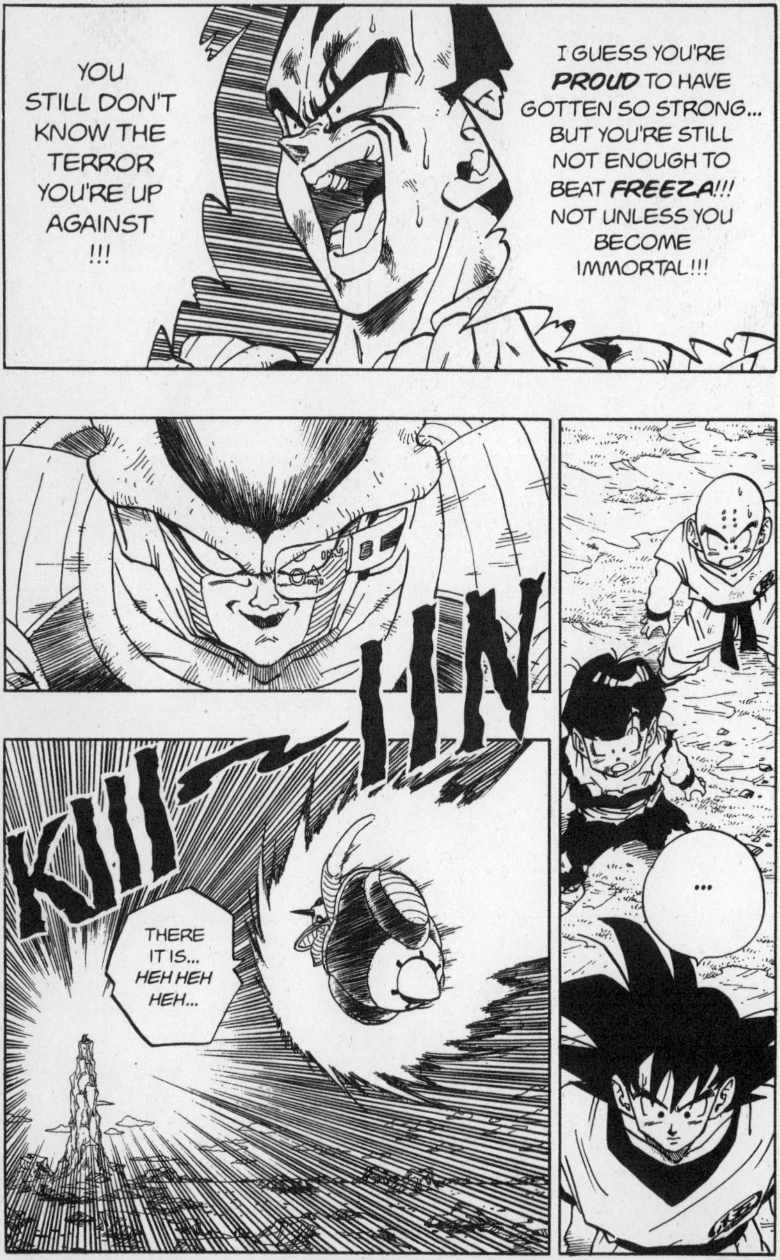

I GUESS YOU'RE PROUD TO HAVE GOTTEN SO STRONG... BUT YOU'RE STILL NOT ENOUGH TO BEAT FREEZA!!! NOT UNLESS YOU BECOME IMMORTAL!!!
YOU STILL DON'T KNOW THE TERROR YOU'RE UP AGAINST !!!
...
KIII—IIN
THERE IT IS... HEH HEH HEH...

NEXT: Ginyu Himself!!

DBZ:89 • Ginyu Steps In

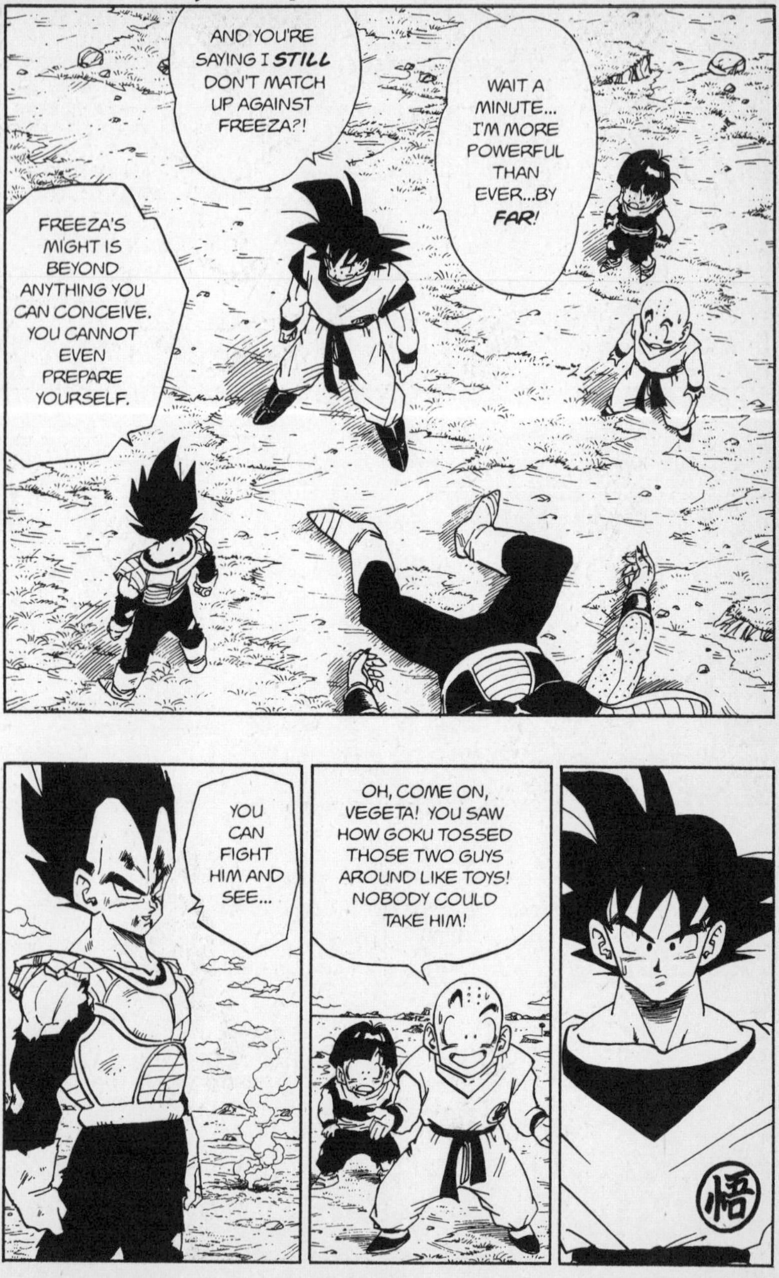
WAIT A MINUTE... I'M MORE POWERFUL THAN EVER...BY FAR!
AND YOU'RE SAYING I STILL DON'T MATCH UP AGAINST FREEZA?!
FREEZA'S MIGHT IS BEYOND ANYTHING YOU CAN CONCEIVE. YOU CANNOT EVEN PREPARE YOURSELF.
OH, COME ON, VEGETA! YOU SAW HOW GOKU TOSSED THOSE TWO GUYS AROUND LIKE TOYS! NOBODY COULD TAKE HIM!
YOU CAN FIGHT HIM AND SEE...

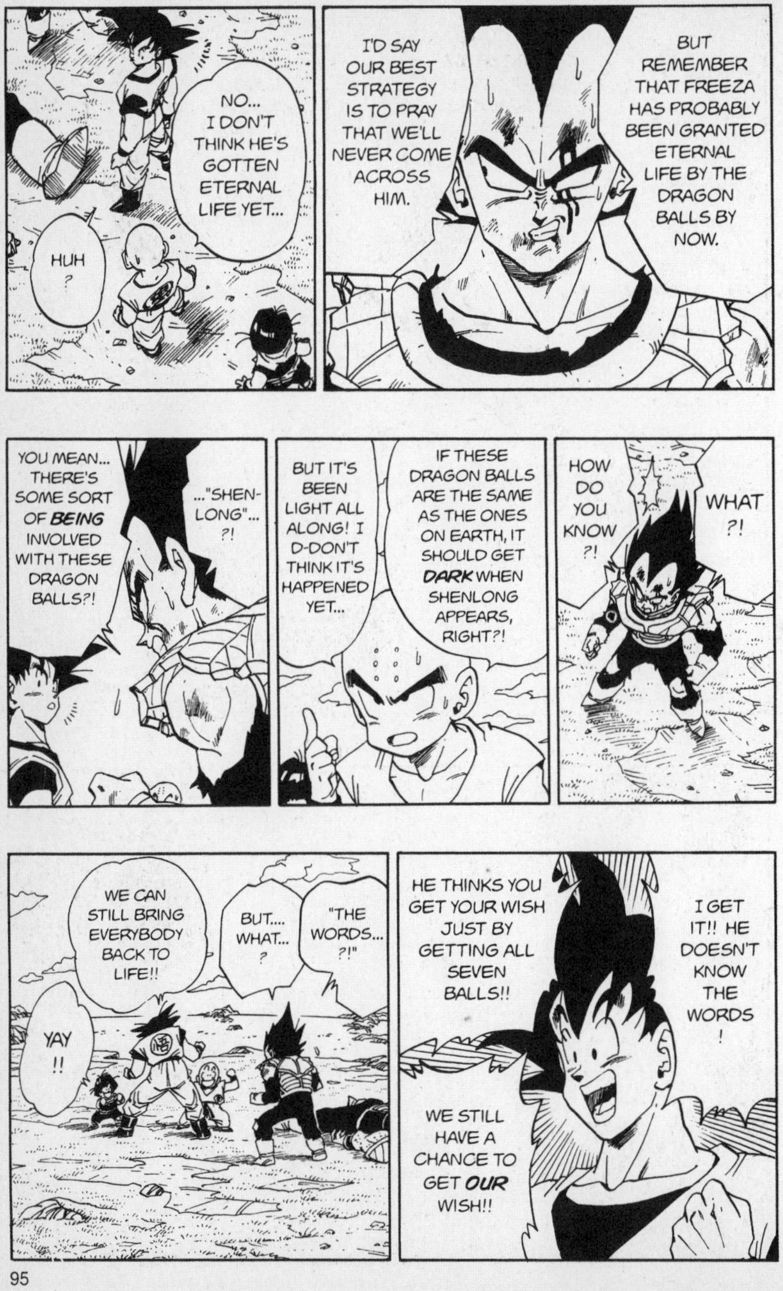
BUT REMEMBER THAT FREEZA HAS PROBABLY BEEN GRANTED ETERNAL LIFE BY THE DRAGON BALLS BY NOW.
I'D SAY OUR BEST STRATEGY IS TO PRAY THAT WE'LL NEVER COME ACROSS HIM.
NO... I DON'T THINK HE'S GOTTEN ETERNAL LIFE YET...
HUH ?
WHAT ?!
HOW DO YOU KNOW ?!
IF THESE DRAGON BALLS ARE THE SAME AS THE ONES ON EARTH, IT SHOULD GET ***DARK*** WHEN SHENLONG APPEARS, RIGHT?!
BUT IT'S BEEN LIGHT ALL ALONG! I D-DON'T THINK IT'S HAPPENED YET...
..."SHEN-LONG"... ?!
YOU MEAN... THERE'S SOME SORT OF ***BEING*** INVOLVED WITH THESE DRAGON BALLS?!
I GET IT!! HE DOESN'T KNOW THE WORDS !
HE THINKS YOU GET YOUR WISH JUST BY GETTING ALL SEVEN BALLS!!
WE STILL HAVE A CHANCE TO GET ***OUR*** WISH!!
"THE WORDS... ?!"
BUT.... WHAT... ?
WE CAN STILL BRING EVERYBODY BACK TO LIFE!!
YAY !!

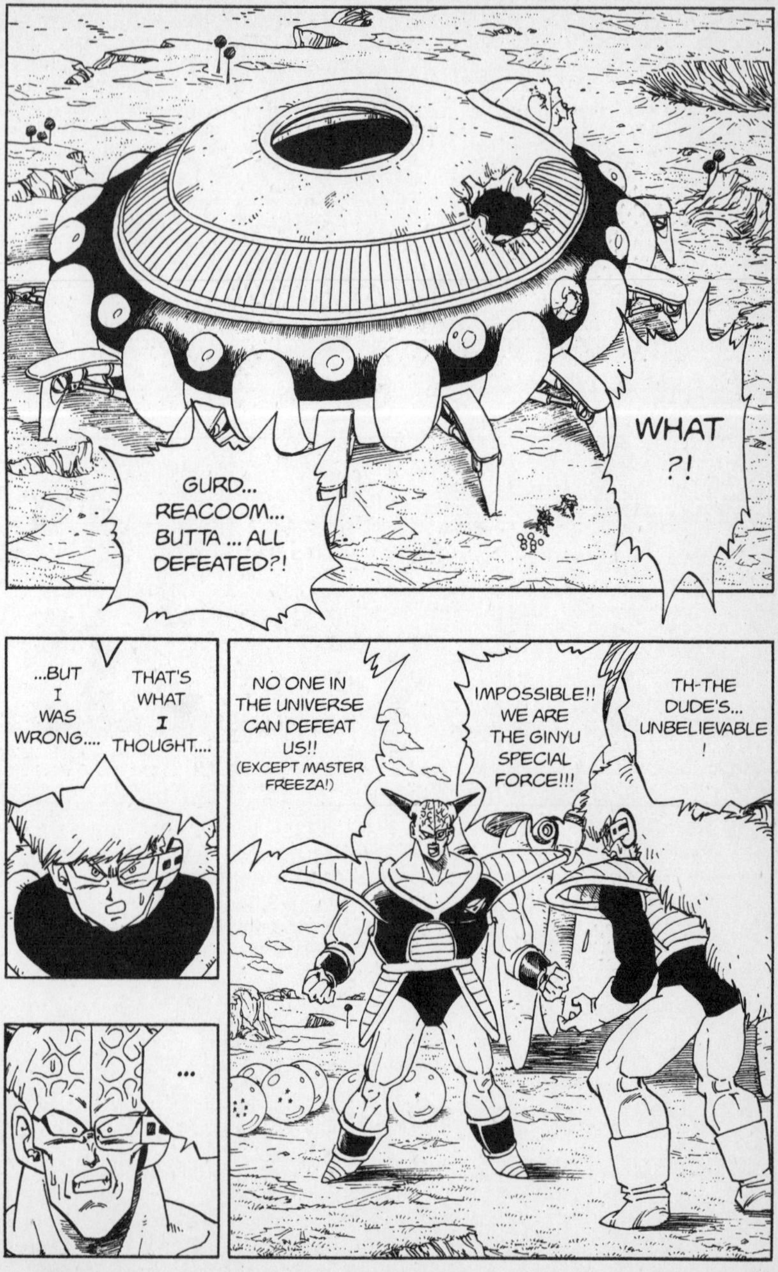
WHAT ?!
GURD... REACOOM... BUTTA ... ALL DEFEATED?!
TH-THE DUDE'S... UNBELIEVABLE!
IMPOSSIBLE!! WE ARE THE GINYU SPECIAL FORCE!!!
NO ONE IN THE UNIVERSE CAN DEFEAT US!! (EXCEPT MASTER FREEZA!)
THAT'S WHAT I THOUGHT....
...BUT I WAS WRONG....
...

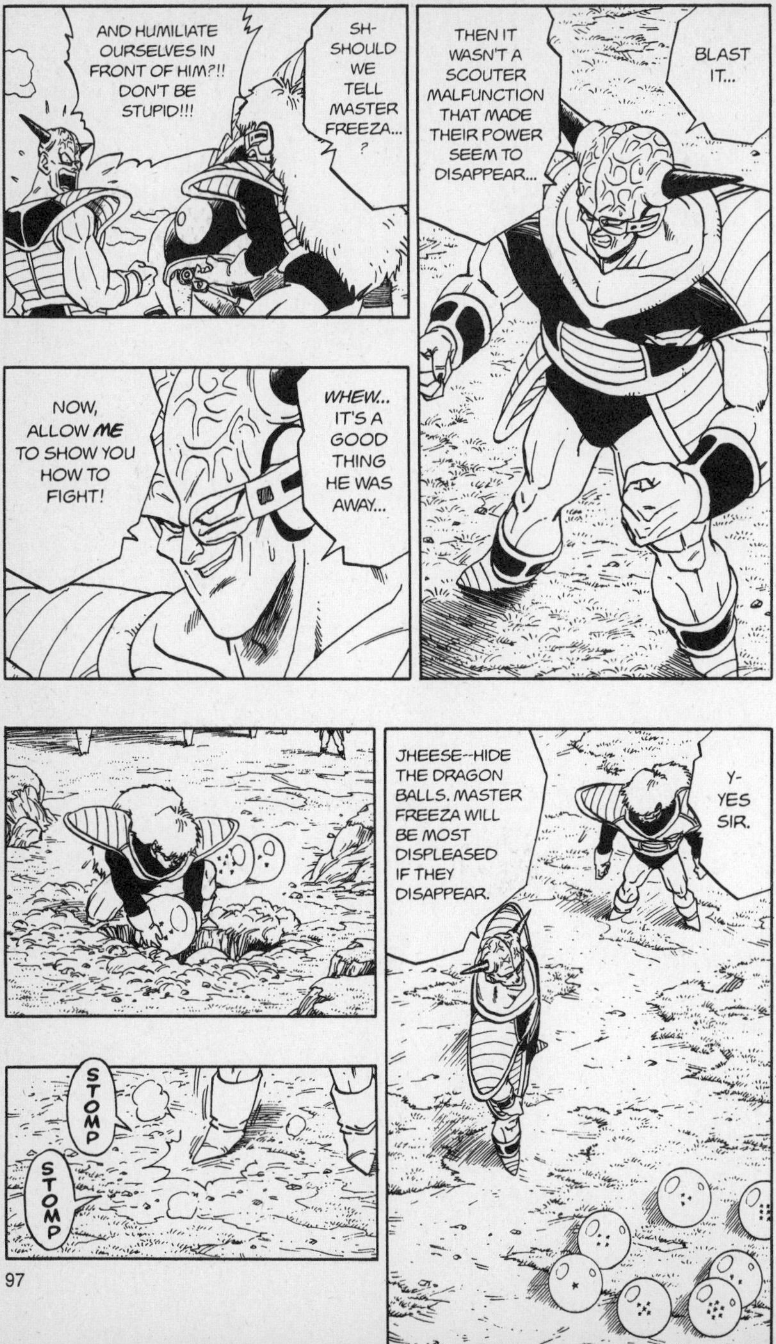
BLAST IT...
THEN IT WASN'T A SCOUTER MALFUNCTION THAT MADE THEIR POWER SEEM TO DISAPPEAR...
SH-SHOULD WE TELL MASTER FREEZA...?
AND HUMILIATE OURSELVES IN FRONT OF HIM?!! DON'T BE STUPID!!!
WHEW... IT'S A GOOD THING HE WAS AWAY...
NOW, ALLOW ME TO SHOW YOU HOW TO FIGHT!
Y-YES SIR.
JHEESE--HIDE THE DRAGON BALLS. MASTER FREEZA WILL BE MOST DISPLEASED IF THEY DISAPPEAR.
STOMP
STOMP

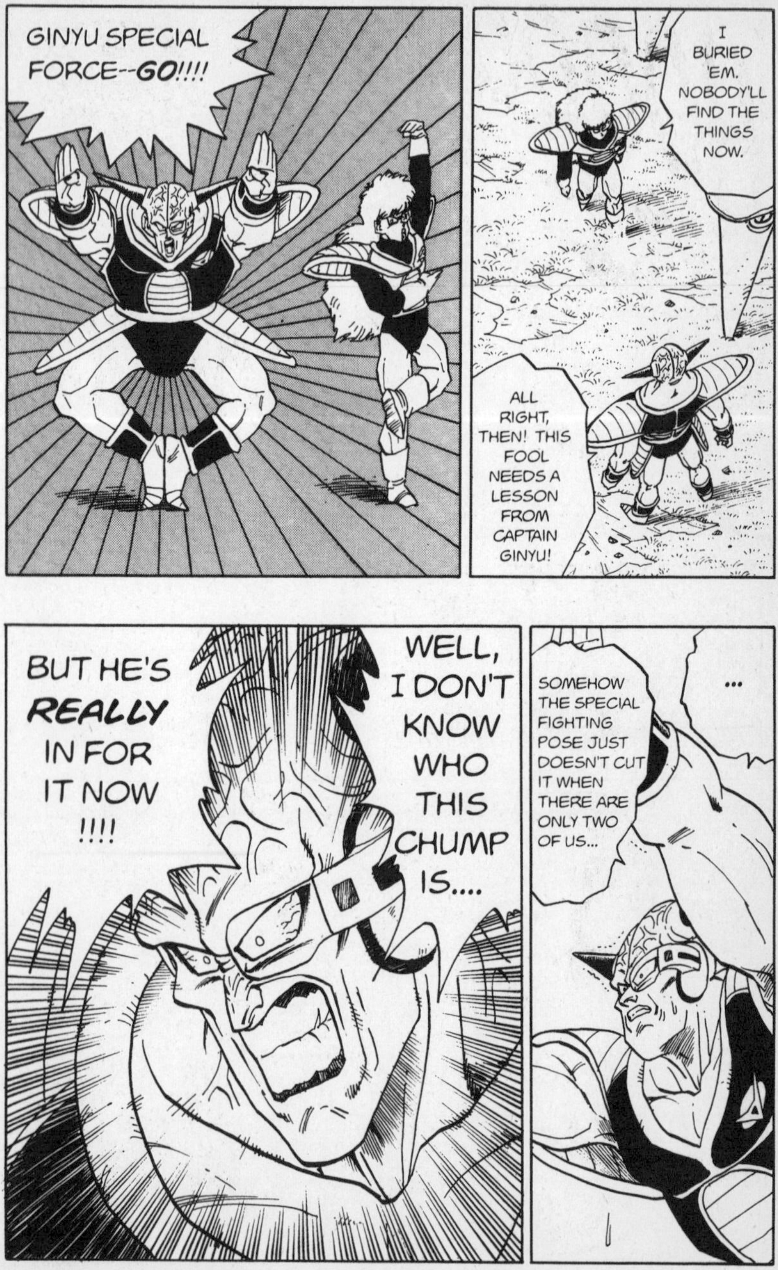
I BURIED 'EM. NOBODY'LL FIND THE THINGS NOW.
ALL RIGHT, THEN! THIS FOOL NEEDS A LESSON FROM CAPTAIN GINYU!
GINYU SPECIAL FORCE--GO!!!!
...
SOMEHOW THE SPECIAL FIGHTING POSE JUST DOESN'T CUT IT WHEN THERE ARE ONLY TWO OF US...
WELL, I DON'T KNOW WHO THIS CHUMP IS....
BUT HE'S REALLY IN FOR IT NOW !!!!

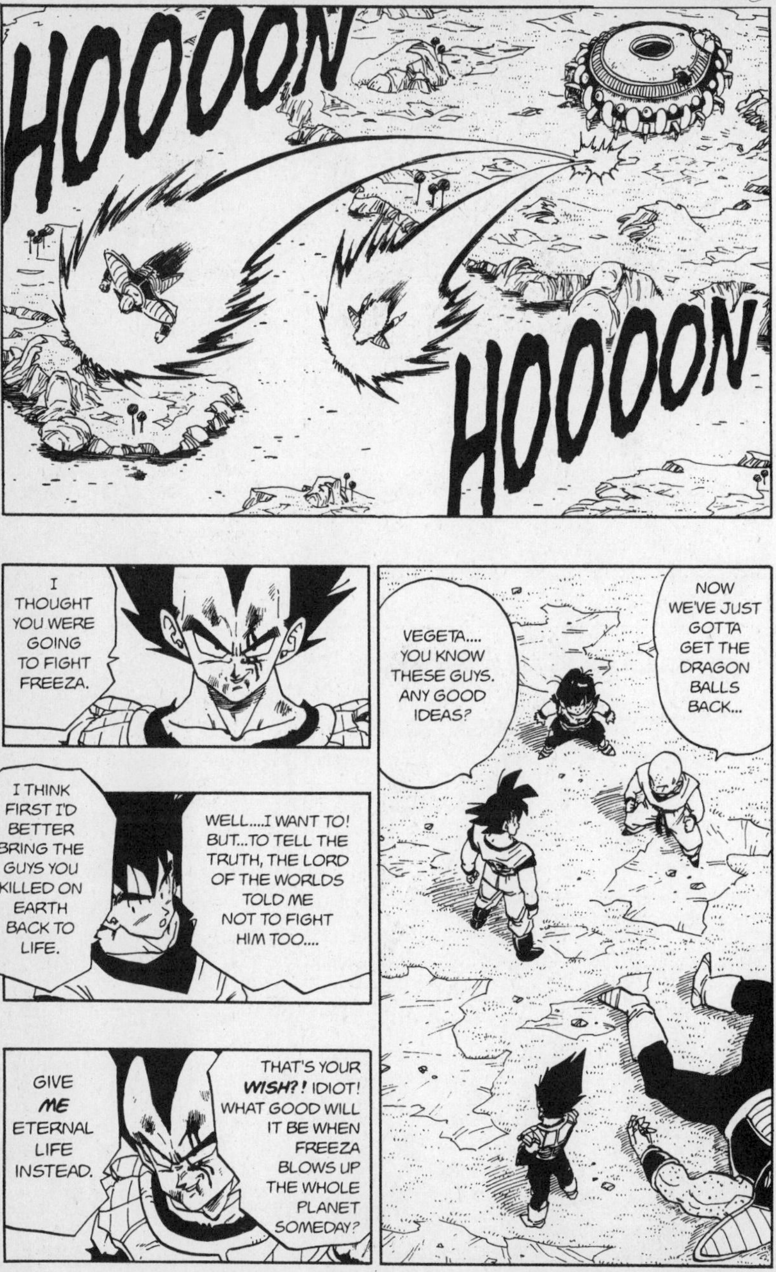
HOOOON
HOOOON
NOW WE'VE JUST GOTTA GET THE DRAGON BALLS BACK...
VEGETA.... YOU KNOW THESE GUYS. ANY GOOD IDEAS?
I THOUGHT YOU WERE GOING TO FIGHT FREEZA.
WELL....I WANT TO! BUT...TO TELL THE TRUTH, THE LORD OF THE WORLDS TOLD ME NOT TO FIGHT HIM TOO....
I THINK FIRST I'D BETTER BRING THE GUYS YOU KILLED ON EARTH BACK TO LIFE.
THAT'S YOUR *WISH?!* IDIOT! WHAT GOOD WILL IT BE WHEN FREEZA BLOWS UP THE WHOLE PLANET SOMEDAY?
GIVE *ME* ETERNAL LIFE INSTEAD.

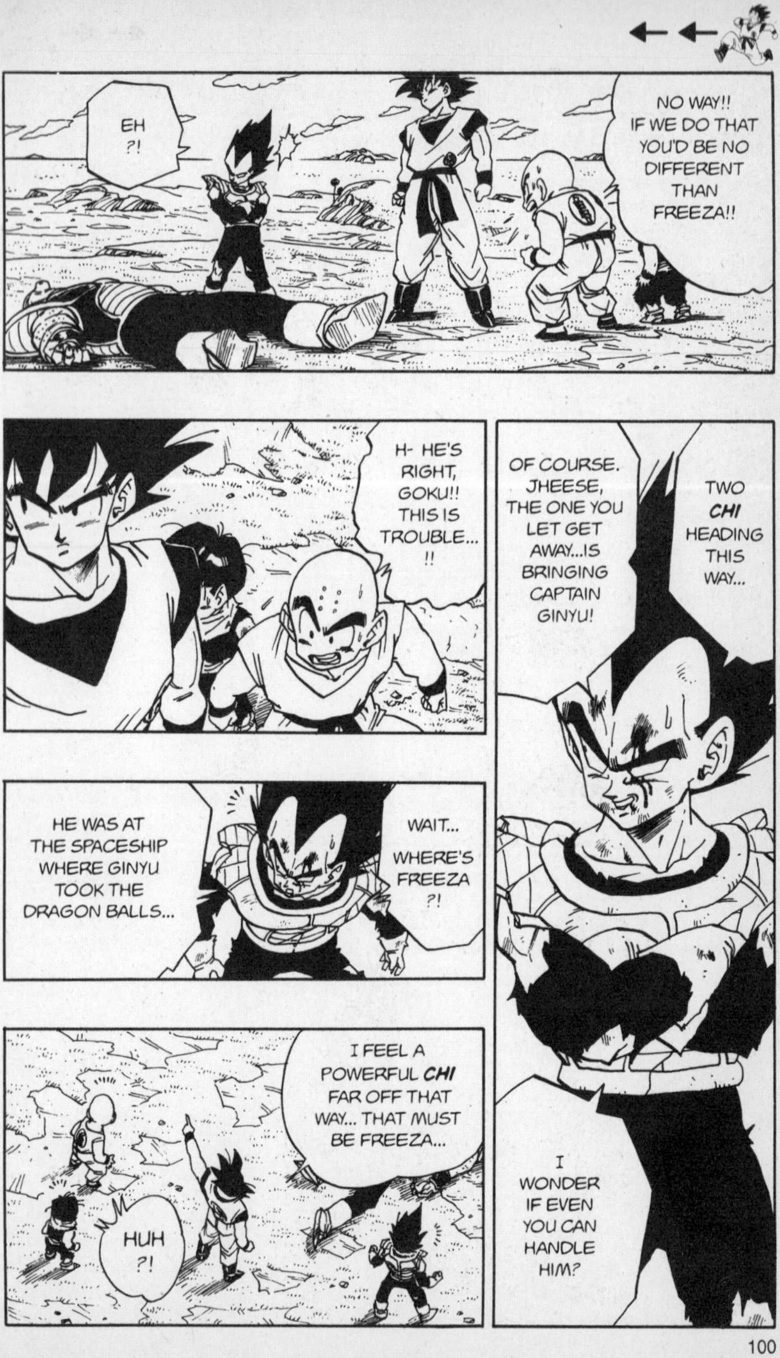
NO WAY!! IF WE DO THAT YOU'D BE NO DIFFERENT THAN FREEZA!!
EH ?!
TWO CHI HEADING THIS WAY...
OF COURSE. JHEESE, THE ONE YOU LET GET AWAY...IS BRINGING CAPTAIN GINYU!
I WONDER IF EVEN YOU CAN HANDLE HIM?
H- HE'S RIGHT, GOKU!! THIS IS TROUBLE... !!
WAIT... WHERE'S FREEZA ?!
HE WAS AT THE SPACESHIP WHERE GINYU TOOK THE DRAGON BALLS...
I FEEL A POWERFUL CHI FAR OFF THAT WAY... THAT MUST BE FREEZA...
HUH ?!

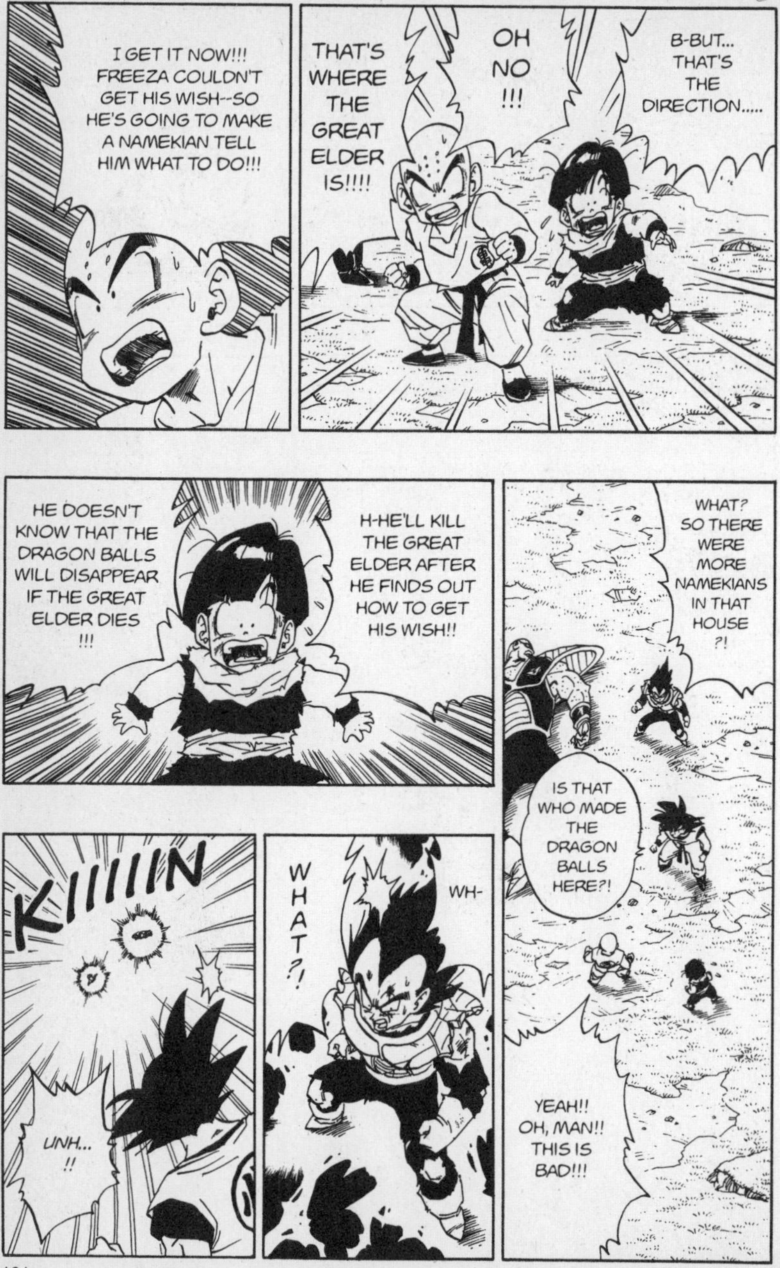
B-BUT... THAT'S THE DIRECTION.....
OH NO !!!
THAT'S WHERE THE GREAT ELDER IS!!!!
I GET IT NOW!!! FREEZA COULDN'T GET HIS WISH--SO HE'S GOING TO MAKE A NAMEKIAN TELL HIM WHAT TO DO!!!
WHAT? SO THERE WERE MORE NAMEKIANS IN THAT HOUSE ?!
IS THAT WHO MADE THE DRAGON BALLS HERE?!
YEAH!! OH, MAN!! THIS IS BAD!!!
H-HE'LL KILL THE GREAT ELDER AFTER HE FINDS OUT HOW TO GET HIS WISH!!
HE DOESN'T KNOW THAT THE DRAGON BALLS WILL DISAPPEAR IF THE GREAT ELDER DIES !!!
WH-
WHAT?!
KIIIIN
UNH... !!

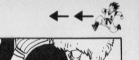

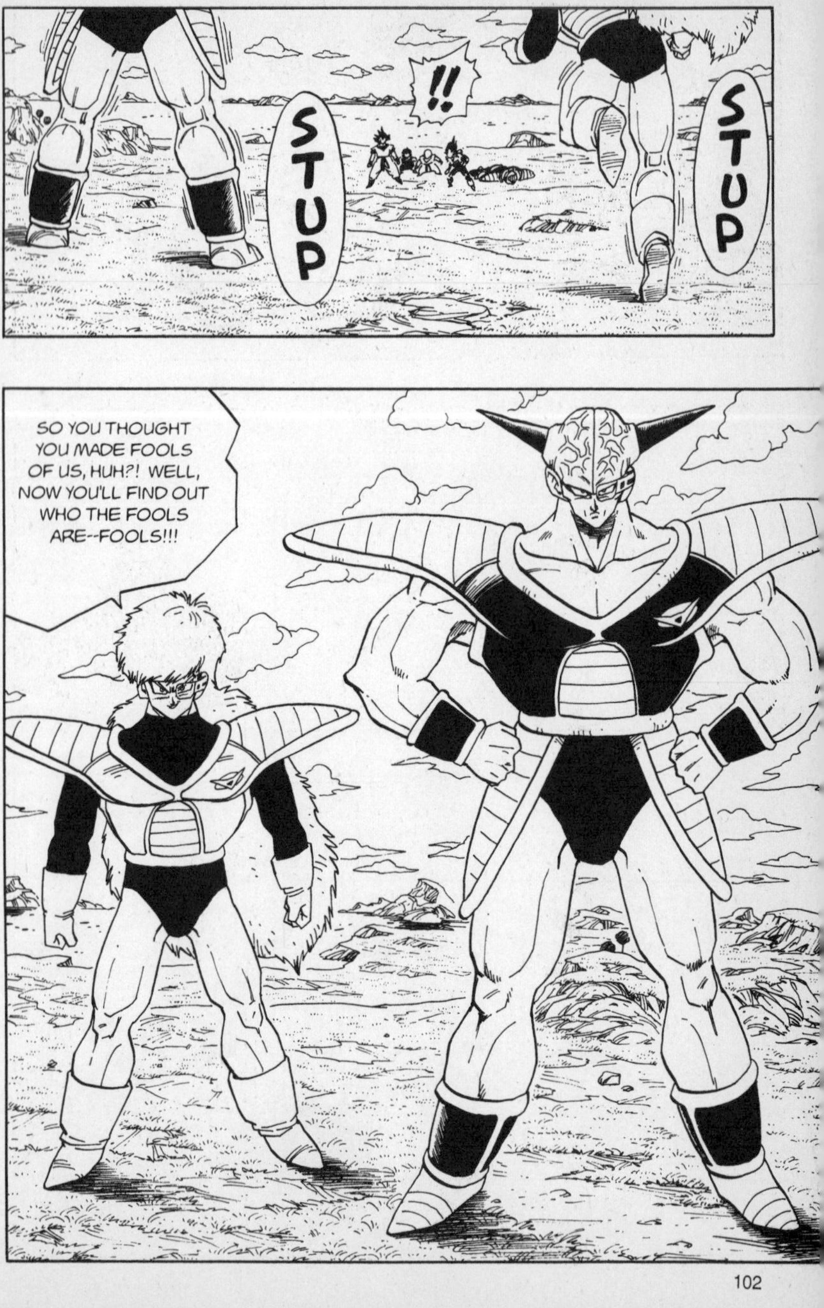
STUP
!!
STUP
SO YOU THOUGHT YOU MADE FOOLS OF US, HUH?! WELL, NOW YOU'LL FIND OUT WHO THE FOOLS ARE--FOOLS!!!

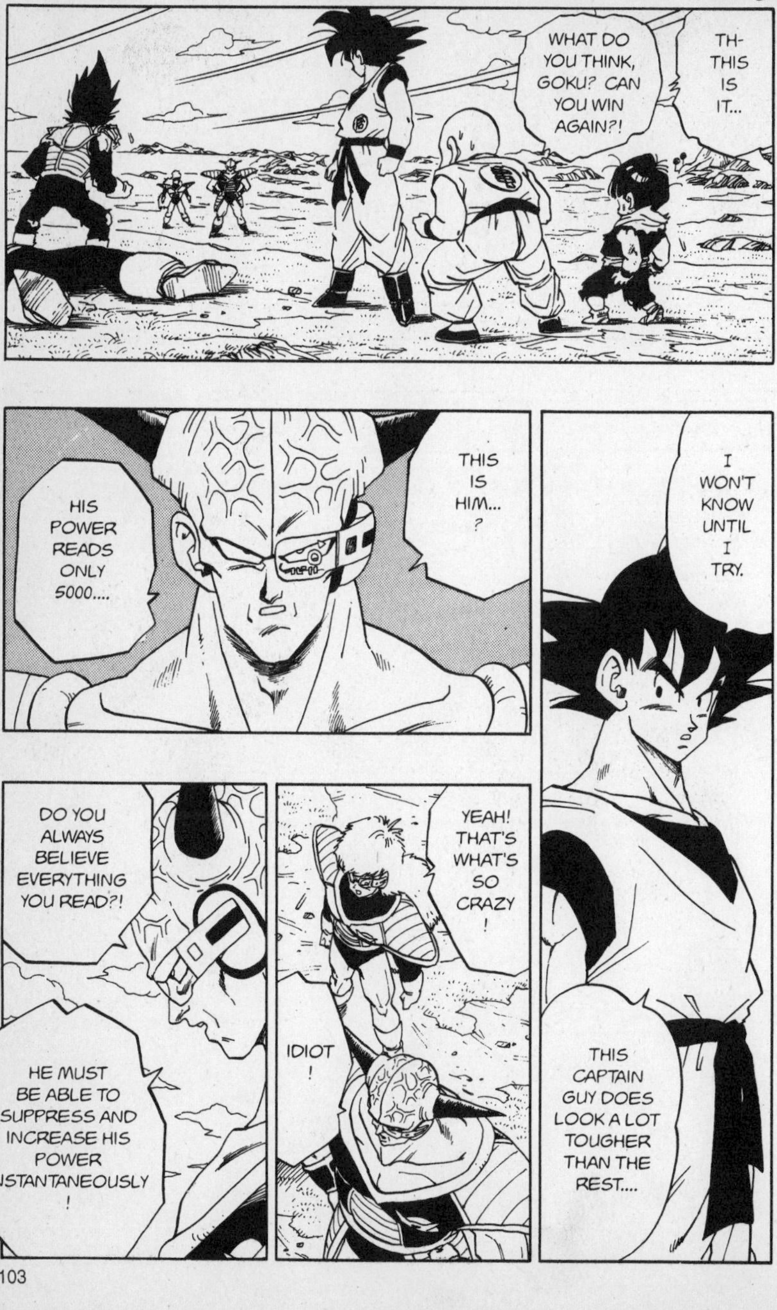
TH- THIS IS IT...
WHAT DO YOU THINK, GOKU? CAN YOU WIN AGAIN?!
I WON'T KNOW UNTIL I TRY.
THIS CAPTAIN GUY DOES LOOK A LOT TOUGHER THAN THE REST....
THIS IS HIM...?
HIS POWER READS ONLY 5000....
YEAH! THAT'S WHAT'S SO CRAZY!
IDIOT!
DO YOU ALWAYS BELIEVE EVERYTHING YOU READ?!
HE MUST BE ABLE TO SUPPRESS AND INCREASE HIS POWER INSTANTANEOUSLY!

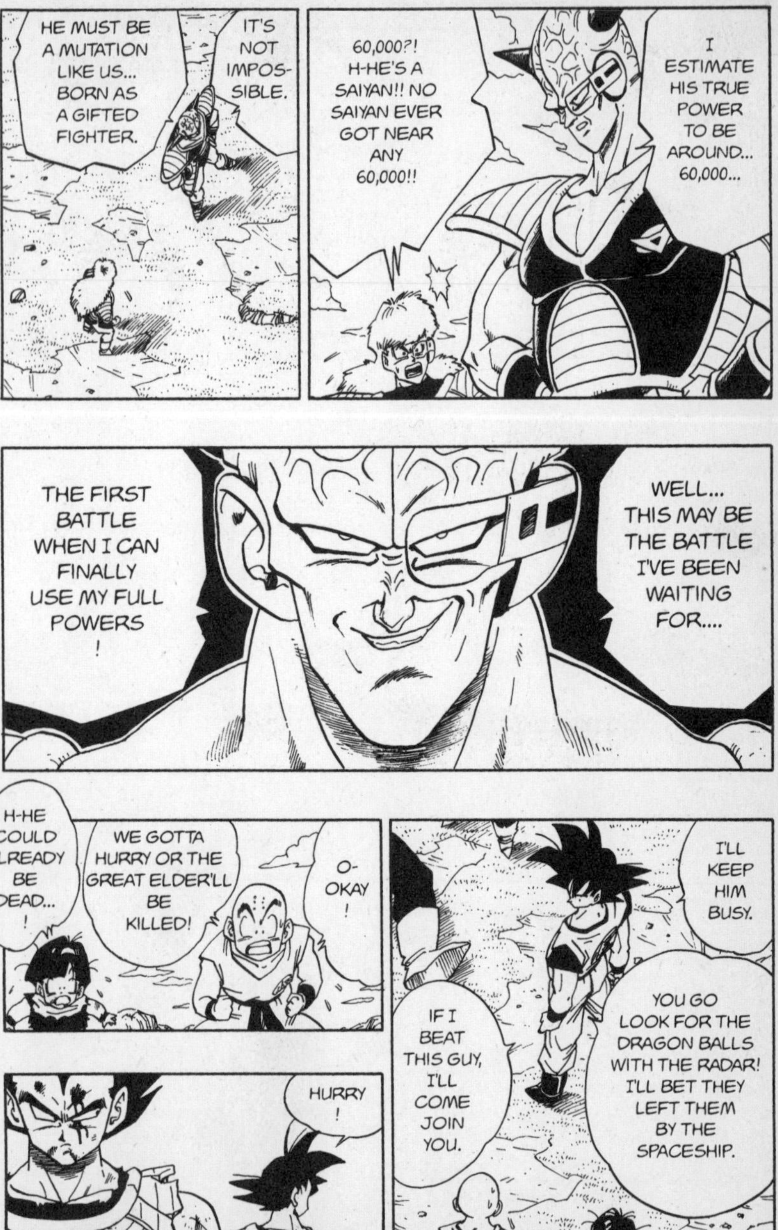
I ESTIMATE HIS TRUE POWER TO BE AROUND... 60,000...
60,000?! H-HE'S A SAIYAN!! NO SAIYAN EVER GOT NEAR ANY 60,000!!
IT'S NOT IMPOSSIBLE.
HE MUST BE A MUTATION LIKE US... BORN AS A GIFTED FIGHTER.
WELL... THIS MAY BE THE BATTLE I'VE BEEN WAITING FOR....
THE FIRST BATTLE WHEN I CAN FINALLY USE MY FULL POWERS!
I'LL KEEP HIM BUSY.
YOU GO LOOK FOR THE DRAGON BALLS WITH THE RADAR! I'LL BET THEY LEFT THEM BY THE SPACESHIP.
IF I BEAT THIS GUY, I'LL COME JOIN YOU.
O-OKAY!
WE GOTTA HURRY OR THE GREAT ELDER'LL BE KILLED!
H-HE COULD ALREADY BE DEAD...!
HURRY!

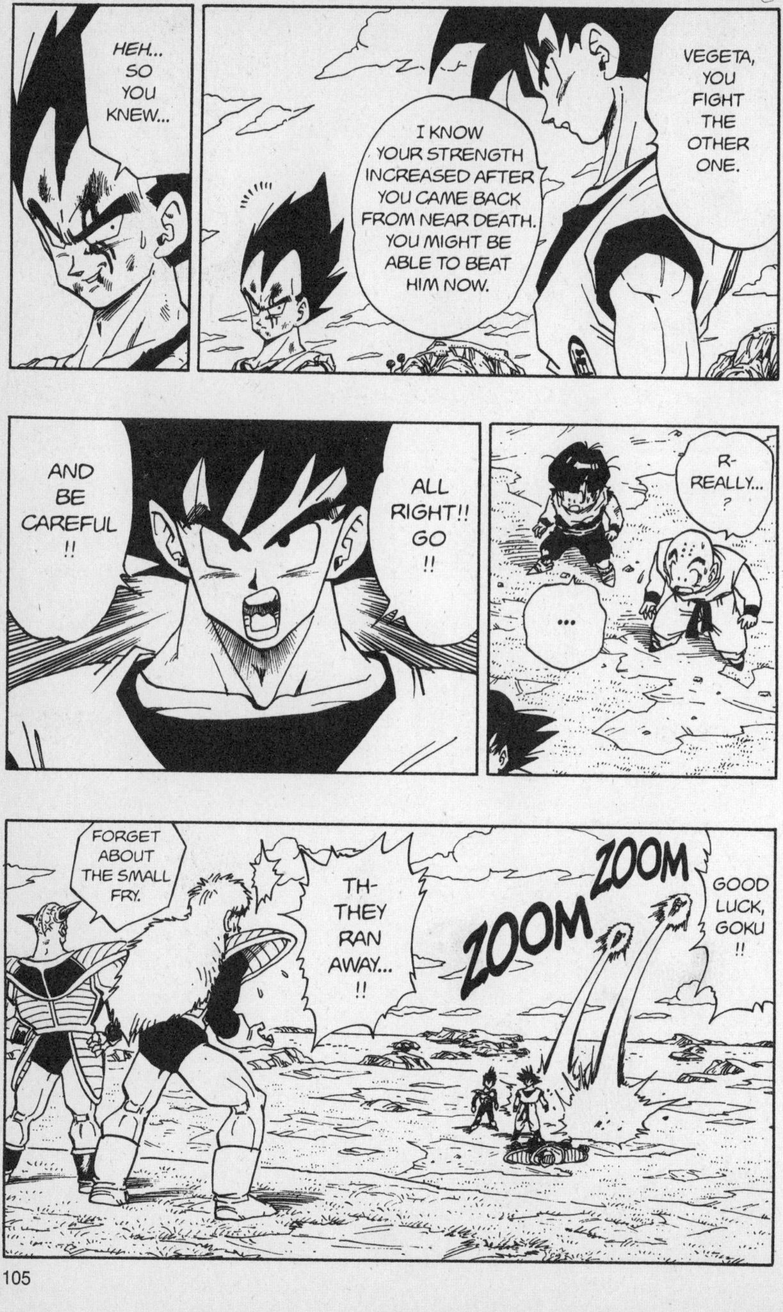
VEGETA, YOU FIGHT THE OTHER ONE.
I KNOW YOUR STRENGTH INCREASED AFTER YOU CAME BACK FROM NEAR DEATH. YOU MIGHT BE ABLE TO BEAT HIM NOW.
HEH... SO YOU KNEW...
R-REALLY...?
...
ALL RIGHT!! GO!!
AND BE CAREFUL!!
GOOD LUCK, GOKU!!
ZOOM
ZOOM
TH-THEY RAN AWAY...!!
FORGET ABOUT THE SMALL FRY.

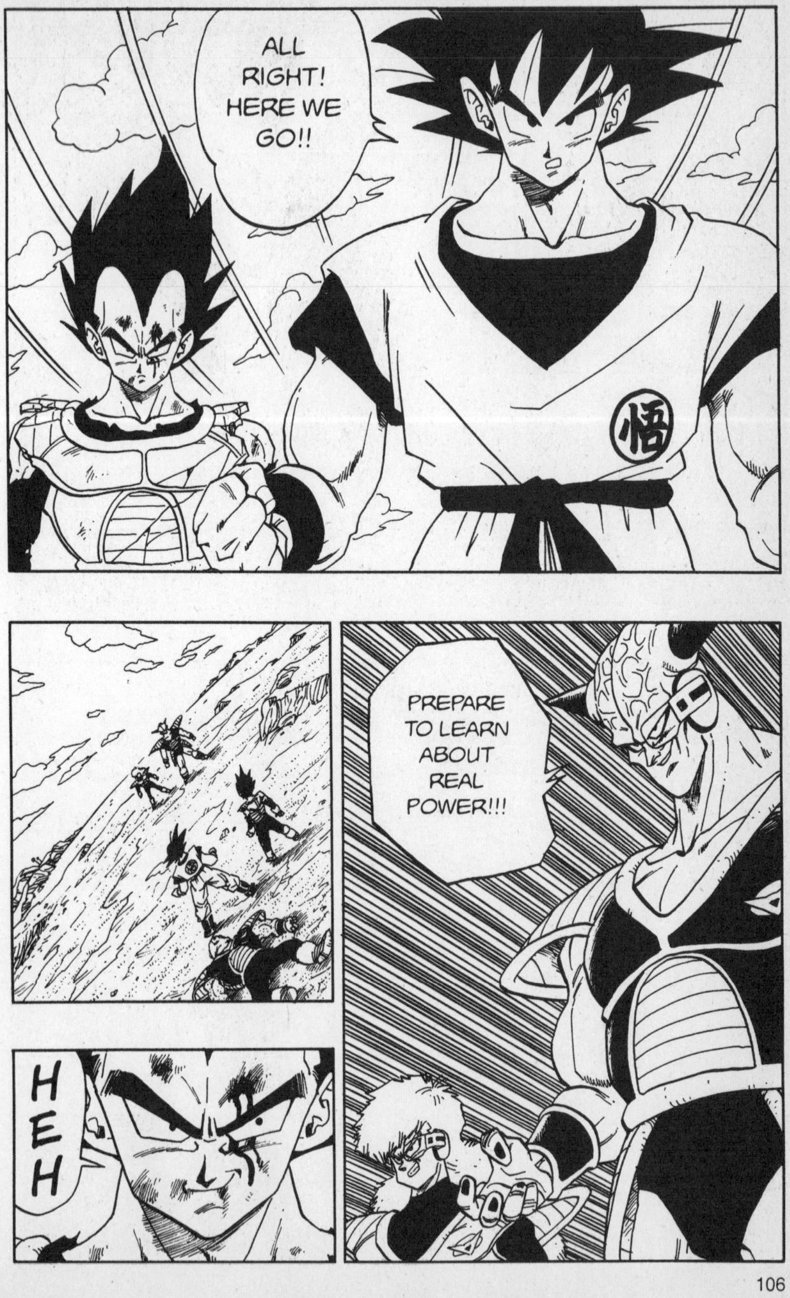
ALL RIGHT! HERE WE GO!!
PREPARE TO LEARN ABOUT REAL POWER!!!
HEH

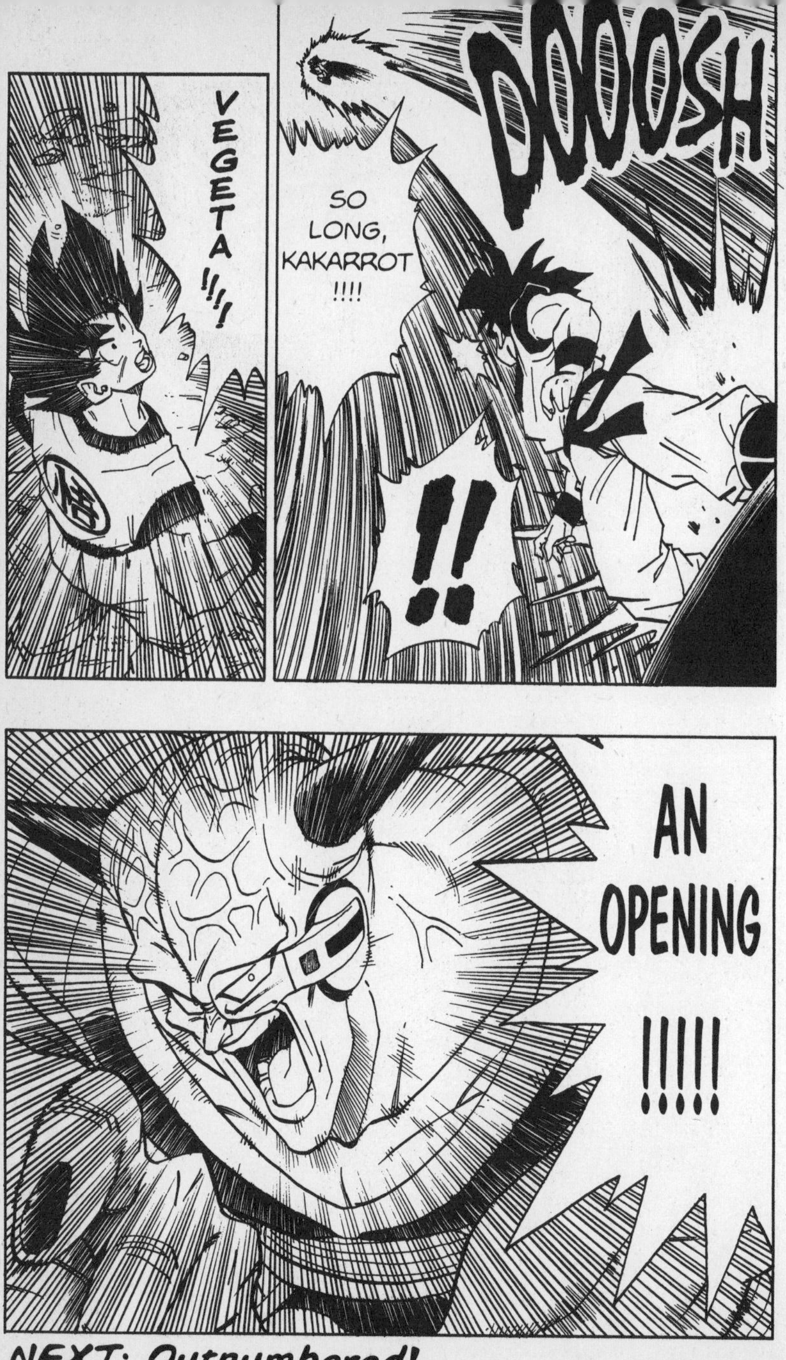
DOOOSH
SO LONG, KAKARROT !!!!
!!
VEGETA !!!!
AN OPENING !!!!!

NEXT: Outnumbered!

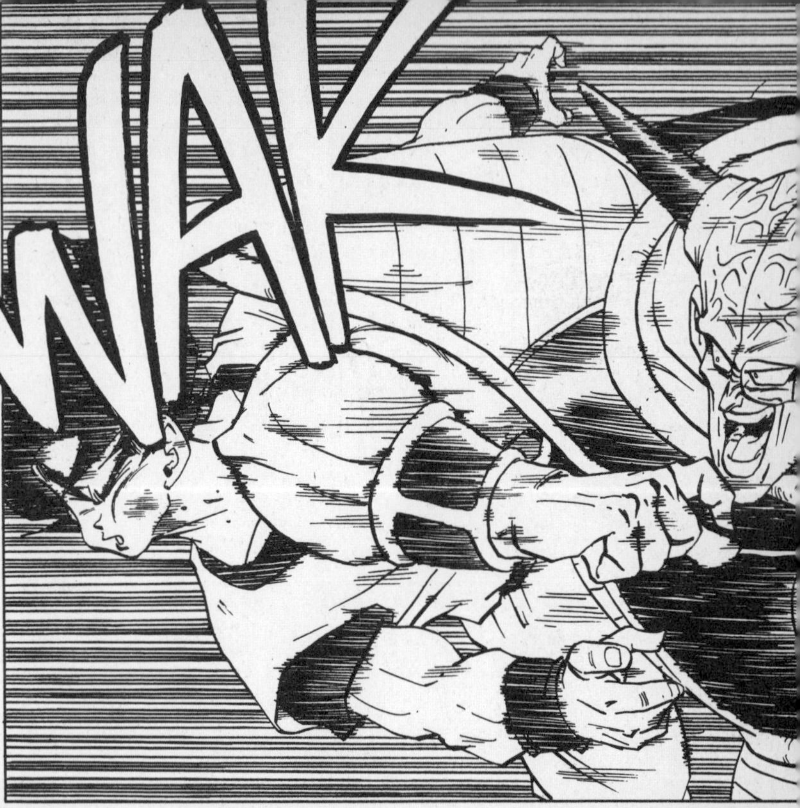
WAK

DBZ:90 • A Matter of Pride

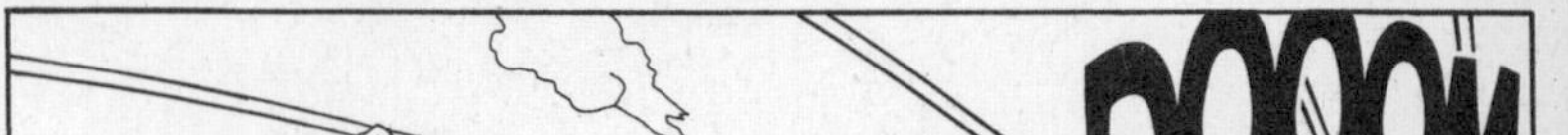
DOOOM

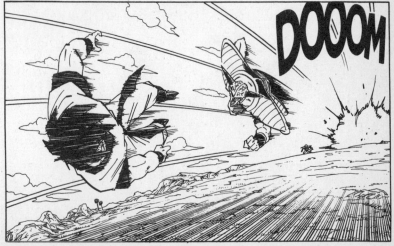

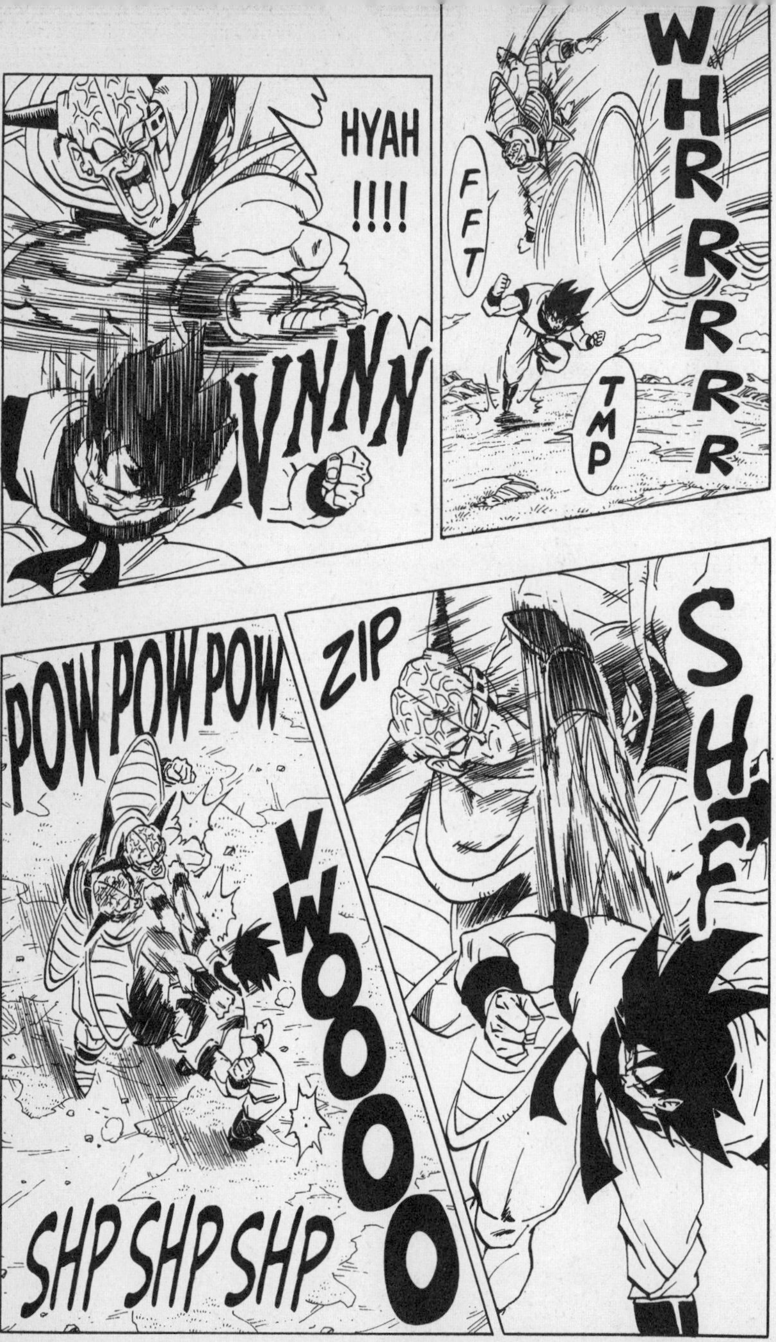
FFT
TMP
WHRRRRR
HYAH!!!!
VNNNN
ZIP
SHFF
POW POW POW
VWOOOO
SHP SHP SHP

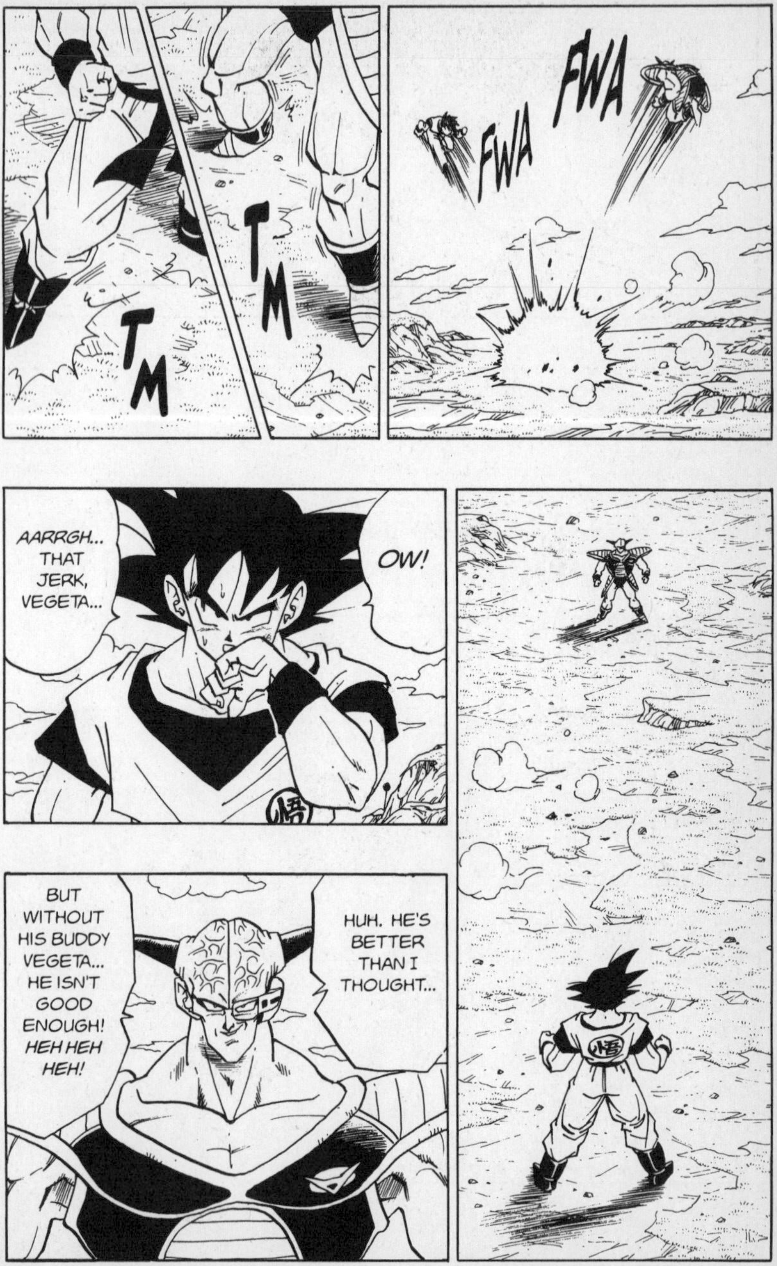
FWA
FWA
TM
TM
OW!
AARRGH... THAT JERK, VEGETA...
HUH. HE'S BETTER THAN I THOUGHT...
BUT WITHOUT HIS BUDDY VEGETA... HE ISN'T GOOD ENOUGH! HEH HEH HEH!

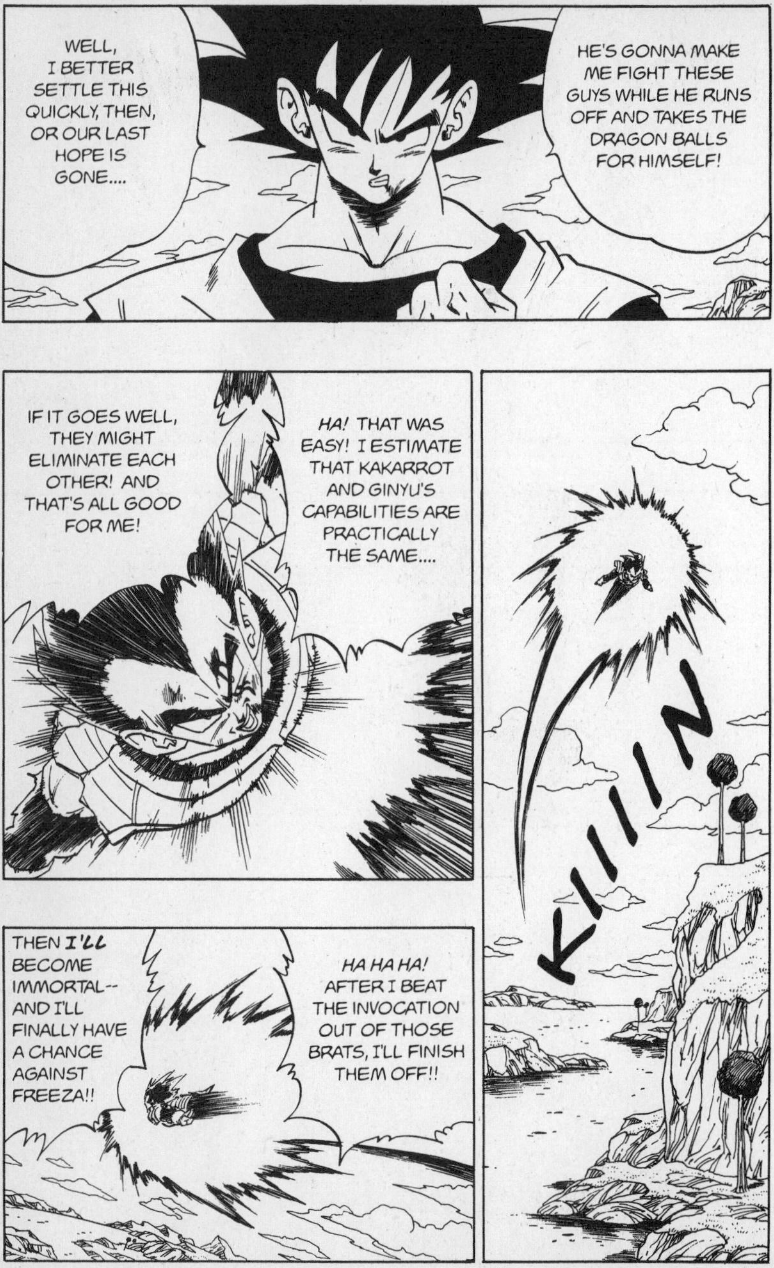
HE'S GONNA MAKE ME FIGHT THESE GUYS WHILE HE RUNS OFF AND TAKES THE DRAGON BALLS FOR HIMSELF!
WELL, I BETTER SETTLE THIS QUICKLY, THEN, OR OUR LAST HOPE IS GONE....
KIIIIN
HA! THAT WAS EASY! I ESTIMATE THAT KAKARROT AND GINYU'S CAPABILITIES ARE PRACTICALLY THE SAME....
IF IT GOES WELL, THEY MIGHT ELIMINATE EACH OTHER! AND THAT'S ALL GOOD FOR ME!
HA HA HA! AFTER I BEAT THE INVOCATION OUT OF THOSE BRATS, I'LL FINISH THEM OFF!!
THEN **I'LL** BECOME IMMORTAL--AND I'LL FINALLY HAVE A CHANCE AGAINST FREEZA!!

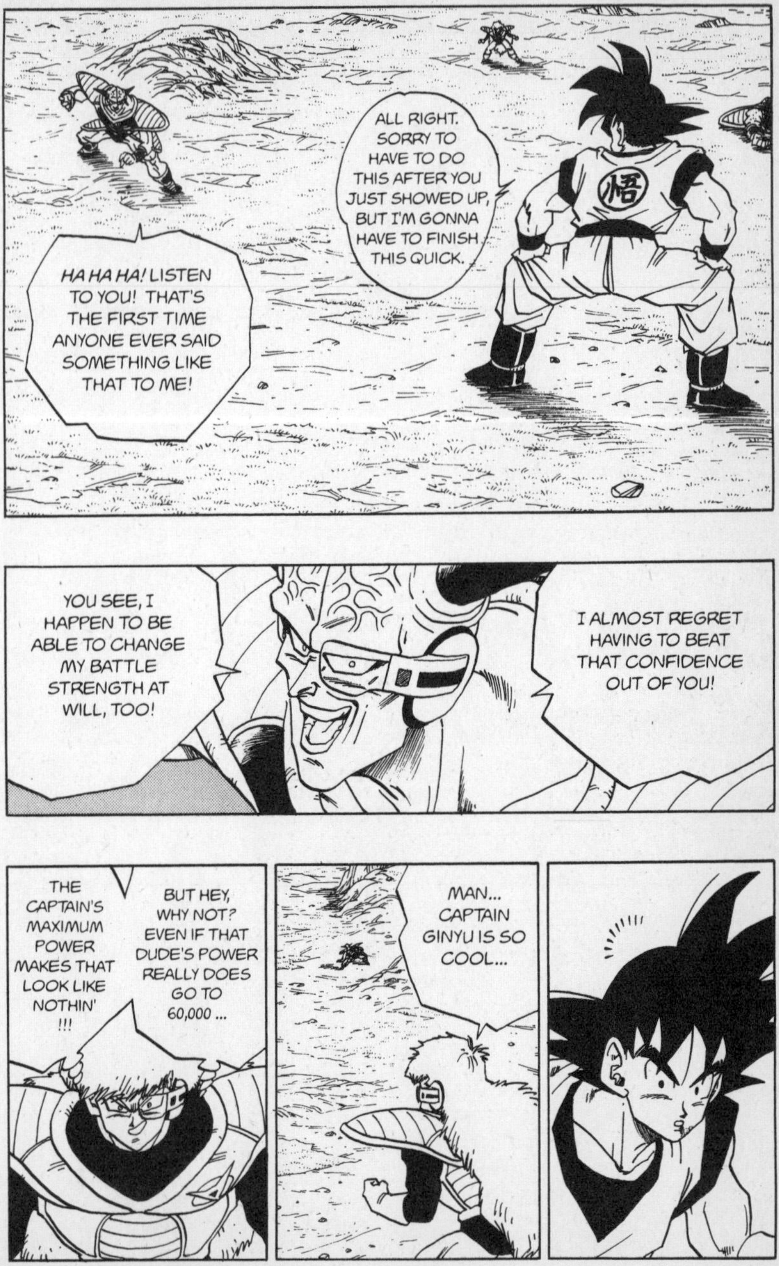
ALL RIGHT. SORRY TO HAVE TO DO THIS AFTER YOU JUST SHOWED UP, BUT I'M GONNA HAVE TO FINISH THIS QUICK.
HA HA HA! LISTEN TO YOU! THAT'S THE FIRST TIME ANYONE EVER SAID SOMETHING LIKE THAT TO ME!
I ALMOST REGRET HAVING TO BEAT THAT CONFIDENCE OUT OF YOU!
YOU SEE, I HAPPEN TO BE ABLE TO CHANGE MY BATTLE STRENGTH AT WILL, TOO!
MAN... CAPTAIN GINYU IS SO COOL...
BUT HEY, WHY NOT? EVEN IF THAT DUDE'S POWER REALLY DOES GO TO 60,000 ...
THE CAPTAIN'S MAXIMUM POWER MAKES THAT LOOK LIKE NOTHIN' !!!

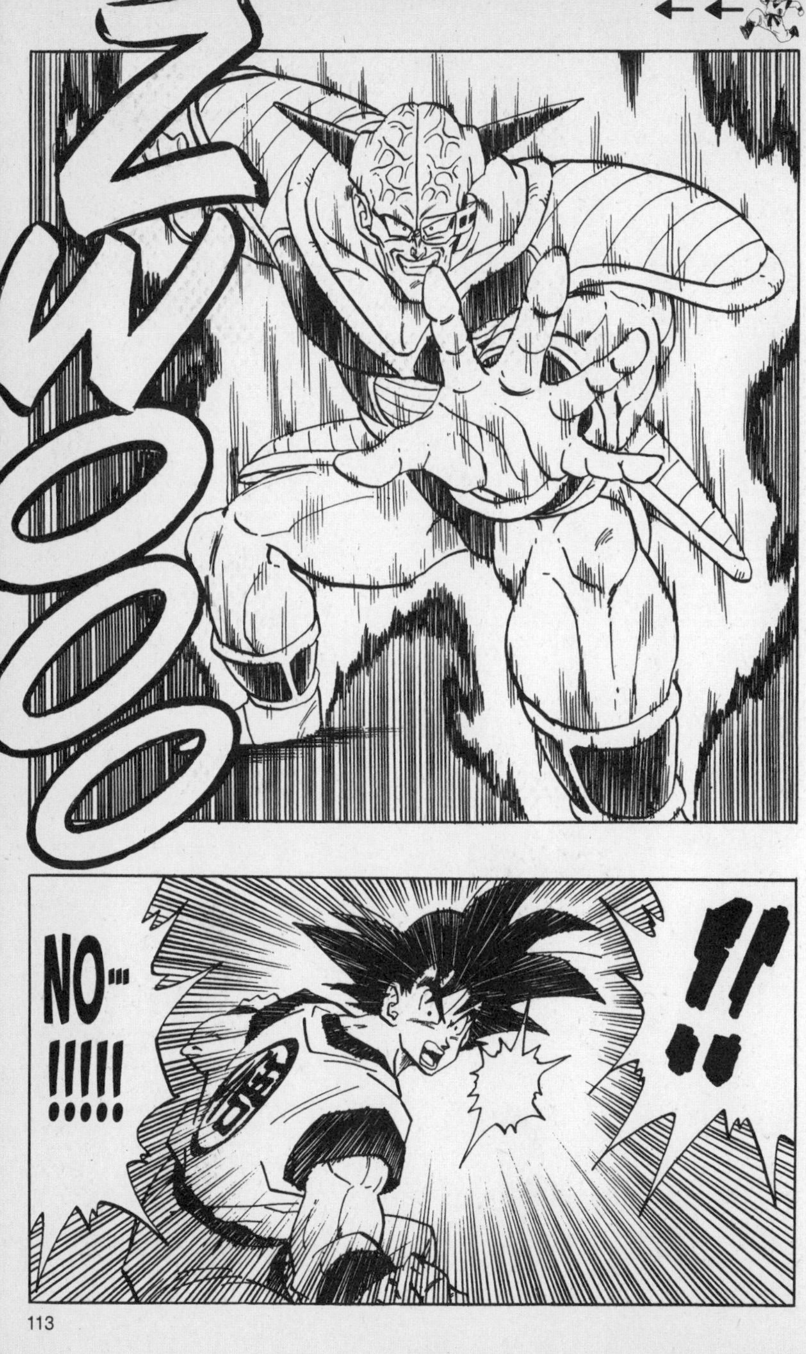
!!
NO... !!!!!

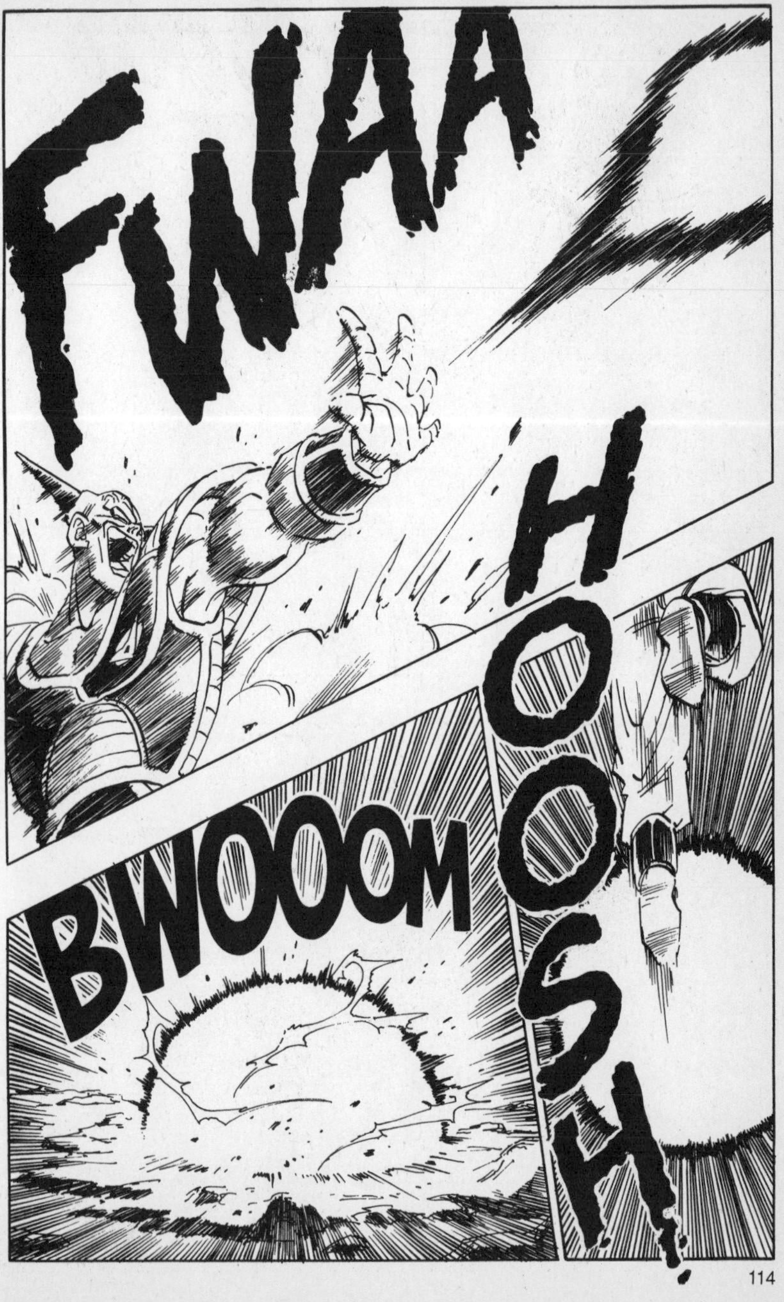
FWAA
HOOOSH
BWOOOM

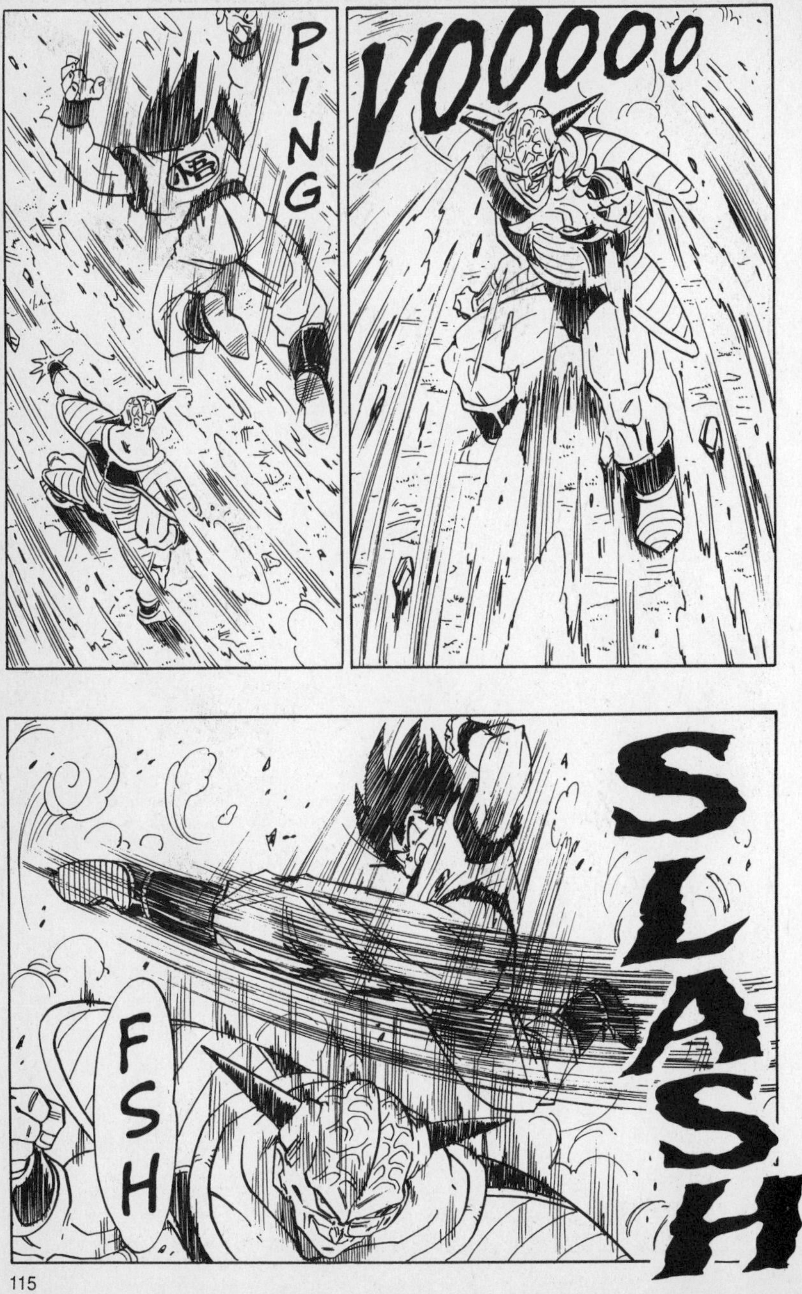
VOOOOO
PING
SLASH
FSH

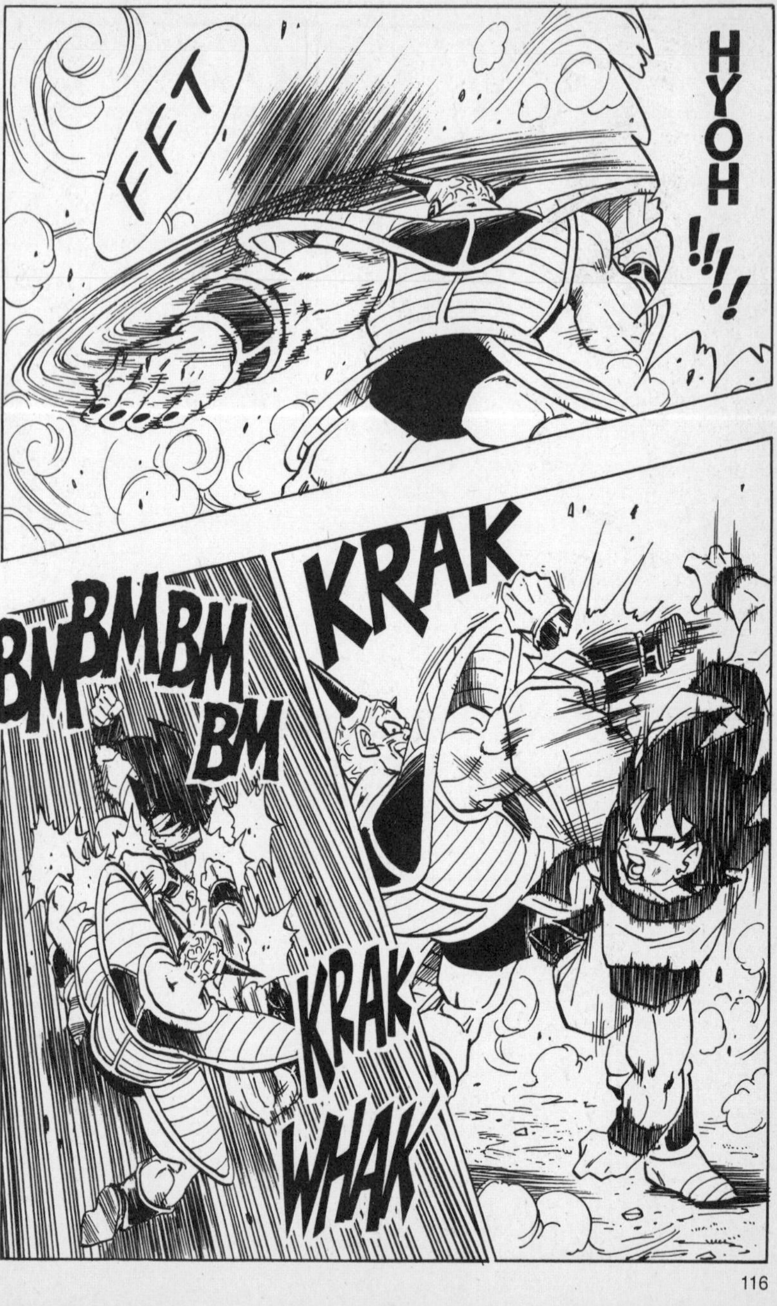
HYOH!!!!
FFT
KRAK
KRAK
WHAK
BMBMBMBM
BM
BM

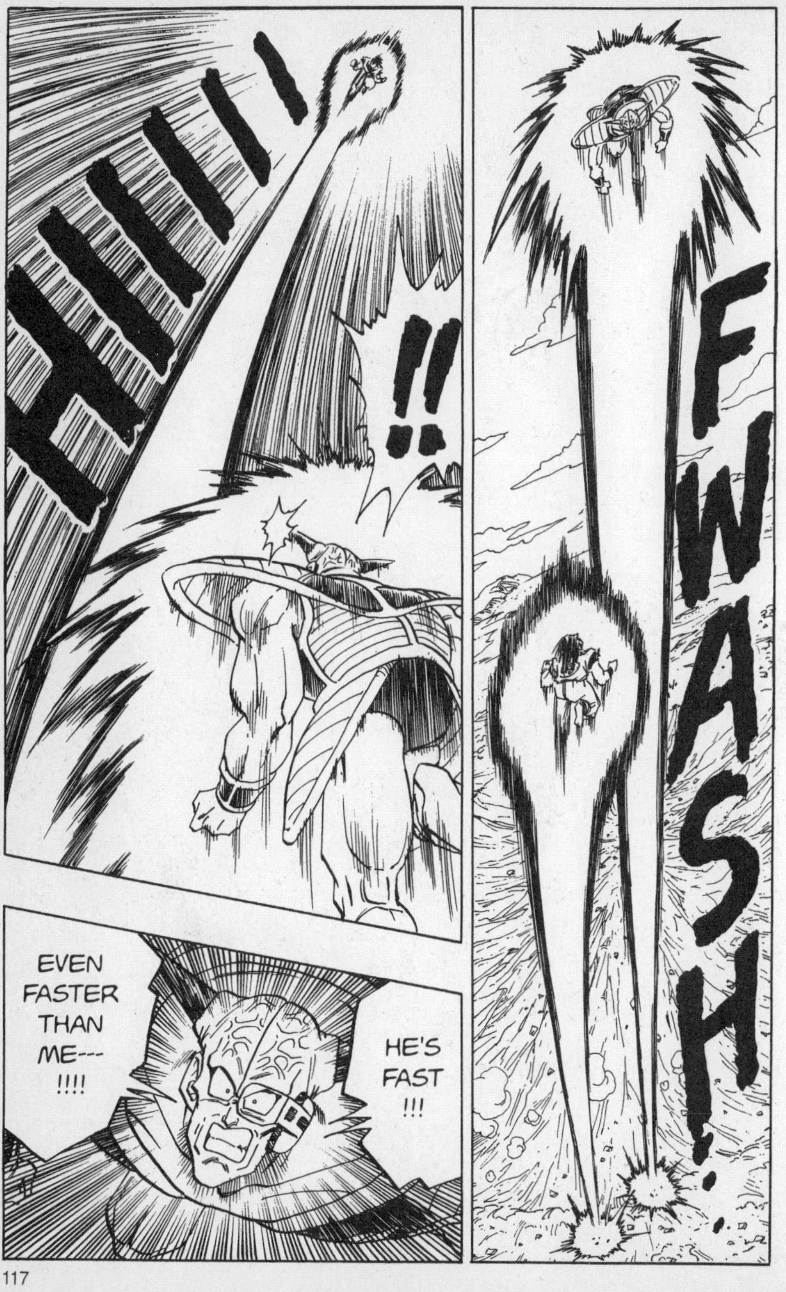
FWASH!
!!
HE'S FAST !!!
EVEN FASTER THAN ME--- !!!!

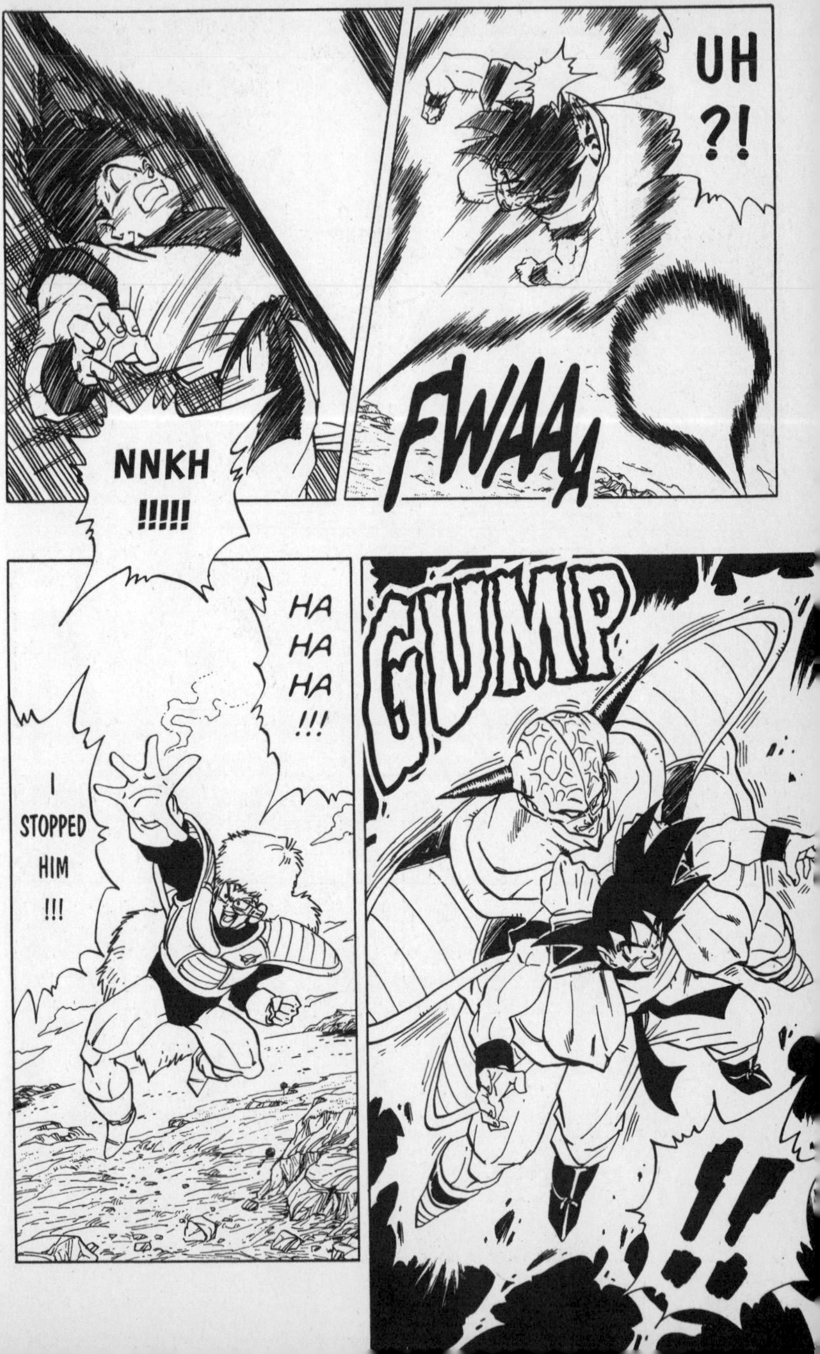
UH ?!
FWAAA
NNKH !!!!!
GUMP
!!
HA HA HA !!!
I STOPPED HIM !!!

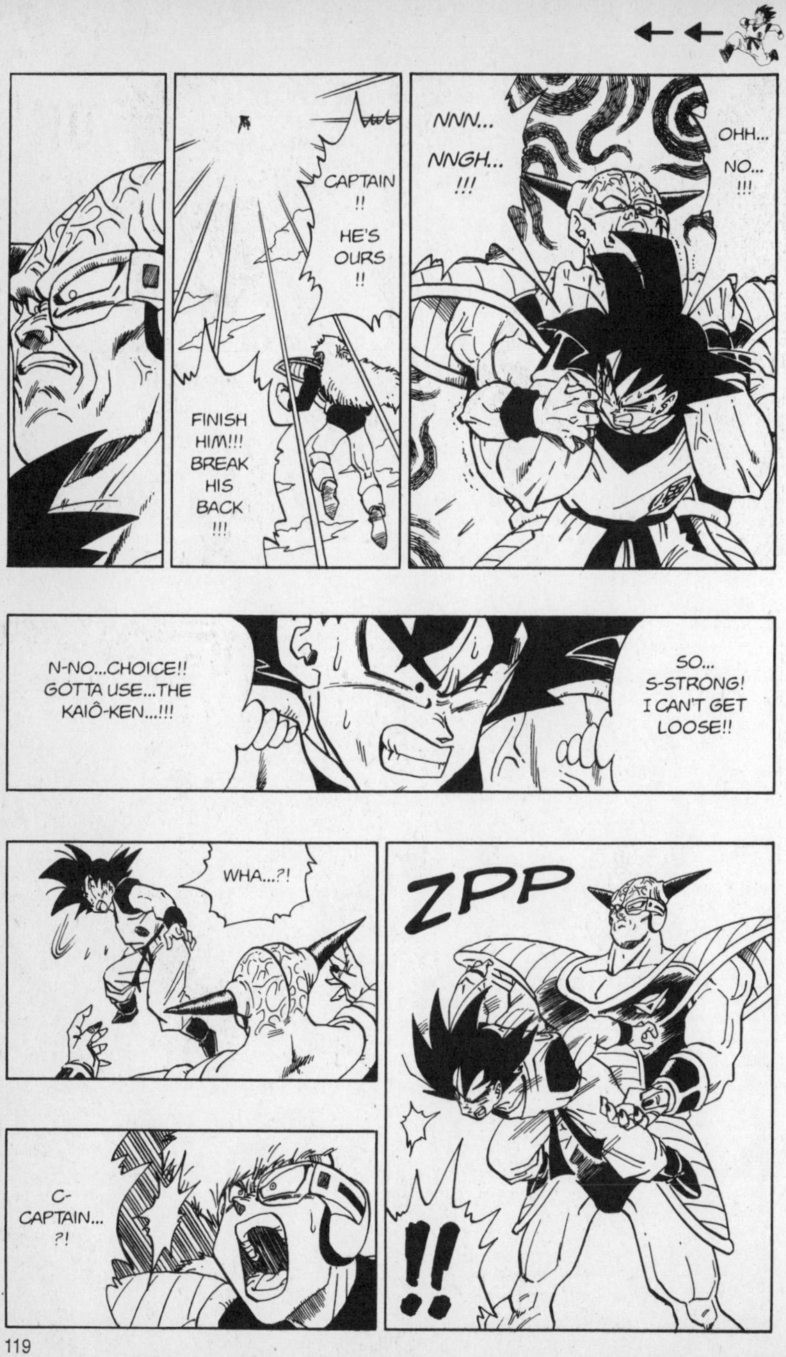
OHH... NO... !!!
NNN... NNGH... !!!
CAPTAIN!! HE'S OURS!!
FINISH HIM!!! BREAK HIS BACK!!!
SO... S-STRONG! I CAN'T GET LOOSE!!
N-NO...CHOICE!! GOTTA USE...THE KAIÔ-KEN...!!!
ZPP
!!
WHA...?!
C-CAPTAIN...?!

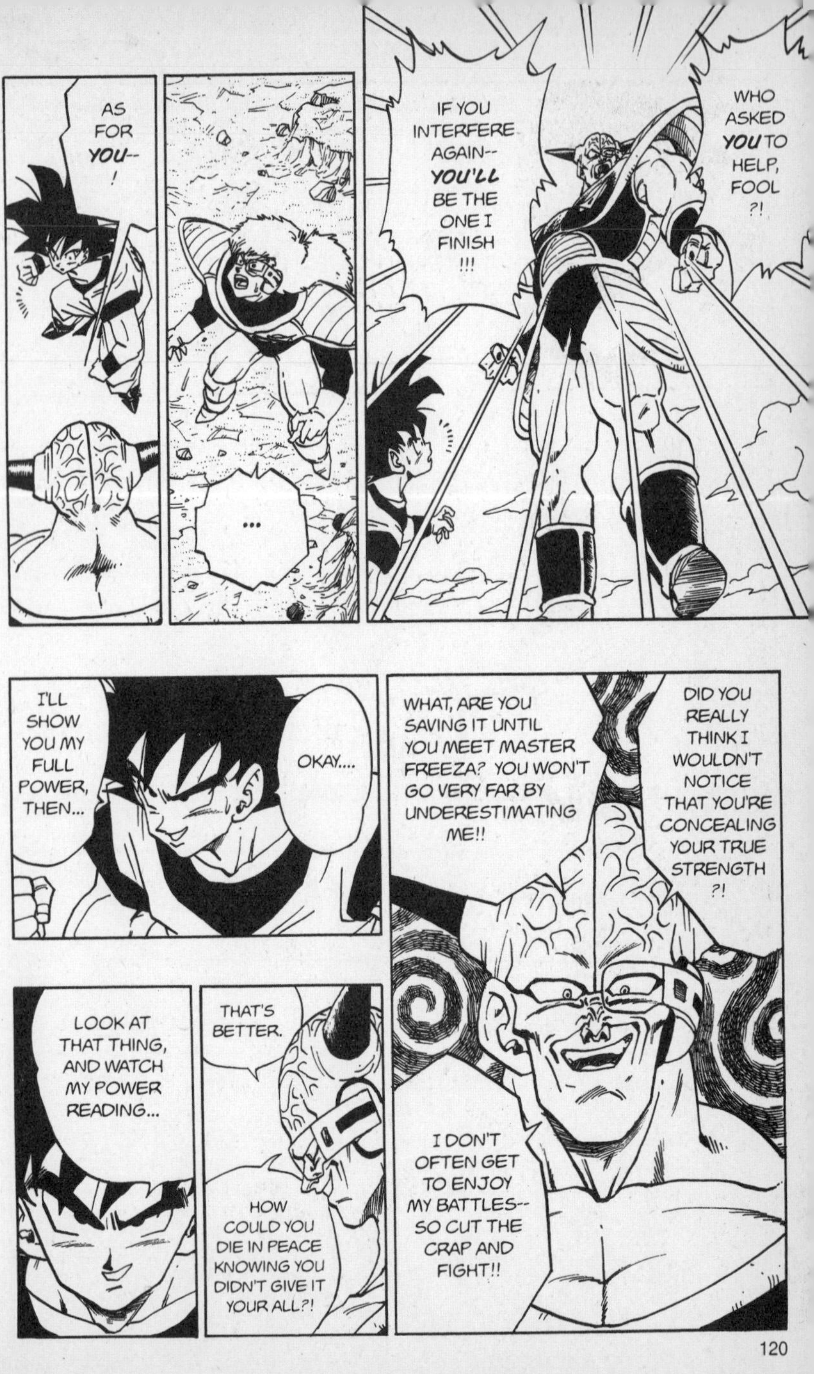
WHO ASKED YOU TO HELP, FOOL ?!
IF YOU INTERFERE AGAIN-- YOU'LL BE THE ONE I FINISH !!!
...
AS FOR YOU--!
DID YOU REALLY THINK I WOULDN'T NOTICE THAT YOU'RE CONCEALING YOUR TRUE STRENGTH ?!
WHAT, ARE YOU SAVING IT UNTIL YOU MEET MASTER FREEZA? YOU WON'T GO VERY FAR BY UNDERESTIMATING ME!!
I DON'T OFTEN GET TO ENJOY MY BATTLES-- SO CUT THE CRAP AND FIGHT!!
OKAY....
I'LL SHOW YOU MY FULL POWER, THEN...
THAT'S BETTER.
HOW COULD YOU DIE IN PEACE KNOWING YOU DIDN'T GIVE IT YOUR ALL?!
LOOK AT THAT THING, AND WATCH MY POWER READING...

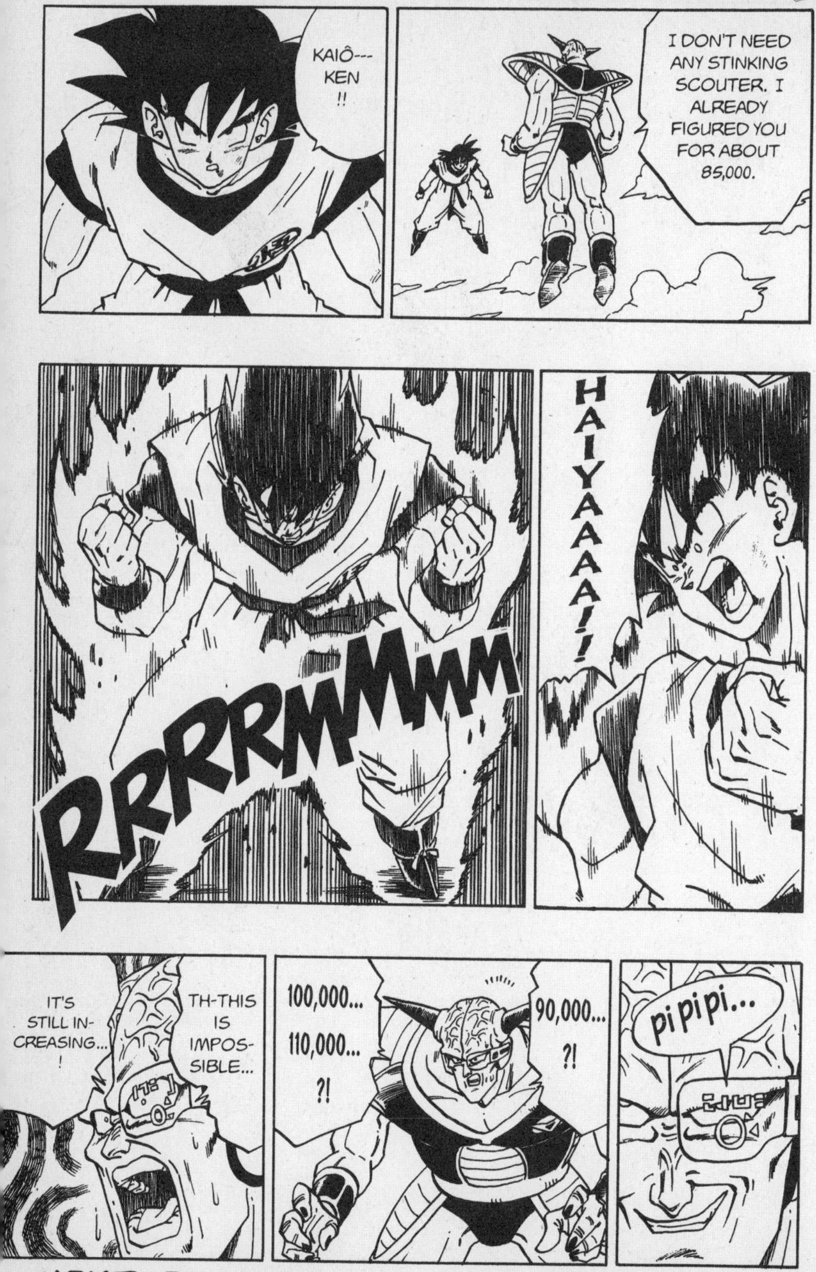
I DON'T NEED ANY STINKING SCOUTER. I ALREADY FIGURED YOU FOR ABOUT 85,000.
KAIÔ---KEN!!
HAIYAAAAA!!
RRRRMMMM
pi pi pi...
90,000...?!
100,000... 110,000...?!
TH-THIS IS IMPOSSIBLE...
IT'S STILL INCREASING...!

NEXT: Escalation

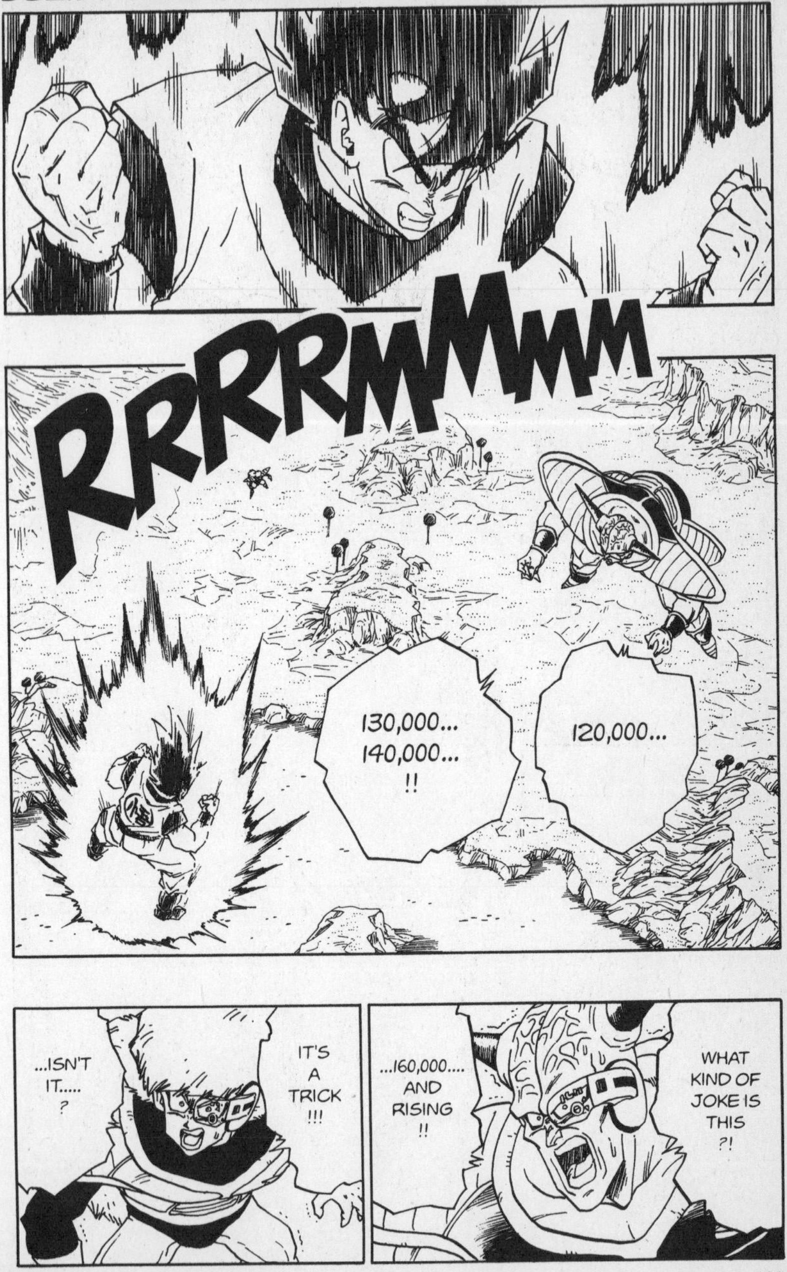
RRRRMMMM
120,000...
130,000... 140,000... !!
WHAT KIND OF JOKE IS THIS ?!
...160,000.... AND RISING !!
IT'S A TRICK !!!
...ISN'T IT..... ?

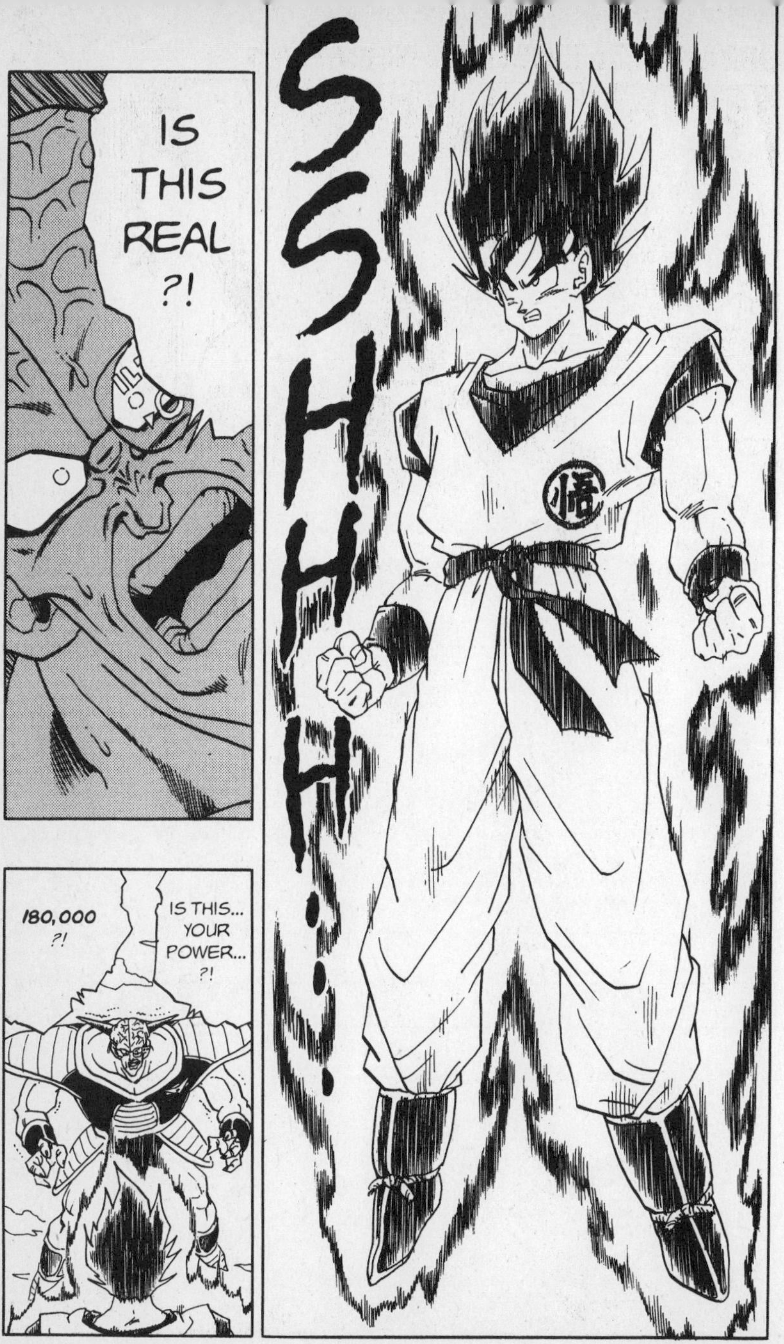
SSHHH...
IS THIS REAL ?!
IS THIS... YOUR POWER... ?!
180,000 ?!

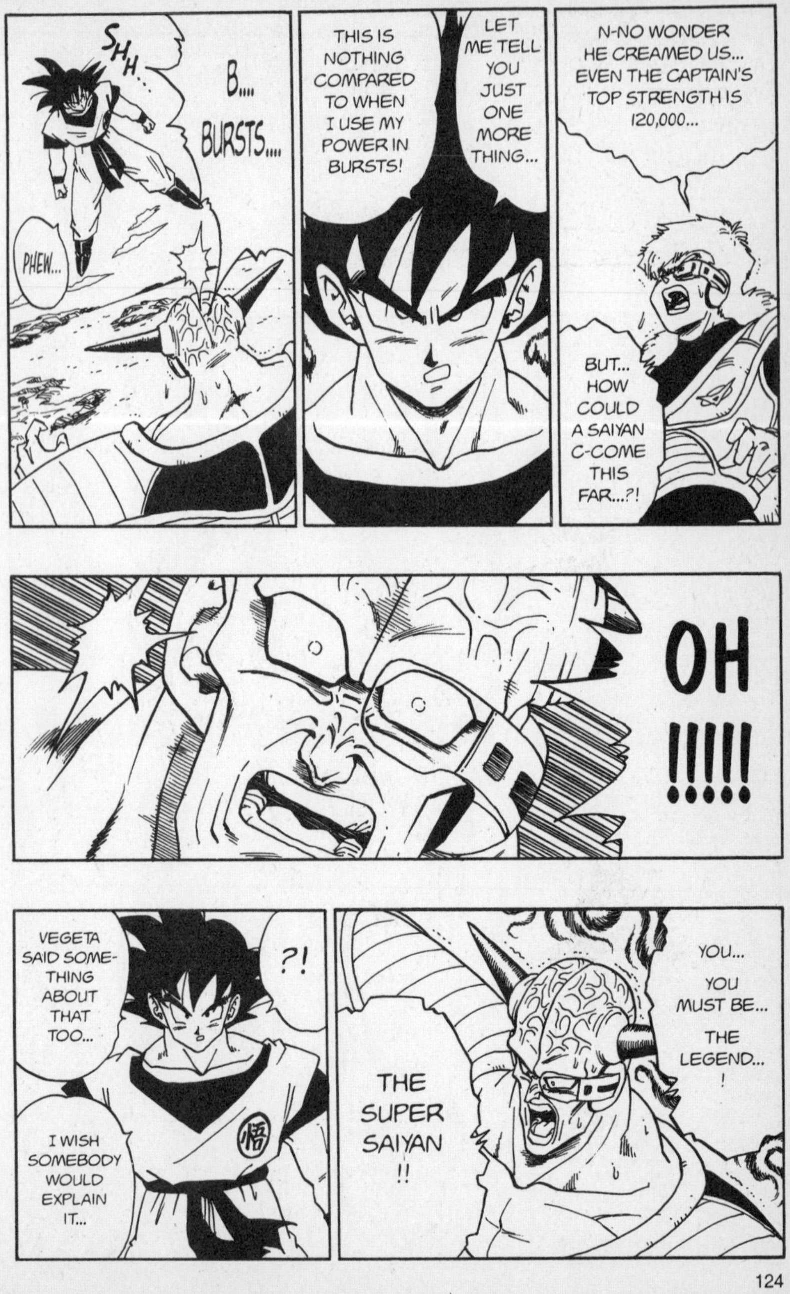
N-NO WONDER HE CREAMED US... EVEN THE CAPTAIN'S TOP STRENGTH IS 120,000...
BUT... HOW COULD A SAIYAN C-COME THIS FAR...?!
LET ME TELL YOU JUST ONE MORE THING...
THIS IS NOTHING COMPARED TO WHEN I USE MY POWER IN BURSTS!
B.... BURSTS....
SHH...
PHEW...
OH !!!!!!
YOU... YOU MUST BE... THE LEGEND... !
THE SUPER SAIYAN !!
?!
VEGETA SAID SOME-THING ABOUT THAT TOO...
I WISH SOMEBODY WOULD EXPLAIN IT...

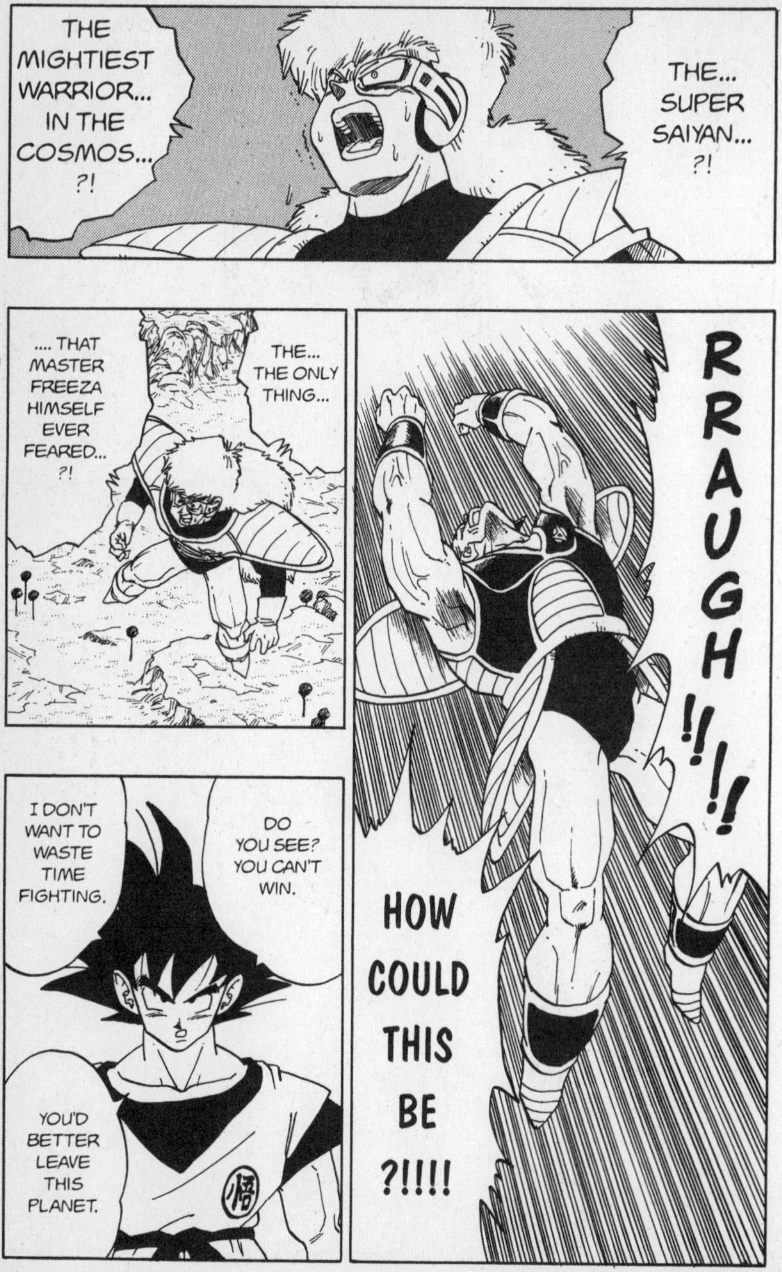
THE... SUPER SAIYAN... ?!
THE MIGHTIEST WARRIOR... IN THE COSMOS... ?!
RRAUGH !!!!
HOW COULD THIS BE ?!!!!
THE... THE ONLY THING...
.... THAT MASTER FREEZA HIMSELF EVER FEARED... ?!
DO YOU SEE? YOU CAN'T WIN.
I DON'T WANT TO WASTE TIME FIGHTING.
YOU'D BETTER LEAVE THIS PLANET.

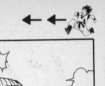

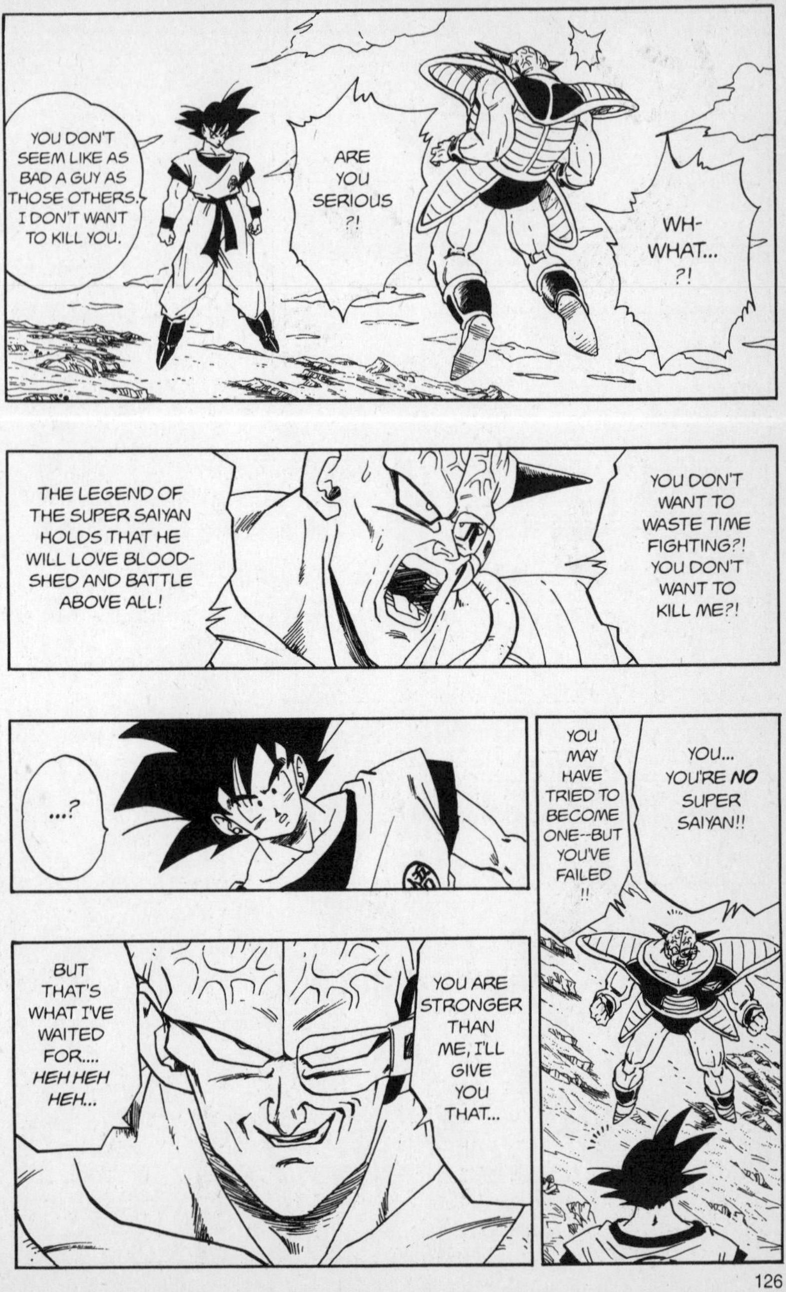
WH- WHAT... ?!
ARE YOU SERIOUS ?!
YOU DON'T SEEM LIKE AS BAD A GUY AS THOSE OTHERS. I DON'T WANT TO KILL YOU.
YOU DON'T WANT TO WASTE TIME FIGHTING?! YOU DON'T WANT TO KILL ME?!
THE LEGEND OF THE SUPER SAIYAN HOLDS THAT HE WILL LOVE BLOOD-SHED AND BATTLE ABOVE ALL!
YOU... YOU'RE ***NO*** SUPER SAIYAN!!
YOU MAY HAVE TRIED TO BECOME ONE--BUT YOU'VE FAILED !!
...?
YOU ARE STRONGER THAN ME, I'LL GIVE YOU THAT...
BUT THAT'S WHAT I'VE WAITED FOR.... *HEH HEH HEH...*

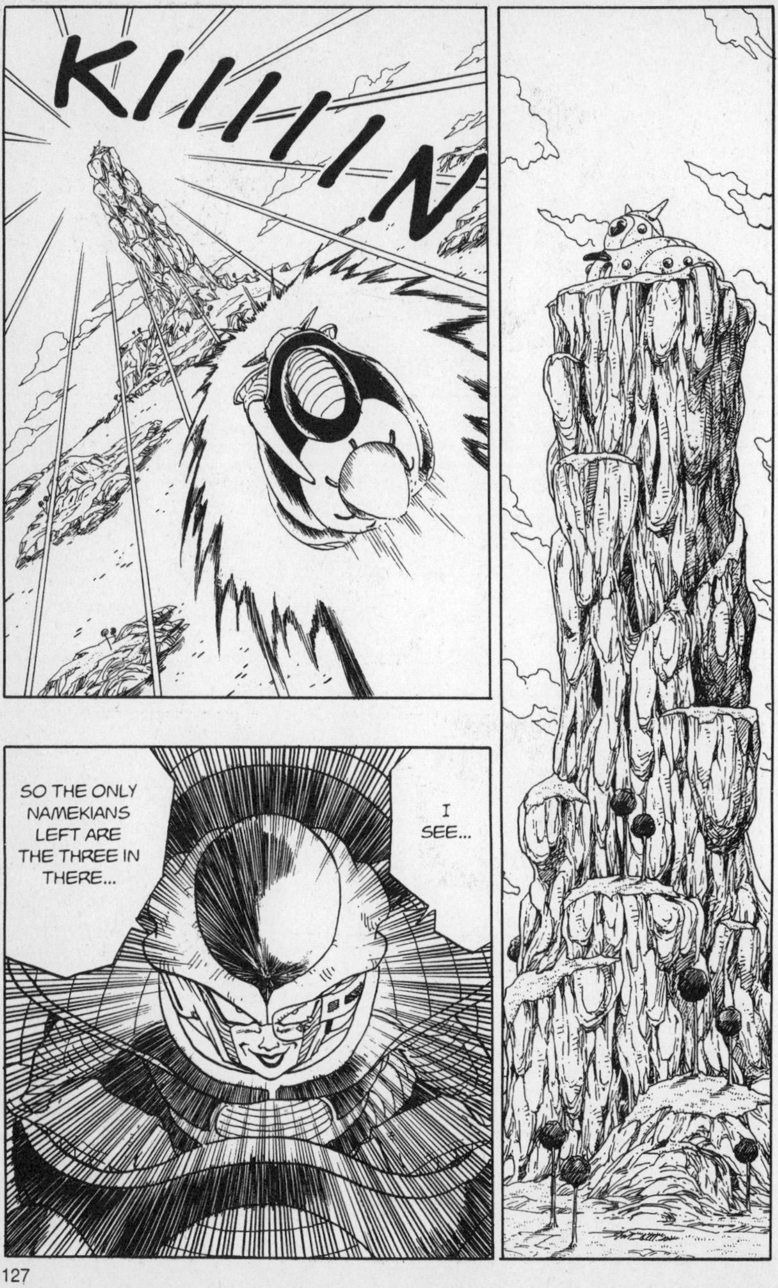
KIIIIN
SO THE ONLY NAMEKIANS LEFT ARE THE THREE IN THERE...
I SEE...

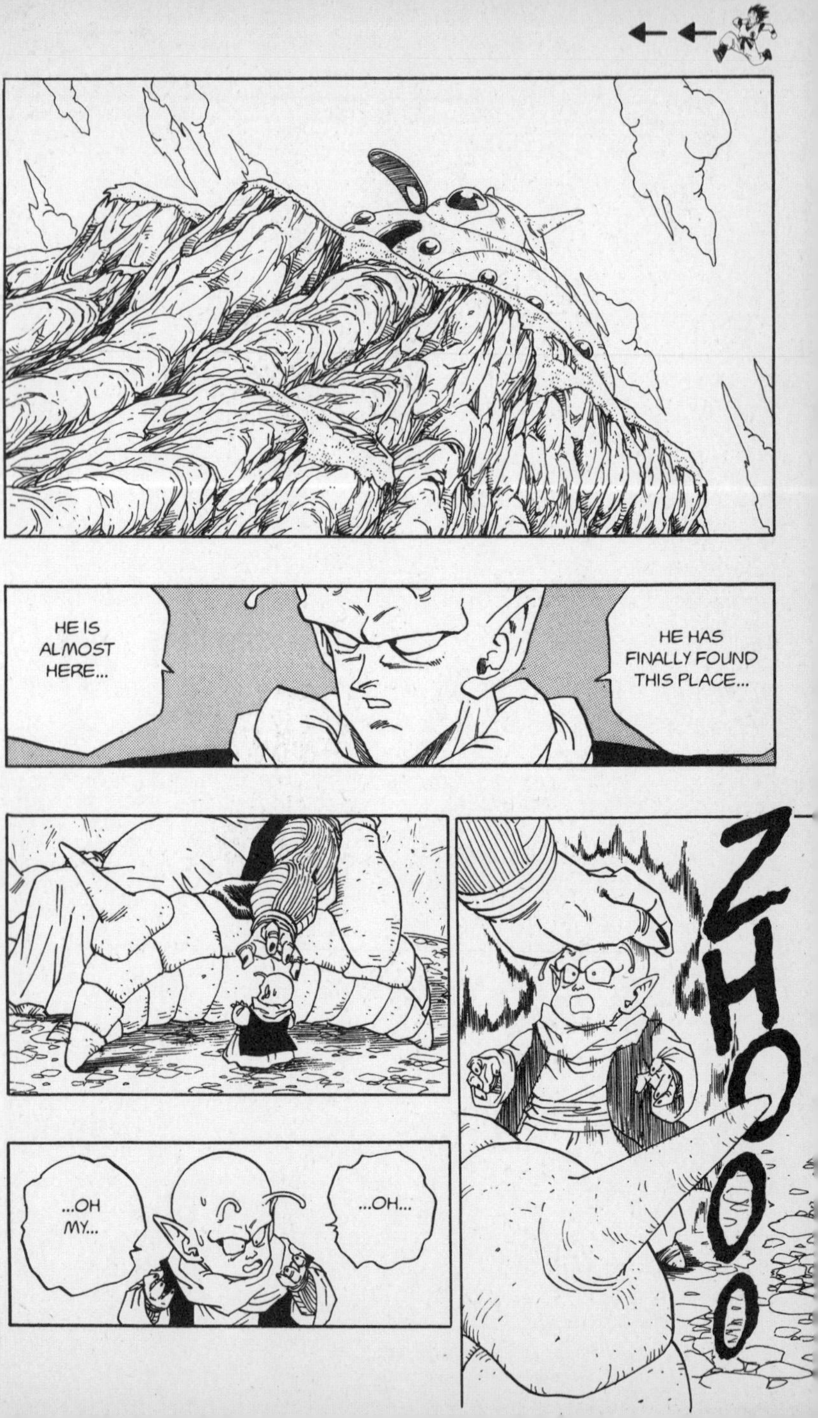
HE HAS FINALLY FOUND THIS PLACE...
HE IS ALMOST HERE...
ZHOOO
...OH...
...OH MY...

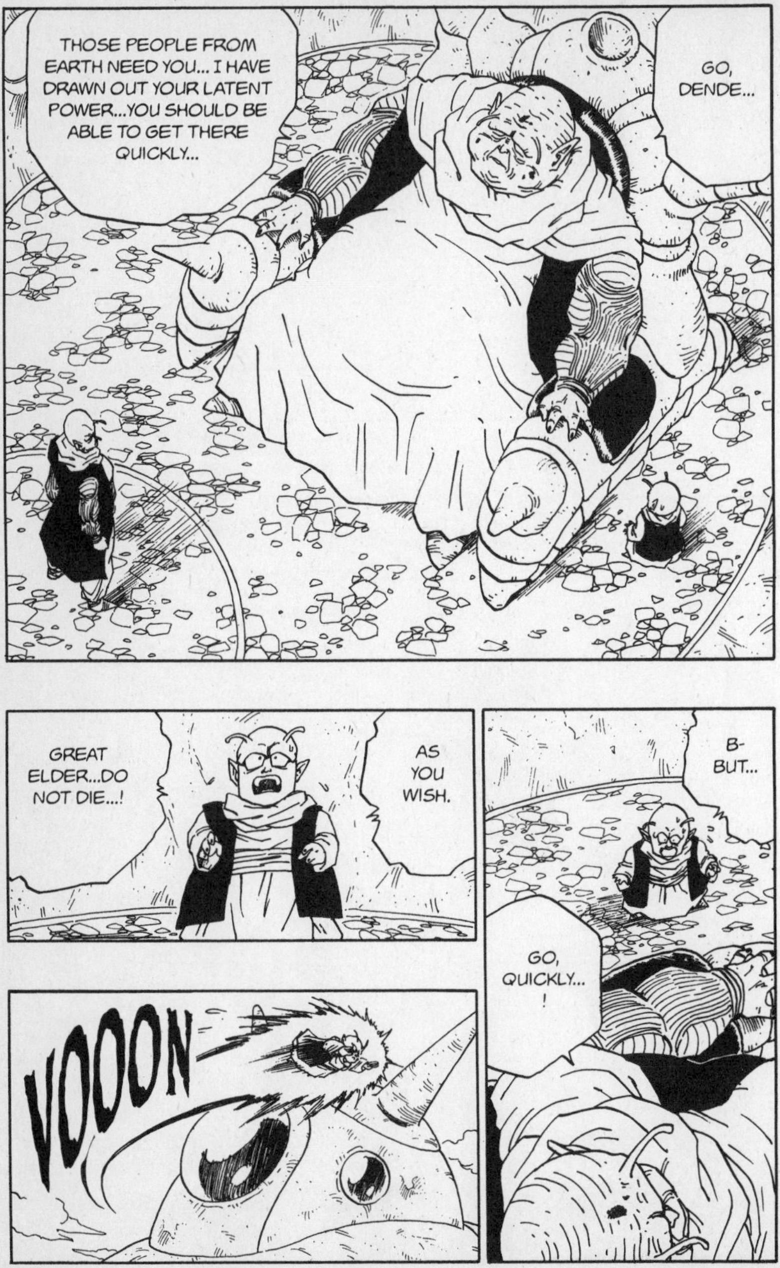
GO, DENDE...
THOSE PEOPLE FROM EARTH NEED YOU... I HAVE DRAWN OUT YOUR LATENT POWER...YOU SHOULD BE ABLE TO GET THERE QUICKLY...
B-BUT...
GO, QUICKLY...!
AS YOU WISH.
GREAT ELDER...DO NOT DIE...!
VOOON

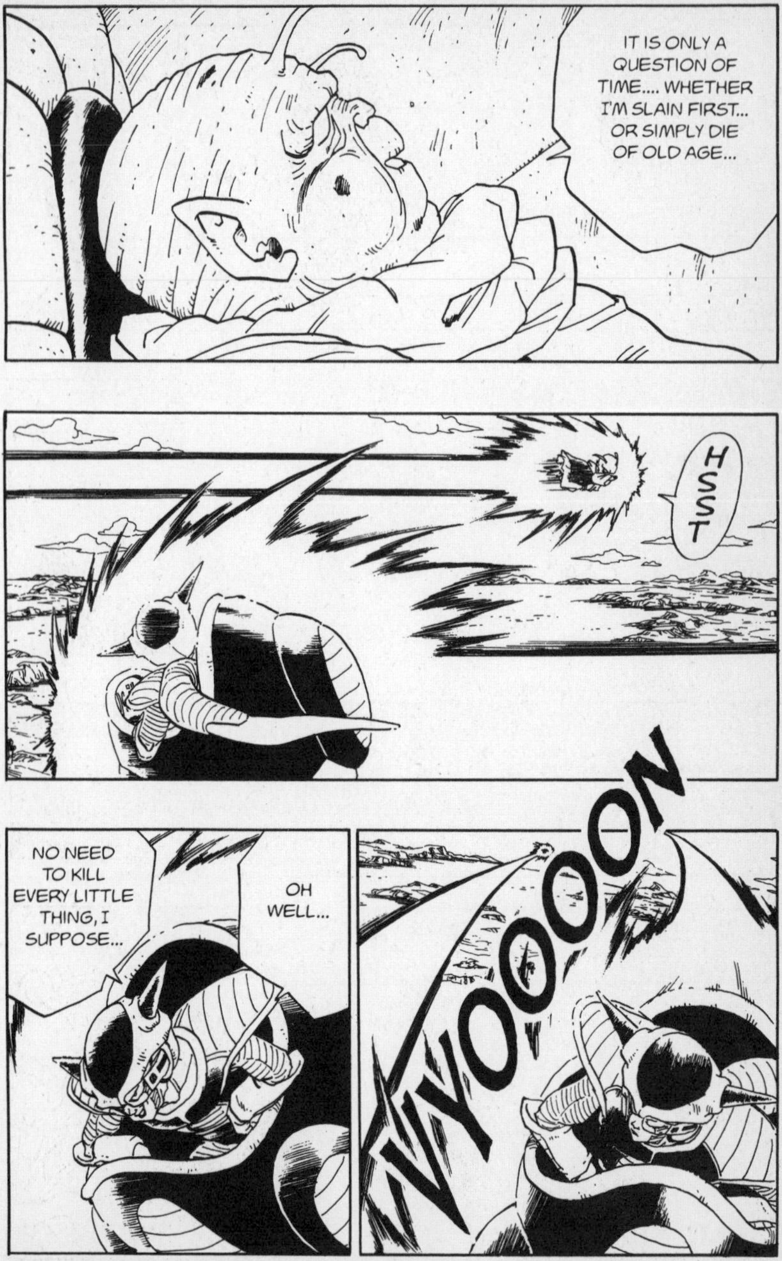
IT IS ONLY A QUESTION OF TIME.... WHETHER I'M SLAIN FIRST... OR SIMPLY DIE OF OLD AGE...
HSST
WYOOOON
OH WELL...
NO NEED TO KILL EVERY LITTLE THING, I SUPPOSE...

KRIII

TMP

MAY
I HELP
YOU?

  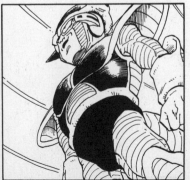

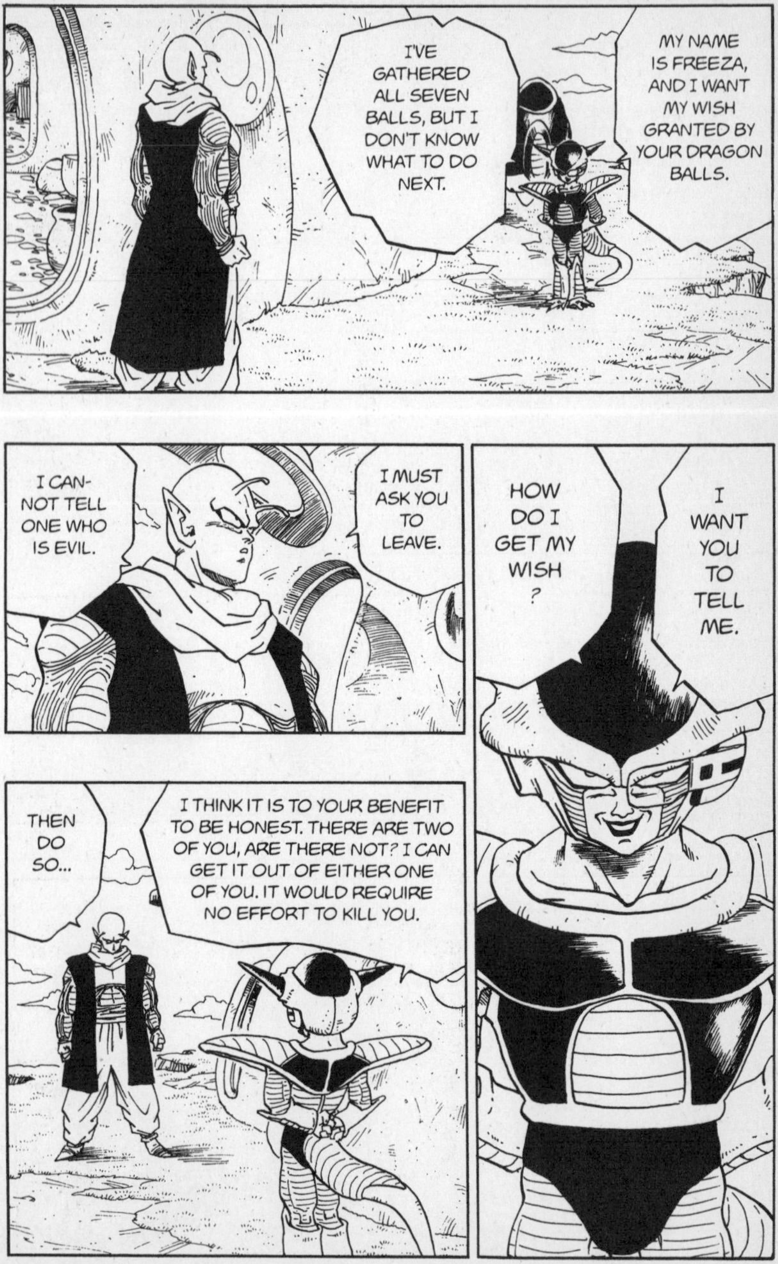
MY NAME IS FREEZA, AND I WANT MY WISH GRANTED BY YOUR DRAGON BALLS.
I'VE GATHERED ALL SEVEN BALLS, BUT I DON'T KNOW WHAT TO DO NEXT.
I WANT YOU TO TELL ME.
HOW DO I GET MY WISH?
I MUST ASK YOU TO LEAVE.
I CAN-NOT TELL ONE WHO IS EVIL.
I THINK IT IS TO YOUR BENEFIT TO BE HONEST. THERE ARE TWO OF YOU, ARE THERE NOT? I CAN GET IT OUT OF EITHER ONE OF YOU. IT WOULD REQUIRE NO EFFORT TO KILL YOU.
THEN DO SO...

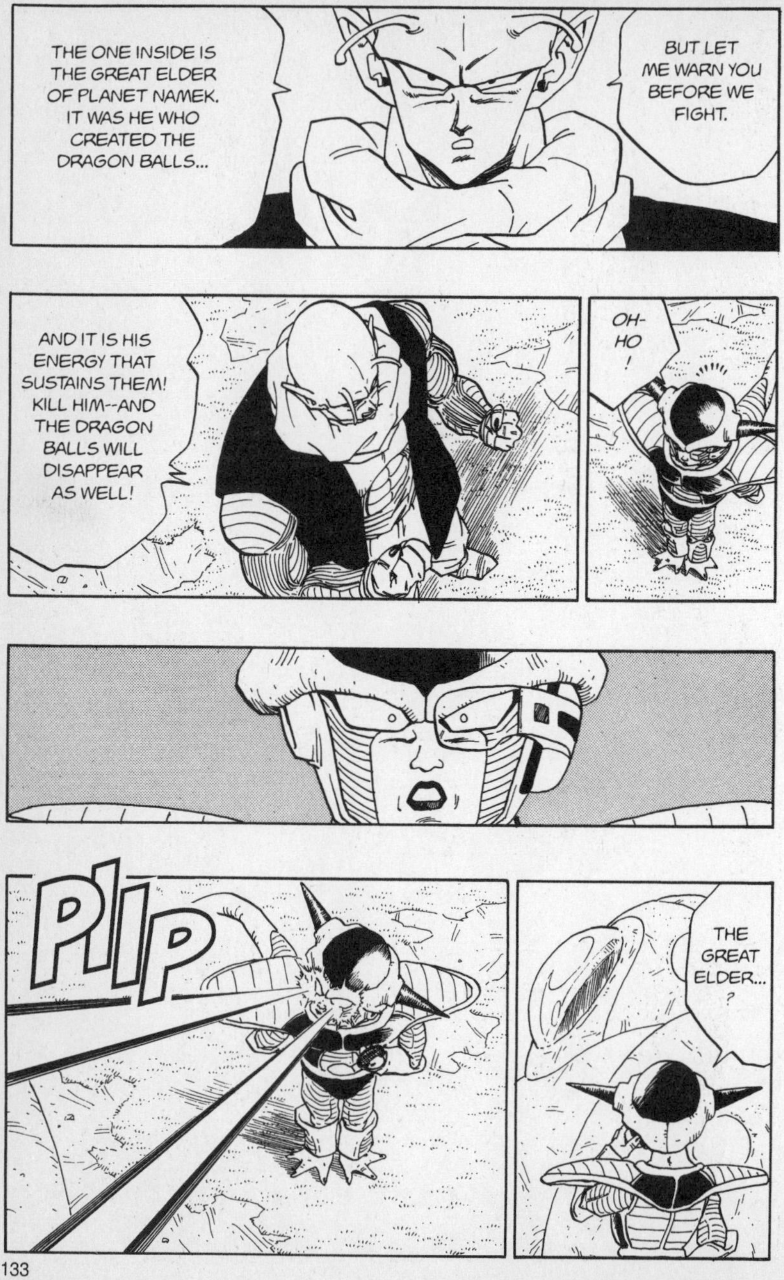
BUT LET ME WARN YOU BEFORE WE FIGHT.
THE ONE INSIDE IS THE GREAT ELDER OF PLANET NAMEK. IT WAS HE WHO CREATED THE DRAGON BALLS...
OH-HO!
AND IT IS HIS ENERGY THAT SUSTAINS THEM! KILL HIM--AND THE DRAGON BALLS WILL DISAPPEAR AS WELL!
THE GREAT ELDER... ?
PIP

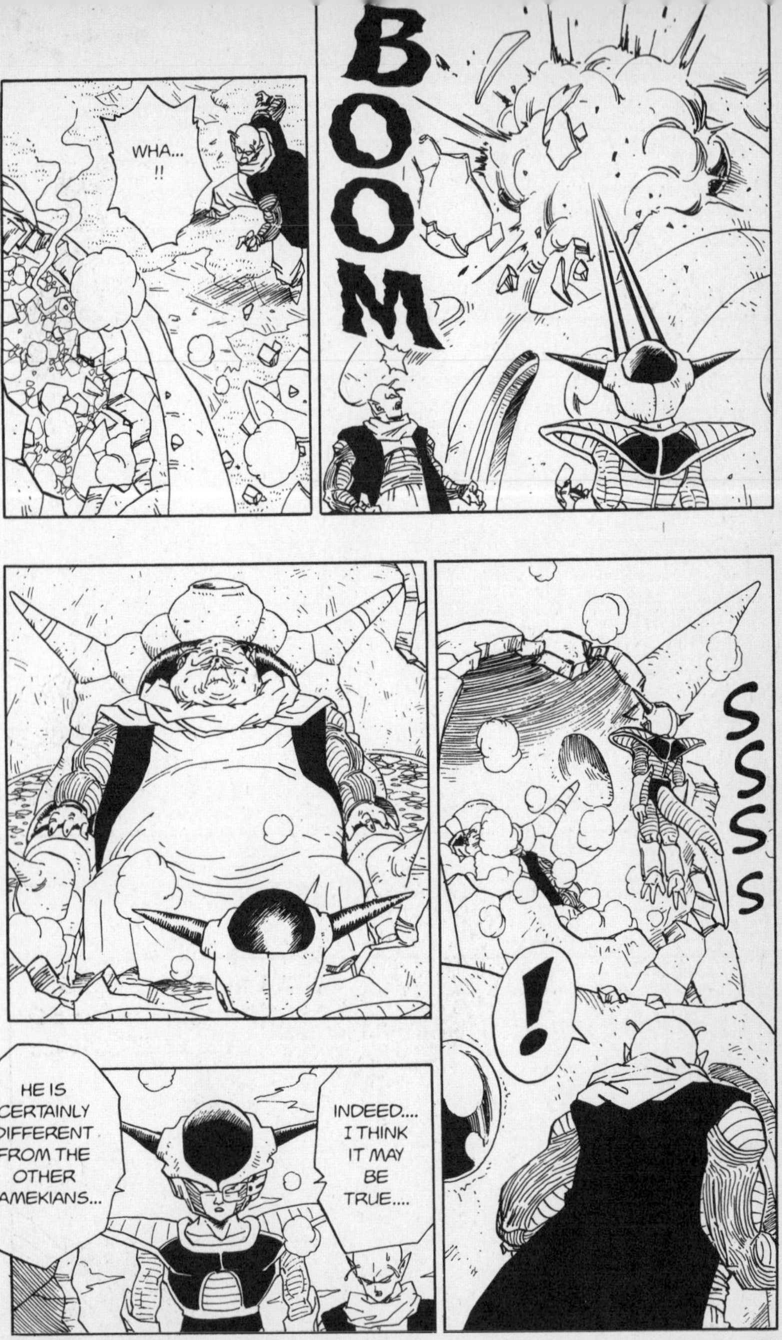
BOOM
WHA... !!
SSSS
!
HE IS CERTAINLY DIFFERENT FROM THE OTHER NAMEKIANS...
INDEED.... I THINK IT MAY BE TRUE....

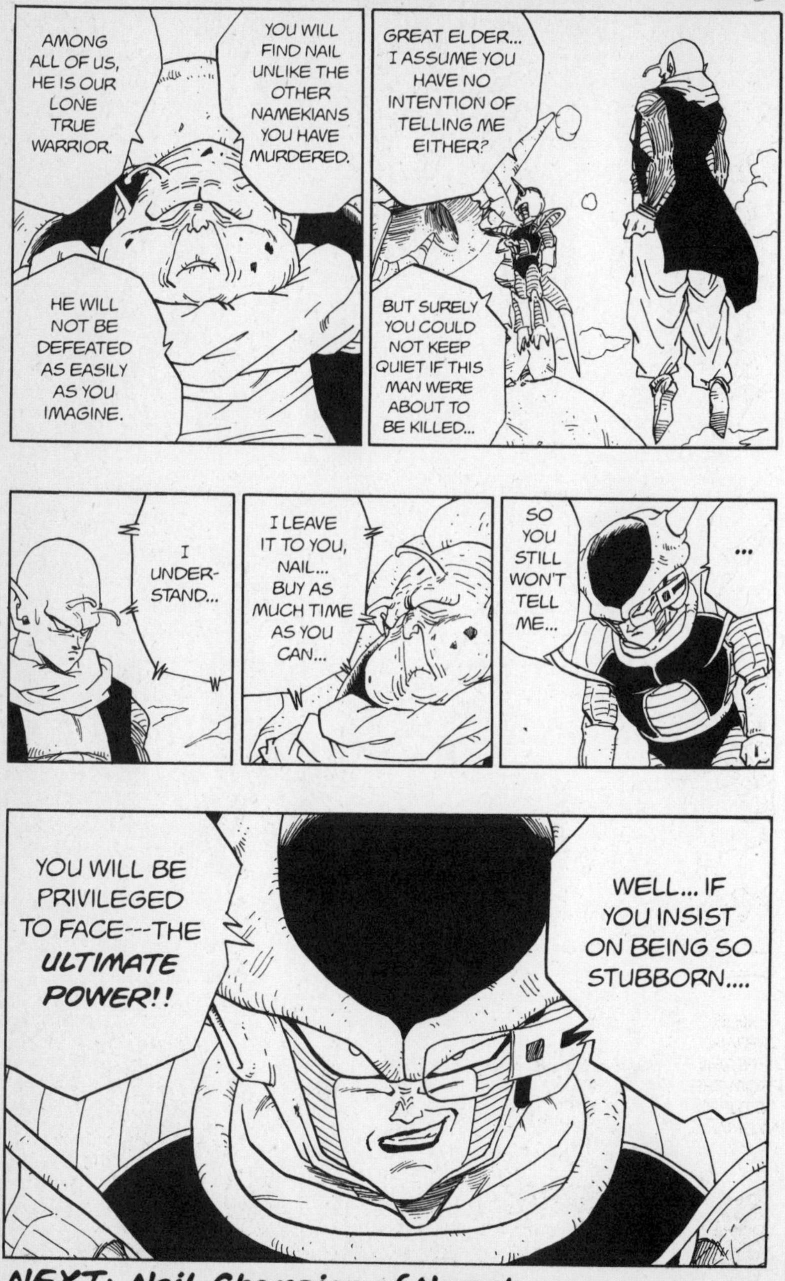
GREAT ELDER... I ASSUME YOU HAVE NO INTENTION OF TELLING ME EITHER?
BUT SURELY YOU COULD NOT KEEP QUIET IF THIS MAN WERE ABOUT TO BE KILLED...
YOU WILL FIND NAIL UNLIKE THE OTHER NAMEKIANS YOU HAVE MURDERED.
AMONG ALL OF US, HE IS OUR LONE TRUE WARRIOR.
HE WILL NOT BE DEFEATED AS EASILY AS YOU IMAGINE.
...
SO YOU STILL WON'T TELL ME...
I LEAVE IT TO YOU, NAIL... BUY AS MUCH TIME AS YOU CAN...
I UNDER-STAND...
WELL... IF YOU INSIST ON BEING SO STUBBORN....
YOU WILL BE PRIVILEGED TO FACE---THE ULTIMATE POWER!!

NEXT: Nail, Champion of Namek

DBZ:92 • Nail, Champion of Namek

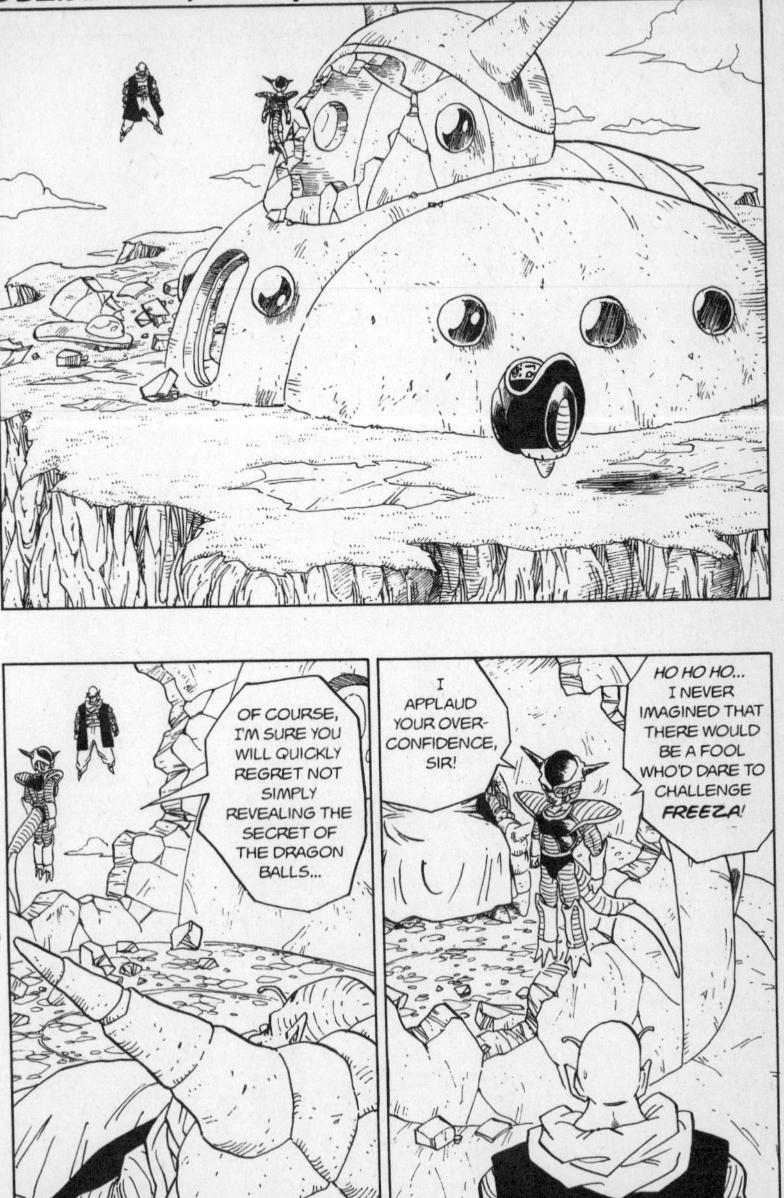
HO HO HO... I NEVER IMAGINED THAT THERE WOULD BE A FOOL WHO'D DARE TO CHALLENGE FREEZA!
I APPLAUD YOUR OVER-CONFIDENCE, SIR!
OF COURSE, I'M SURE YOU WILL QUICKLY REGRET NOT SIMPLY REVEALING THE SECRET OF THE DRAGON BALLS...

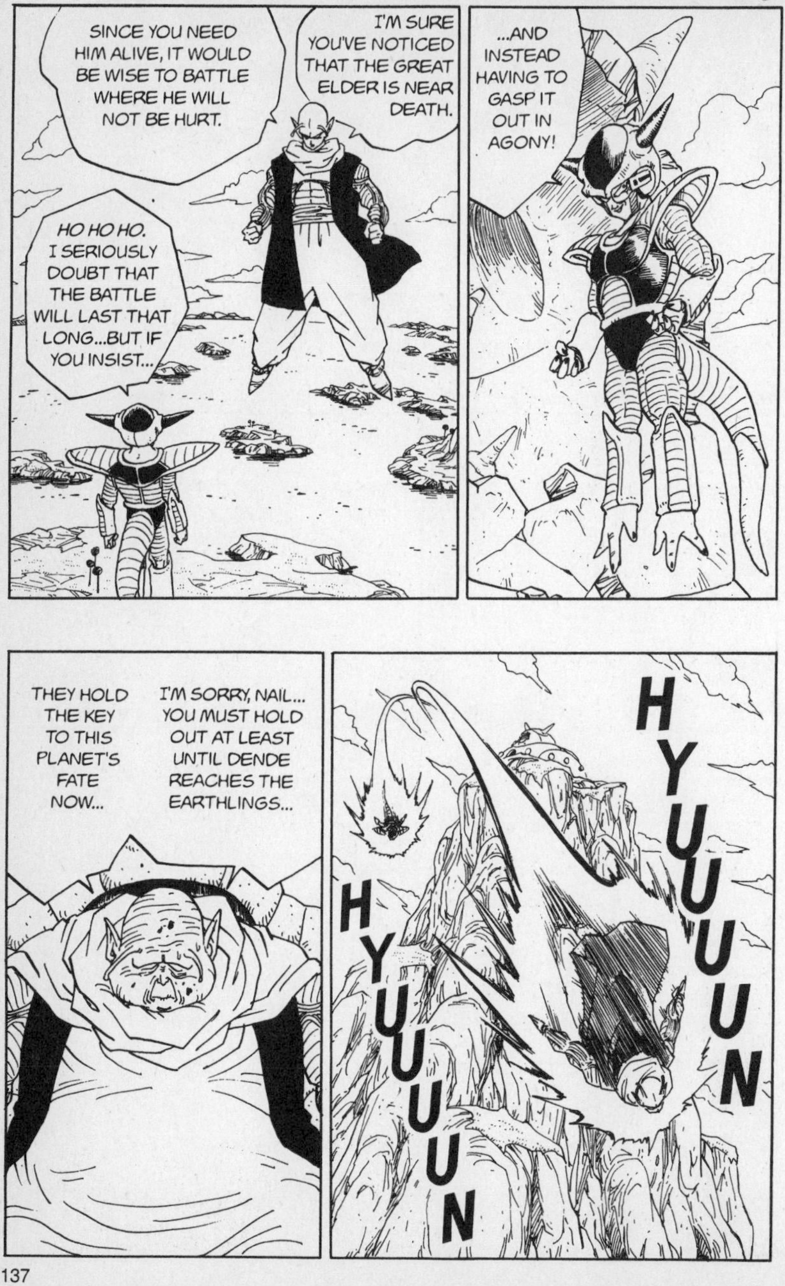
...AND INSTEAD HAVING TO GASP IT OUT IN AGONY!
I'M SURE YOU'VE NOTICED THAT THE GREAT ELDER IS NEAR DEATH.
SINCE YOU NEED HIM ALIVE, IT WOULD BE WISE TO BATTLE WHERE HE WILL NOT BE HURT.
HO HO HO. I SERIOUSLY DOUBT THAT THE BATTLE WILL LAST THAT LONG...BUT IF YOU INSIST...
HYUUUUN
HYUUUUN
I'M SORRY, NAIL... YOU MUST HOLD OUT AT LEAST UNTIL DENDE REACHES THE EARTHLINGS...
THEY HOLD THE KEY TO THIS PLANET'S FATE NOW...

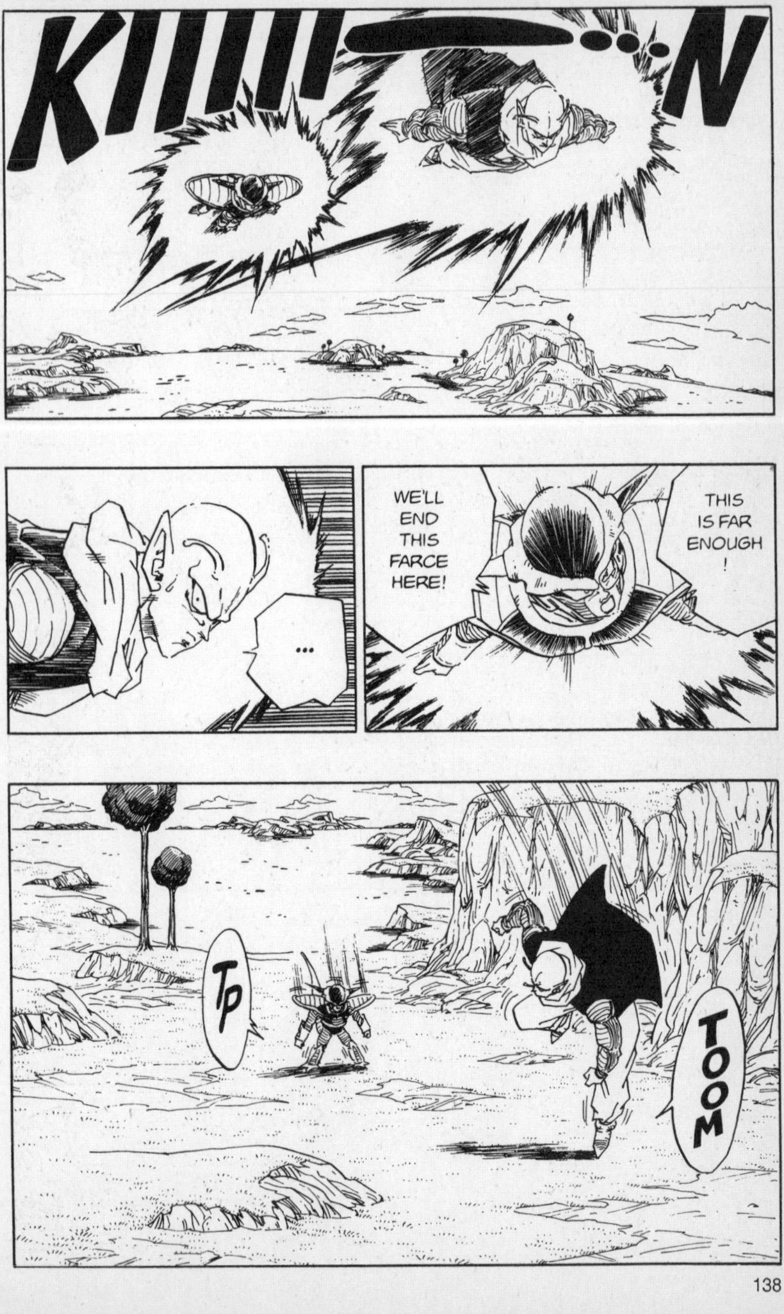
KIIII—...N
THIS IS FAR ENOUGH!
WE'LL END THIS FARCE HERE!
...
TOOM
TP

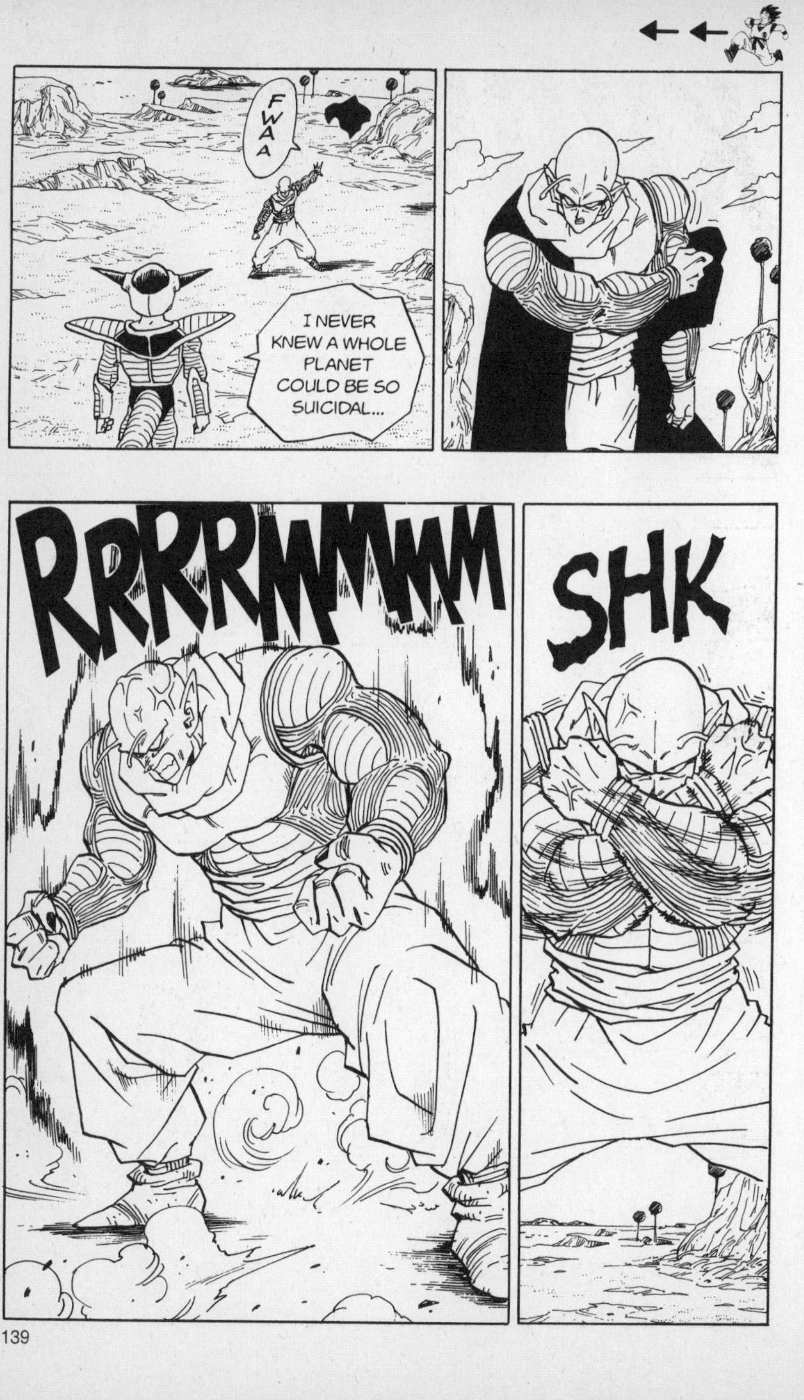
FWAA
I NEVER KNEW A WHOLE PLANET COULD BE SO SUICIDAL...
SHK
RRRRMMMMM

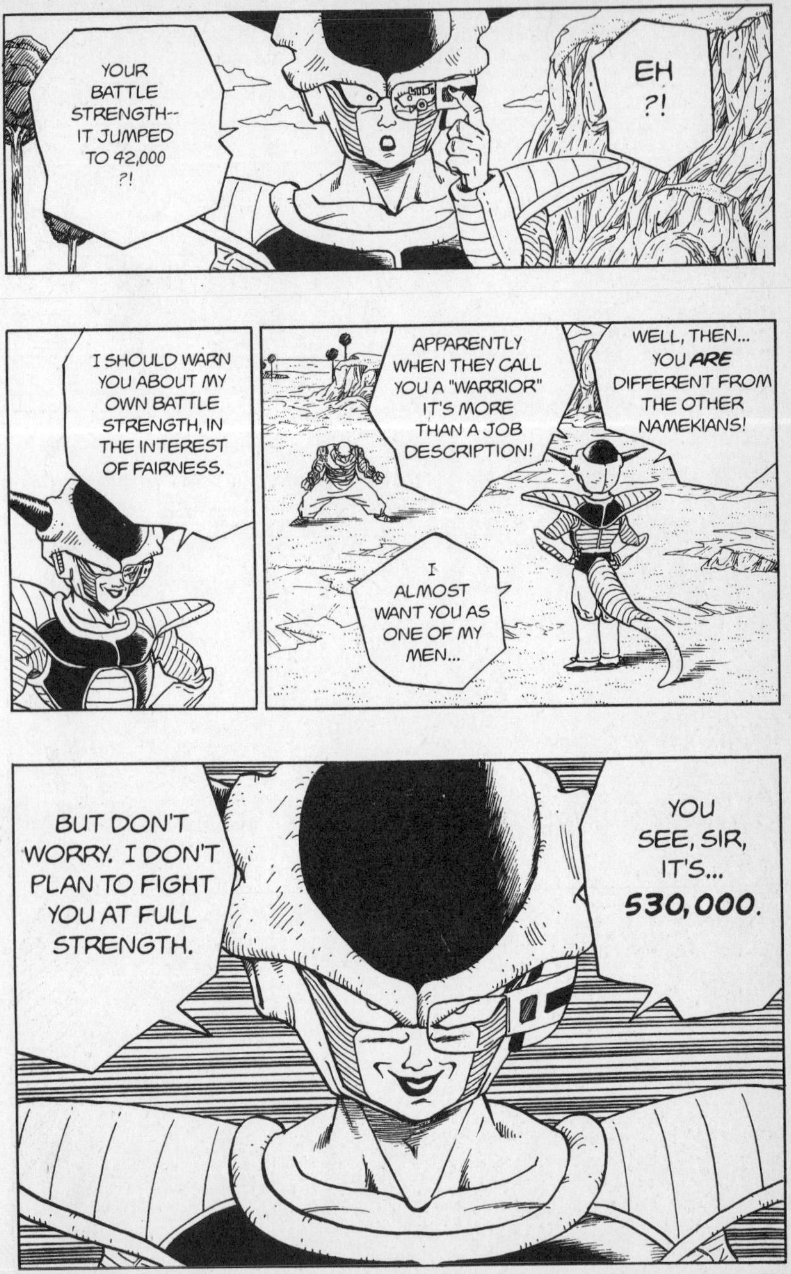
EH ?!
YOUR BATTLE STRENGTH-- IT JUMPED TO 42,000 ?!
WELL, THEN... YOU **ARE** DIFFERENT FROM THE OTHER NAMEKIANS!
APPARENTLY WHEN THEY CALL YOU A "WARRIOR" IT'S MORE THAN A JOB DESCRIPTION!
I ALMOST WANT YOU AS ONE OF MY MEN...
I SHOULD WARN YOU ABOUT MY OWN BATTLE STRENGTH, IN THE INTEREST OF FAIRNESS.
YOU SEE, SIR, IT'S... **530,000.**
BUT DON'T WORRY. I DON'T PLAN TO FIGHT YOU AT FULL STRENGTH.

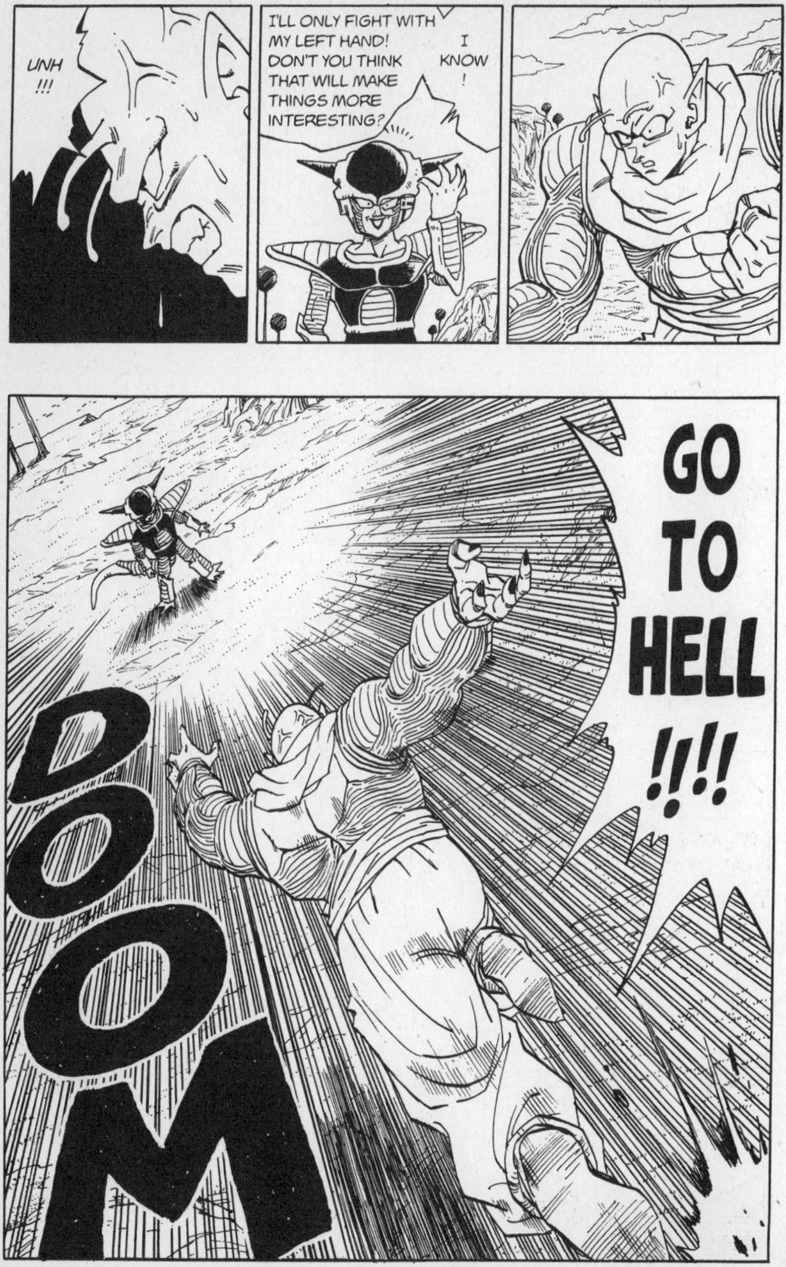
I KNOW!
I'LL ONLY FIGHT WITH MY LEFT HAND! DON'T YOU THINK THAT WILL MAKE THINGS MORE INTERESTING?
UNH!!!
GO TO HELL!!!!
DOOM

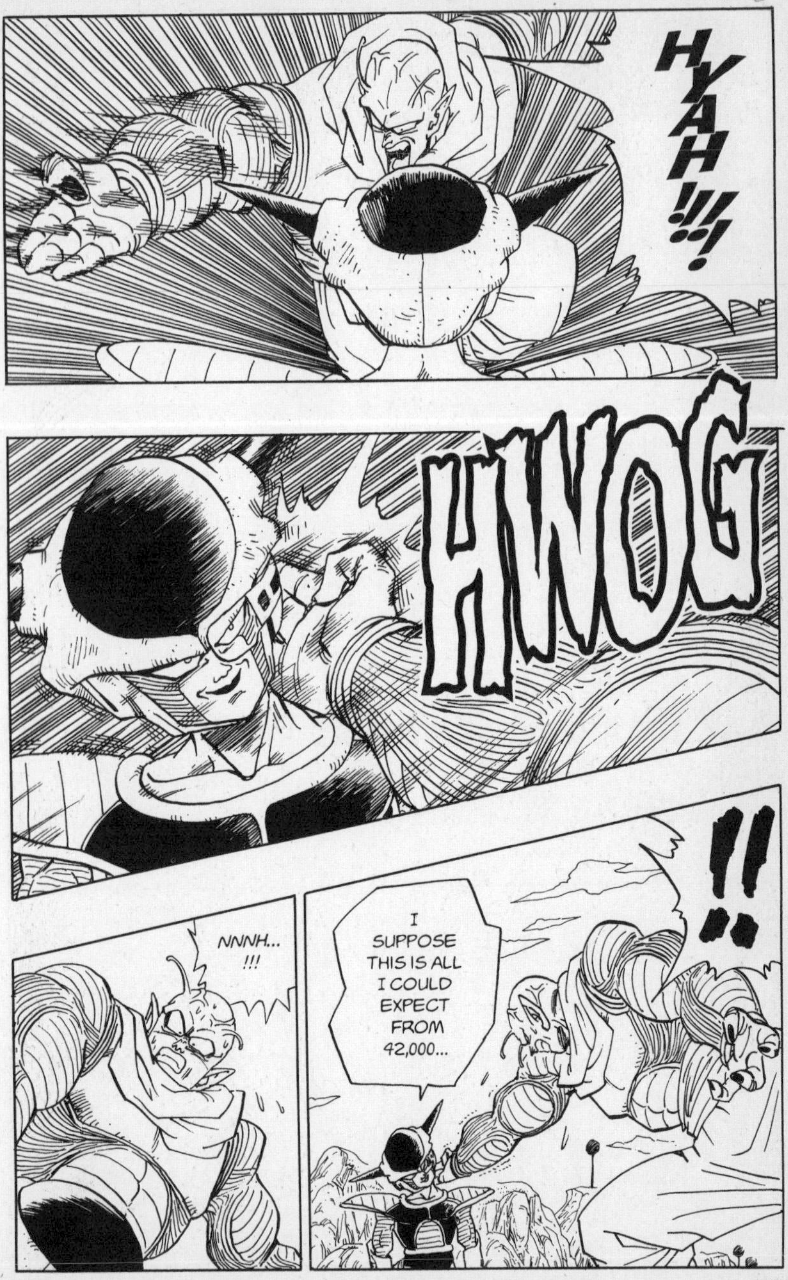
HYAH!!!!
HWOG
!!
I SUPPOSE THIS IS ALL I COULD EXPECT FROM 42,000...
NNNH... !!!

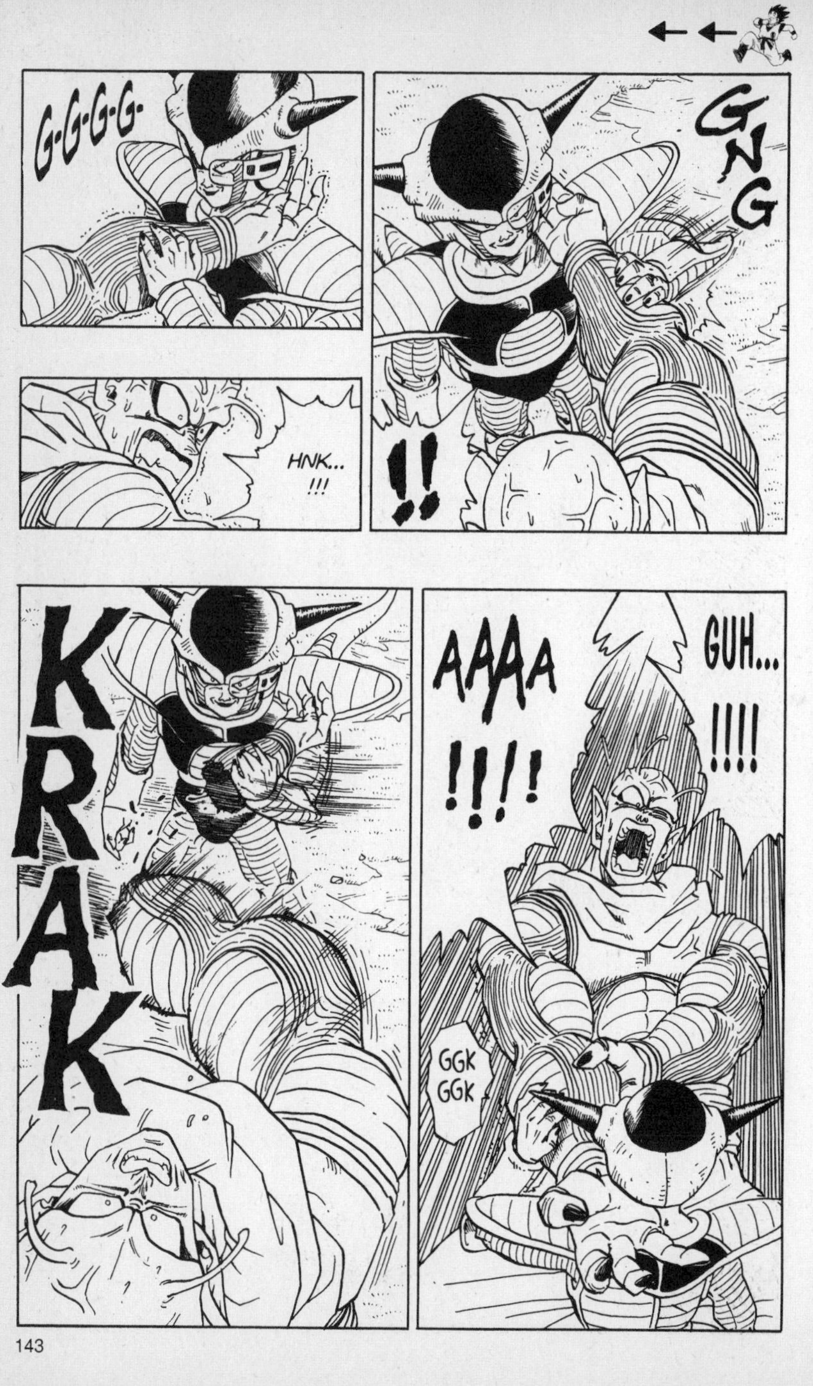
GNG
!!
G-G-G-G-
HNK... !!!
GUH... !!!!
AAAA !!!!
GGK GGK
KRAK

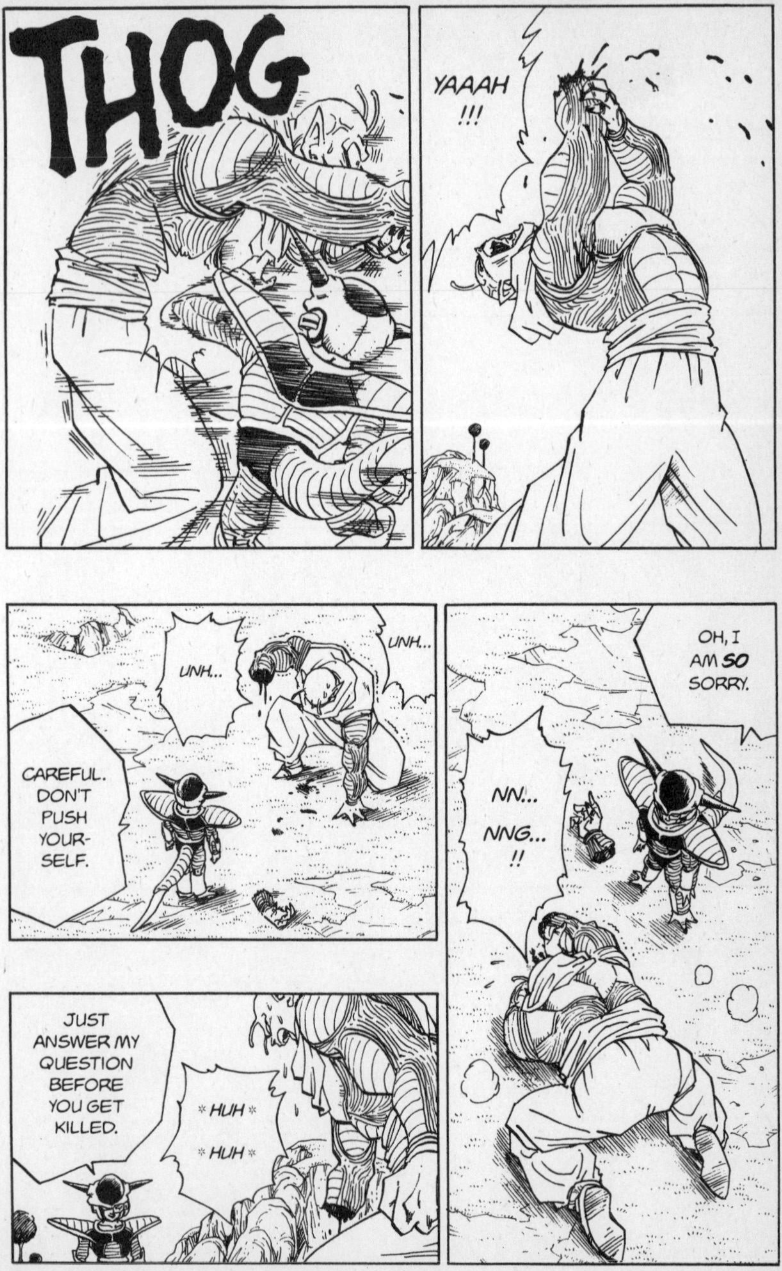

YAAAH !!!
THOG
OH, I AM **SO** SORRY.
NN... NNG... !!
UNH...
UNH...
CAREFUL. DON'T PUSH YOURSELF.
✲HUH✲ ✲HUH✲
JUST ANSWER MY QUESTION BEFORE YOU GET KILLED.

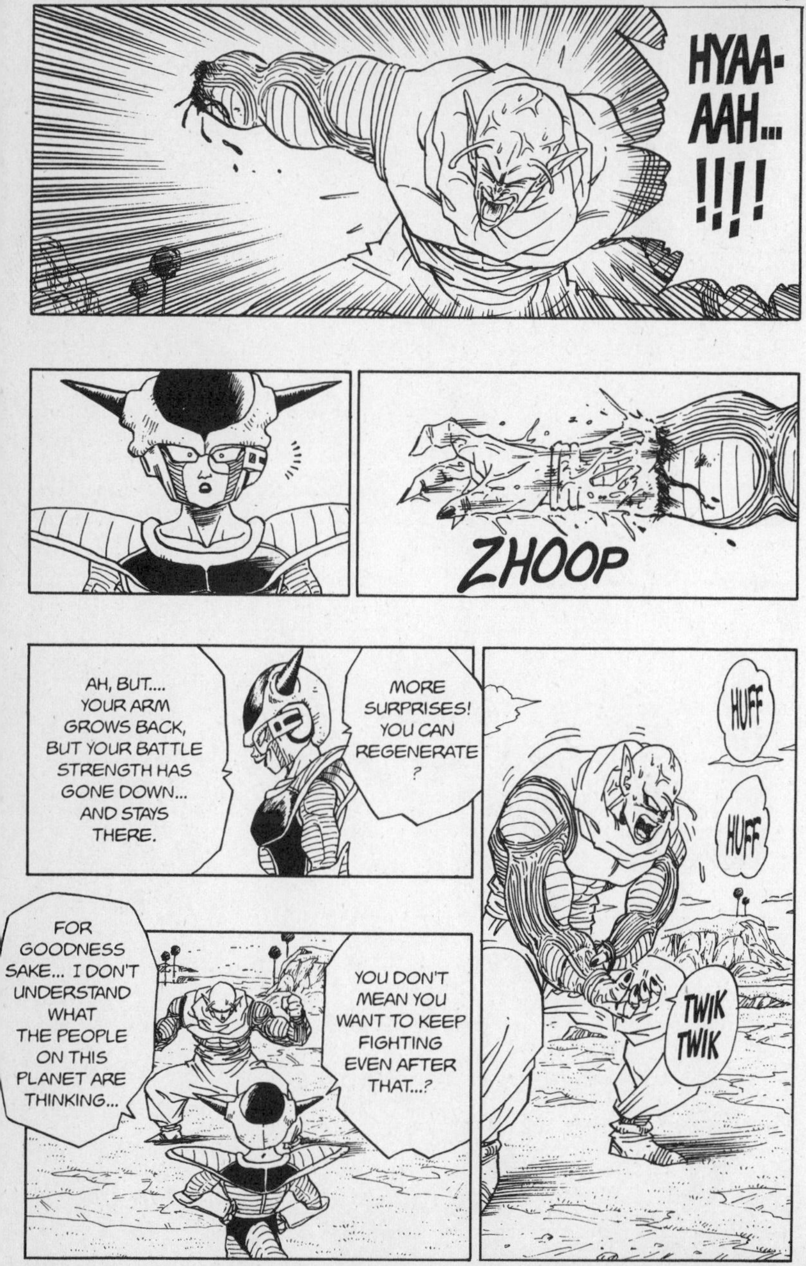
HYAA-AAH...!!!!
ZHOOP
HUFF
HUFF
TWIK TWIK
MORE SURPRISES! YOU CAN REGENERATE?
AH, BUT.... YOUR ARM GROWS BACK, BUT YOUR BATTLE STRENGTH HAS GONE DOWN... AND STAYS THERE.
YOU DON'T MEAN YOU WANT TO KEEP FIGHTING EVEN AFTER THAT...?
FOR GOODNESS SAKE... I DON'T UNDERSTAND WHAT THE PEOPLE ON THIS PLANET ARE THINKING...

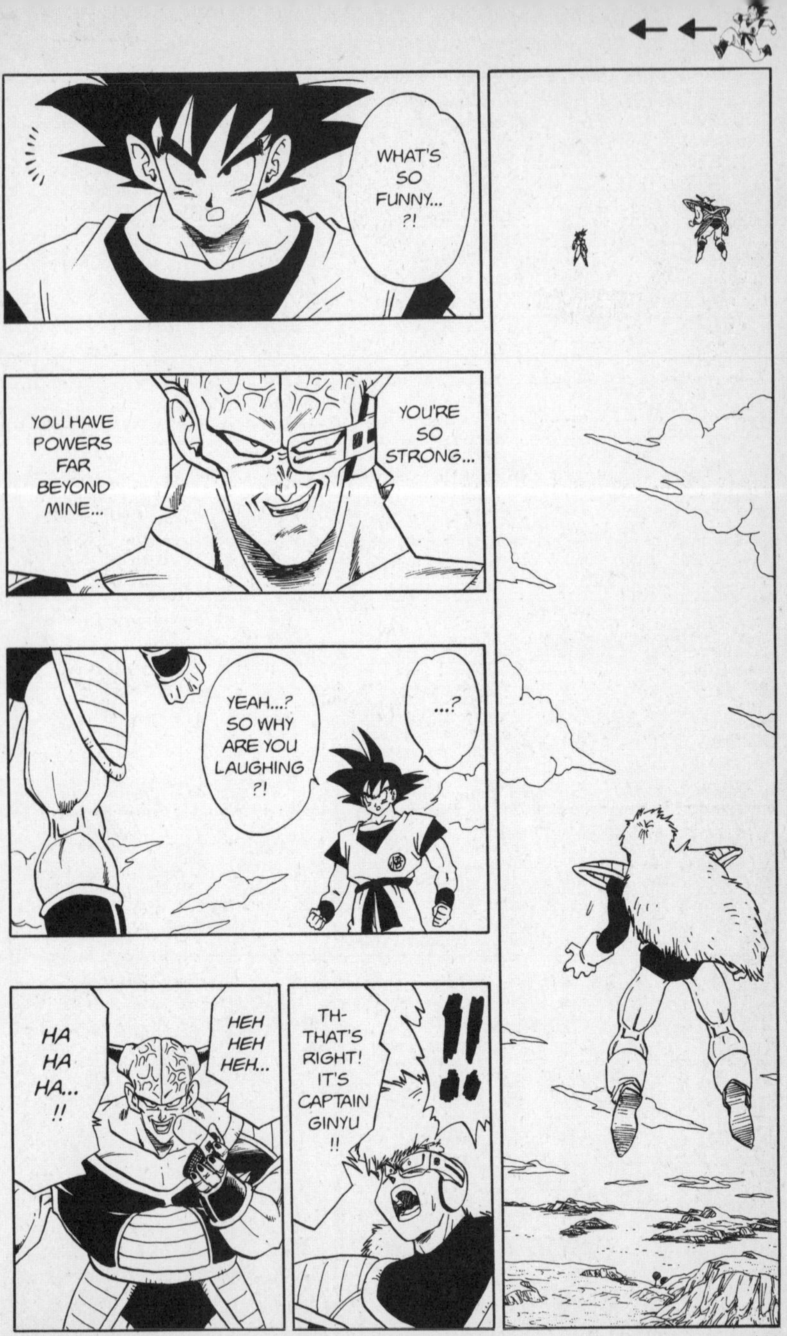
WHAT'S SO FUNNY... ?!
YOU'RE SO STRONG...
YOU HAVE POWERS FAR BEYOND MINE...
...?
YEAH...? SO WHY ARE YOU LAUGHING ?!
!!
TH-THAT'S RIGHT! IT'S CAPTAIN GINYU !!
HEH HEH HEH...
HA HA HA... !!

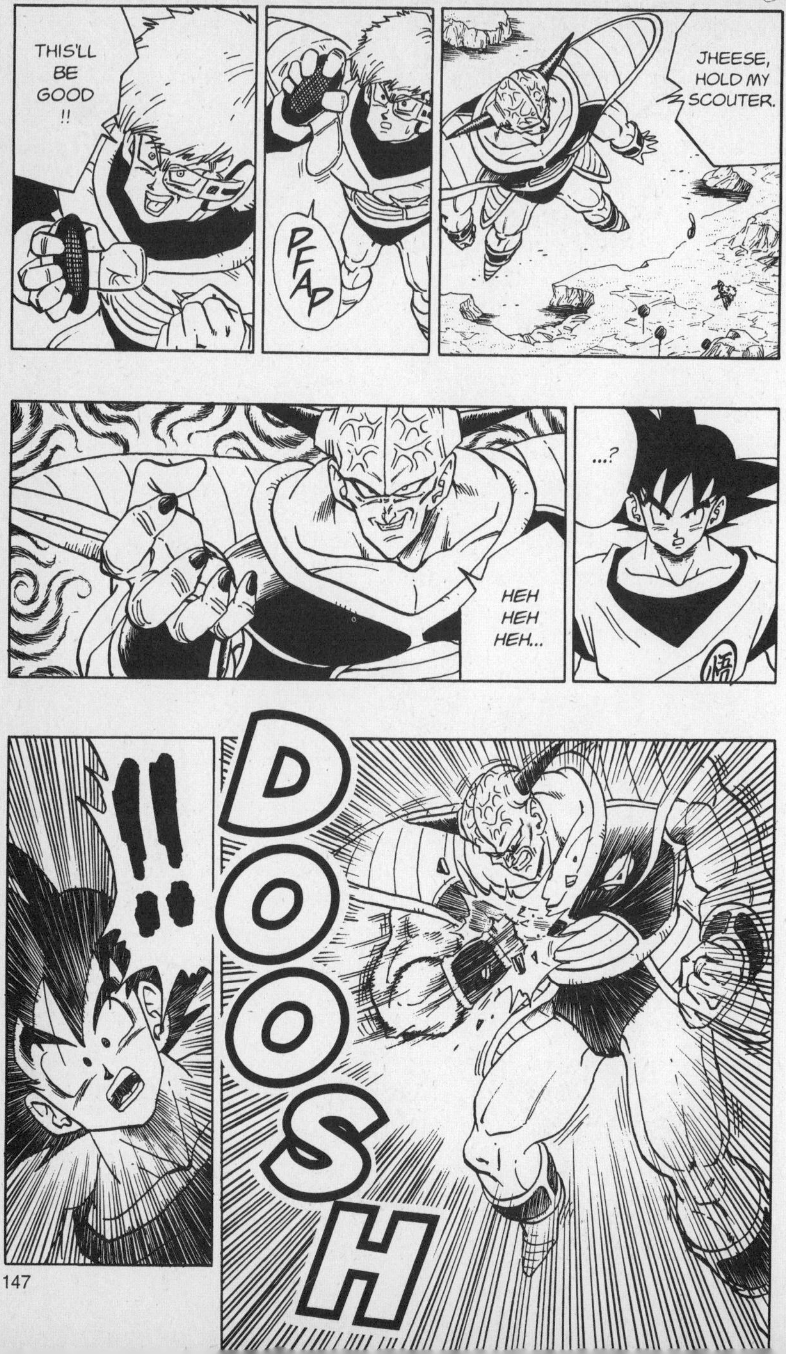
JHEESE, HOLD MY SCOUTER.
PFAP
THIS'LL BE GOOD !!
...?
HEH HEH HEH...
DOOSH
!!

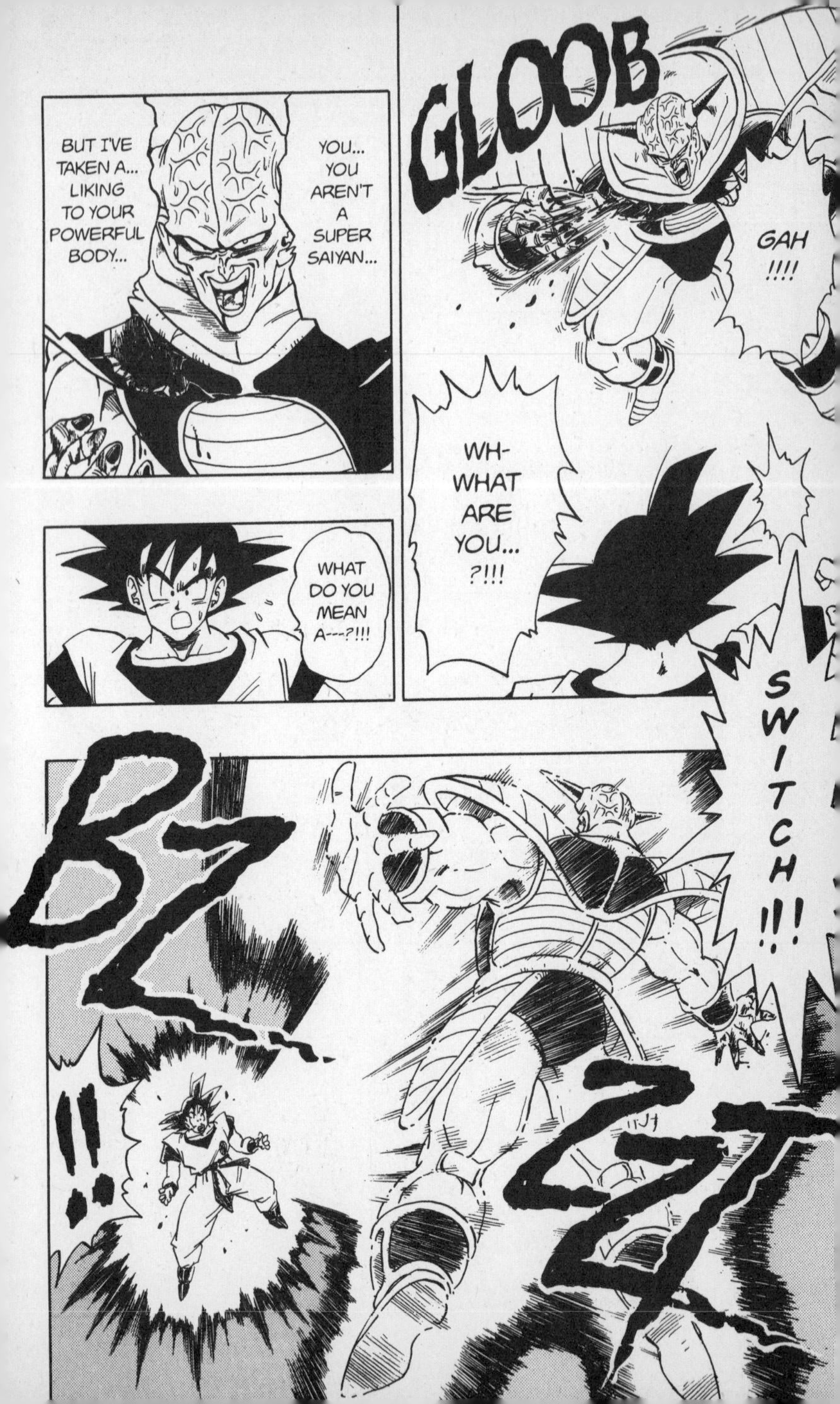
GLOOB
GAH !!!!
WH- WHAT ARE YOU... ?!!!
YOU... YOU AREN'T A SUPER SAIYAN...
BUT I'VE TAKEN A... LIKING TO YOUR POWERFUL BODY...
WHAT DO YOU MEAN A---?!!!
SWITCH !!!
!!

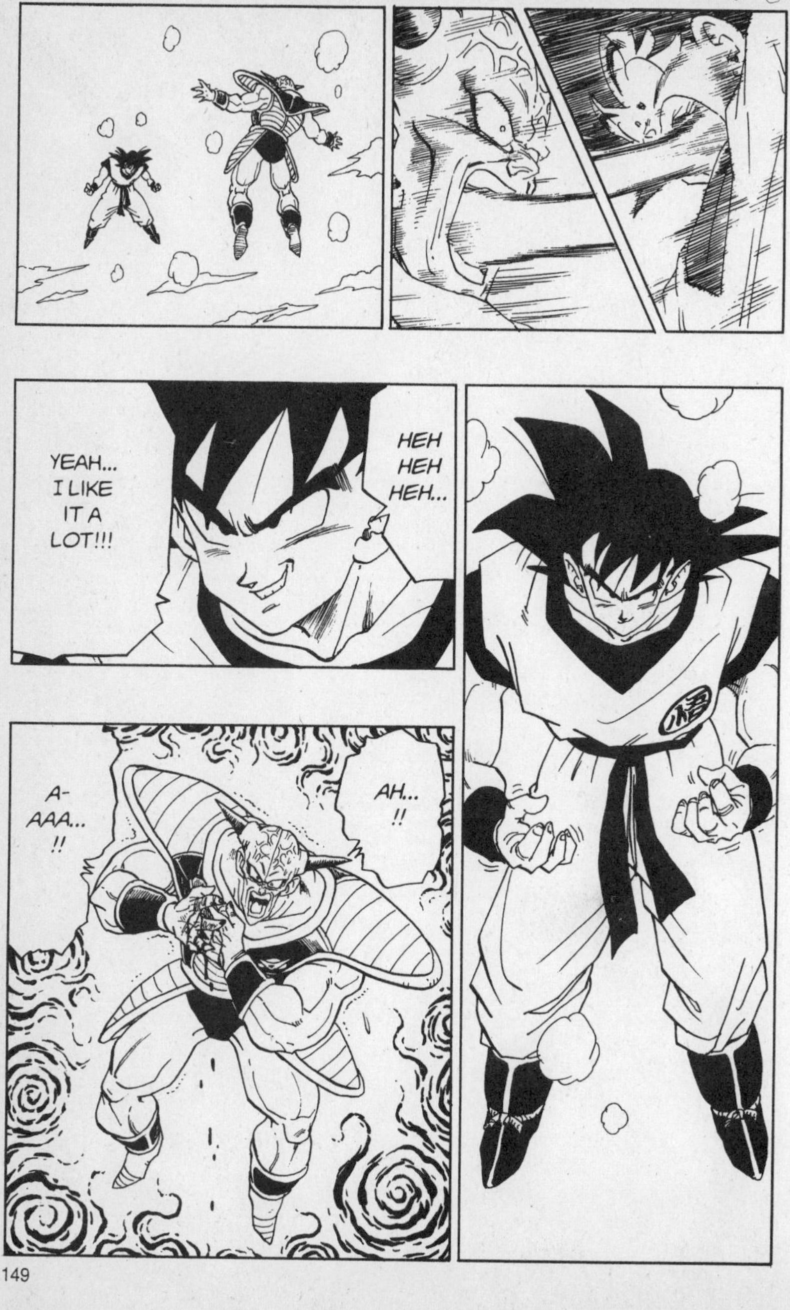
HEH HEH HEH...
YEAH... I LIKE IT A LOT!!!
AH... !!
A-AAA... !!

DBZ:93 • The Switch

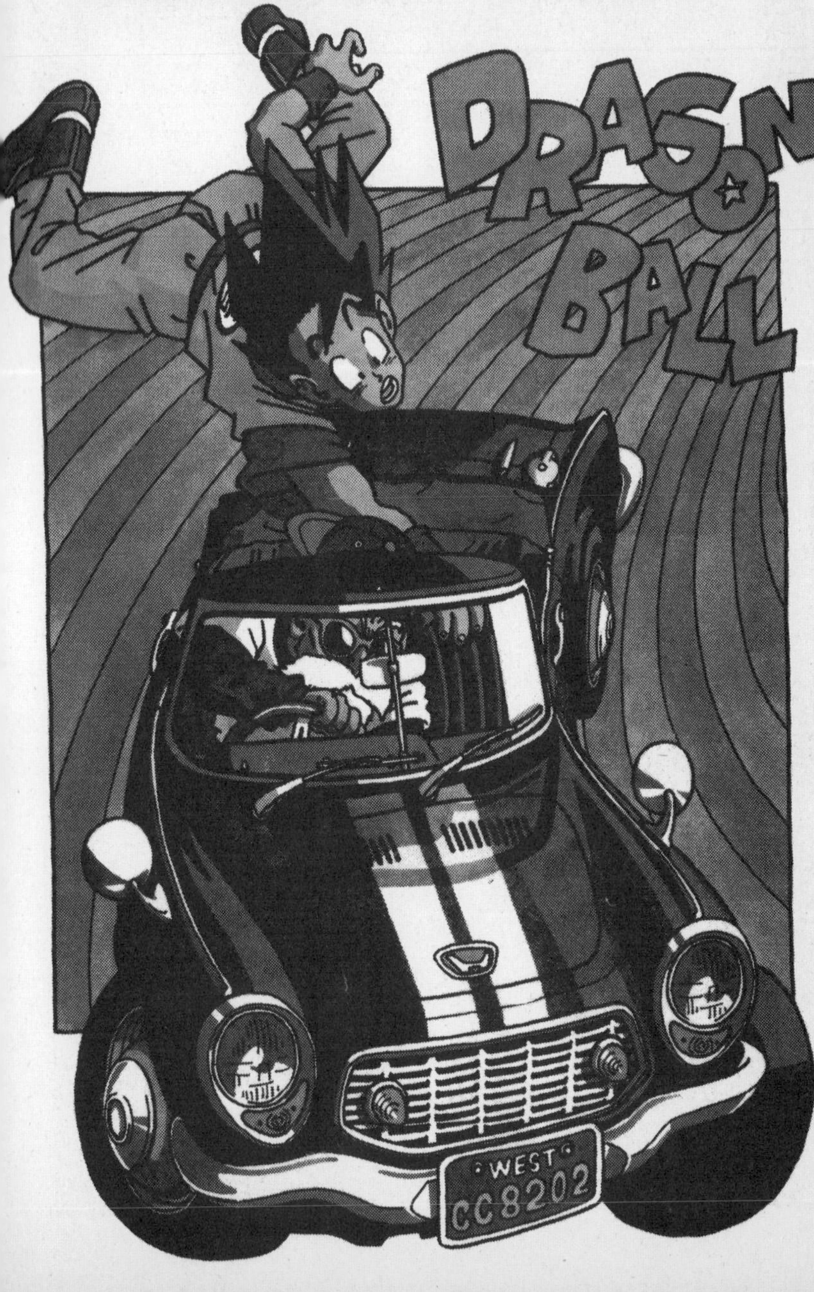
DRAGON BALL
WEST
CC8202

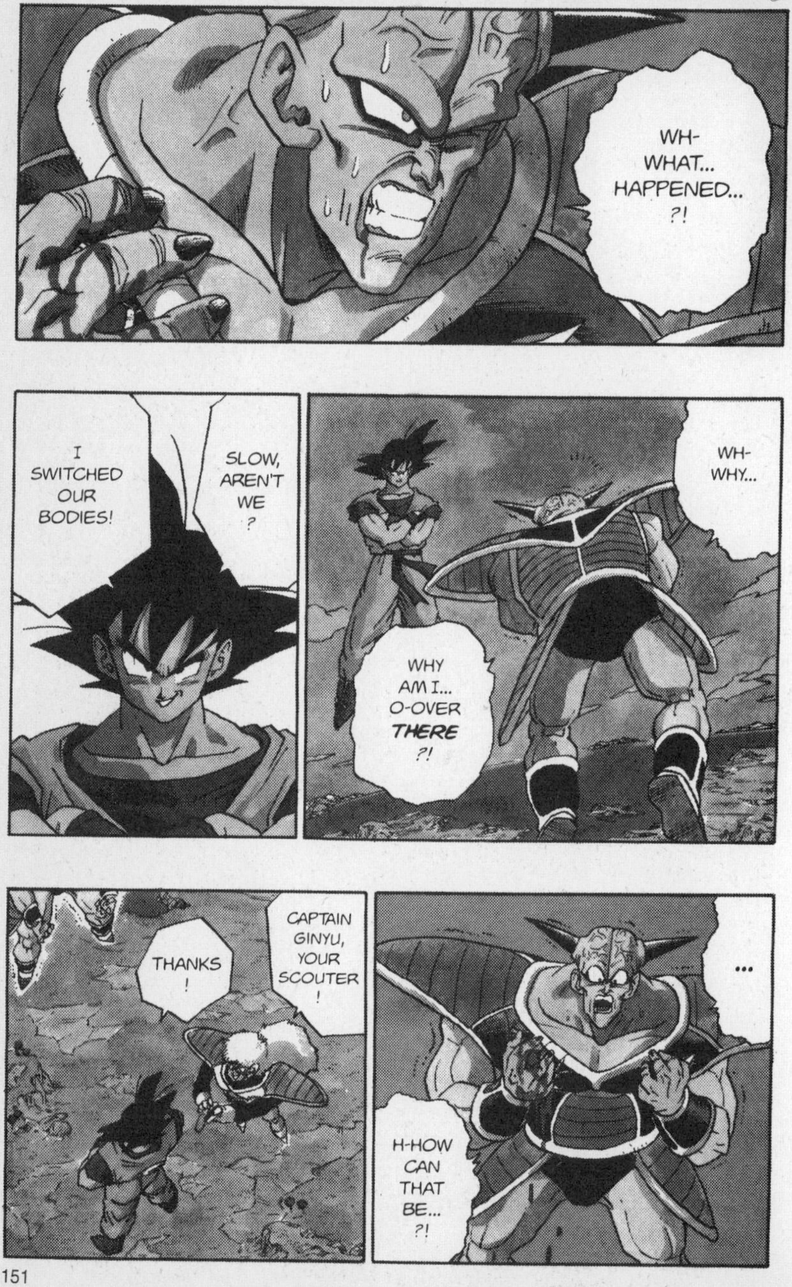
WH- WHAT... HAPPENED... ?!
WH- WHY...
WHY AM I... O-OVER THERE ?!
SLOW, AREN'T WE ?
I SWITCHED OUR BODIES!
...
H-HOW CAN THAT BE... ?!
CAPTAIN GINYU, YOUR SCOUTER !
THANKS !

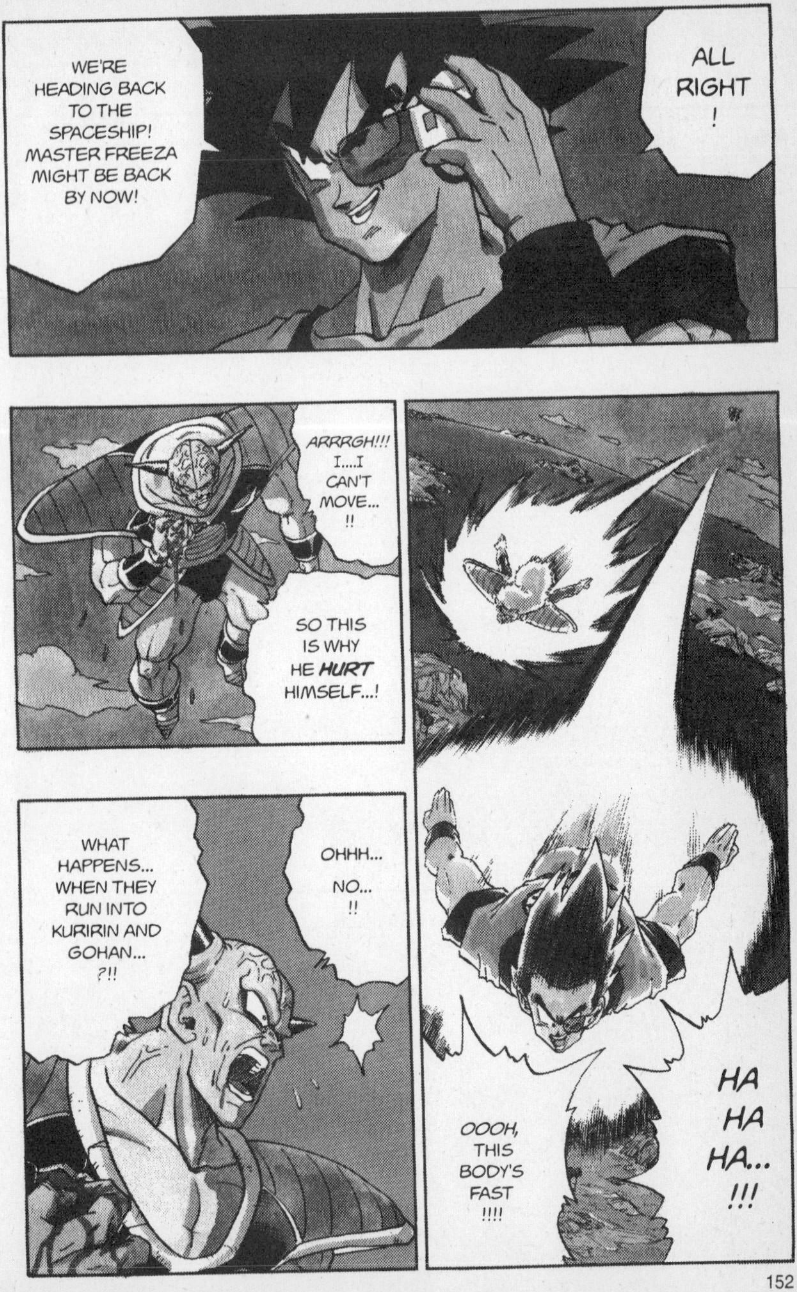
ALL RIGHT !
WE'RE HEADING BACK TO THE SPACESHIP! MASTER FREEZA MIGHT BE BACK BY NOW!
HA HA HA... !!!
OOOH, THIS BODY'S FAST !!!!
ARRRGH!!! I....I CAN'T MOVE... !!
SO THIS IS WHY HE *HURT* HIMSELF...!
OHHH... NO... !!
WHAT HAPPENS... WHEN THEY RUN INTO KURIRIN AND GOHAN... ?!!

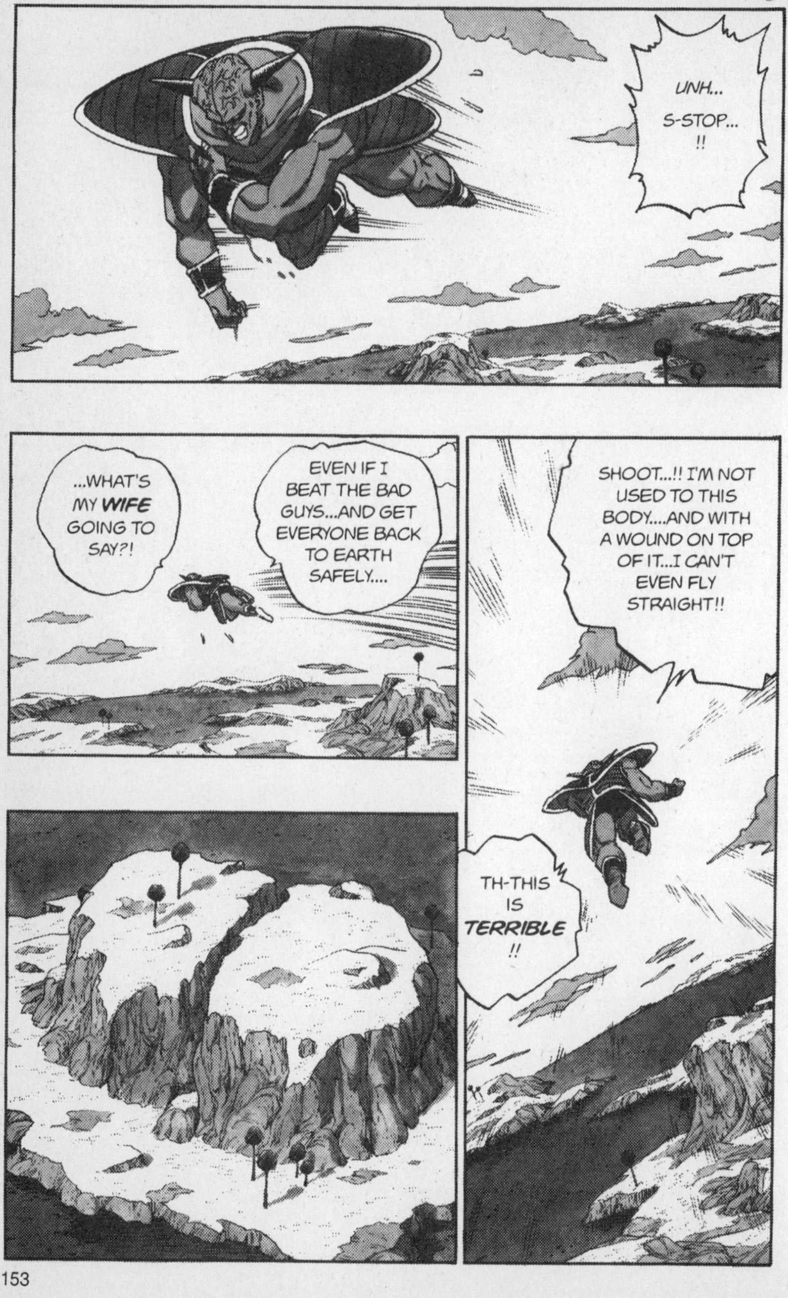
UNH... S-STOP... !!
SHOOT...!! I'M NOT USED TO THIS BODY....AND WITH A WOUND ON TOP OF IT...I CAN'T EVEN FLY STRAIGHT!!
TH-THIS IS TERRIBLE !!
EVEN IF I BEAT THE BAD GUYS...AND GET EVERYONE BACK TO EARTH SAFELY....
...WHAT'S MY WIFE GOING TO SAY?!

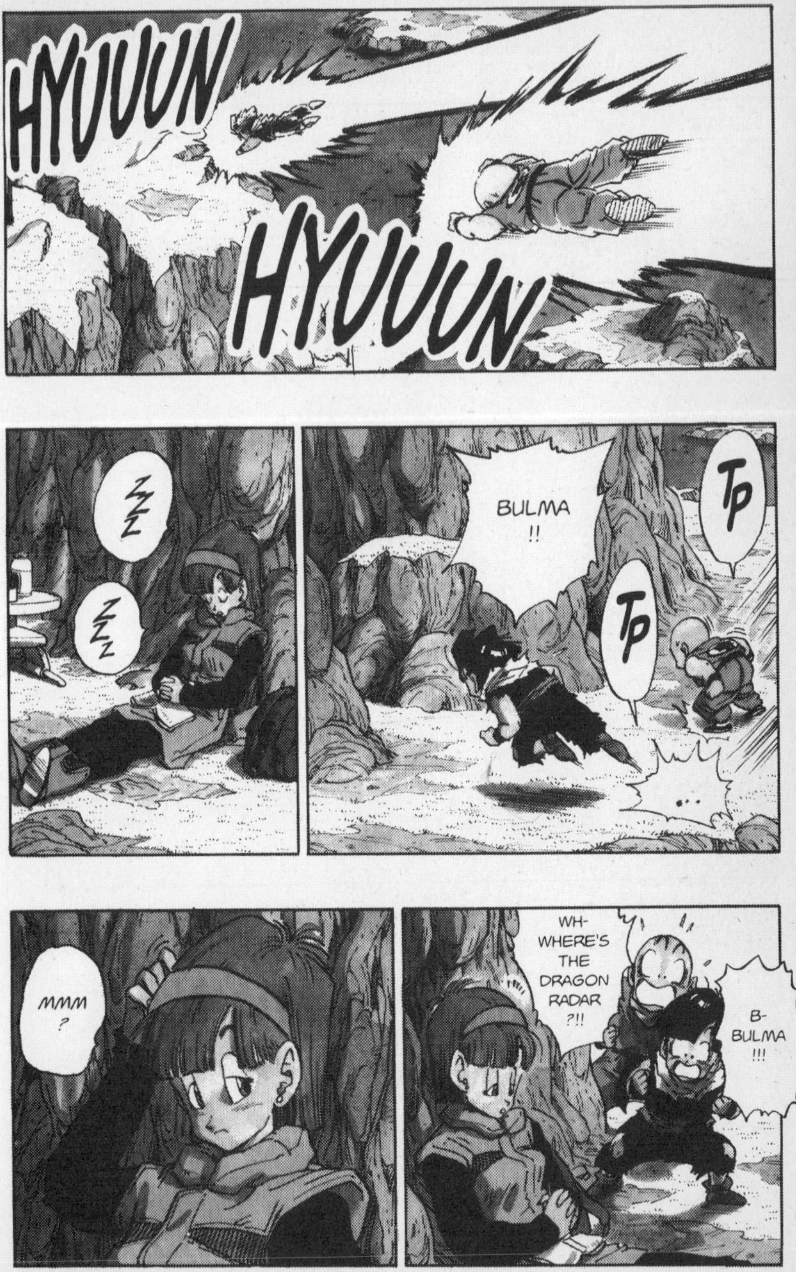
HYUUUN
HYUUUN
BULMA !!
TP
TP
...
ZZZ
ZZZ
WH- WHERE'S THE DRAGON RADAR ?!!
B- BULMA !!!
MMM ?

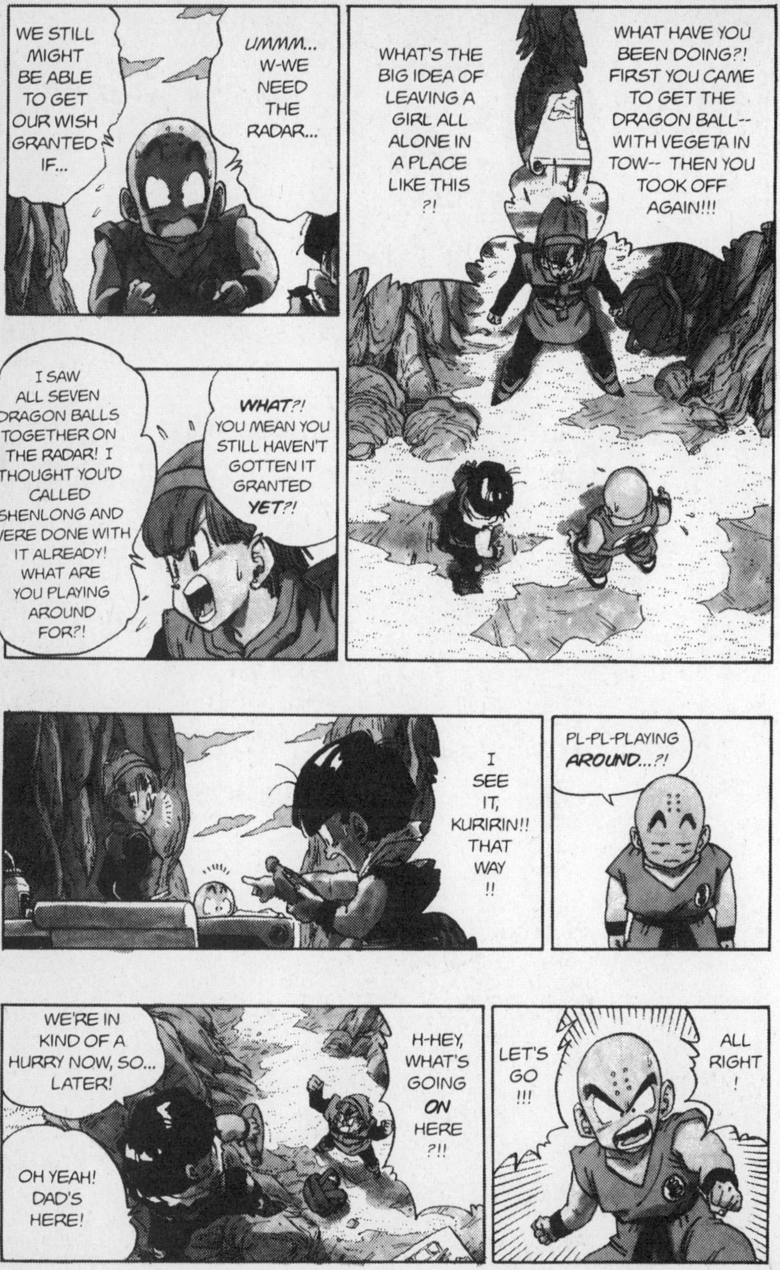
WHAT HAVE YOU BEEN DOING?! FIRST YOU CAME TO GET THE DRAGON BALL-- WITH VEGETA IN TOW-- THEN YOU TOOK OFF AGAIN!!!
WHAT'S THE BIG IDEA OF LEAVING A GIRL ALL ALONE IN A PLACE LIKE THIS ?!
UMMM... W-WE NEED THE RADAR...
WE STILL MIGHT BE ABLE TO GET OUR WISH GRANTED IF...
WHAT?! YOU MEAN YOU STILL HAVEN'T GOTTEN IT GRANTED YET?!
I SAW ALL SEVEN DRAGON BALLS TOGETHER ON THE RADAR! I THOUGHT YOU'D CALLED SHENLONG AND WERE DONE WITH IT ALREADY! WHAT ARE YOU PLAYING AROUND FOR?!
PL-PL-PLAYING AROUND...?!
I SEE IT, KURIRIN!! THAT WAY !!
ALL RIGHT !
LET'S GO !!!
H-HEY, WHAT'S GOING ON HERE ?!!
WE'RE IN KIND OF A HURRY NOW, SO... LATER!
OH YEAH! DAD'S HERE!

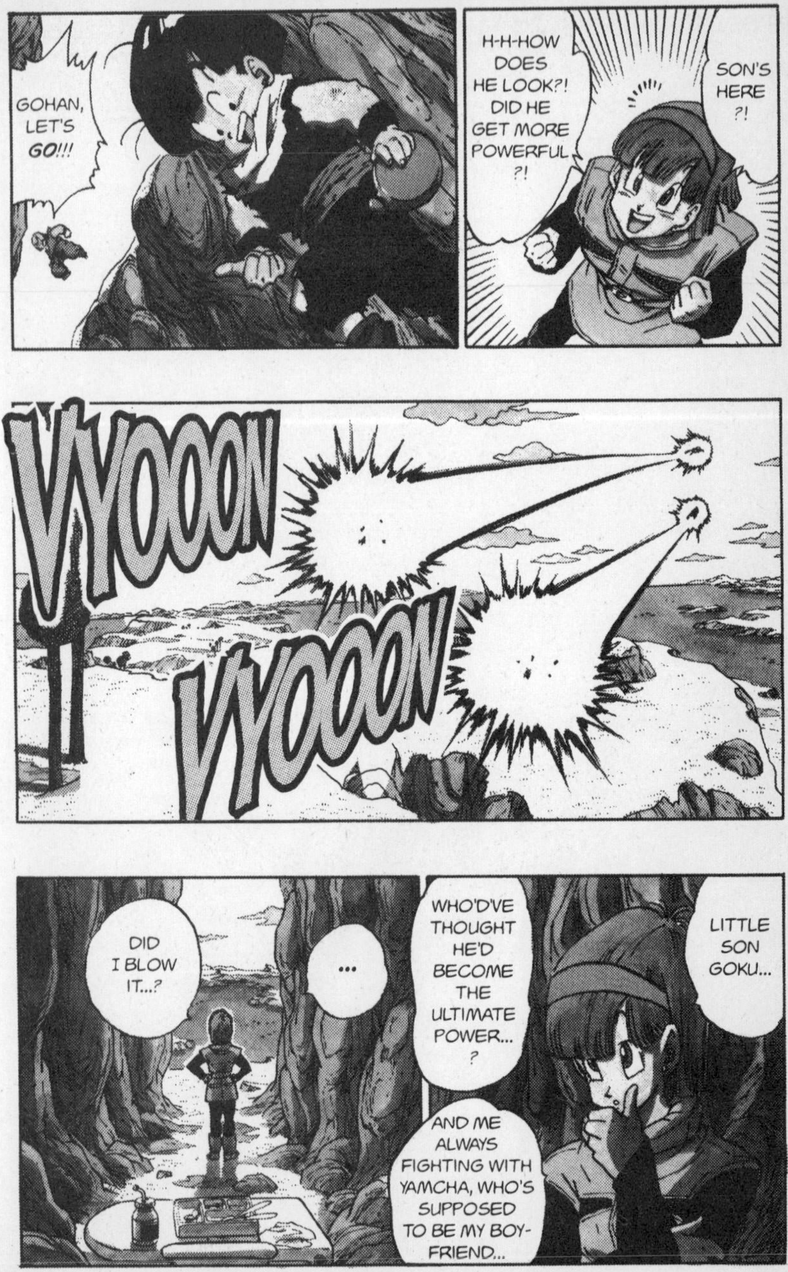
SON'S HERE ?!
H-H-HOW DOES HE LOOK?! DID HE GET MORE POWERFUL ?!
GOHAN, LET'S *GO*!!!
VYOOON
VYOOON
LITTLE SON GOKU...
WHO'D'VE THOUGHT HE'D BECOME THE ULTIMATE POWER... ?
AND ME ALWAYS FIGHTING WITH YAMCHA, WHO'S SUPPOSED TO BE MY BOY-FRIEND...
...
DID I BLOW IT...?

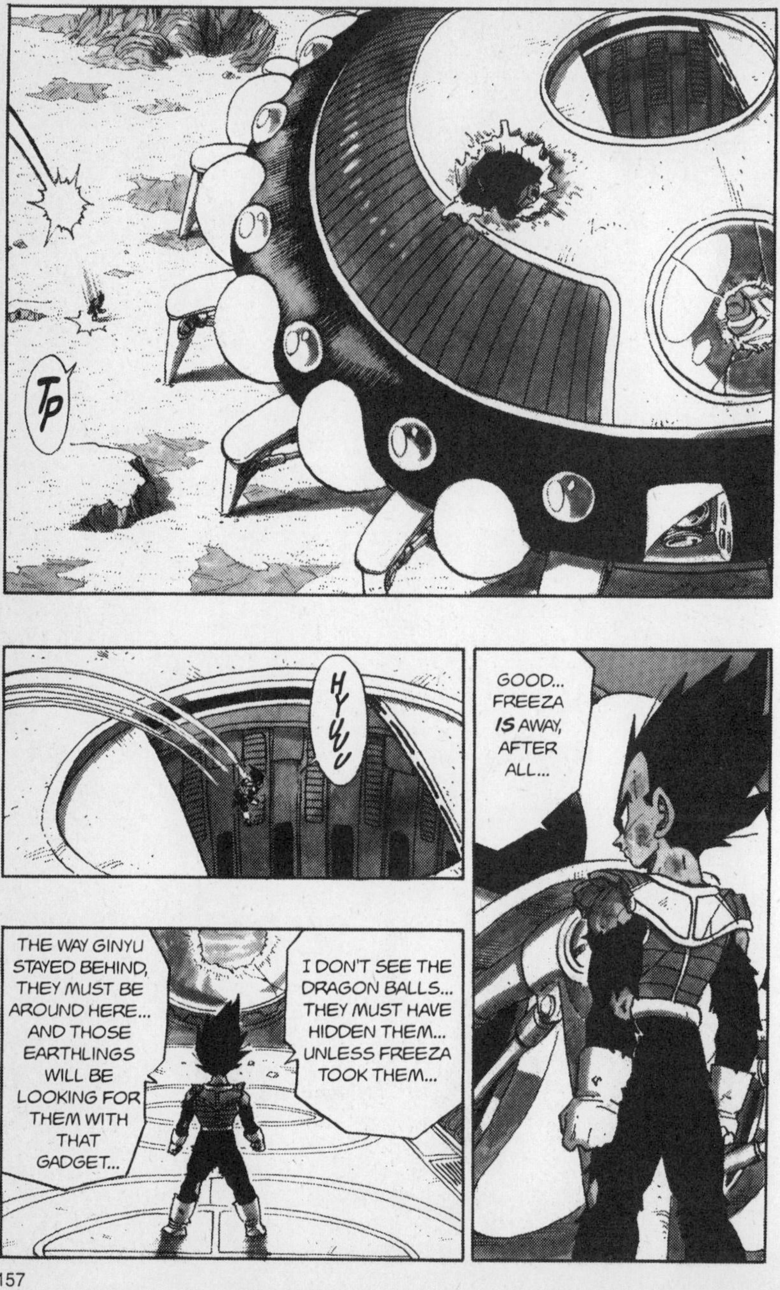
TP
GOOD... FREEZA IS AWAY, AFTER ALL...
HYUUU
I DON'T SEE THE DRAGON BALLS... THEY MUST HAVE HIDDEN THEM... UNLESS FREEZA TOOK THEM...
THE WAY GINYU STAYED BEHIND, THEY MUST BE AROUND HERE... AND THOSE EARTHLINGS WILL BE LOOKING FOR THEM WITH THAT GADGET...

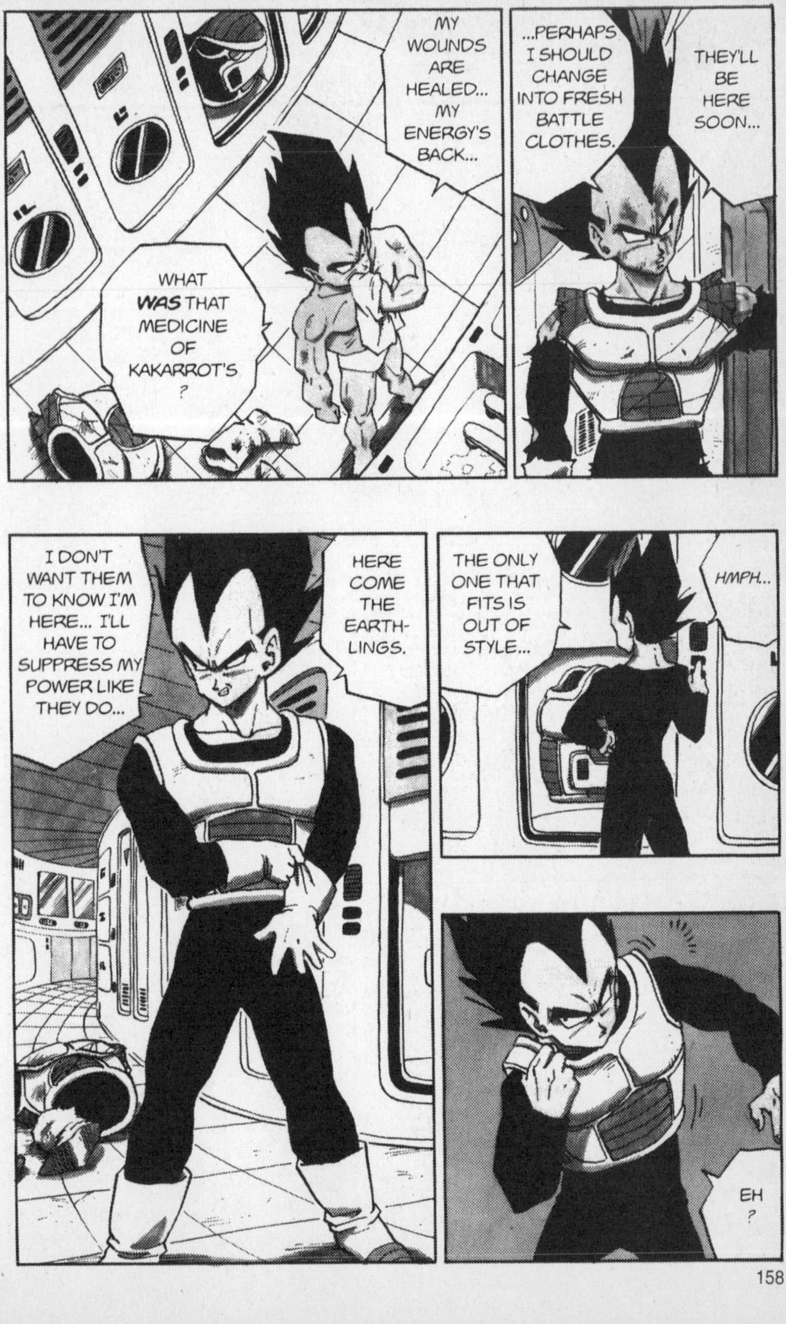
THEY'LL BE HERE SOON...
...PERHAPS I SHOULD CHANGE INTO FRESH BATTLE CLOTHES.
MY WOUNDS ARE HEALED... MY ENERGY'S BACK...
WHAT *WAS* THAT MEDICINE OF KAKARROT'S?
HMPH...
THE ONLY ONE THAT FITS IS OUT OF STYLE...
EH?
HERE COME THE EARTH-LINGS.
I DON'T WANT THEM TO KNOW I'M HERE... I'LL HAVE TO SUPPRESS MY POWER LIKE THEY DO...

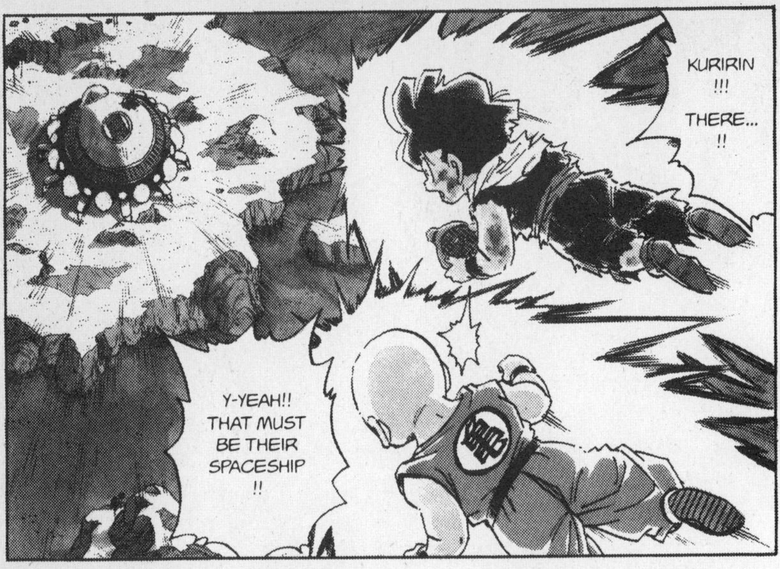
KURIRIN !!! THERE... !!
Y-YEAH!! THAT MUST BE THEIR SPACESHIP !!

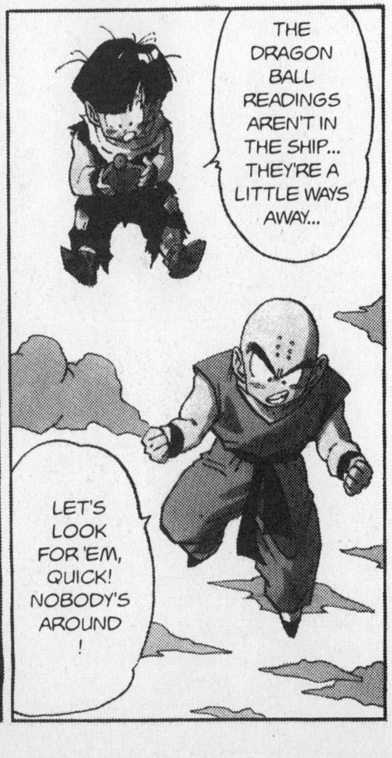
THE DRAGON BALL READINGS AREN'T IN THE SHIP... THEY'RE A LITTLE WAYS AWAY...
LET'S LOOK FOR 'EM, QUICK! NOBODY'S AROUND !

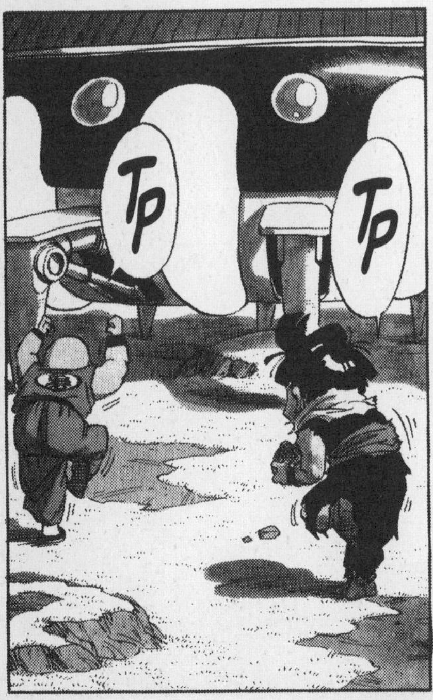
TP
TP

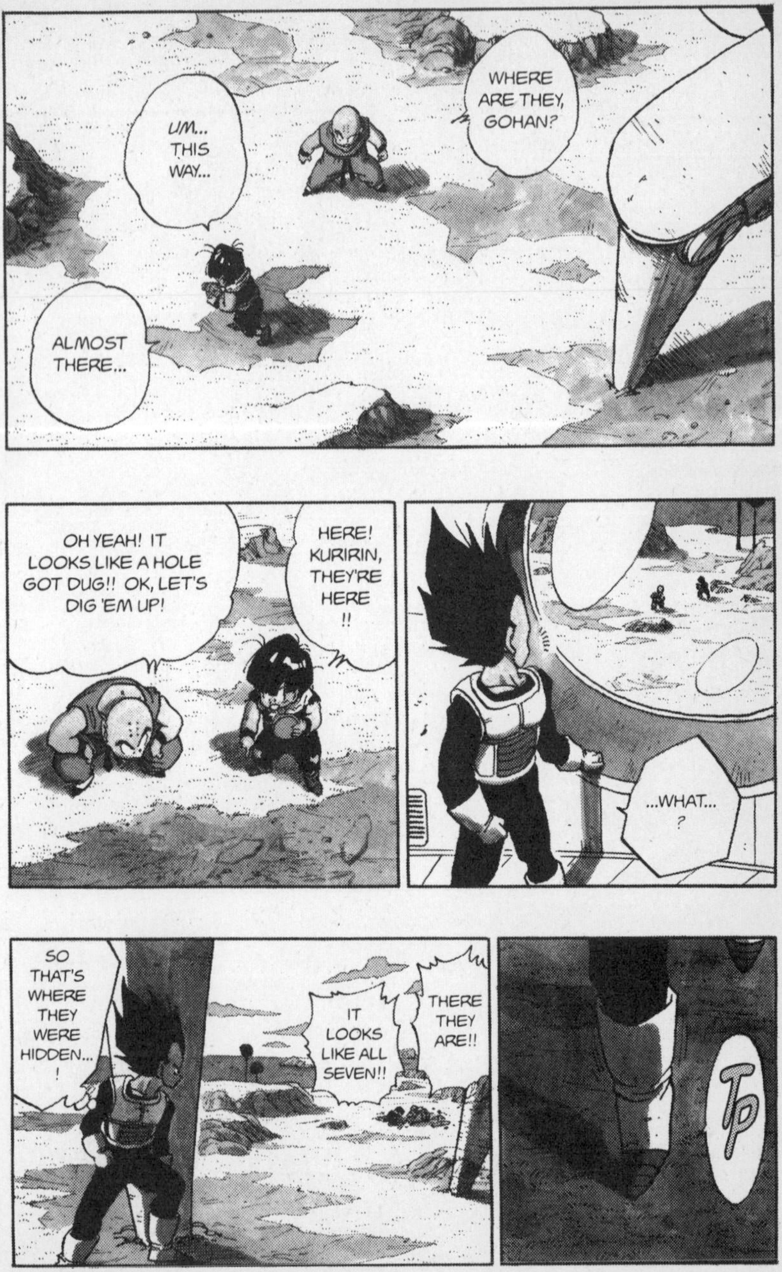
WHERE ARE THEY, GOHAN?
UM... THIS WAY...
ALMOST THERE...
...WHAT... ?
HERE! KURIRIN, THEY'RE HERE !!
OH YEAH! IT LOOKS LIKE A HOLE GOT DUG!! OK, LET'S DIG 'EM UP!
Tp
THERE THEY ARE!!
IT LOOKS LIKE ALL SEVEN!!
SO THAT'S WHERE THEY WERE HIDDEN... !

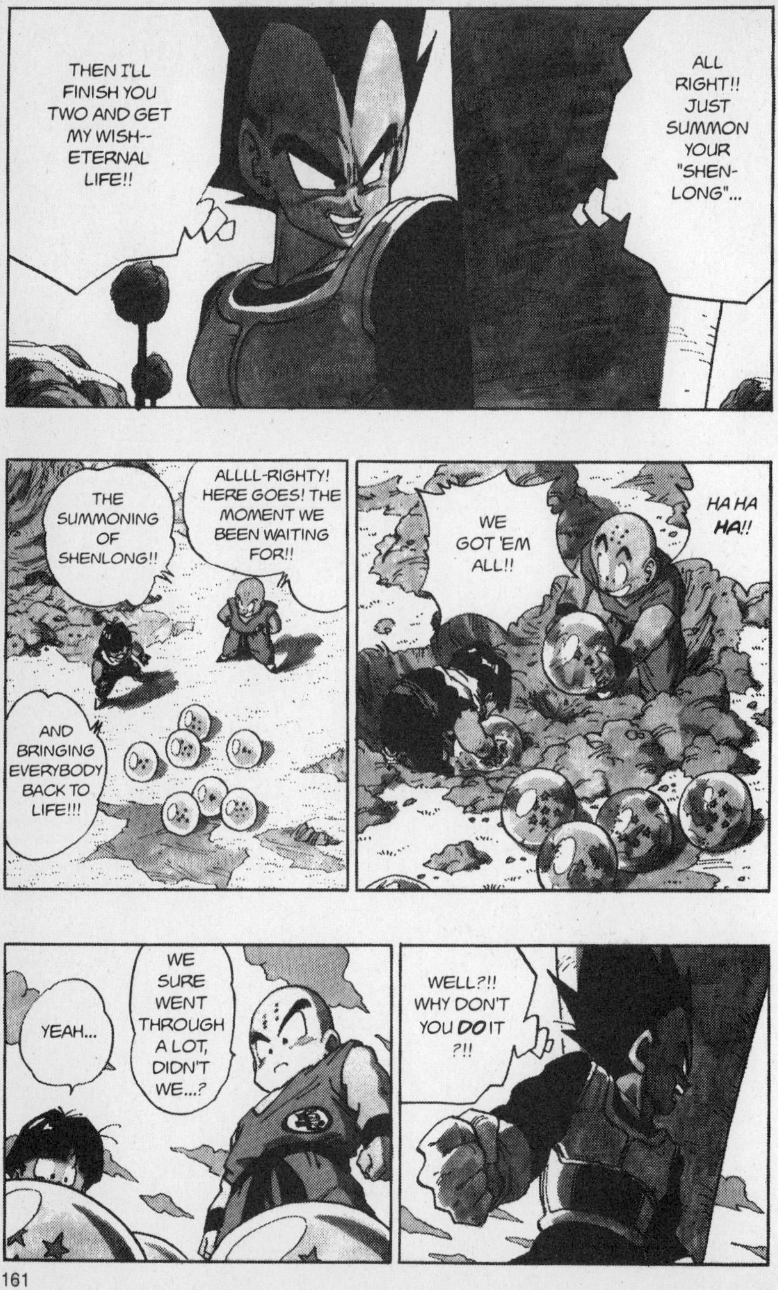

ALL RIGHT!! JUST SUMMON YOUR "SHEN-LONG"...
THEN I'LL FINISH YOU TWO AND GET MY WISH--ETERNAL LIFE!!
HA HA **HA!!**
WE GOT 'EM ALL!!
ALLLL-RIGHTY! HERE GOES! THE MOMENT WE BEEN WAITING FOR!!
THE SUMMONING OF SHENLONG!!
AND BRINGING EVERYBODY BACK TO LIFE!!!
WELL?!! WHY DON'T YOU **DO** IT ?!!
WE SURE WENT THROUGH A LOT, DIDN'T WE...?
YEAH...

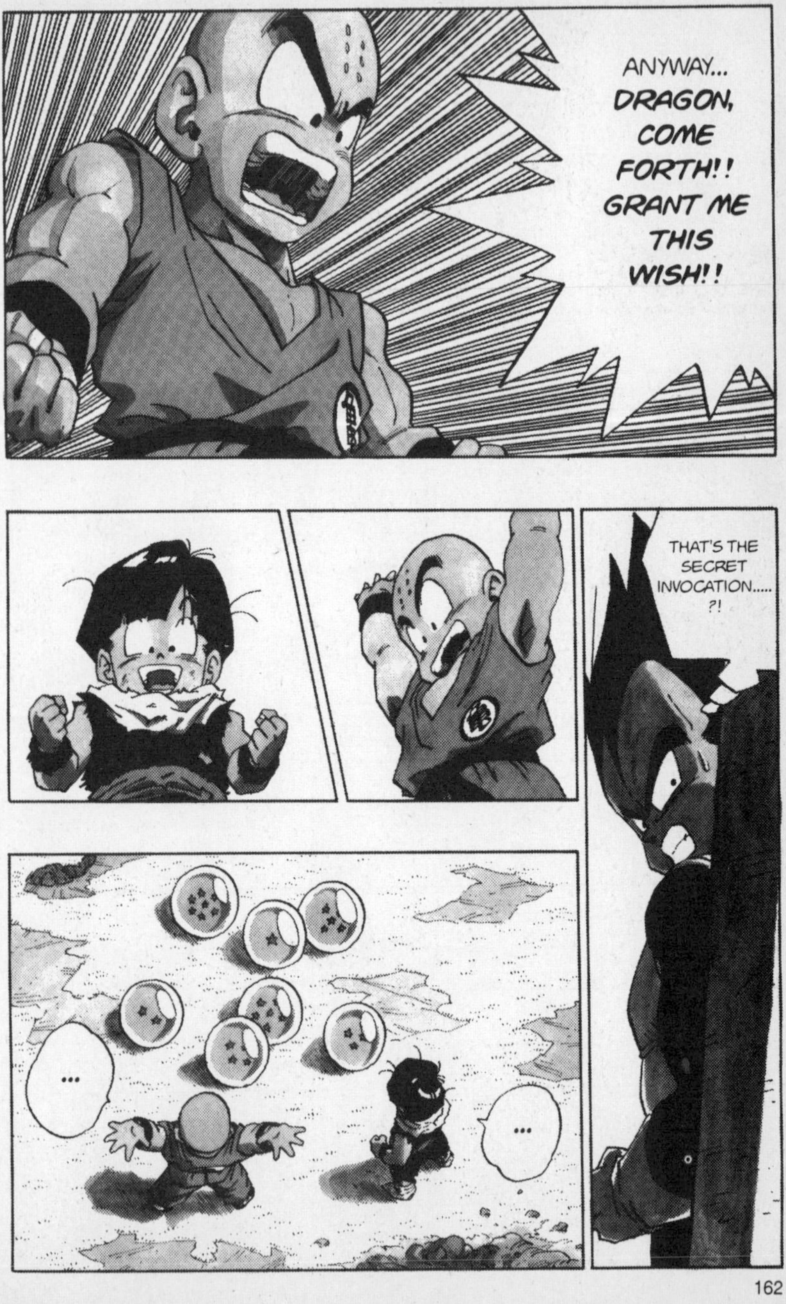
ANYWAY... DRAGON, COME FORTH!! GRANT ME THIS WISH!!
THAT'S THE SECRET INVOCATION.....?!
...
...

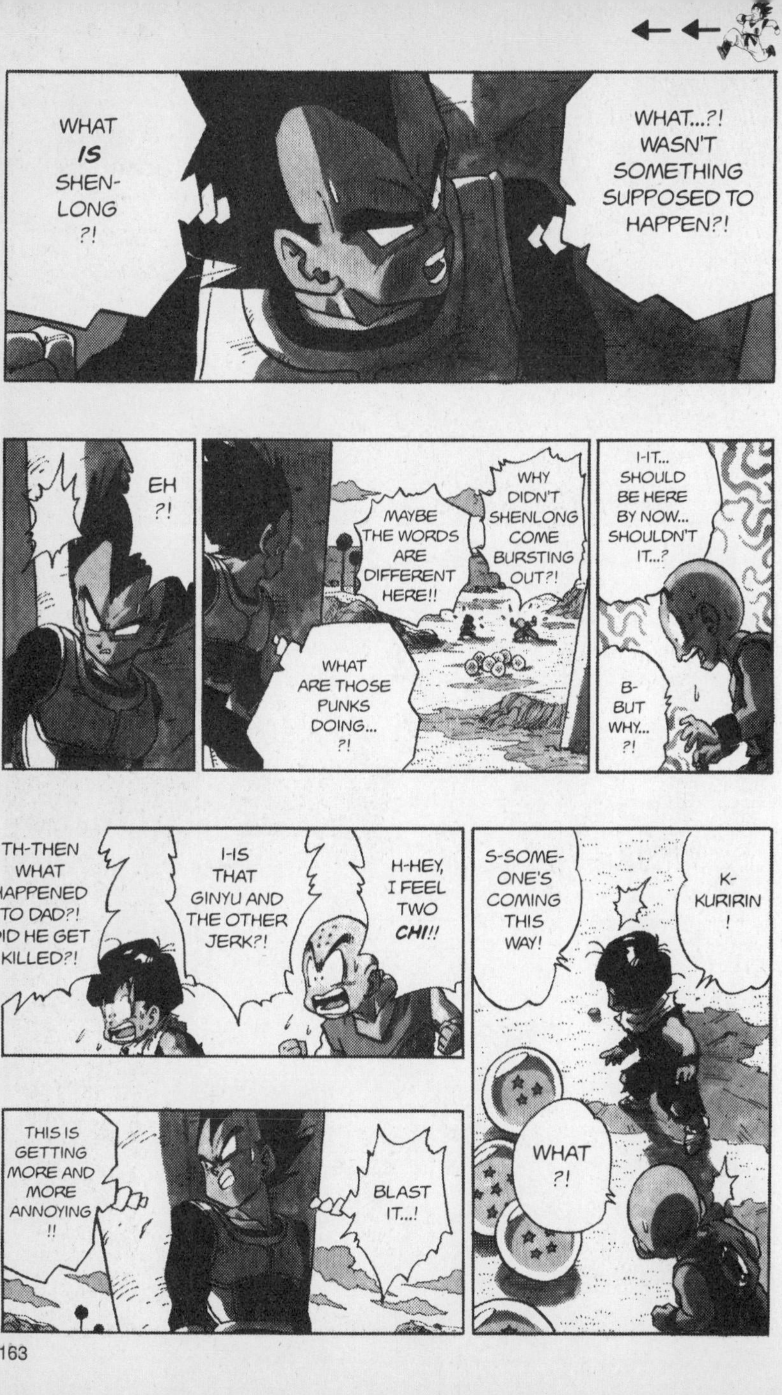
WHAT...?! WASN'T SOMETHING SUPPOSED TO HAPPEN?!
WHAT *IS* SHEN-LONG?!
I-IT... SHOULD BE HERE BY NOW... SHOULDN'T IT...?
B-BUT WHY...?!
WHY DIDN'T SHENLONG COME BURSTING OUT?!
MAYBE THE WORDS ARE DIFFERENT HERE!!
WHAT ARE THOSE PUNKS DOING...?!
EH?!
K-KURIRIN!
S-SOMEONE'S COMING THIS WAY!
WHAT?!
H-HEY, I FEEL TWO *CHI*!!
I-IS THAT GINYU AND THE OTHER JERK?!
TH-THEN WHAT HAPPENED TO DAD?! DID HE GET KILLED?!
BLAST IT...!
THIS IS GETTING MORE AND MORE ANNOYING!!

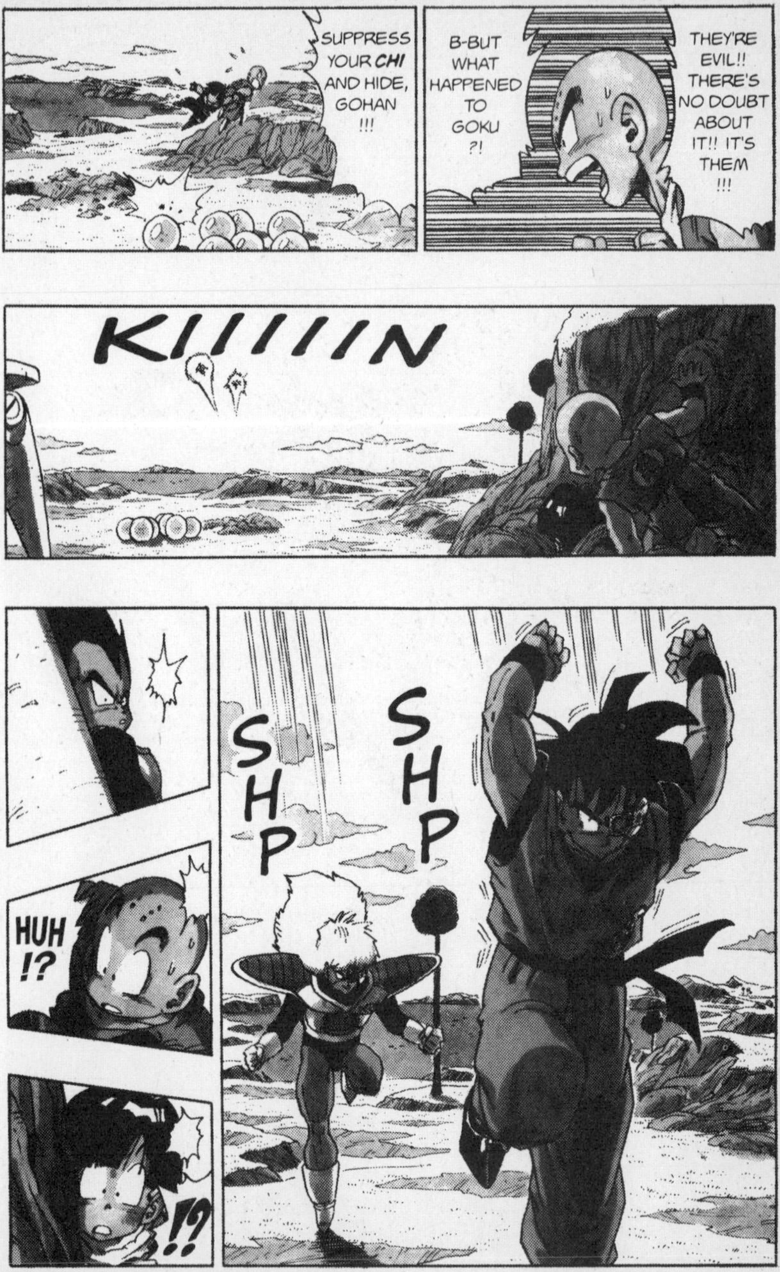
THEY'RE EVIL!! THERE'S NO DOUBT ABOUT IT!! IT'S THEM!!!
B-BUT WHAT HAPPENED TO GOKU?!
SUPPRESS YOUR CHI AND HIDE, GOHAN!!!
KIIIIN
SHP
SHP
HUH!?
!!?

DBZ:94 • Goku or Ginyu?

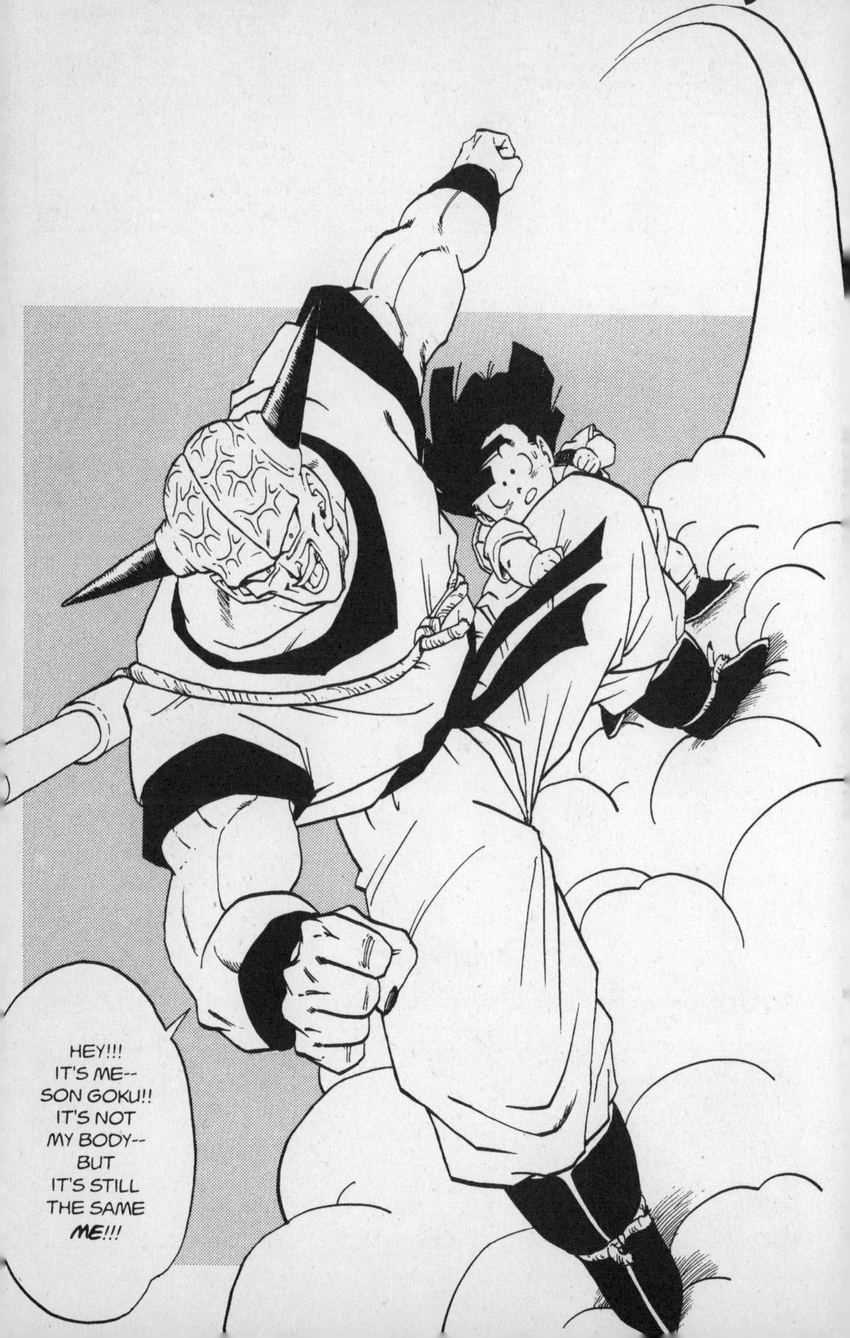
HEY!!! IT'S ME-- SON GOKU!! IT'S NOT MY BODY-- BUT IT'S STILL THE SAME *ME*!!!

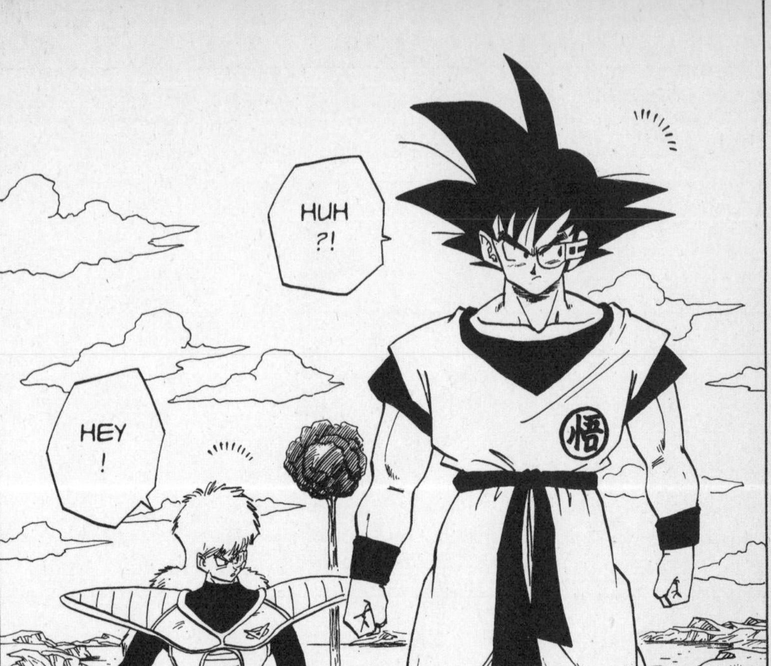
HUH ?!
HEY !

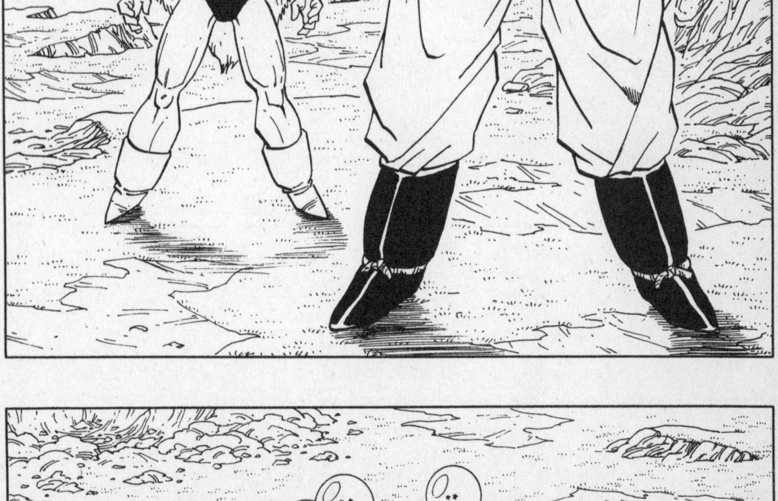

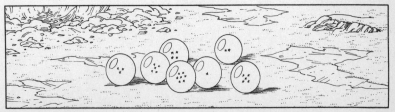

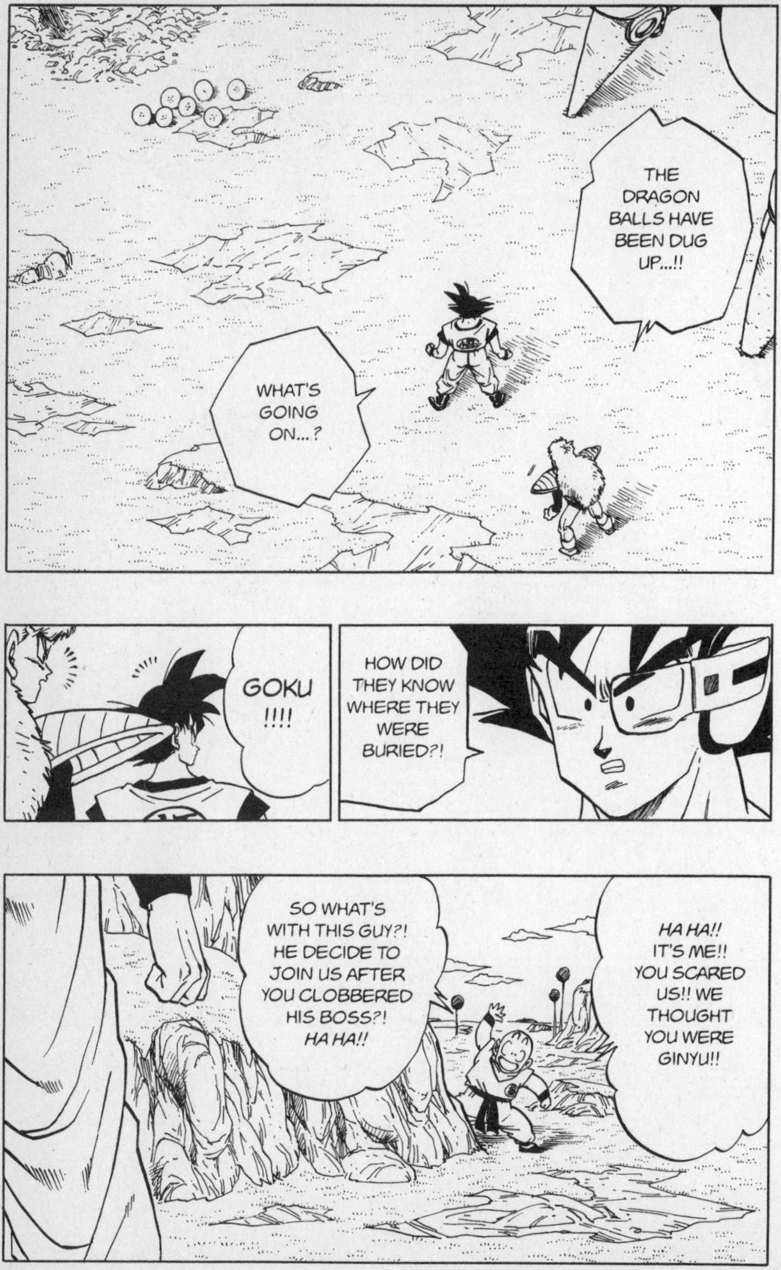

THE DRAGON BALLS HAVE BEEN DUG UP...!!
WHAT'S GOING ON...?
HOW DID THEY KNOW WHERE THEY WERE BURIED?!
GOKU !!!!
HA HA!! IT'S ME!! YOU SCARED US!! WE THOUGHT YOU WERE GINYU!!
SO WHAT'S WITH THIS GUY?! HE DECIDE TO JOIN US AFTER YOU CLOBBERED HIS BOSS?! *HA HA!!*

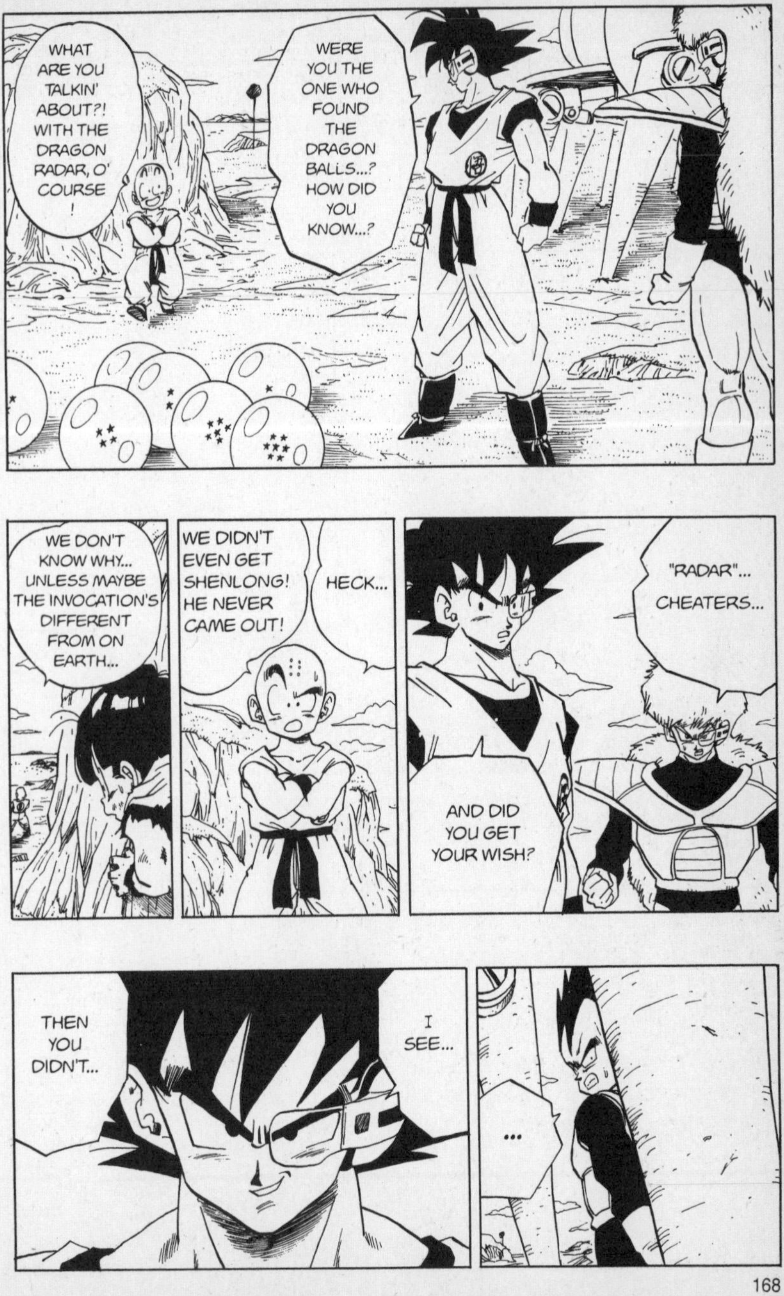

WERE YOU THE ONE WHO FOUND THE DRAGON BALLS...? HOW DID YOU KNOW...?
WHAT ARE YOU TALKIN' ABOUT?! WITH THE DRAGON RADAR, O' COURSE!
"RADAR"... CHEATERS...
AND DID YOU GET YOUR WISH?
HECK...
WE DIDN'T EVEN GET SHENLONG! HE NEVER CAME OUT!
WE DON'T KNOW WHY... UNLESS MAYBE THE INVOCATION'S DIFFERENT FROM ON EARTH...
...
I SEE...
THEN YOU DIDN'T...

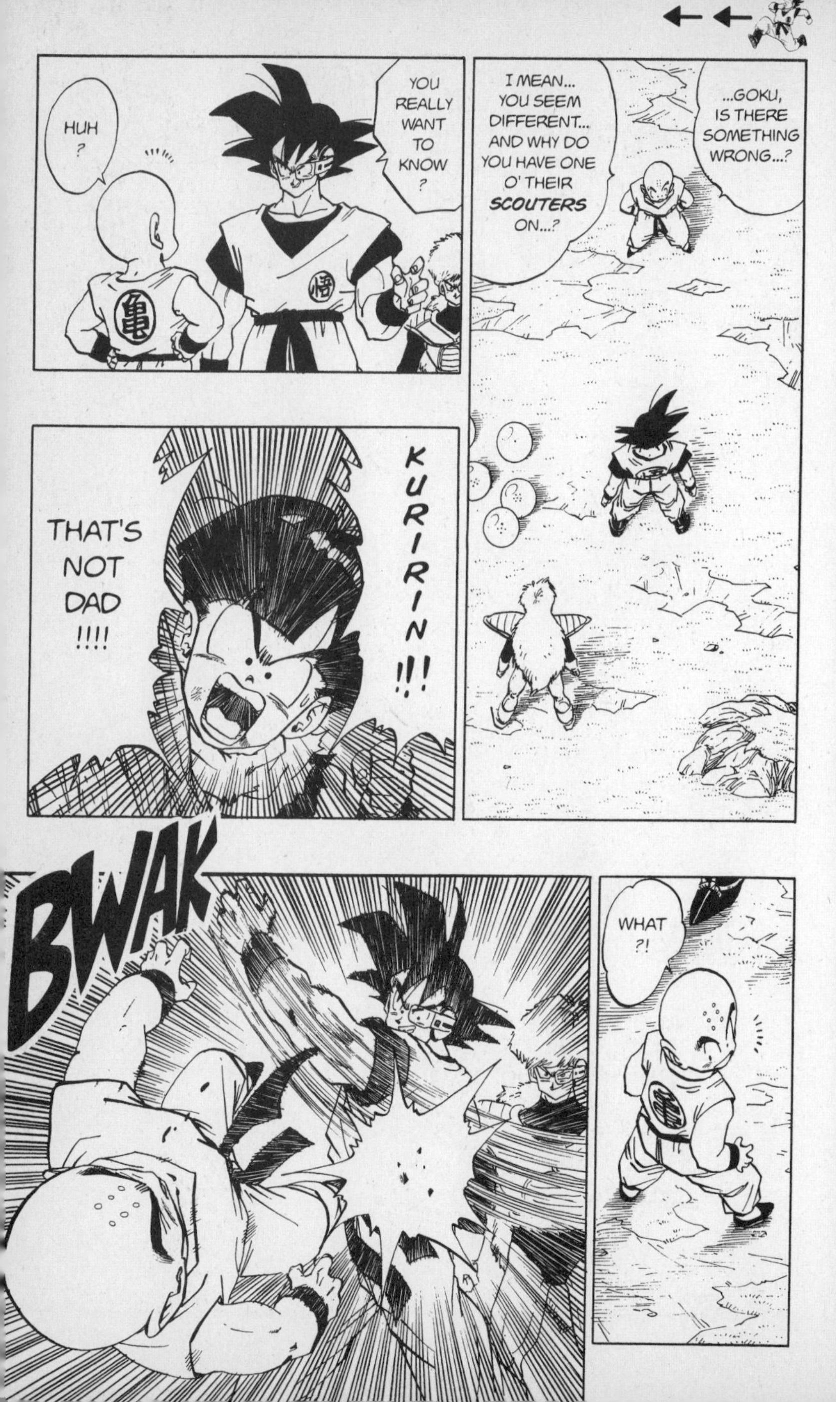
...GOKU, IS THERE SOMETHING WRONG...?
I MEAN... YOU SEEM DIFFERENT... AND WHY DO YOU HAVE ONE O' THEIR **SCOUTERS** ON...?
YOU REALLY WANT TO KNOW ?
HUH ?
KURIRIN !!!
THAT'S NOT DAD !!!!
WHAT ?!
BWAK

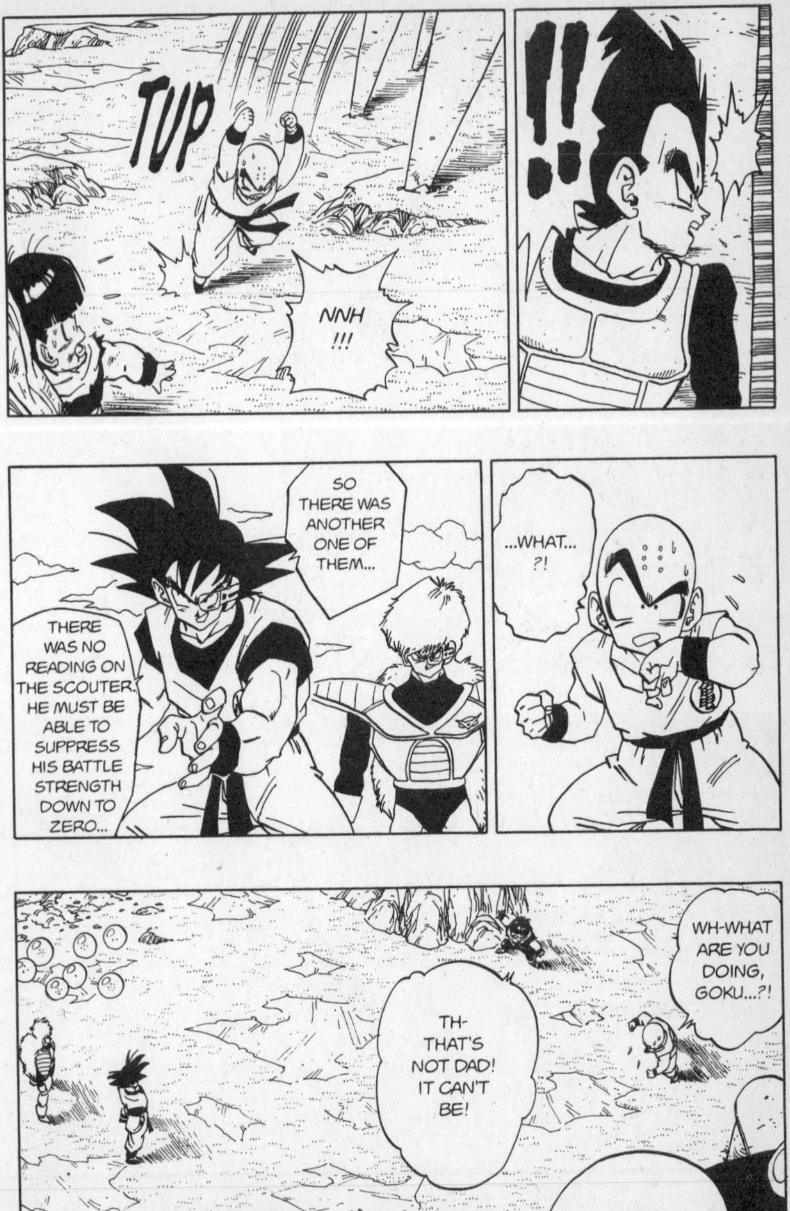
!!
TUP
NNH !!!
...WHAT... ?!
SO THERE WAS ANOTHER ONE OF THEM...
THERE WAS NO READING ON THE SCOUTER. HE MUST BE ABLE TO SUPPRESS HIS BATTLE STRENGTH DOWN TO ZERO...
WH-WHAT ARE YOU DOING, GOKU...?!
TH- THAT'S NOT DAD! IT CAN'T BE!

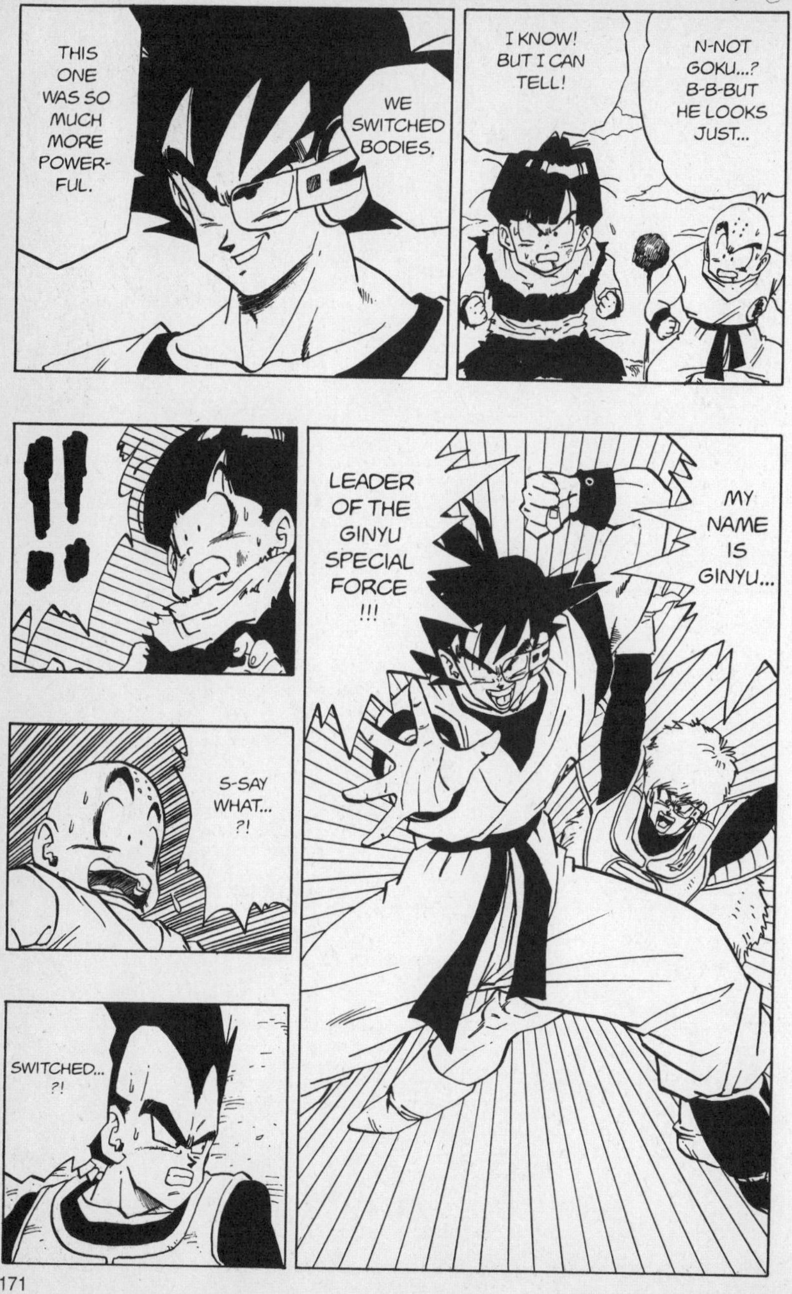

N-NOT GOKU...? B-B-BUT HE LOOKS JUST...
I KNOW! BUT I CAN TELL!
WE SWITCHED BODIES.
THIS ONE WAS SO MUCH MORE POWER-FUL.
MY NAME IS GINYU...
LEADER OF THE GINYU SPECIAL FORCE !!!
!!
S-SAY WHAT... ?!
SWITCHED... ?!

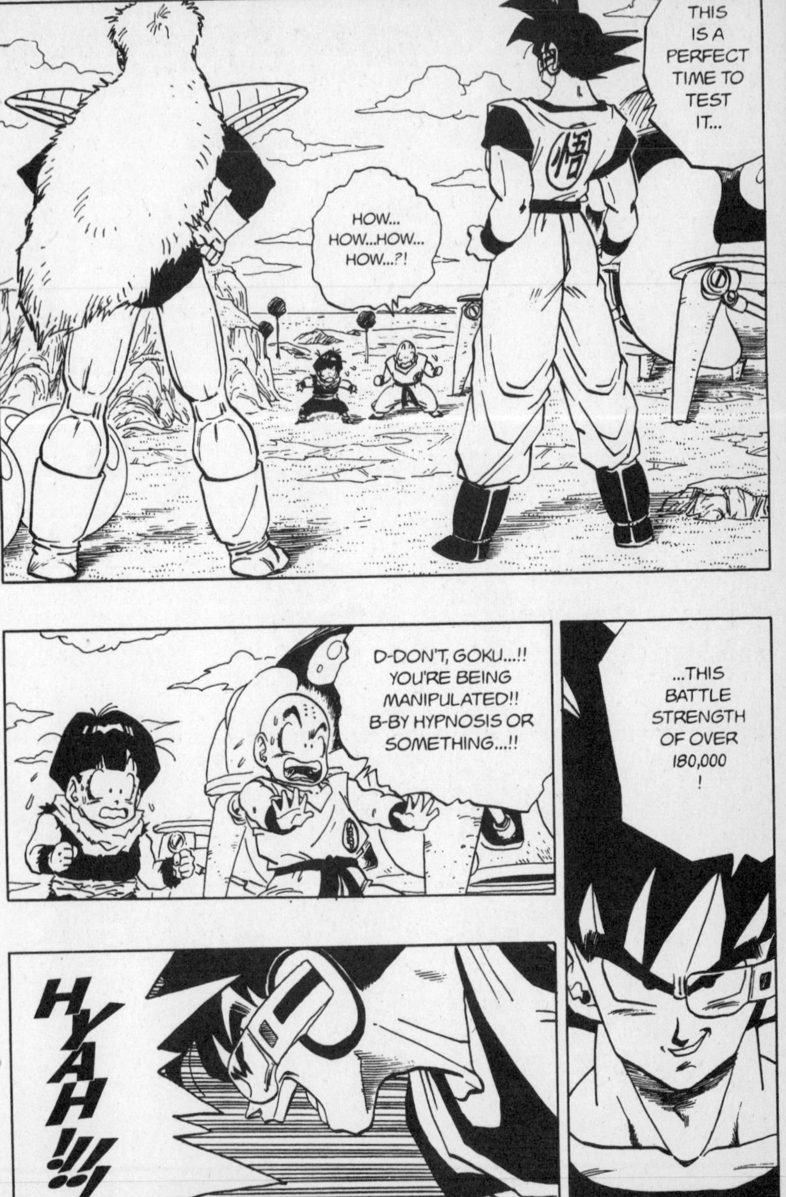
THIS IS A PERFECT TIME TO TEST IT...
HOW... HOW...HOW... HOW...?!
...THIS BATTLE STRENGTH OF OVER 180,000 !
D-DON'T, GOKU...!! YOU'RE BEING MANIPULATED!! B-BY HYPNOSIS OR SOMETHING...!!
HYAH!!!!!

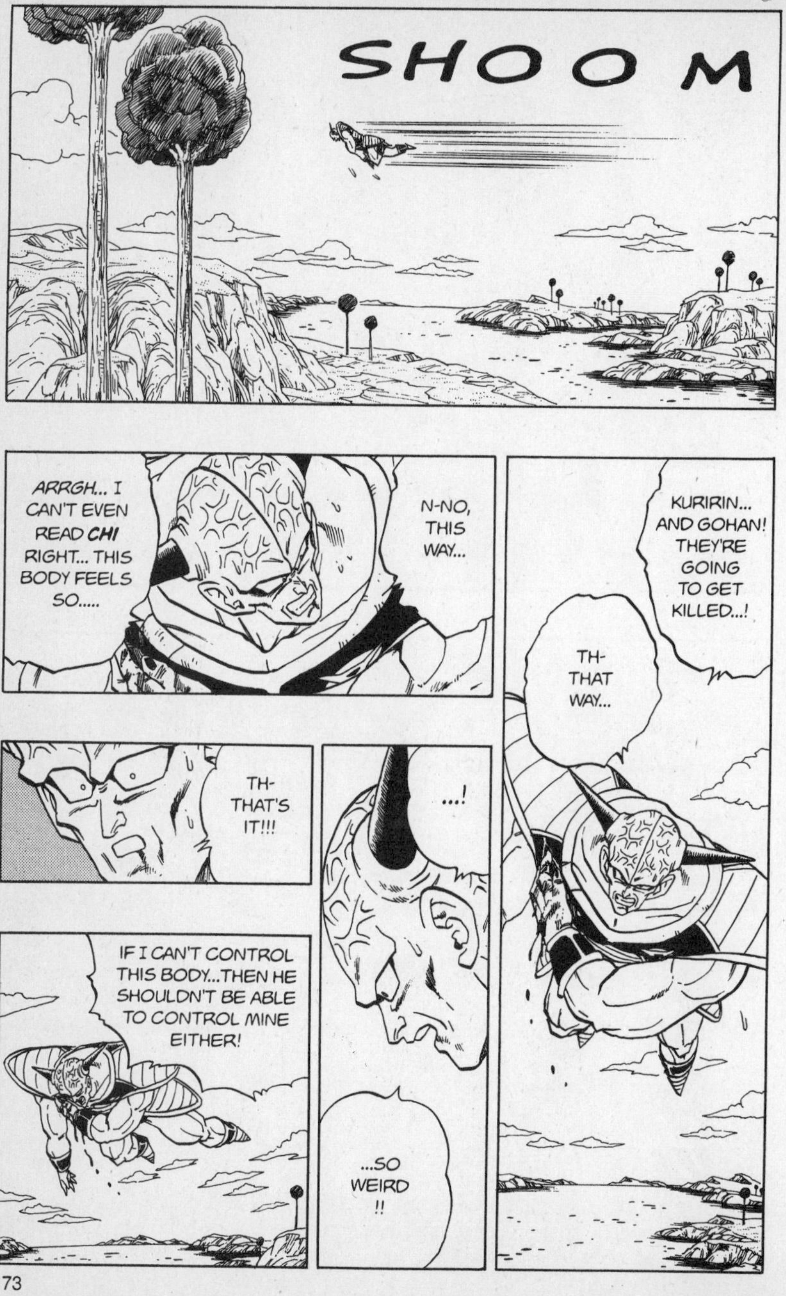
SHOOM
KURIRIN... AND GOHAN! THEY'RE GOING TO GET KILLED...!
TH- THAT WAY...
N-NO, THIS WAY...
ARRGH... I CAN'T EVEN READ **CHI** RIGHT... THIS BODY FEELS SO.....
...!
...SO WEIRD !!
TH- THAT'S IT!!!
IF I CAN'T CONTROL THIS BODY...THEN HE SHOULDN'T BE ABLE TO CONTROL MINE EITHER!

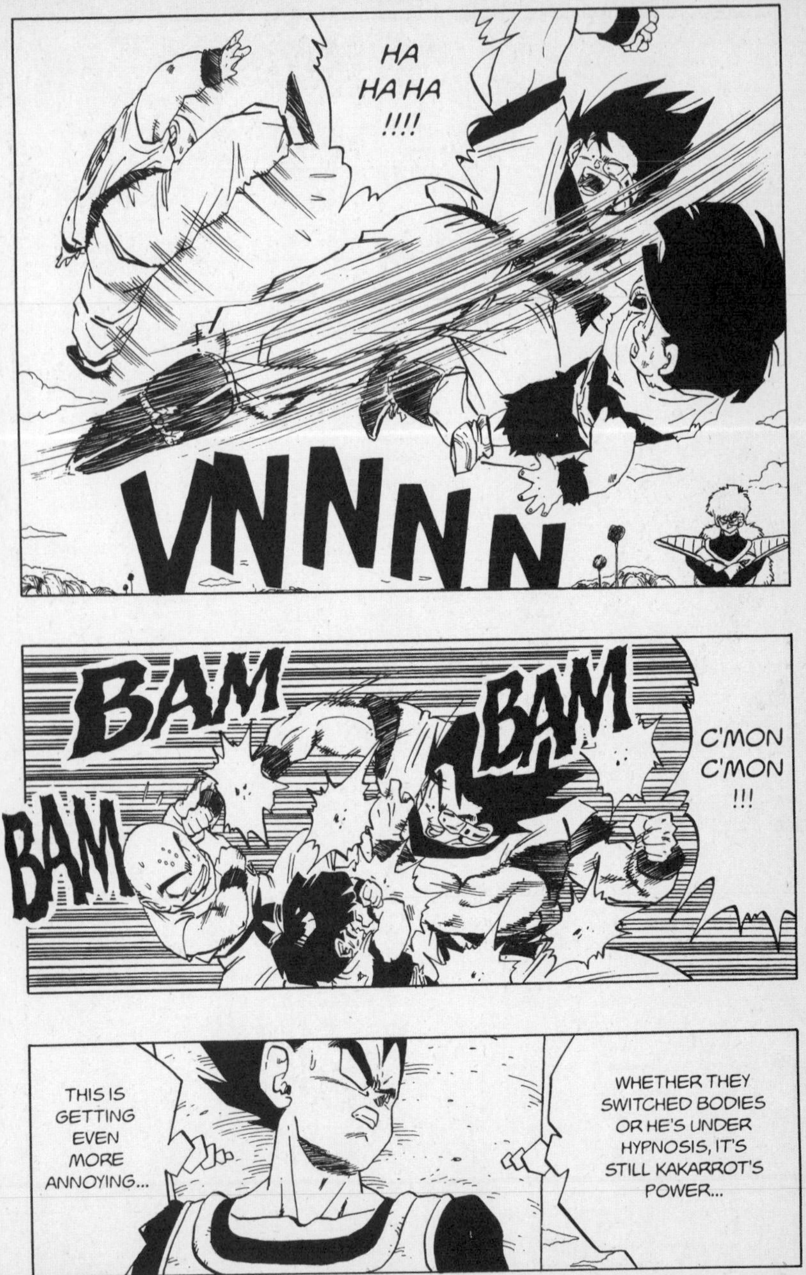

HA HA HA !!!!
VNNNN
C'MON C'MON !!!
BAM
BAM
BAM
WHETHER THEY SWITCHED BODIES OR HE'S UNDER HYPNOSIS, IT'S STILL KAKARROT'S POWER...
THIS IS GETTING EVEN MORE ANNOYING...

PI PIII

BMM

BMM BMM

HUH ?

HA HA HA !!

I'M GOING TO INCREASE MY POWER BIT BY BIT!! ARE YOU READY?!

WHAT ?

CAPTAIN GINYU !

HE'S COME AFTER US!

ACK !

HUFF *HUFF* I...I FOUND THEM...!

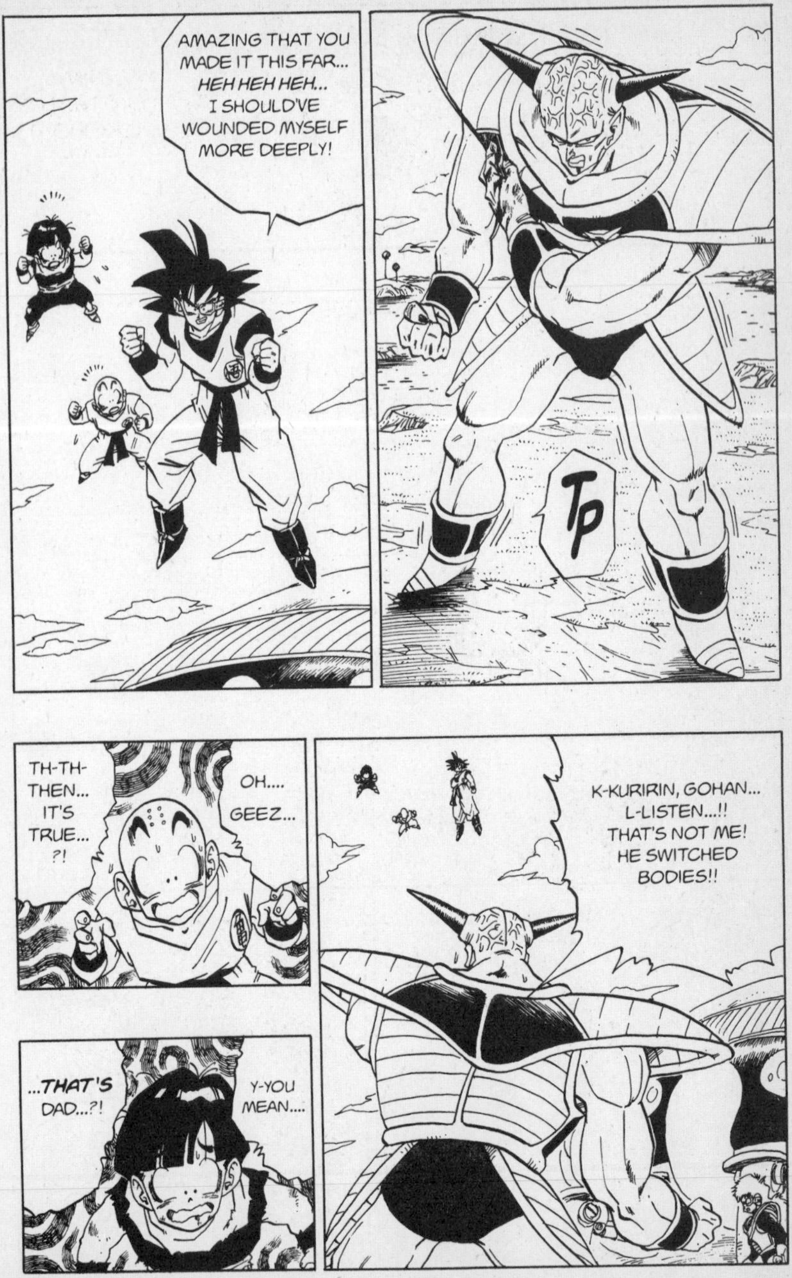
TP
AMAZING THAT YOU MADE IT THIS FAR... HEH HEH HEH... I SHOULD'VE WOUNDED MYSELF MORE DEEPLY!
K-KURIRIN, GOHAN... L-LISTEN...!! THAT'S NOT ME! HE SWITCHED BODIES!!
OH.... GEEZ...
TH-TH-THEN... IT'S TRUE... ?!
Y-YOU MEAN....
...THAT'S DAD...?!

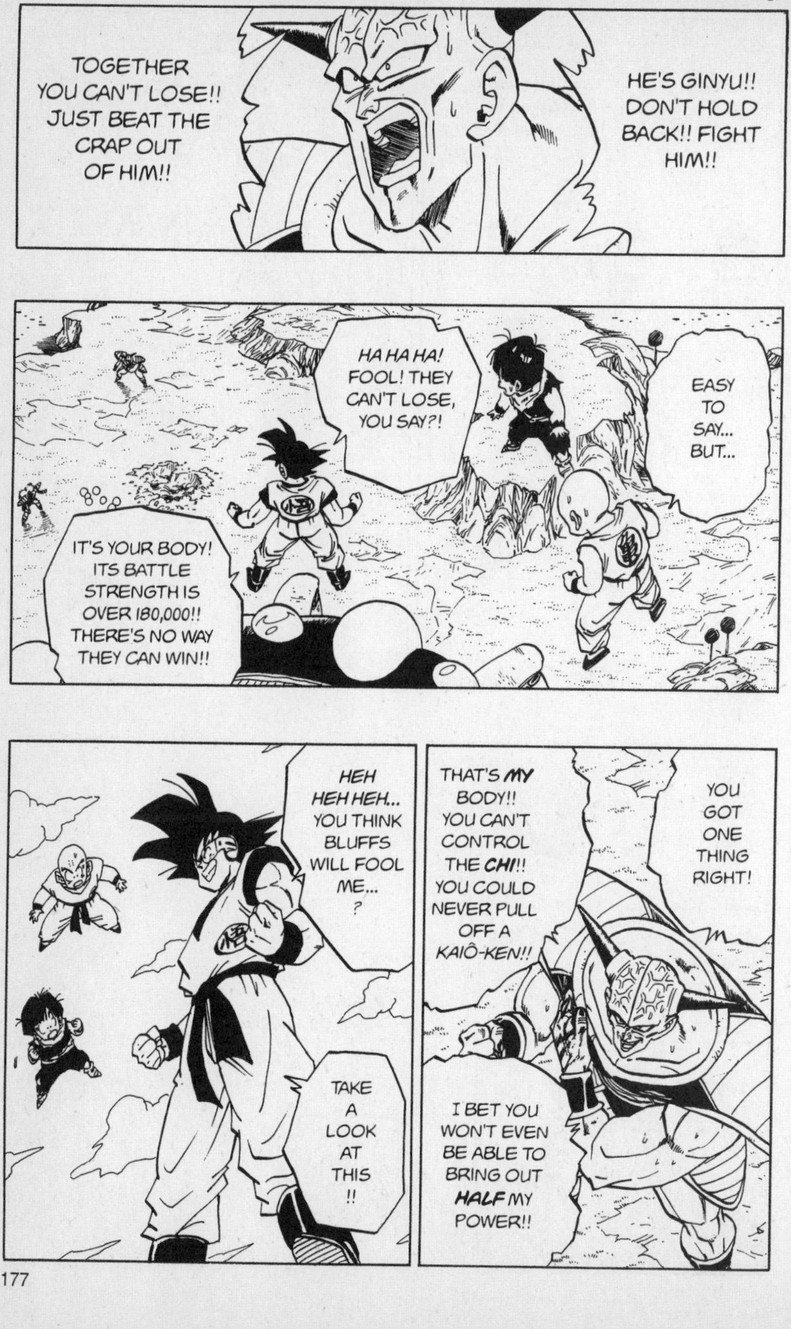
HE'S GINYU!! DON'T HOLD BACK!! FIGHT HIM!!
TOGETHER YOU CAN'T LOSE!! JUST BEAT THE CRAP OUT OF HIM!!
EASY TO SAY... BUT...
HA HA HA! FOOL! THEY CAN'T LOSE, YOU SAY?!
IT'S YOUR BODY! ITS BATTLE STRENGTH IS OVER 180,000!! THERE'S NO WAY THEY CAN WIN!!
YOU GOT ONE THING RIGHT!
THAT'S ***MY*** BODY!! YOU CAN'T CONTROL THE ***CHI***!! YOU COULD NEVER PULL OFF A *KAIÔ-KEN*!!
I BET YOU WON'T EVEN BE ABLE TO BRING OUT ***HALF*** MY POWER!!
HEH HEH HEH... YOU THINK BLUFFS WILL FOOL ME...?
TAKE A LOOK AT THIS !!

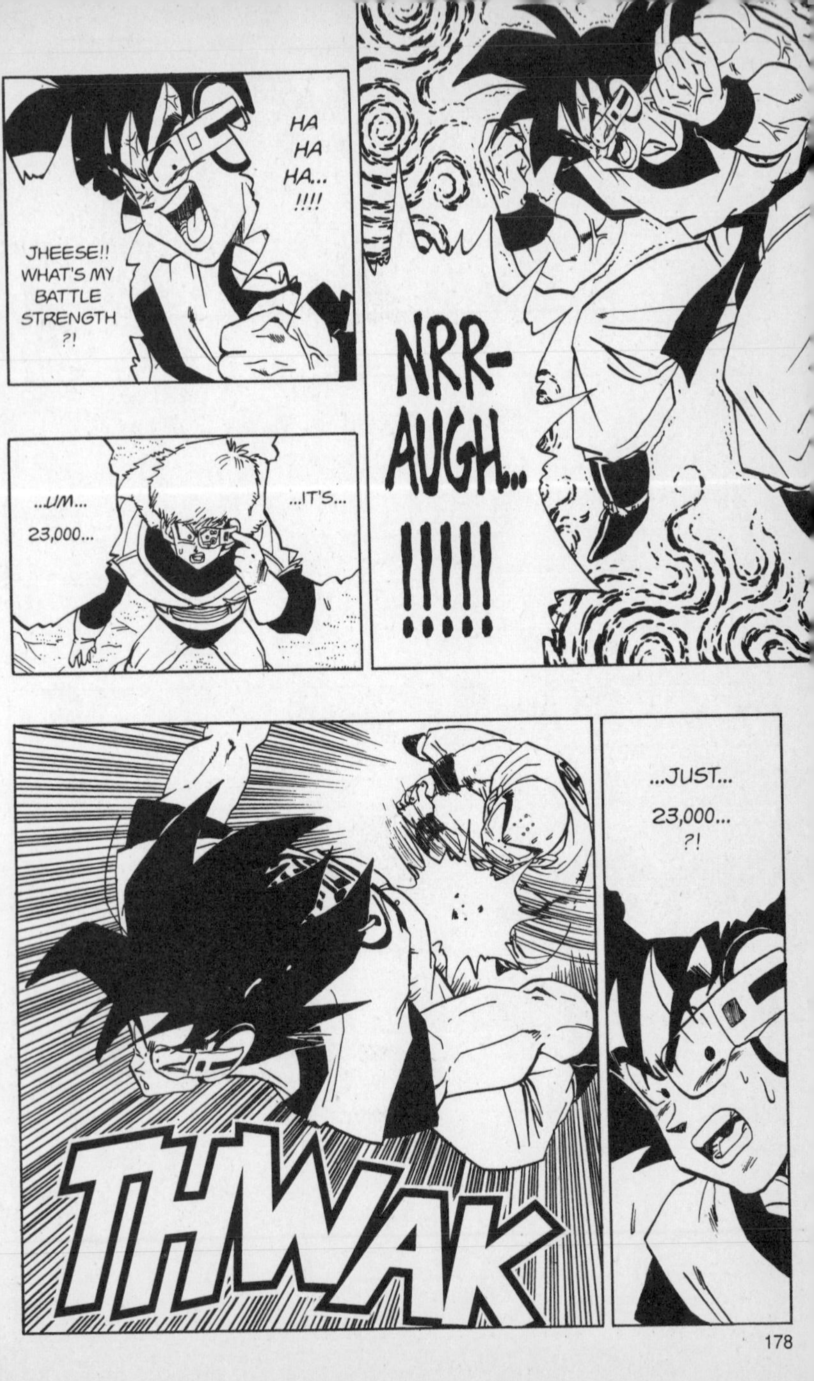
NRR-AUGH...!!!!!
HA HA HA... !!!!
JHEESE!! WHAT'S MY BATTLE STRENGTH ?!
...IT'S...
...UM... 23,000...
...JUST... 23,000... ?!
THWAK

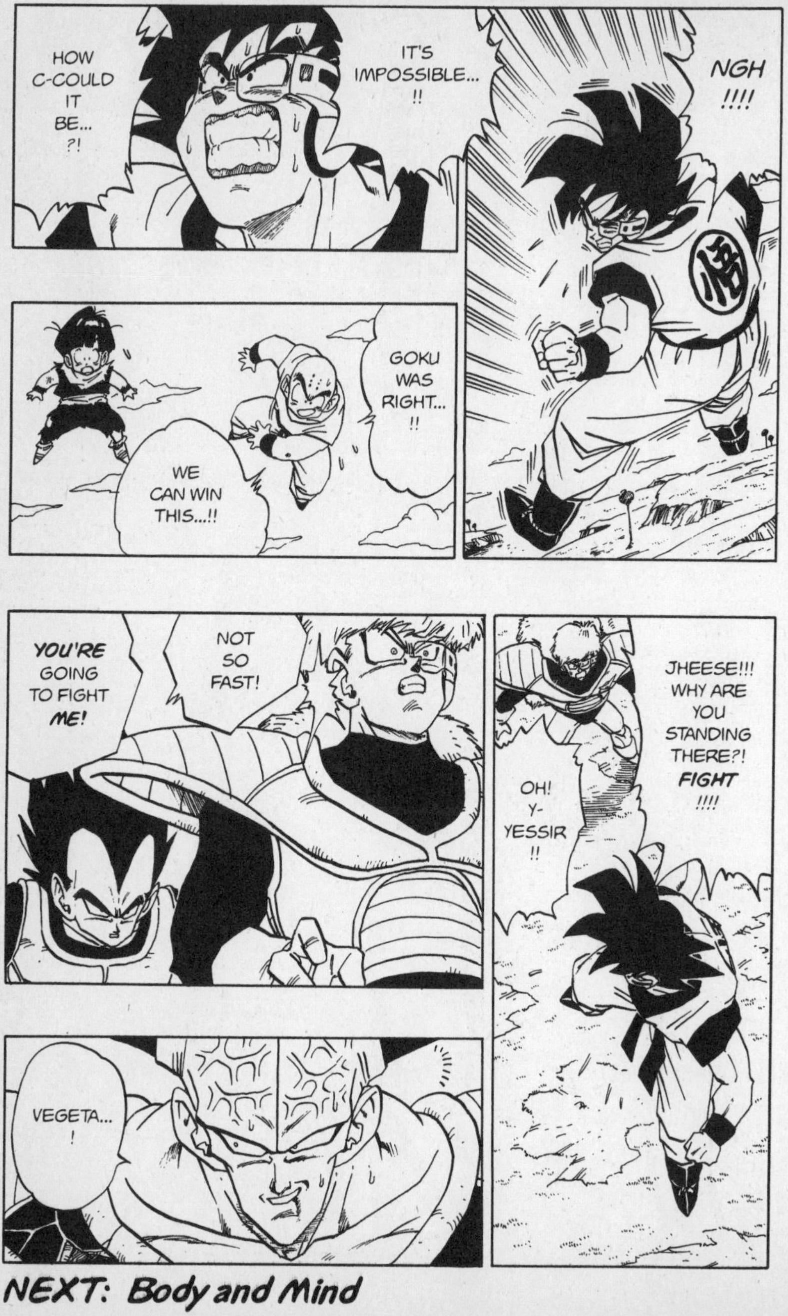
NGH!!!!
IT'S IMPOSSIBLE...!!
HOW C-COULD IT BE...?!
GOKU WAS RIGHT...!!
WE CAN WIN THIS...!!
JHEESE!!! WHY ARE YOU STANDING THERE?! **FIGHT**!!!!
OH! Y-YESSIR!!
NOT SO FAST!
YOU'RE GOING TO FIGHT ***ME!***
VEGETA...!

NEXT: Body and Mind

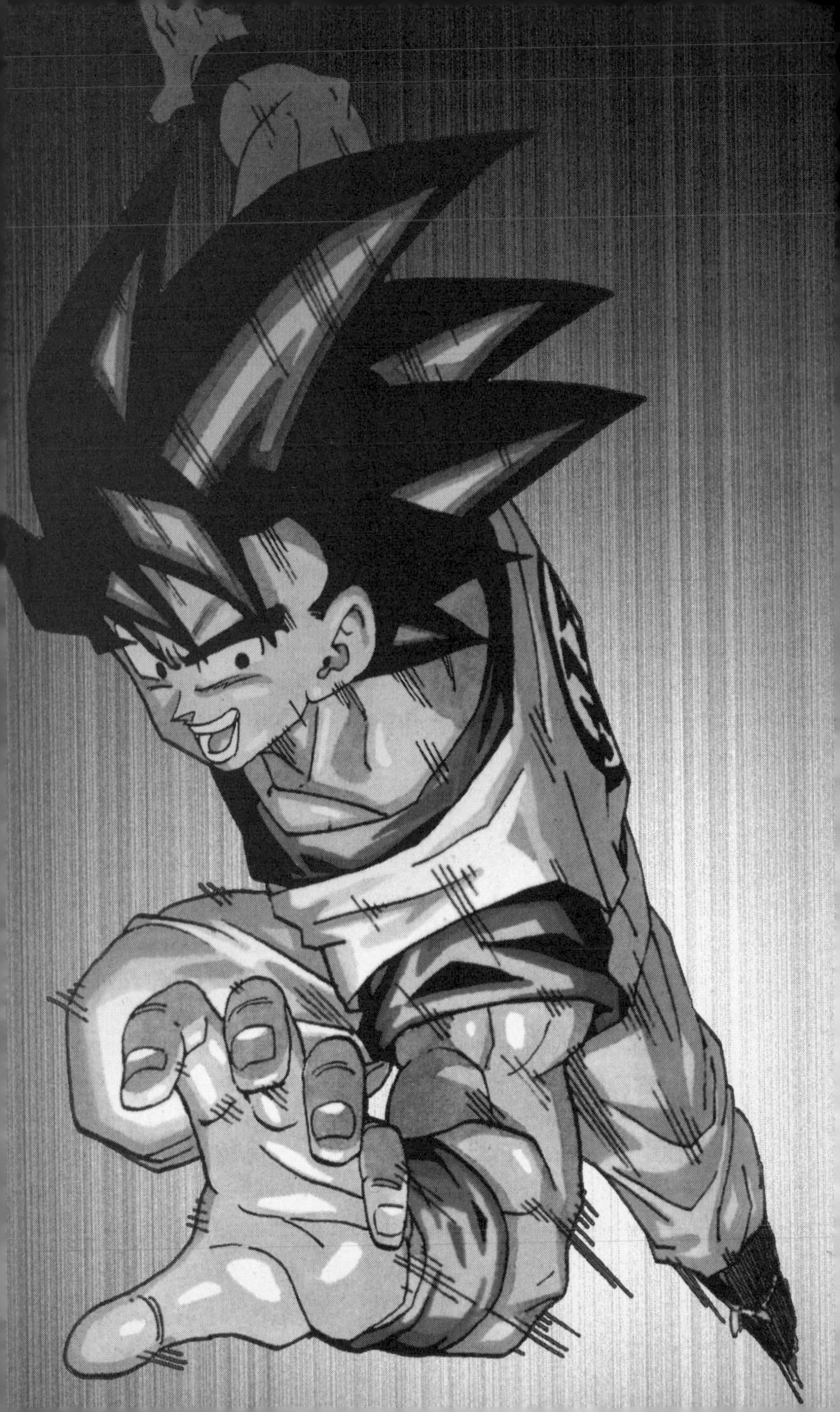

TITLE PAGE GALLERY

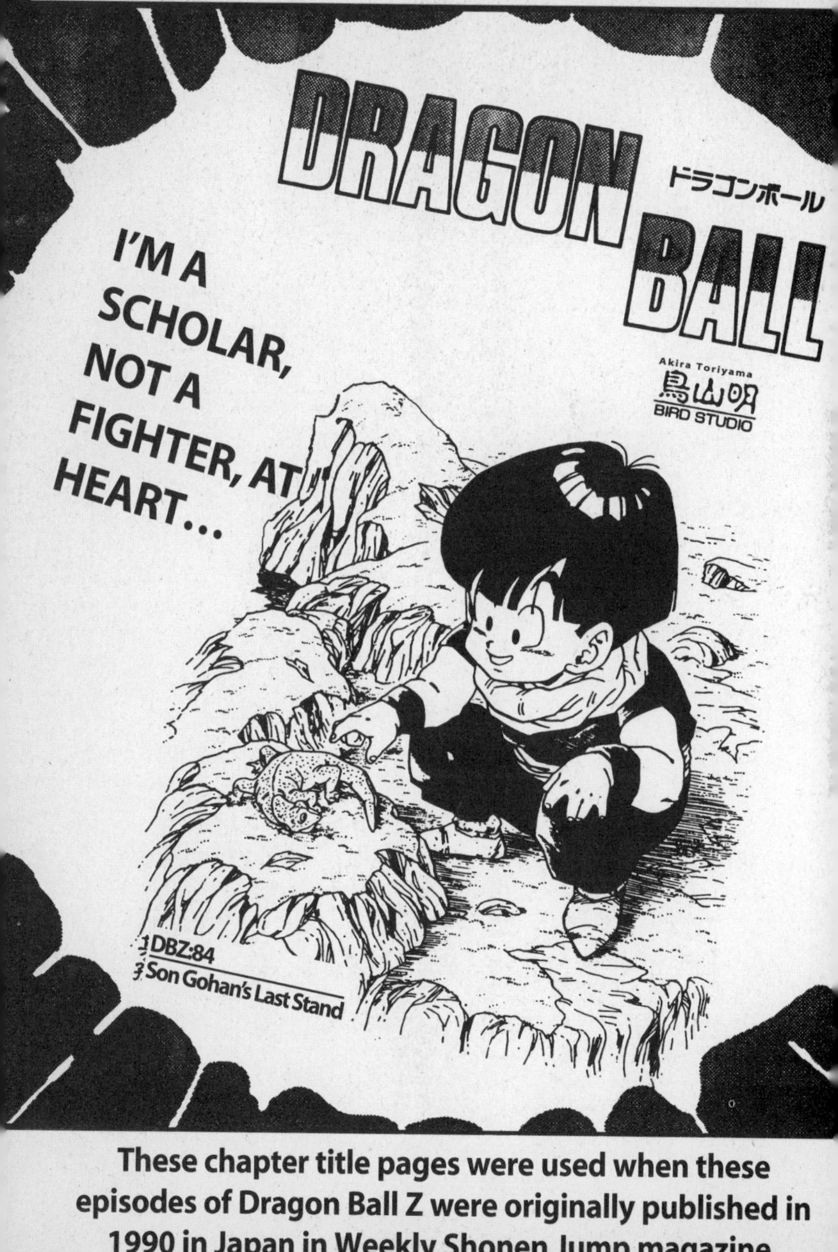
DRAGON BALL
ドラゴンボール
I'M A SCHOLAR, NOT A FIGHTER, AT HEART...
Akira Toriyama
鳥山明
BIRD STUDIO
DBZ:84
Son Gohan's Last Stand

These chapter title pages were used when these episodes of Dragon Ball Z were originally published in 1990 in Japan in Weekly Shonen Jump magazine.

DRAGON BALL

I'M READY!!!

DBZ:85 • Son Goku Has Landed!

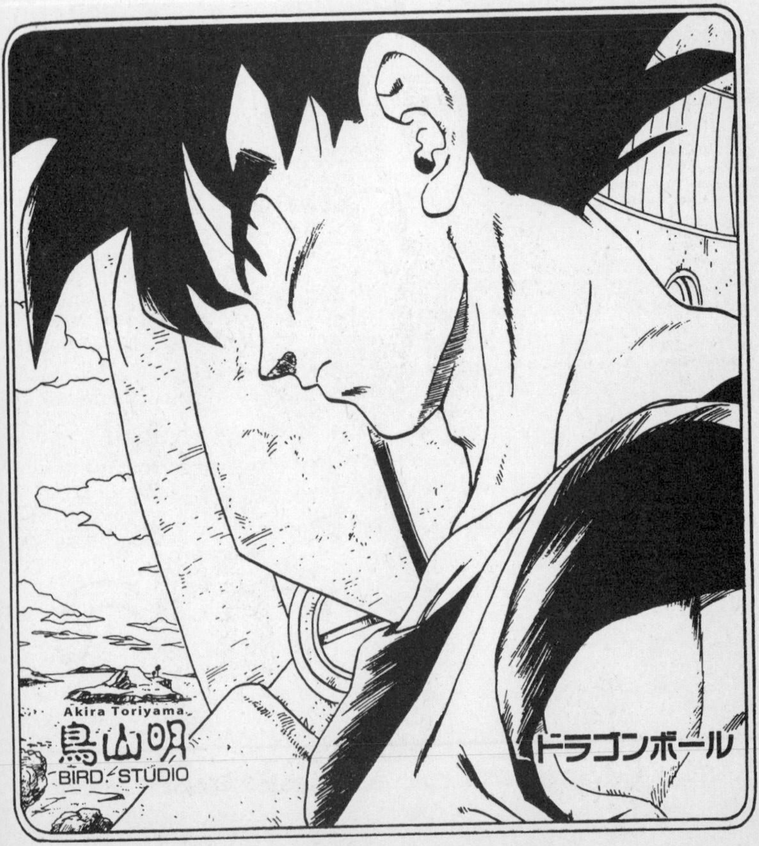
Akira Toriyama
鳥山明
BIRD STUDIO
ドラゴンボール

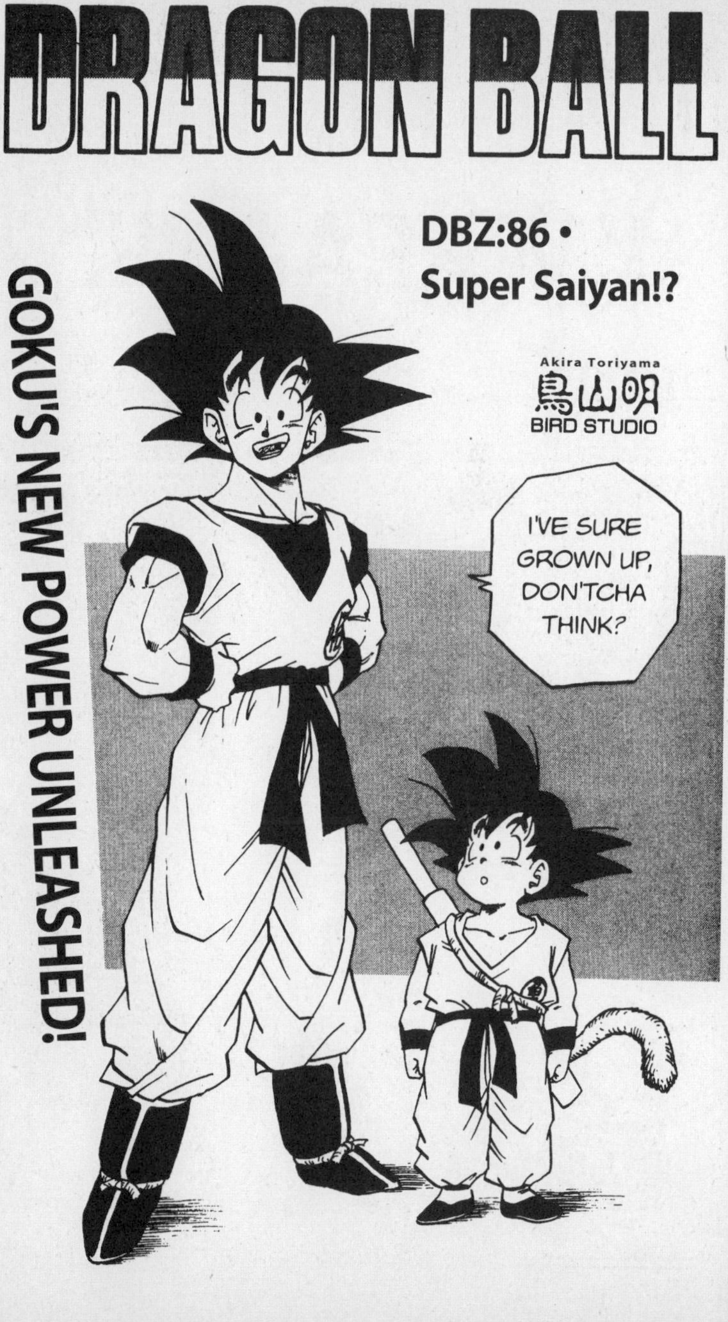
DRAGON BALL
DBZ:86 • Super Saiyan!?
Akira Toriyama
鳥山明
BIRD STUDIO
GOKU'S NEW POWER UNLEASHED!
I'VE SURE GROWN UP, DON'TCHA THINK?

DRAGON BALL

DO YOU REALLY THINK YOU CAN FIGHT ME?

DBZ:87 • Jheese and Butta

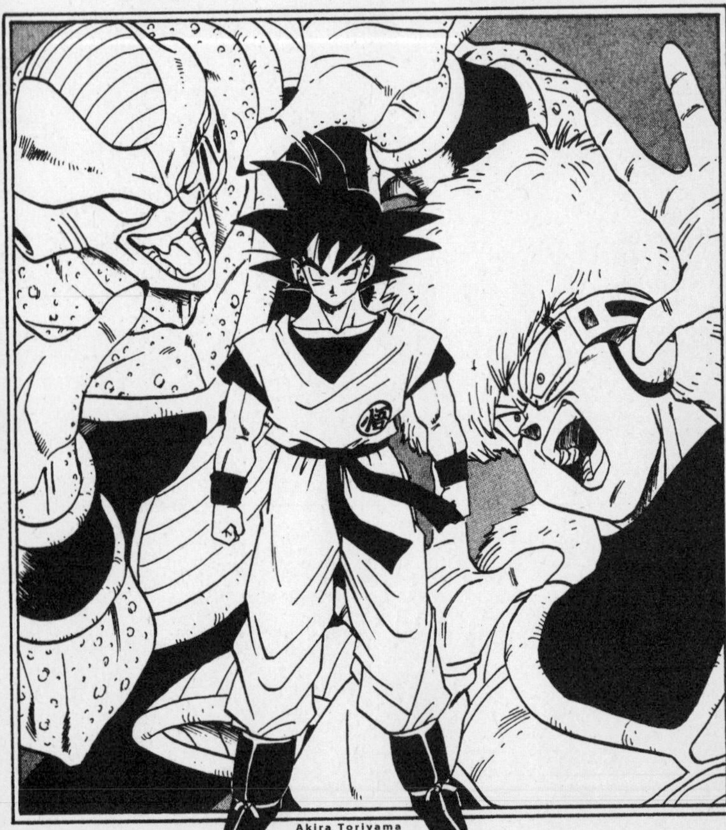

Akira Toriyama
鳥山明
BIRD STUDIO

DRAGON BALL

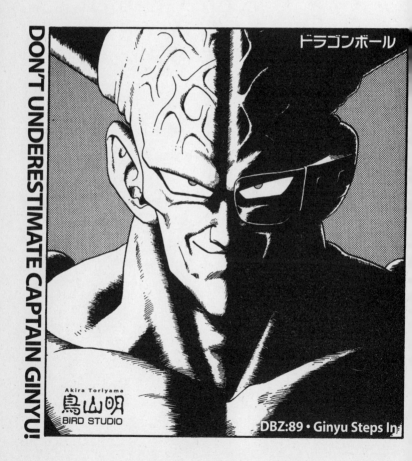

ドラゴンボール
Akira Toriyama
鳥山明
BIRD STUDIO
DBZ:89 • Ginyu Steps In!

DON'T UNDERESTIMATE CAPTAIN GINYU!

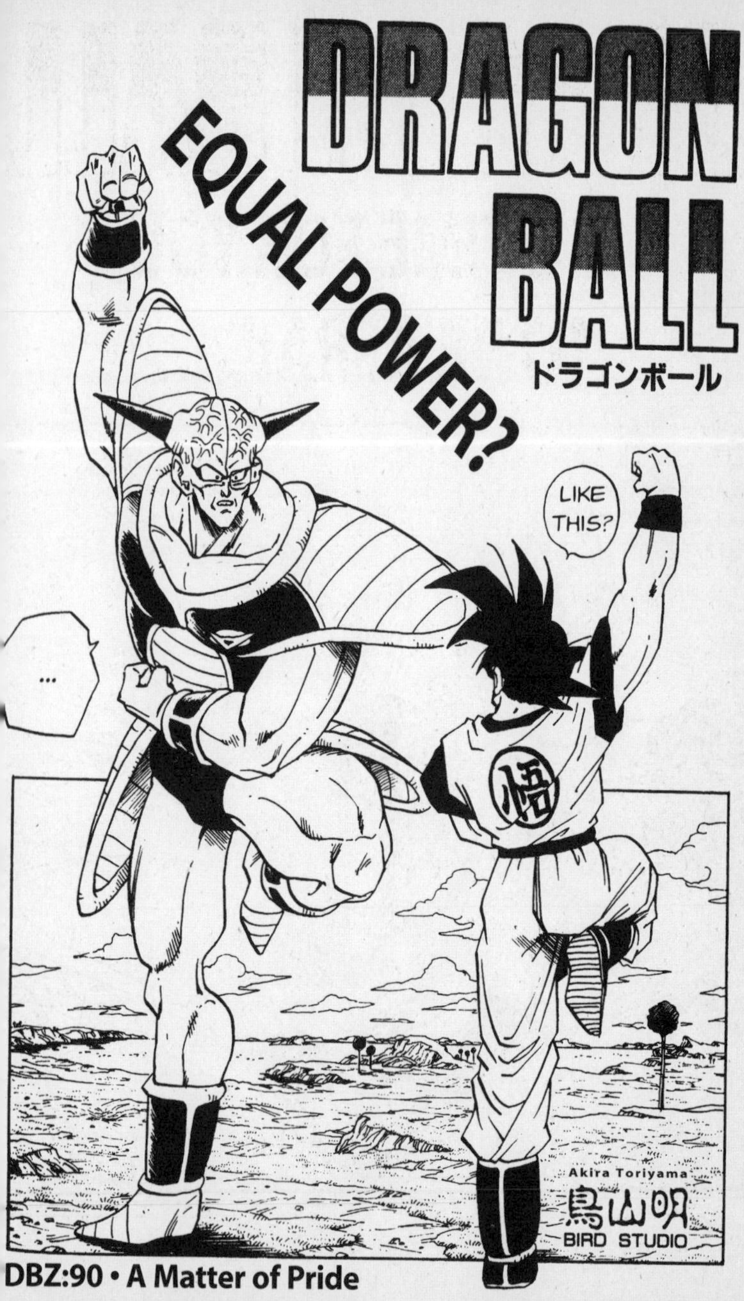

DRAGON BALL
ドラゴンボール
EQUAL POWER?
LIKE THIS?
...
Akira Toriyama
鳥山明
BIRD STUDIO

DBZ:90 • A Matter of Pride

DRAGON BALL

IT'S TIME FOR YOU TO BE AFRAID...

DBZ:91 • The Last Three Namekians

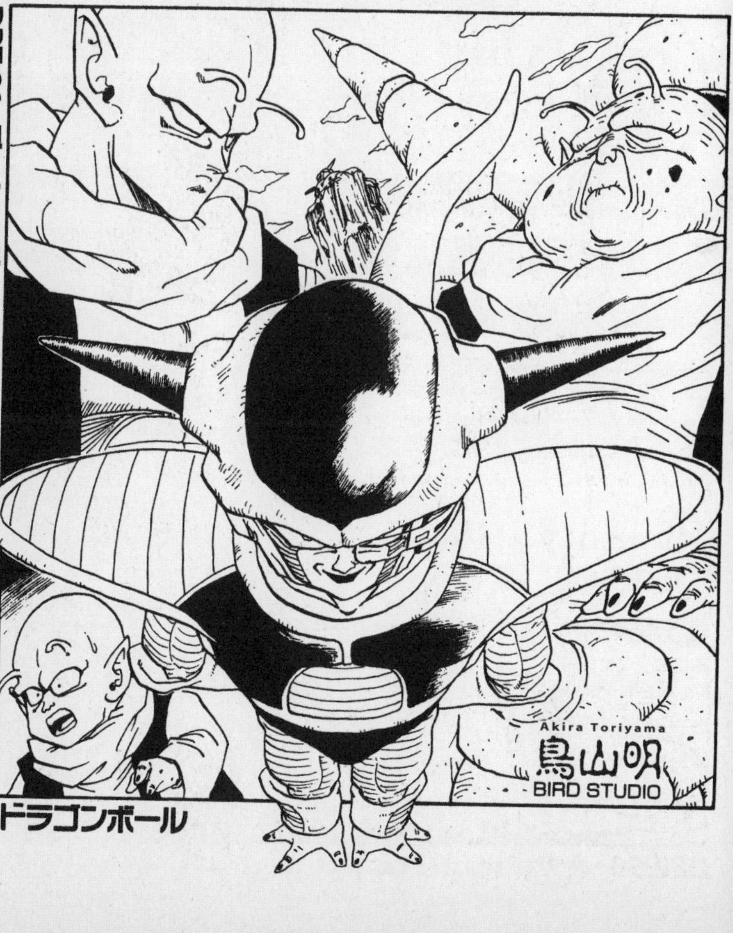
Akira Toriyama
鳥山明
BIRD STUDIO

ドラゴンボール

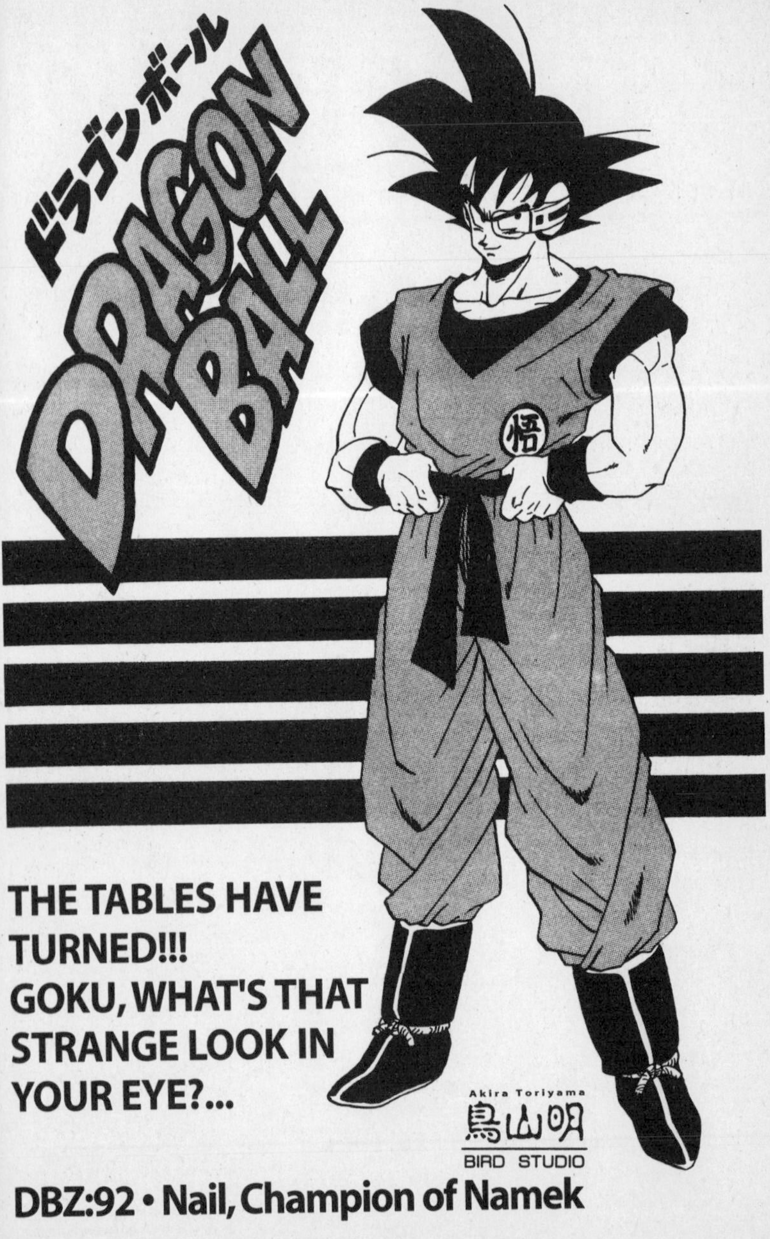
ドラゴンボール
DRAGON BALL
Akira Toriyama
鳥山明
BIRD STUDIO

THE TABLES HAVE TURNED!!! GOKU, WHAT'S THAT STRANGE LOOK IN YOUR EYE?...

DBZ:92 • Nail, Champion of Namek

ho will win the Tenka'ichi Budokai? See the battle unfold!

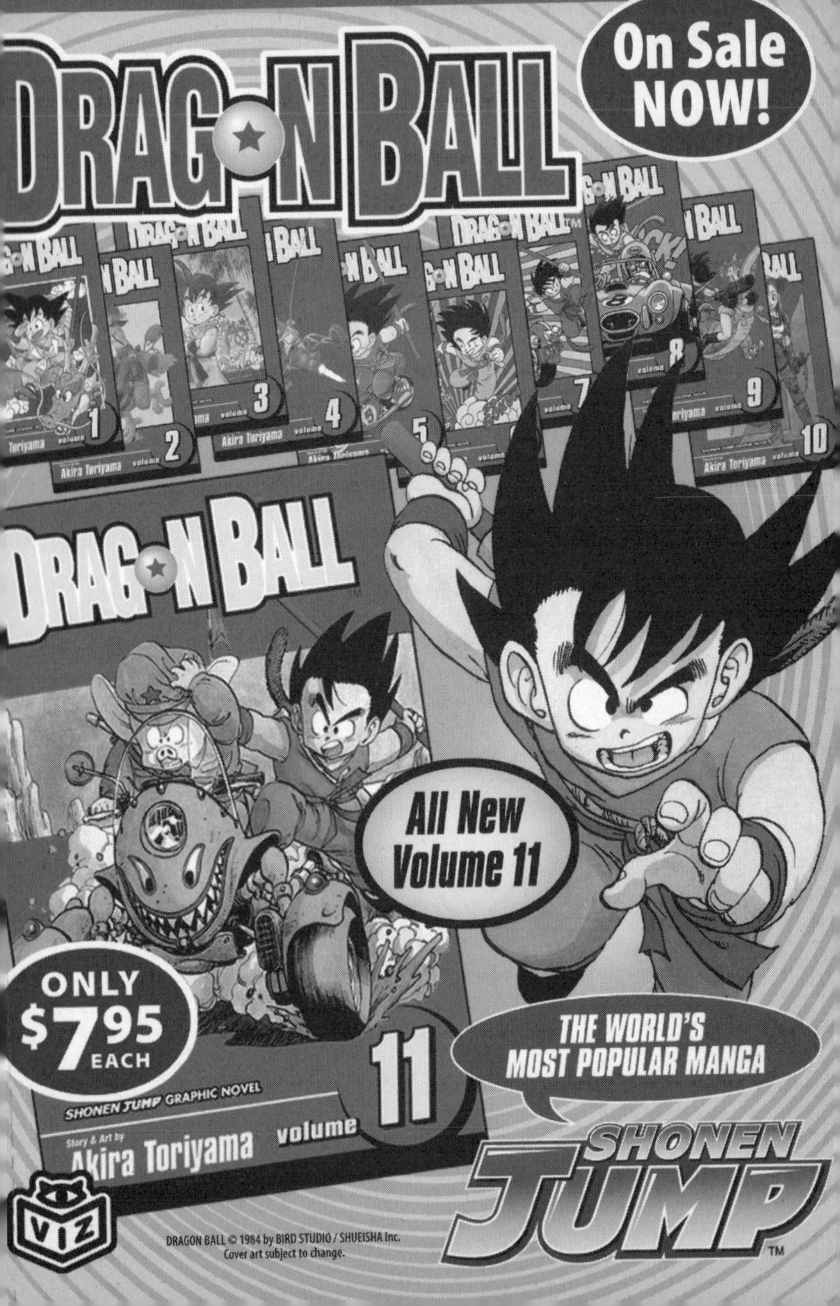
DRAGON BALL
On Sale NOW!
All New Volume 11
ONLY $7.95 EACH
SHONEN JUMP GRAPHIC NOVEL
Story & Art by Akira Toriyama volume 11
THE WORLD'S MOST POPULAR MANGA
SHONEN JUMP™
VIZ
DRAGON BALL © 1984 by BIRD STUDIO / SHUEISHA Inc.
Cover art subject to change.

COMPLETE OUR SURVEY AND LET US KNOW WHAT YOU THINK!

☐ Please check here if you DO NOT wish to receive information or future offers from VIZ

Name: _____

Address: _____

City: _____ **State:** _____ **Zip:** _____

E-mail: _____

☐ Male ☐ Female   **Date of Birth** (mm/dd/yyyy): ___ / ___ / _____   (Under 13? Parental consent required)

What race/ethnicity do you consider yourself? (please check one)

☐ Asian/Pacific Islander   ☐ Black/African American   ☐ Hispanic/Latino

☐ Native American/Alaskan Native   ☐ White/Caucasian   ☐ Other: _____

What VIZ product did you purchase? (check all that apply and indicate title purchased)

☐ DVD/VHS _____

☐ Graphic Novel _____

☐ Magazines _____

☐ Merchandise _____

Reason for purchase: (check all that apply)

☐ Special offer   ☐ Favorite title   ☐ Gift

☐ Recommendation   ☐ Other _____

Where did you make your purchase? (please check one)

☐ Comic store   ☐ Bookstore   ☐ Mass/Grocery Store

☐ Newsstand   ☐ Video/Video Game Store ☐ Other: _____

☐ Online (site: _____)

What other VIZ properties have you purchased/own? _____

_____

How many anime and/or manga titles have you purchased in the last year? How many were VIZ titles? (please check one from each column)

ANIME	MANGA	VIZ
☐ None	☐ None	☐ None
☐ 1-4	☐ 1-4	☐ 1-4
☐ 5-10	☐ 5-10	☐ 5-10
☐ 11+	☐ 11+	☐ 11+

I find the pricing of VIZ products to be: (please check one)

☐ Cheap ☐ Reasonable ☐ Expensive

What genre of manga and anime would you like to see from VIZ? (please check two)

☐ Adventure ☐ Comic Strip ☐ Detective ☐ Fighting

☐ Horror ☐ Romance ☐ Sci-Fi/Fantasy ☐ Sports

What do you think of VIZ's new look?

☐ Love It ☐ It's OK ☐ Hate It ☐ Didn't Notice ☐ No Opinion

THANK YOU! Please send the completed form to:

NJW Research
42 Catharine St.
Poughkeepsie, NY 12601

All information provided will be used for internal purposes only. We promise not to sell or otherwise divulge your information.